The War for North America

The War for North America
The Struggle between France & Britain for a Continent

The Conquest of New France

The Fall of Canada

George M. Wrong

The War for North America
The Struggle between France & Britain for a Continent
The Conquest of New France
and
The Fall of Canada
by George M. Wrong

First published under the titles
The Conquest of New France
and
The Fall of Canada

Leonaur is an imprint of Oakpast Ltd

Copyright in this form © 2016 Oakpast Ltd

ISBN: 978-1-78282-551-7 (hardcover)
ISBN: 978-1-78282-552-4 (softcover)

http://www.leonaur.com

Publisher's Notes

In the interests of authenticity, the spellings, grammar and place names used have been retained from the original editions.

The opinions of the authors represent a view of events in which he was a participant related from his own perspective, as such the text is relevant as an historical document.

The views expressed in this book are not necessarily those of the publisher.

Contents

The Conquest of New France   7

The Fall of Canada   135

The Conquest of New France

William Pitt, Earl of Chatham

Contents

The Conflict Opens: Frontenac and Phips	11
Quebec and Boston	22
France Loses Acadia	31
Louisbourg and Boston	42
The Great West	59
The Valley of the Ohio	82
The Expulsion of the Acadians	93
The Victories of Montcalm	100
Montcalm at Quebec	112
The Strategy of Pitt	118
The Fall of Canada	128

CHAPTER 1

The Conflict Opens: Frontenac and Phips

Many centuries of European history had been marked by war almost ceaseless between France and England when these two states first confronted each other in America. The conflict for the New World was but the continuation of an age-long antagonism in the Old, intensified now by the savagery of the wilderness and by new dreams of empire. There was another potent cause of strife which had not existed in the earlier days. When, during the fourteenth and fifteenth centuries, the antagonists had fought through the interminable Hundred Years' War, they had been of the same religious faith. Since then, however, England had become Protestant, while France had remained Catholic. When the rivals first met on the shores of the New World, colonial America was still very young.

It was in 1607 that the English occupied Virginia. At the same time the French were securing a foothold in Acadia, now Nova Scotia. Six years had barely passed when the English Captain Argall sailed to the north from Virginia and destroyed the rising French settlements. Sixteen years after this another English force attacked and captured Quebec. Presently these conquests were restored. France remained in possession of the St. Lawrence and in virtual possession of Acadia. The English colonies, holding a great stretch of the Atlantic seaboard, increased in number and power. New France also grew stronger. The steady hostility of the rivals never wavered. There was, indeed, little open warfare as long as the two crowns remained at peace.

From 1660 to 1688, the Stuart rulers of England remained subservient to their cousin the Bourbon King of France and at one with him in religious faith. But after the fall of the Stuarts France bitterly denounced the new King, William of Orange, as both a heretic and a usurper, and attacked the English in America with a savage fury unknown in Europe. From 1690 to 1760 the combatants fought with little more than pauses for renewed preparation; and the conflict ended only when France yielded to England the mastery of her empire in America. It is the story of this struggle, covering a period of seventy years, which is told in the following pages.

The career of Louis de Buade, Comte de Frontenac, who was Governor of Canada from 1672 to 1682 and again from 1689 to his death in 1698, reveals both the merits and the defects of the colonising genius of France. Frontenac was a man of noble birth whose life had been spent in court and camp. The story of his family, so far as it is known, is a story of attendance upon the royal house of France. His father and uncles had been playmates of the young *Dauphin*, afterwards Louis XIII. The thoughts familiar to Frontenac in his youth remained with him through life; and, when he went to rule at Quebec, the very spirit that dominated the court at Versailles crossed the sea with him.

A man is known by the things he loves. The things which Frontenac most highly cherished were marks of royal favour, the ceremony due to his own rank, the right to command. He was an egoist, supremely interested in himself. He was poor, but at his country seat in France, near Blois, he kept open house in the style of a great noble. Always he bore himself as one to whom much was due. His guests were expected to admire his indifferent horses as the finest to be seen, his gardens as the most beautiful, his clothes as of the most effective cut and finish, the plate on his table as of the best workmanship, and the food as having superior flavour. He scolded his equals as if they were naughty children.

Yet there was genius in this showy court figure. In 1669, when the Venetian Republic had asked France to lend her an efficient soldier to lead against the rampant Turk, the great Marshal Turenne had chosen Frontenac for the task. Crete, which Frontenac was to rescue, the Turk indeed had taken; but, it is said, at the fearful cost of a hundred and eighty thousand men. Three years later, Frontenac had been sent to Canada to war with the savage Iroquois and to hold in check the aggressive designs of the English. He had been recalled in 1682, after ten years of service, chiefly on account of his arbitrary temper. He had quarrelled with the bishop. He had bullied the *intendant* until at one time that harried official had barricaded his house and armed his servants.

He had told the Jesuit missionaries that they thought more of selling beaver-skins than of saving souls. He had insulted those about him, sulked, threatened, foamed at the mouth in rage, revealed a childish vanity in regard to his dignity, and a hunger insatiable for marks of honour from the king—"more grateful," he once said, "than anything else to a heart shaped alter the right pattern."

France, however, now required at Quebec a man who could do the needed man's tasks. The real worth of Frontenac had been tested; and so, in 1689, when England had driven from her shores her Catholic king and when France's colony across the sea seemed to be in grave danger from the Iroquois allies of the English, Frontenac was sent again to Quebec to subdue these savages and, if he could, to destroy in America the power of the age-long enemy of his country.

Perched high above the St. Lawrence, on a noble site where now is a public terrace and a great hotel, stood the Château St. Louis, the scene of Frontenac's rule as head of the colony. No other spot in the world commanded such a highway linking the inland waters with the sea. The French had always an eye for points of strategic value; and in holding Quebec they hoped to possess the pivot on which the destinies of North America should turn. For a long time, it seemed, indeed, as if this glowing vision might become a reality. The imperial ideas which were working at Quebec were based upon the substantial realities of trade. The instinct for business was hardly less strong in these keen adventurers than the instinct for empire. In promise of trade the interior of North America was rich. Today its vast agriculture and its wealth in minerals have brought rewards beyond the dreams of two hundred years ago. The wealth, however, sought by the leaders of that time came from furs. In those wastes of river, lake, and forest were the richest preserves in the world for fur-bearing animals.

This vast wilderness was not an unoccupied land. In those wild regions dwelt many savage tribes. Some of the natives were by no means without political capacity. On the contrary, they were long clever enough to pit English against French to their own advantage as the real sovereigns in North America. One of them, whose fluent oratory had won for him the name of Big Mouth, told the Governor of Canada, in 1688, that his people held their lands from the Great Spirit, that they yielded no lordship to either the English or the French, that they well understood the weakness of the French and were quite able to destroy them, but that they wished to be friends with both French and English who brought to them the advantages of trade. In sagacity of council and dignity of carriage some of these Indians so bore themselves that to trained observers they seemed not unequal to the diplomats of Europe. They were, however, weak before the superior knowledge of the white men.

In all their long centuries in America they had learned nothing of the use of iron. Their sharpest tool had been made of chipped obsidian or of hammered copper. Their most potent weapons had been the stone hatchet or axe and the bow and arrow. It thus happened that, when steel and gunpowder reached America, the natives soon came to despise their primitive implements. More and more they craved the supplies from Europe which multiplied in a hundred ways their strength in the conflict with nature and with man. To the Indian tribes trade with the French or English soon became a vital necessity. From the far northwest for a thousand miles to the bleak shores of Hudson Bay, from the banks of the Mississippi to the banks of the St. Lawrence and the Hudson, they came each year on laborious journeys, paddling their canoes and carrying them over portages, to barter furs for the things which they must have and which the white man alone could supply.

The Iroquois, the ablest and most resolute of the native tribes, held the lands bordering on Lake Ontario which commanded the approaches from both the Hudson and the St. Lawrence by the Great Lakes to the spacious regions of the West. The five tribes known as the Iroquois had shown marked political talent by forming themselves into a confederacy. From the time of Champlain, the founder of Quebec, there had been trouble between the French and the Iroquois. In spite of this bad beginning, the French had later done their best to make friends with the powerful confederacy. They had sent to them devoted missionaries, many of whom met the martyr's reward of torture and massacre. But the opposing influence of the English, with whom the Iroquois chiefly traded, proved too strong.

With the Iroquois hostile, it was too dangerous for the French to travel inland by way of Lake Ontario. They had, it is true, a shorter and, indeed, a better route farther north, by way of the Ottawa River and Lake Nipissing to Lake Huron. In time, however, the Iroquois made even this route unsafe. Their power was far-reaching and their ambition limitless. They aimed to be masters of North America. Like all virile but backward peoples, they believed themselves superior to every other race. Their orators declared that the fate of the world was to turn on their policy.

On Frontenac's return to Canada he had a stormy inheritance in confronting the Iroquois. They had real grievances against France. Denonville, Frontenac's predecessor, had met their treachery by treachery of his own. Louis XIV had found that these lusty savages made excellent galley slaves and had ordered Denonville to secure a supply in Canada. In consequence the Frenchman seized even friendly Iroquois and sent them overseas to France. The savages in retaliation exacted a fearful vengeance in the butchery of French colonists. The bloodiest story in the annals of Canada is the massacre at Lachine, a village a few miles above Montreal. On the night of August 4, 1689, fourteen hundred Iroquois burst in on the village and a wild orgy of massacre followed. All Canada was in a panic. Some weeks later Frontenac arrived at Quebec and took command.

To the old soldier, now in his seventieth year, his hard task was not uncongenial. He had fought the savage Iroquois before and the no less savage Turk. He belonged to that school of military action which knows no scruple in its methods, and he was prepared to make war with all the frightfulness practised by the savages themselves. His resolute, blustering demeanour was well fitted to impress the red men of the forest, for an imperious eye will sometimes cow an Indian as well as a lion, and Frontenac's mien was imperious. In his life in court and camp he had learned how to command.

The English in New York had professed to be brothers to the Iroquois and had called them by that name. This title of equality, however, Frontenac would not yield. Kings speak of "my people"; Frontenac spoke to the Indians not as his brothers but as his children and as children of the great king whom he served. He was their father, their protector, the disposer and controller of mighty reserves of power, who loved and cared for those putting their trust in him. He could unbend to play with their children and give presents to their squaws. At times he seemed patient, gentle, and forgiving. At times, too, he swaggered and boasted in terms which the event did not always justify.

La Potherie, a cultivated Frenchman in Canada during Frontenac's regime, describes an amazing scene at Montreal, which seems to show that, whether Frontenac recognised the title or not, he had qualities which made him the real brother of the savages. In 1690 Huron and other Indian allies of the French had come from the far interior to trade and also to consider the eternal question of checking the Iroquois. At the council, which began with grave decorum, a Huron orator begged the French to make no terms with the Iroquois. Frontenac answered in the high tone which he could so well assume. He would fight them until they should humbly crave peace; he would make with them no treaty except in concert with his Indian allies, whom he would never fail in fatherly care.

To impress the council by the reality of his oneness with the Indians, Frontenac now seized a tomahawk and brandished it in the air shouting at the same time the Indian war-song. The whole assembly, French and Indians, joined in a wild orgy of war passion, and the old man of seventy, fresh from the court of Louis XIV, led in the war-dance, yelled with the Indians their savage war-whoops, danced round the circle of the council, and showed himself in spirit a brother of the wildest of them. This was good diplomacy. The savages swore to make war to the end under his lead. Many a frontier outrage, many a village attacked in the dead of night and burned, amidst bloody massacre of its few toil-worn settlers, was to be the result of that strange mingling of Europe with wild America.

Frontenac's task was to make war on the English and their Iroquois allies. He had before him the king's instructions as to the means for effecting this. The king aimed at nothing less than the conquest of the English colonies in America. In 1664 the English, by a sudden blow in time of peace, had captured New Netherland, the Dutch colony on the Hudson, which then became New York. Now, a quarter of a century later. France thought to strike a similar blow against the English, and Louis XIV was resolved that the conquest should be thoroughgoing. The Dutch power had fallen before a meagre naval force. The English now would have to face one much more formidable. Two French ships were to cross the sea and to lie in wait near New York. Meanwhile from Canada, sixteen hundred armed men, a thousand of them French regular troops, were to advance by land into the heart of the colony, seize Albany and all the boats there available, and descend by the Hudson to New York.

The warships, hovering off the coast, would then enter New York harbour at the same time that the land forces made their attack. The village, for it was hardly more than this, contained, as the French believed, only some two hundred houses and four hundred fighting men and it was thought that a month would suffice to complete this whole work of conquest. Once victors, the French were to show no pity. All private property, but that of Catholics, was to be confiscated. Catholics, whether English or Dutch, were to be left undisturbed if not too numerous and if they would take the oath of allegiance to Louis XIV and show some promise of keeping it. Rich Protestants were to be held for ransom. All the other inhabitants, except those whom the French might find useful for their own purposes, were to be driven out of the colony, homeless wanderers, to be scattered far so that they could not combine to recover what they had lost. With New York taken.

New England would be so weakened that in time it too would fall. Such was the plan of conquest which came from the brilliant chambers at Versailles. New York did not fall. The expedition so carefully planned came to nothing. Frontenac had never shown much faith in the enterprise. At Quebec, on his arrival in the autumn of 1689, he was planning something less ideally perfect, but certain to produce results. The scarred old courtier intended so to terrorize the English that they should make no aggressive advance, to encourage the French to believe themselves superior to their rivals, and, above all, to prove to the Indian tribes that prudence dictated alliance with the French and not with the English.

Frontenac wrote a tale of blood. There were three war parties; one set out from Montreal against New York, and one from Three Rivers and one from Quebec against the frontier settlements of New Hampshire and Maine. To describe one is to describe all. A band of one hundred and sixty Frenchmen, with nearly as many Indians, gathers at Montreal in mid-winter. The ground is deep with snow and they troop on snowshoes across the white wastes. Dragging on sleds the needed supplies, they march up the Richelieu River and over the frozen surface of Lake Champlain. As they advance with caution into the colony of New York they suffer terribly, now from bitter cold, now from thaws which make the soft trail almost impassable.

On a February night their scouts tell them that they are near Schenectady, on the English frontier. There are young members of the Canadian *noblesse* in the party. In the dead of night, they creep up to the paling which surrounds the village. The signal is given and the village is awakened by the terrible war-whoop. Doors are smashed by axes and hatchets, and women and children are killed as they lie in bed, or kneel, shrieking for mercy. Houses are set on fire and living human beings are thrown into the flames. By midday the assailants have finished their dread work and are retreating along the forest paths dragging with them a few miserable captives. In this winter of 1689-90 raiding parties also came back from the borders of New Hampshire and of Maine with news of similar exploits, and Quebec and Montreal glowed with the joy of victory.

Far away an answering attack was soon on foot. Sir William Phips of Massachusetts, the son of a poor settler on the Kineme River, had made his first advance in life by taking up the trade of carpenter in Boston. Only when grown up had he learned to read and write. He married a rich wife, and ease of circumstances freed his mind for great designs. Some fifty years before he was thus relieved of material cares, a Spanish *galleon* carrying vast wealth had been wrecked in the West Indies. Phips now planned to raise the ship and get the money. For this enterprise he obtained support in England and set out on his exacting adventure. On the voyage his crew mutinied. Armed with cutlasses, they told Phips that he must turn pirate or perish; but he attacked the leader with his fists and triumphed by sheer strength of body and will. A second mutiny he also quelled, and then took his ship to Jamaica where he got rid of its worthless crew.

His enterprise had apparently failed; but the second Duke of Albemarle and other powerful men believed in him and helped him to make another trial. This time he succeeded in finding the wreck on the coast of Hispaniola, and took possession of its cargo of precious metals and jewels—treasure to the value of three hundred thousand pounds sterling. Of the spoil Phips himself received sixteen thousand pounds, a great fortune for a New Englander in those days. He was also knighted for his services and, in the end, was named by William and Mary the first royal Governor of Massachusetts.

Massachusetts, whose people had been thoroughly aroused by the French incursions, resolved to retaliate by striking at the heart of Canada by sea and to take Quebec. Sir William Phips, though not yet made governor, would lead the expedition. The first blow fell in Acadia. Phips sailed up the Bay of Fundy and on May 11, 1690, landed a force before Port Royal. The French governor surrendered on terms. The conquest was intended to be final, and the people were offered their lives and property on the condition of taking the oath to be loyal subjects of William and Mary. This many of them did and were left unmolested. It was a bloodless victory.

But Phips, the Puritan crusader, was something of a pirate. He plundered private property and was himself accused of taking not merely the silver forks and spoons of the captive governor but even his wigs, shirts, garters, and night caps. The Boston Puritans joyfully pillaged the church at Port Royal, and overturned the high altar and the images. The booty was considerable and by the end of May Phips, a prosperous hero, was back in Boston.

Boston was aflame with zeal to go on and conquer Canada. By the middle of August Phips had set out on the long sea voyage to Quebec, with twenty-two hundred men, a great force for a colonial enterprise of that time, and in all some forty ships. The voyage occupied more than two months.

Apparently the hardy carpenter-sailor, able enough to carry through a difficult undertaking with a single ship, lacked the organising skill to manage a great expedition. He performed, however, the feat of navigating safely with his fleet the treacherous waters of the lower St. Lawrence. On the morning of October 16, 1690, watchers at Quebec saw the fleet, concerning which they had already been warned, rounding the head of the Island of Orleans and sailing into the broad basin. Breathless spectators counted the ships. There were thirty-four in sight, a few large vessels, some mere fishing craft. It was a spectacle well calculated to excite and alarm the good people of Quebec. They might, however, take comfort in the knowledge that their great Frontenac was present to defend them.

A few days earlier he had been in Montreal, but, when there had come the startling news of the approach of the enemy's ships, he had hurried down the river and had been received with shouts of joy by the anxious populace. The situation was one well suited to Frontenac's genius for the dramatic. When a boat under a flag of truce put out from the English ships, Frontenac hurried four canoes to meet it. The English envoy was placed blindfold in one of these canoes and was paddled to the shore. Here two soldiers took him by the arms and led him over many obstacles up the steep ascent to the Château St. Louis. He could see nothing but could hear the beating of drums, the blowing of trumpets, the jeers and shouting of a great multitude in a town which seemed to be full of soldiers and to have its streets heavily barricaded.

When the bandage was taken from his eyes he found himself in a great room of the *château*. Before him stood Frontenac, in brilliant uniform, surrounded by the most glittering array of officers which Quebec could muster. The astonished envoy presented a letter from Phips. It was a curt demand in the name of King William of England for the unconditional surrender of all "forts and castles" in Canada, of Frontenac himself, and all his forces and supplies. On such conditions Phips would show mercy, as a Christian should. Frontenac must answer within an hour.

When the letter had been read the envoy took a watch from his pocket and pointed out the time to Frontenac. It was ten o'clock. The reply must be given by eleven. Loud mutterings greeted the insulting message. One officer cried out that Phips was a pirate and that his messenger should be hanged. Frontenac knew well how to deal with such a situation. He threw the letter in the envoy's face and turned his back upon him. The unhappy man, who understood French, heard the governor give orders that a gibbet should be erected on which he was to be hanged. When the bishop and the *intendant* pleaded for mercy, Frontenac seemed to yield. He would not take, he said, an hour to reply, but would answer at once. He knew no such person as King William. James, though in exile, was the true King of England and the good friend of the King of France. There would be no surrender to a pirate.

After this outburst, the envoy asked if he might have the answer in writing. "No!" thundered Frontenac. "I will answer only from the mouths of my cannon and with my musketry!"

Phips could not take Quebec. In carrying out his plans, he was slow and dilatory. Nature aided his foe. The weather was bad, the waters before Quebec were difficult, and boats grounded unexpectedly in a falling tide. Phips landed a force on the north side of the basin at Beauport but was held in check by French and Indian skirmishing parties. He sailed his ships up close to Quebec and bombarded the stronghold, but then, as now, ships were impotent against well-served land defences. Soon Phips was short of ammunition. A second time he made a landing in order to attack Quebec from the valley of the St. Charles but French regulars fought with militia and Indians to drive off his forces.

Phips held a meeting with his officers for prayer. Heaven, however, denied success to his arms. If he could not take Quebec, it was time to be gone, for in the late autumn the dangers of the St. Lawrence are great. He lay before Quebec for just a week and on the 23rd of October sailed away. It was late in November when his battered fleet began to straggle into Boston. The ways of God had not proved as simple as they had seemed to the Puritan faith, for the stronghold of Satan had not fallen before the attacks of the Lord's people. There were searchings of heart, recriminations, and financial distress in Boston.

For seven years more the war endured. Frontenac's victory over Phips at Quebec was not victory over the Iroquois or victory over the colony of New York. In 1691 this colony sent Peter Schuyler with a force against Canada by way of Lake Champlain. Schuyler penetrated almost to Montreal, gained some indecisive success, and caused much suffering to the unhappy Canadian settlers. Frontenac made his last great stroke in July, 1696, when he led more than two thousand men through the primeval forest to destroy the villages of the Onondaga and the Oneida tribes of the Iroquois. On the journey from the south shore of Lake Ontario, the old man of seventy-five was unable to walk over the rough portages and fifty Indians shouting songs of joy carried his great canoe on their shoulders. When the soldiers left the canoes and marched forward to the fight, they bore Frontenac in an easy chair. He did not destroy his enemy, for many of the Indians fled, but he burned their chief village and taught them a new respect for the power of the French. It was the last great effort of the old warrior. In the next year, 1697, was concluded the Peace of Ryswick; and in 1698 Frontenac died in his seventy-ninth year, a hoary champion of France's imperial designs.

The Peace of Ryswick was an indecisive ending of an indecisive war. It was indeed one of those bad treaties which invite renewed war. The struggle had achieved little but to deepen the conviction of each side that it must make itself stronger for the next fight. Each gave back most of what it had gained. The peace, however, did not leave matters quite as they had been. The position of William was stronger than before, for France had treated with him and now recognised him as King of England. Moreover, France, hitherto always victorious, with generals who had not known defeat, was really defeated when she could not longer advance.

CHAPTER 2

Quebec and Boston

At the end of the seventeenth century it must have seemed a far cry from Versailles to Quebec. The ocean was crossed only by small sailing vessels haunted by both tempest and pestilence, the one likely to prolong the voyage by many weeks, the other to involve the sacrifice of scores of lives through scurvy and other maladies. Yet, remote as the colony seemed, Quebec was the child of Versailles, protected and nourished by Louis XIV and directed by him in its minutest affairs. The king spent laborious hours over papers relating to the cherished colony across the sea. He sent wise counsel to his officials in Canada and with tactful patience rebuked their faults. He did everything for the colonists—gave them not merely land, but muskets, farm implements, even chickens, pigs, and sometimes wives. The defect of his government was that it tended to be too paternal. The vital needs of a colony struggling with the problems of barbarism could hardly be read correctly and provided for at Versailles. Colonies, like men, are strong only when they learn to take care of themselves.

The English colonies present a vivid contrast. London did not direct and control Boston. In London the will, indeed, was not wanting, for the Stuart kings, Charles II and James II, were not less despotic in spirit than Louis XIV. But while in France there was a vast organism which moved only as the king willed, in England power was more widely distributed. It may be claimed with truth that English national liberties are a growth from the local freedom which has existed from time immemorial. When British colonists left the motherland to found a new society, their first instinct was to create institutions which involved local control. The solemn covenant by which in 1620 the worn company of the *Mayflower*, after a long and painful voyage, pledged themselves to create a self-governing society, was the inevitable expression of the English political spirit. Do what it would, London could never control Boston as Versailles controlled Quebec.

The English colonist kept his eyes fixed on his own fortunes. From the state he expected little; from himself, everything. He had no great sense of unity with neighbouring colonists under the same crown. Only when he realised some peril to his interests, some menace which would master him if he did not fight, was he stirred to warlike energy. French leaders, on the other hand, were thinking of world politics. The voyage of Verrazano, the Italian sailor who had been sent out by Francis I of France in 1524, and who had sailed along a great stretch of the Atlantic coast, was deemed by Frenchmen a sufficient title to the whole of North America. They flouted England's claim based upon the voyages of the Cabots nearly thirty years earlier. Spain, indeed, might claim Florida, but the English had no real right to any footing in the New World.

As late as in 1720, when the fortunes of France were already on the wane in the New World, Father Bobé, a priest of the Congregation of Missions, presented to the French court a document which sets forth in uncompromising terms the rights of France to all the land between the thirtieth and the fiftieth parallels of latitude. True, he says, others occupy much of this territory, but France must drive out intruders and in particular the English. Boston rightly belongs to France and so also do New York and Philadelphia. The only regions to which England has any just claim are Acadia, Newfoundland, and Hudson Bay, ceded by France under the Treaty of Utrecht in 1713.

This weak cession all true Frenchmen regret and England must hand the territories back. She owes France compensation for her long occupation of lands not really hers. If she makes immediate restitution, the King of France, generous and kind, will forego some of his rights and allow England to retain a strip some fifty miles wide extending from Maine to Florida. France has the right to the whole of the interior. In the mind of the reverend memorialist, no doubt, there was the conviction that England would soon lose the meagre strip, fifty miles wide, which France might yield.

These dreams of power had a certain substance. It seems to us now that, from the first, the French were dreaming of the impossible. We know what has happened, and after the event it is an easy task to measure political forces. The ambitions of France were not, however, empty fancies. More than once she has seemed on the point of mastering the nations of the West. Just before the year 1690 she had a great opportunity. In England, in 1660, the fall of the system created by Oliver Cromwell brought back to the English throne the House of Stuart, for centuries the ally and usually the pupil of France. Stuart kings of Scotland, allied with France, had fought the Tudor kings of England.

Stuarts in misfortune had been the pensioners of France. Charles II, a Stuart, alien in religion to the convictions of his people, looked to Catholic France to give him security on his throne. Before the first half of the reign of Louis XIV had ended, it was the boast of the French that the King of England was vassal to their king, that the states of continental Europe had become mere pawns in the game of their Grand Monarch, and that France could be master of as much of the world as was really worth mastering. In 1679 the Canadian Intendant, Duchesneau, writing from Quebec to complain of the despotic conduct of the governor, Frontenac, paid a tribute to "the king our master, of whom the whole world stands in awe, who has just given law to all Europe."

To men thus obsessed by the greatness of their own ruler it seemed no impossible task to overthrow a few English colonies in America of whose king their own was the patron and the paymaster. The world of high politics has never been conspicuous for its knowledge of human nature. A strong blow from a strong arm would, it was believed both at Versailles and Quebec, shatter forever a weak rival and give France the prize of North America. Officers in Canada talked loftily of the ease with which France might master all the English colonies. The Canadians, it was said, were a brave and warlike people, trained to endure hardship, while the English colonists were undisciplined, ignorant of war, and cowardly. The link between them and the motherland, said these observers, could be easily broken, for the colonies were longing to be free.

There is no doubt that France could put into the field armies vastly greater than those of England. Had the French been able to cross the Channel, march on London and destroy English power at its root, the story of civilization in a great part of North America might well have been different, and we should perhaps find now on the banks of the Hudson what we find on the banks of the St. Lawrence—villages dominated by great churches and convents, with inhabitants Catholic to a man, speaking the language and preserving the traditions of France. The strip of inviolate sea between Calais and Dover made impossible, however, an assault on London. Sea power kept secure not only England but English effort in America and in the end defeated

France.

England had defences other than her great strength on the sea. In spite of the docility towards France shown by the English king, Charles II, himself half French in blood and at heart devoted to the triumph of the Catholic faith, the English people would tolerate no policies likely to make England subservient to France. This was forbidden by age-long tradition. The struggle had become one of religion as well as of race. A fight for a century and a half with the Roman Catholic Church had made England sternly, fanatically Protestant. In their suspicion of the system which France accepted, Englishmen had sent a king to the scaffold, had overthrown the monarchy, and had created a military republic. This republic, indeed, had fallen, but the distrust of the aims of the Roman Catholic Church remained intense and burst into passionate fury the moment an understanding of the aims of France gained currency.

There are indeed few passages in English history less creditable than the panic fear of Roman Catholic plots which swept the country in the days when Frontenac at Quebec was working to destroy English and Protestant influence in America. In 1678, Titus Gates, a clergyman of the Church of England who had turned Roman Catholic, declared that, while in the secrets of his new church, he had found on foot a plot to restore Roman Catholic dominance in England by means of the murder of Charles II and of any other crimes necessary for that purpose. Gates said that he had left the Church and returned to his former faith because of the terrible character of the conspiracy which he had discovered. His story was not even plausible; he was known to be a man of vicious life; moreover.

Catholic plotters would hardly murder a king who was at heart devoted to Catholic policy. England, however, was in a nervous state of mind; Charles II was known to be intriguing with France; and a cruel fury surged through the nation. For a share in the supposed plots a score of people, among them one of the great nobles of England, the venerable and innocent Earl of Stafford, were condemned to death and executed. Whatever Charles II himself might have thought, he was obliged for his own safety to acquiesce in the policy of persecution.

Catholic France was not less malignant than Protestant England. Though cruel severity had long been shown to Protestants, they seemed to be secure under the law of France in certain limited rights and in a restricted toleration. In 1685, however, Louis XIV revoked the Edict of Nantes by which Henry IV a century earlier had guaranteed this toleration. All over France there had already burst out terrible persecution, and the act of Louis XIV brought a fiery climax. Unhappy heretics who would not accept Roman Catholic doctrine found life intolerable. Tens of thousands escaped from France in spite of a law which, though it exiled the Protestant ministers, forbade other Protestants to leave the country. Stories of plots were made the excuse to seize the property of Protestants. Regiments of soldiers, charged with the task, could boast of many enforced "conversions."

Quartered on Protestant households, they made the life of the inmates a burden until they abandoned their religion. Among the means used were torture before a slow fire, the tearing off of the finger nails, the driving of the whole families naked into the streets and the forbidding of anyone to give them shelter, the violation of women, and the crowding of the heretics in loathsome prisons. By such means it took a regiment of soldiers in Rouen only a few days to "convert" to the old faith some six hundred families. Protestant ministers caught in France were sent to the galleys for life. The persecutions which followed the revocation of the Edict of Nantes outdid even Titus Gates.

Charles II died in 1685 and the scene at his deathbed encouraged in England suspicions of Catholic policy and in France hope that this policy was near its climax of success. Though indolent and dissolute, Charles yet possessed striking mental capacity and insight. He knew well that to preserve his throne he must remain outwardly a Protestant and must also respect the liberties of the English nation. He cherished, however, the Roman Catholic faith and the despotic ideals of his Bourbon mother. On his deathbed he avowed his real belief. With great precautions for secrecy, he was received into the Roman Catholic Church and comforted with the consolations which it offers to the dying. While this secret was suspected by the English people, one further fact was perfectly clear.

Their new king, James II, was a zealous Roman Catholic, who would use all his influence to bring England back to the Roman communion. Suspicion of the king's designs soon became certainty and, after four years of bitter conflict with James, the inevitable happened. The Roman Catholic Stuart king was driven from his throne and his daughter Mary and her Protestant husband, William of Orange, became the sovereigns of England by choice of the English Parliament. Again had the struggle between Roman Catholic and Protestant brought revolution in England, and the politics of Europe dominated America. The revolution in London was followed by revolution in

Boston and New York. The authority of James II was repudiated. His chief agent in New England, Sir Edmund Andros, was seized and imprisoned, and William and Mary reigned over the English colonies in America as they reigned over the motherland.

To the loyal Catholics of France, the English, who had driven out a Catholic king and dethroned an ancient line, were guilty of the double sin of heresy and of treason. To the Jesuit enthusiast in Canada not only were they *infidel* devils in human shape upon whose plans must rest the curse of God; they were also rebels, republican successors of the accursed Cromwell, who had sent an anointed king to the block. It would be a holy thing to destroy this lawless power which ruled from London. The Puritans of Boston were, in turn, not less convinced that theirs was the cause of God, and that Satan, enthroned in the French dominance at Quebec, must soon fall. The smaller the pit the fiercer the rats. Passions raged in the petty colonial capitals more bitterly than even in London and Paris. This intensity of religious differences embittered the struggle for the mastery of the new continent.

The English colonies had twenty white men to one in Canada. Yet Canada was long able to wage war on something like equal terms. She had the supreme advantage of a single control. There was no trouble at Quebec about getting a reluctant legislature to vote money for war purposes. No semblance of an elected legislating existed and the money for war came not from the Canadians, but from the capacious, if now usually depleted, coffers of the French court at Versailles. In the English colonies the legislatures preferred, of all political struggles, one about money with the governor, the representative of the king. At least one of the English colonies, Pennsylvania, believing that evil is best conquered by non-resistance, was resolutely against war for any reason, good or bad.

Other colonies often raised the more sordid objection that they were too poor to help in war. The colonial legislatures, indeed, with their eternal demand for the privileges and rights which the British House of Commons had won in the long centuries of its history, constitute the most striking of all the contrasts with Canada. In them were always the sparks of an independent temper. The English diarist, Evelyn, wrote, in 1671, that New England was in "a peevish and touchy humour." Colonists who go out to found a new state will always demand rights like those which they have enjoyed at home.

It was unthinkable that men of Boston, who, themselves, or whose party in England, had fought against a despotic king, had sent him to the block and driven his son from the throne, would be content with anything short of controlling the taxes which they paid, making the laws which they obeyed, and carrying on their affairs in their own way. When obliged to accept a governor from England, they were resolved as far as possible to remain his paymaster. In a majority of the colonies they insisted that the salary of the governor should be voted each year by their representatives, in order that they might be able always to use against him the cogent logic of financial need. On questions of this kind Quebec had nothing to say. To the king in France and to him alone went all demands for pay and honours. If, in such things, the people of Canada had no remote voice, they were still as well off as Frenchmen in France. New England was a copy of Old England and New France a copy of Old France. There was, as yet, no "peevish and touchy humour" at either Quebec or Versailles in respect to political rights.

Canada, in spite of its scanty population, was better equipped for war than was any of the English colonies. The French were largely explorers and hunters, familiar with hardship and danger and led by men with a love of adventure. The English, on the other hand, were chiefly traders and farmers who disliked and dreaded the horrors of war. There was not to be found in all the English colonies a family of the type of the Canadian family of Le Moyne. Charles Le Moyne, of Montreal, a member of the Canadian *noblesse*, had ten sons, every one of whom showed the spirit and capacity of the adventurous soldier. They all served in the time of Frontenac.

The most famous of them, Pierre Le Moyne d'Iberville, shines in varied roles. He was a frontier leader who made his name a terror in the English settlements; a sailor who seized and ravaged the English settlements in Newfoundland, who led a French squadron to the remote and chill waters of Hudson Bay, and captured there the English strongholds of the fur trade; and a leader in the more peaceful task of founding, at the mouth of the Mississippi, the colony of Louisiana. Canada had the advantage over the English colonies in bold pioneers of this type.

Canada was never doubtful of the English peril or divided in the desire to destroy it. Nearly always, a soldier or a naval officer ruled in the Château St. Louis, at Quebec, with eyes alert to see and arms ready to avert military danger. England sometimes sent to her colonies in America governors who were disreputable and inefficient, needy hangers-on, too well-known at home to make it wise there to give them office, but thought good enough for the colonies. It would not have been easy to find a governor less fitted to maintain the dignity and culture of high office than Sir William Phips, Governor of Massachusetts in the time of Frontenac.

Phips, however, though a rough brawler, was reasonably efficient, but Lord Cornbury, who became Earl of Clarendon, owed his appointment as Governor of New Jersey and New York in 1701, only to his necessities and to the desire of his powerful connections to provide for him. Queen Anne was his cousin. He was a profligate, feeble in mind but arrogant in spirit, with no burden of honesty and a great burden of debt, and he made no change in his scandalous mode of life when he represented his sovereign at New York. There were other governors only slightly better. Canada had none as bad. Her viceroys as a rule kept up the dignity of their office and respected the decencies of life. In English colonies, governors eked out their incomes by charging heavy fees for official acts and anyone who refused to pay such fees was not likely to secure attention to his business.

In Canada the population was too scanty and the opportunity too limited to furnish happy hunting-grounds of this kind. The governors, however, badly paid as they were, must live, and, in the case of a man like Frontenac, repair fortunes shattered at court. To do so they were likely to have some concealed interest in the fur trade. This was forbidden by the court but was almost a universal practice. Some of the governors carried trading to great lengths and aroused the bitter hostility of rival trading interests. The fur trade was easily controlled as a government monopoly and it was unfair that a needy governor should share its profits. But, after all, such a quarrel was only between rival monopolists. Better a trading governor than one who plundered the people or who by drunken profligacy discredited his office.

While all Canada was devoted to the Roman Catholic Church, the diversity of religious beliefs in the English colonies was a marked feature of social life. In Virginia, by law of the colony, the Church of England was the established Church. In Massachusetts, founded by stern Puritans, the public services of the Church of England were long prohibited. In Pennsylvania there was dominant the sect derisively called "Quakers," who would have no ecclesiastical organisation and believed that religion was purely a matter for the individual soul. Boston jeered at the superstitions of Quebec, such as the belief of the missionaries that a drop of water, with the murmured words of baptism, transformed a dying Indian child from an outcast savage into an angel of light. Quebec might, however, deride Boston with equal justice.

Sir William Phips believed that malignant and invisible devils had made a special invasion of Massachusetts, dragging people from their houses, pushing them into fire and water, and carrying them through the air for miles over trees and hills. These devils, it was thought, took visible form, of which the favourite was that of a black cat. Witches were thought to be able to pass through keyholes and to exercise charms which would destroy their victims. While Phips and Frontenac were struggling for the mastery of Canada, a fever of excitement ran through New England about these perils of witchcraft. When, in 1692, Phips became Governor of Massachusetts, he named a special court to try accused persons. The court considered hundreds of cases and condemned and hanged nineteen persons for wholly imaginary crimes. Whatever the faults of the rule of the priests at Quebec, they never equalled this in brutality or surpassed it in blind superstition. In New England we find bitter religious persecution. In Canada there was none: the door was completely closed to Protestants and the family within were all of one mind. There was no one to persecute.

The old contrast between French and English ideals still endures. At Quebec there was an early zeal for education. In 1638, the year in which Harvard College was organised, a college and a school for training the French youth and the natives were founded at Quebec. In the next year the Ursuline nuns established at Quebec the convent which through all the intervening years has continued its important work of educating girls. In zeal for education Quebec was therefore not behind Boston. But the spirit was different. Quebec believed that safety lay in control by the Church, and this control it still maintains. Massachusetts came in time to believe that safety lay in freeing education from any spiritual authority.

Today, (1918), Laval University at Quebec and Harvard University at Cambridge represent the outcome of these differing modes of thought. Other forces were working to produce essentially different types. The printing-press Quebec did not know; and, down to the final overthrow of the French power in 1763, no newspaper or book was issued in Canada. Massachusetts, on the other hand, had a printing-press as early as in 1688 and soon books were being printed in the colony. Of course, in the spirit of the time, there was a strict censorship. But, by 1722, this had come to an end, and after that the newspaper, unknown in Canada, was busy and free in its task of helping to mould the thought of the English colonies in America.

CHAPTER 3

France Loses Acadia

The Peace of Ryswick in 1697 had settled nothing finally. France was still strong enough to aim at the mastery of Europe and America. England was torn by internal faction and would not prepare to face her menacing enemy. Always the English have disliked a great standing army. Now, despite the entreaties of a king who knew the real danger, they reduced the army to the pitiable number of seven thousand men. Louis XIV grew ever more confident. In 1700 he was able to put his own grandson on the throne of Spain and to dominate Europe from the Straits of Gibraltar to the Netherlands. Another event showing his resolve soon startled the world.

In 1701 died James II, the dethroned King of England, and Louis went out of his way to insult the English people. William III was king by the will of Parliament. Louis had recognised him as such. Yet, on the death of James, Louis declared that James's son was now the true King of England. This impudent defiance meant, and Louis intended that it should mean, renewed war. England had invited it by making her forces weak. William III died in 1702 and the war went on under his successor, Queen Anne.

Thus it happened that once more war-parties began to prowl on the Canadian frontier, and women and children in remote clearings in the forest shivered at the prospect of the savage scourge. The English colonies suffered terribly. Everywhere France was aggressive. The warlike Iroquois were now so alarmed by the French menace that, to secure protection, they ceded their territory to Queen Anne and became British subjects, a humiliating step indeed for a people who had once thought themselves the most important in all the world. By 1703 the butchery on the frontier was in full operation.

The Jesuit historian Charlevoix, with complacent exaggeration, says that in that year alone three hundred men were killed on the New England frontier by the Abenaki Indians incited by the French. The numbers slain were in fact fewer and the slain were not always men but sometimes old women and young babies. The policy of France was to make the war so ruthless that a gulf of hatred should keep their Indian allies from ever making friends and resuming trade with the English, whose hatchets, blankets, and other supplies were, as the French well knew, better and cheaper than their own. The French hoped to seize Boston, to destroy its industries and sink its ships, then to advance beyond Boston and deal out to other places the same fate. The rivalry of New England was to be ended by making that region a desert.

The first fury of the war raged on the frontier of Maine, which was an outpost of Massachusetts. On an August day in 1703 the people of the rugged little settlement of Wells were at their usual tasks when they heard gunshots and war-whoops. Indians had crept up to attack the place. They set the village on fire and killed or carried off some two-score prisoners, chiefly women and children. The village of Deerfield, on the northwestern frontier of Massachusetts, consisted of a wooden meeting-house and a number of rough cabins which lodged the two or three hundred inhabitants.

On a February night in 1704 savages led by a young member of the Canadian *noblesse*, Hertel de Rouville, approached the village silently on snowshoes, waited on the outskirts during the dead of night, and then just before dawn burst in upon the sleeping people. The work was done quickly. Within an hour after dawn the place had been plundered and set on fire, forty or fifty dead bodies of men and women and children lay in the village, and a hundred and eleven miserable prisoners were following their captors on snowshoes through the forest, each prisoner well knowing that to fall by the way meant to have his head split by a tomahawk and the scalp torn off. When on the first night one of them slipped away, Rouville told the others that, should a further escape occur, he would burn alive all those remaining in his hands.

The minister of the church at Deerfield, the Reverend John Williams, was a captive, together with his wife and five children. The wife, falling by the way, was killed by a stroke of a tomahawk and the body was left lying on the snow. The children were taken from their father and scattered among different bands. After a tramp of two hundred miles through the wilderness to the outlying Canadian settlements, the minister in the end reached Quebec. Every effort was made, even by his Indian guard, to make him accept the Roman Catholic faith, but the stern Puritan was obdurate. His daughter, Eunice, on the other hand, caught young, became a Catholic so devoted that later she would not return to New England lest the contact with Protestants should injure her faith. She married a Caughnawaga Indian and became to all outward appearance a squaw. Williams himself lived to resume his career in New England and to write the story of the raid at Deerfield.

It may be that there were men in New England and New York capable of similar barbarities. It is true that the savage allies of the English, when at their worst, knew no restraint. There is nothing in the French raids on a scale as great as that of the murderous raid by the Iroquois on the French village of Lachine. But the Puritans of New England, while they were ready to hew down savages, did not like and rarely took part in the massacre of Europeans.

As the outrages went on year after year the temper of New England towards the savages grew more ruthless. The General Court, the Legislature of Massachusetts, offered forty pounds for every Indian scalp brought in. Indians, like wolves, were vermin to be destroyed. The anger of New England was further kindled by what was happening on the sea. Privateers from Port Royal, in Acadia, attacked New England commerce and New England fishermen and made unsafe the approaches to Boston. This was to touch a commercial community on its most tender spot; and a deep resolve was formed that Canada should be conquered and the menace ended once for all.

It was only an occasional spirit in Massachusetts who made comprehensive political plans. One of these was Samuel Vetch, a man somewhat different from the usual type of New England leader, for he was not of English but of Scottish origin, of the Covenanter strain. Vetch, himself an adventurous trader, had taken a leading part in the ill-fated Scottish attempt to found on the Isthmus of Panama a colony, which, in easy touch with both the Pacific and the Atlantic, should carry on a gigantic commerce between the East and the West. The colony failed, chiefly, perhaps, because Spain would not have this intrusion into territory which she claimed. Tropical disease and the disunion and incompetence of the colonists themselves were Spain's allies in the destruction. After this, Vetch had found his way to Boston, where he soon became prominent.

In 1707 Scotland and England were united under one Parliament, and the active mind of Vetch was occupied with something greater than a Scottish colony at Panama. Queen Anne, Vetch was resolved, should be "Sole Empress of the vast North American Continent." Massachusetts was ready for just such a cry. The General Court took up eagerly the plan of Vetch. The scheme required help from England and the other colonies. To England Vetch went in 1708. Marlborough had just won the great victory of Oudenarde. It was good, the English ministry thought, to hit France wherever she raised her head. In the spring of 1709 Vetch returned to Boston with promises of powerful help at once for an attack on Canada, and with the further promise that, the victory won, he himself should be the first British Governor of Canada. New York was to help with nine hundred men. Other remoter colonies were to aid on a smaller scale. These contingents were to attack Canada by way of Lake Champlain. Twelve hundred men from New England were to join the regulars from England and go against Quebec by way of the sea and master Canada once for all.

The plan was similar to the one which Amherst and Wolfe carried to success exactly fifty years later, and with a Wolfe in command it might now have succeeded. The troops from England were to be at Boston before the end of May, 1709. The colonial forces gathered. New Jersey and Pennsylvania refused, indeed, to send any soldiers; but New York and the other colonies concerned did their full share. By the early summer Colonel Francis Nicholson, with some fifteen hundred men, lay fully equipped in camp on Wood Creek near Lake Champlain, ready to descend on Montreal as soon as news came of the arrival of the British fleet at Boston for the attack on Quebec. On the shores of Boston harbour lay another colonial army, large for the time—the levies from New England which were to sail to Quebec.

Officers had come out from England to drill these hardy men, and as soldiers they were giving a good account of themselves. They watched, fasted, and prayed, and watched again for the fleet from England. Summer came and then autumn and still the fleet did not arrive. Far away, in the crowded camp on Wood Creek, pestilence broke out and as time wore on this army slowly melted away either by death or withdrawal. At last, on October 11, 1709, word came from the British ministry, dated the 27th of July, two months after the promised fleet was to arrive at Boston, that it had been sent instead to Portugal.

In spite of this disappointment the resolution endured to conquer Canada. New York joined New England in sending deputations to London to ask again for help. Four Mohawk chiefs went with Peter Schuyler from New York and were the wonder of the day in London.

It is something to have a plan talked about. Malplaquet, the last of Marlborough's great victories, had been won in the autumn of 1709 and the thought of a new enterprise was popular. Nicholson, who had been sent from Boston, urged that the first step should be to take Port Royal. What the colonies required for this expedition was the aid of four frigates and five hundred soldiers who should reach Boston by March.

The help arrived, though not in March but in July, 1710. Boston was filled with enthusiasm for the enterprise. The legislature made military service compulsory, quartered soldiers in private houses without consent of the owners, impressed sailors, and altogether was quite arbitrary and high-handed. The people, however, would bear almost anything if only they could crush Port Royal, the den of privateers who seized many New England vessels. On the 18th of September, to the great joy of Boston, the frigates and the transports sailed away, with Nicholson in command of the troops and Vetch as adjutant-general.

What we know today as Digby Basin on the east side of the Bay of Fundy, is a great harbour, landlocked but for a narrow entrance about a mile wide. Through this "gut," as it is called, the tide rushes in a torrential and dangerous stream, but soon loses its violence in the spacious and quiet harbour. Here the French had made their first enduring colony in America. On the shores of the beautiful basin the *fleurs-de-lis* had been raised over a French fort as early as 1605. A lovely valley opens from the head of the basin to the interior.

It is now known as the Annapolis Valley, a fertile region dotted by the homesteads of a happy and contented people. These people, however, are not French in race nor do they live under a French Government. When on the 24th of September, 1710, the fleet from Boston entered the basin, and in doing so lost a ship and more than a score of men through the destructive current, the decisive moment had come for all that region. Fate had decreed that the land should not remain French but should become English.

Port Royal was at that time a typical French community of the New World. The village consisted of some poor houses made of logs or planks, a wooden church, and, lying apart, a fort defended by earthworks. The governor, Subercase, was a brave French officer. He ruled the little community with a despotism tempered only by indignant protests to the king from those whom he ruled when his views and theirs did not coincide. The peasants in the village counted for nothing. Connected with the small garrison there were ladies and gentlemen who had no light opinion of their own importance and were so peppery that Subercase wished he had a madhouse in which to confine some of them. He thought well of the country. It produced, he said, everything that France produced except olives. The fertile land promised abundance of grain and there was an inexhaustible supply of timber. There were many excellent harbours. Had he a million *livres*, he would, he said, invest it gladly in the country and be certain of a good return. His enthusiasm had produced, however, no answering enthusiasm at Versailles, for there the interests of Port Royal were miserably neglected. Yet it was a thorn in the flesh of the English. In 1708 privateers from Port Royal had destroyed no less than thirty-five English vessels, chiefly from Boston, and had carried to the fort four hundred and seventy prisoners. Even in winter months French ships would flit out of Port Royal and bring in richly laden prizes. Can we wonder at Boston's deep resolve that now at last the pest should end!

It was an imposing force which sailed into the basin. The four frigates and thirty transports carried an army far greater than Subercase had thought possible. The English landed some fourteen hundred men. Subercase had less than three hundred. Within a few days, when the English began to throw shells into the town, he asked for terms. On the 16th of October the little garrison, neglected by France and left ragged and half-starved, marched out with drums beating and colours flying. The English, drawn up before the gate, showed the usual honours to a brave foe.

The French flag was hauled down and in its place floated that of Britain. Port Royal was renamed Annapolis and Vetch was made its governor. Three times before had the English come to Port Royal as conquerors and then gone away, but now they were to remain. Ever since that October day, when autumn was colouring the abundant foliage of the lovely harbour, the British flag has waved over Annapolis. Because the flag waved there it was destined to wave over all Acadia, or Nova Scotia, and with Acadia in time went Canada.

A partial victory, however, such as the taking of Port Royal, was not enough for the aroused spirit of the English. They and their allies had beaten Louis XIV on the battlefields of Europe and had so worn out France that clouds and darkness were about the last days of the grand monarch now nearing his end. In America his agents were still drawing up papers outlining grandiose designs for mastering the continent and for proving that England's empire was near its fall, but Europe knew that France in the long war had been beaten. The right way to smite France in America was to rely upon England's naval power, to master the great highway of the St. Lawrence, to isolate Canada, and to strangle one by one the French settlements, beginning with Quebec.

There was malignant intrigue at the court of Queen Anne. One favourite, the Duchess of Marlborough, had just been disgraced, and another, Mrs. Masham, had been taken on by the weak and stupid queen. The conquest of Canada, if it could be achieved without the aid of Marlborough, would help in his much desired overthrow. Petty motives were unhappily at the root of the great scheme. Who better to lead such an expedition than the brother of the new favourite whose success might discredit the husband of the old one? Accordingly General "Jack" Hill, brother of Mrs. Masham, was appointed to the chief military command and an admiral hitherto little known but of good habits and quick wit, Sir Hovenden Walker, was to lead the fleet.

The expedition against Quebec was on a scale adequate for the time. Britain dispatched seven regiments of regulars, numbering in all five thousand five hundred men, and there were besides in the fleet some thousands of sailors and marines. Never before had the English sent to North America a force so great. On June 24, 1711, Admiral Walker arrived at Boston with his great array. Boston was impressed, but Boston was also a little hurt, for the British leaders were very lofty and superior in their tone towards colonials and gave orders as if Boston were a provincial city of England which must learn respect and obedience to His Majesty's officers "vested with the Queen's Royal Power and Authority."

More than seventy ships, led by nine men-of-war, sailed from Boston for the attack on Canada. On board were nearly twelve thousand men. Compared with this imposing fleet, that of Phips, twenty-one years earlier, seems feeble. Phips had set out too late. This fleet was in good time, for it sailed on the 30th of July. Vetch, always competent, was in command of the colonial military forces, but never had any chance to show his mettle, for during the voyage the seamen were in control. The admiral had left England with secret instructions. He had not been informed of the task before him and for it he was hardly prepared. There were no competent pilots to correct his ignorance. Now that he knew where he was going he was anxious about the dangers of the northern waters. The St. Lawrence River, he believed, froze solidly to the bottom in winter and he feared that the ice would crush the sides of his ships.

As he had provisions for only eight or nine weeks, his men might starve. His mind was filled, as he himself says, with melancholy and dismal horror at the prospect of seamen and soldiers, worn to skeletons by hunger, drawing lots to decide who should die first amidst the "adamantine frosts" and "mountains of snow" of bleak and barren Canada.

The Gulf and River St. Lawrence spell death to an incompetent sailor. The fogs, the numerous shoals and islands, make skilful seamanship necessary. It is a long journey from Boston to Quebec by water. For three weeks, however, all went well. On the 22nd of August, Walker was out of sight of land in the Gulf where it is about seventy miles wide above the Island of Anticosti. A strong east wind with thick fog is dreaded in those waters even now, and on the evening of that day a storm of this kind blew up. In the fog Walker lost his bearings. When in fact he was near the north shore he thought he was not far from the south shore.

At half-past ten at night Paddon, the captain of the *Edgar*, Walker's flagship, came to tell him that land was in sight. Walker assumed that it was the south shore and gave a fatal order for the fleet to turn and head northward, a change which turned them straight towards cliffs and breakers. He then went to bed. Soon one of the military officers rushed to his cabin and begged him to come on deck as the ships were among breakers. Walker, who was an irascible man, resented the intrusion and remained in bed. A second time the officer appeared and said the fleet would be lost if the admiral did not act.

Why it was left for a military rather than a naval officer to rouse the admiral in such a crisis we do not know. Perhaps the sailors were afraid of the great man. Walker appeared on deck in dressing gown and slippers. The fog had lifted, and in the moonlight there could be seen breaking surf to leeward. A French pilot, captured in the Gulf, had taken pains to give what he could of alarming information. He now declared that the ships were off the north shore. Walker turned his own ship sharply and succeeded in beating out into deep water and safety. For the fleet the night was terrible. Some ships dropped anchor which held, for happily the storm abated. Fog guns and lights as signals of distress availed little to the ships in difficulty. Eight British transports laden with troops and two ships carrying supplies were dashed to pieces on the rocks. The shrieks of drowning men could be heard in the darkness. The scene was the rocky Isle aux Œufs and adjacent reefs off the north shore. About seven hundred soldiers, including twenty-nine officers, and in addition perhaps two hundred sailors, were lost on that awful night.

The disaster was not overwhelming and Walker might have gone on and captured Quebec. He had not lost a single war-ship and he had still some eleven thousand men. General Hill might have stiffened the back of the forlorn Admiral, but Hill himself was no better. Vetch spoke for going on. He knew the St. Lawrence waters for he had been at Quebec and had actually charted a part of the river and was more familiar with it, he believed, than were the Canadians themselves. What pilots there were declared, however, that to go on was impossible and the helpless captains of the ships were of opinion that, with the warning of such a disaster, they could not disregard this counsel.

Though the character of the English is such that usually a reverse serves to stiffen their backs, in this case it was not so. A council of war yielded to the panic of the hour and the great fleet turned homeward. Soon it was gathered in what is now Sydney harbour in Cape Breton. From here the New England ships went home and Walker sailed for England. At Spithead the *Edgar*, the flag-ship, blew up and all on board perished. Walker was on shore at the time. So far was he from being disgraced that he was given a new command. Later, when the Whigs came in, he was dismissed from the service, less, it seems, in blame for the disaster than for his Tory opinions. It is not an unusual irony of life that Vetch, the one wholly efficient leader in the expedition, ended his days in a debtor's prison.

Quebec had shivered before a menace, the greatest in its history. Through the long months of the summer of 1711 there had been prayer and fasting to avert the danger. Apparently trading ships had deserted the lower St. Lawrence in alarm, for no word had arrived at Quebec of the approach of Walker's fleet. Nor had the great disaster been witnessed by any onlookers. The island where it occurred was then and still remains desert. Up to the middle of October, nearly two months after the disaster, the watchers at Quebec feared that they might see any day a British fleet rounding the head of the Island of Orleans. On the 19th of October the first news of the disaster arrived and then it was easy for Quebec to believe that God had struck the English wretches with a terrible vengeance. Three thousand men, it was said, had reached land and then perished miserably. Many bodies had been found naked and in attitudes of despair. Other thousands had perished in the water. Vessel-loads of spoil had been gathered, rich plate, beautiful swords, magnificent clothing, gold, silver, jewels.

The truth seems to be that some weeks after the disaster the evidences of the wrecks were discovered. Even to this day ships are battered to pieces in those rock-strewn waters and no one survives to tell the story. Some fishermen landing on the island had found human bodies, dead horses and other animals, and the hulls of seven ships. They had gathered some wreckage—and that was the whole story. Quebec sang *Te Deum.* From attacks by sea there had now been two escapes which showed God's love for Canada. In the little church of *Notre Dame des Victoires,* consecrated at that time to the memory of the deliverance from Phips and Walker, daily prayers are still poured out for the well-being of Canada. God had been a present help on land as well as on the sea. Nicholson, with more than two thousand men, had been waiting at his camp near Lake Champlain to descend on Montreal as soon as Walker reached Quebec. When he received the news of the disaster he broke up his force and retired. For the moment Canada was safe from the threatened invasion.

In spite of this apparent deliverance, the long war, now near its end, brought a destructive blow to French power in America. Though France still possessed vigour and resources which her enemies were apt to underrate, the war had gone against her in Europe. Her finest armies had been destroyed by Marlborough, her taxation was crushing, her credit was ruined, her people were suffering for lack of food. The allies had begun to think that there was no humiliation which they might not put upon France. Louis XIV, they said, must give up Alsace, which, with Lorraine, he had taken some years earlier, and he must help to drive his own grandson from the Spanish throne. This exorbitant demand stirred the pride not only of Louis but of the French nation, and the allies found that they could not trample France under their feet.

The Treaty of Utrecht, concluded in 1713, shows that each side was too strong as yet to be crushed. In dismissing Marlborough, Great Britain had lost one of her chief assets. His name had become a terror to France. To this day, both in France and in French Canada, is sung the popular ditty "*Monsieur Malbrouck est mort,*" a song of delight at a report that Marlborough was dead. When in place of Marlborough leaders of the type of General Hill were appointed to high command, France could not be finally beaten. The Treaty of Utrecht was the outcome of war-weariness. It marks, however, a double check to Louis XIV. He could not master Europe and he could not master America. France now ceded to Britain her claim to Acadia, Newfoundland, and

Hudson Bay. She regarded this, however, as only a temporary set-back and was soon planning and plotting great designs far surpassing the narrower vision of the English colonies.

It was with a wry face, however, that France yielded Acadia. To retain it she offered to give up all rights in the Newfoundland fisheries, the nursery of her marine. Britain would not yield Acadia, dreading chiefly perhaps the wrath of New England which had conquered Port Royal. Britain, however, compromised on the question of boundaries in a way so dangerous that the long war settled finally no great issues in America. She took Acadia "according to its ancient limits,"—but no one knew these limits. They were to be defined by a joint commission of the two nations which, after forty years, reached no agreement. The Island of Cape Breton and the adjoining Ile St. Jean, now Prince Edward Island, remained to France. Though Britain secured sovereignty over Newfoundland, France retained extensive rights in the Newfoundland fisheries. The treaty left unsettled the boundary between Canada and the English colonies. While it yielded Hudson Bay to Britain, it settled nothing as to frontiers in the wilderness which stretched beyond the Great Lakes into the Far West and which had vast wealth in furs.

CHAPTER 4

Louisbourg and Boston

For thirty years England and France now remained at peace, and England had many reasons for desiring peace to continue. Anne, the last of the Stuart rulers, died in 1714. The new king, George I, Elector of Hanover, was a German and a German unchangeable, for he was already fifty-four, with little knowledge of England and none of the English, and with an undying love for the dear despotic ways easily followed in a small German principality. He and his successor George II were thinking eternally of German rather than of English problems, and with German interests chiefly regarded it was well that England should make a friend of France. It was well, too, that under a new dynasty, with its title disputed, England should not encourage France to continue the friendly policy of Louis XIV towards James, the deposed Stuart Pretender.

England had just made a new, determined, and arrogant enemy by forcing upon Spain the deep humiliation of ceding Gibraltar, which had been taken in 1704 by Admiral Rooke with allied forces. The proudest monarchy in Europe was compelled to see a spot of its own sacred territory held permanently by a rival nation. Gibraltar Spain was determined to recover. Its loss drove her into the arms of the enemies of England and remains to this day a grievance which on occasion Spanish politicians know well how to make useful.

Great Britain was now under the direction of a leader whose policy was peace. A nation is happy when a born statesman with a truly liberal mind and a genuine love of his country comes to the front in its affairs. Such a man was Sir Robert Walpole. He was a Whig squire, a plain country gentleman, with enough of culture to love good pictures and the ancient classics, but delighting chiefly in sports and agriculture, hard drinking and politics. When only twenty-seven he was already a leader among the Whigs; at thirty-two he was Secretary for War; and before he was forty he had become Prime Minister, a post which he really created and was the first Englishman to hold. Friendship with France marked a new phase of British policy.

Walpole's baffled enemies said that he was bribed by France. His shrewd insight kept France lukewarm in its support of the Stuart rising in 1715, which he punished with great severity. But it was as a master of finance that he was strongest. While continental nations were wasting men and money Walpole gloried in saving English lives and English gold. He found new and fruitful modes of taxation, but when urged to tax the colonies he preferred, as he said, to leave that to a bolder man. It is a pity that anyone was ever found bold enough to do it.

Walpole's policy endured for a quarter of a century. He abandoned it only after a bitter struggle in which he was attacked as sacrificing the national honour for the sake of peace. Spain was an easy mark for those who wished to arouse the warlike spirit. She still persecuted and burned heretics, a great cause of offense in Protestant Britain, and she was rigorous in excluding foreigners from trading with her colonies. To be the one exception in this policy of exclusion was the privilege enjoyed by Britain. When the fortunes of Spain were low in 1713, she had been forced not merely to cede Gibraltar but also to give to the British the monopoly of supplying the Spanish colonies with negro slaves and the right to send one ship a year to trade at Porto Bello in South America.

It seems a sufficiently ignoble bargain for a great nation to exact: the monopoly of carrying and selling cargoes of black men and the right to send a single ship yearly to a Spanish colony. We can hardly imagine grave diplomats of our day haggling over such terms. But the eighteenth century was not the twentieth. From the treaty the British expected amazing results. The South Sea Company was formed to carry on a vast trade with South America. One ship a year could, of course, carry little, but the ships laden with negroes could smuggle into the colonies merchandise and the one trading ship could be and was reloaded fraudulently from lighters so that its cargo was multiplied many-fold.

Out of the belief in huge profits from this trade with its exaggerated visions of profit grew in 1720 the famous South Sea Bubble which inaugurated a period of frantic speculation in England. Worthless shares in companies formed for trade in the South Seas sold at a thousand *per*

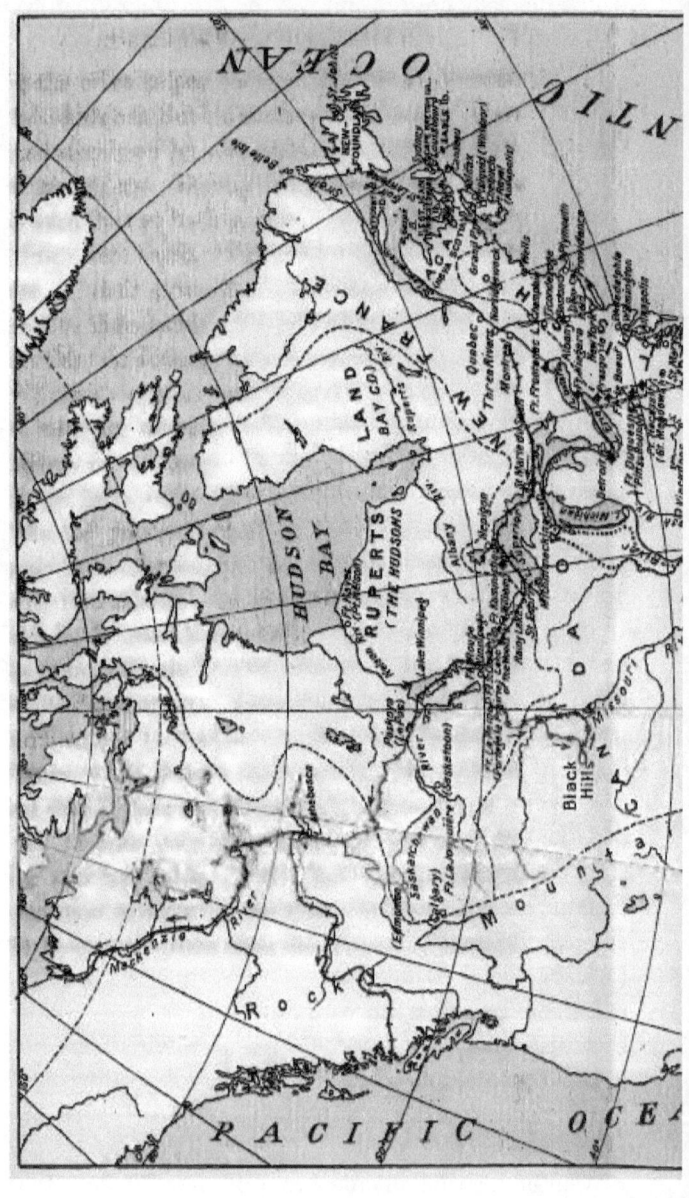

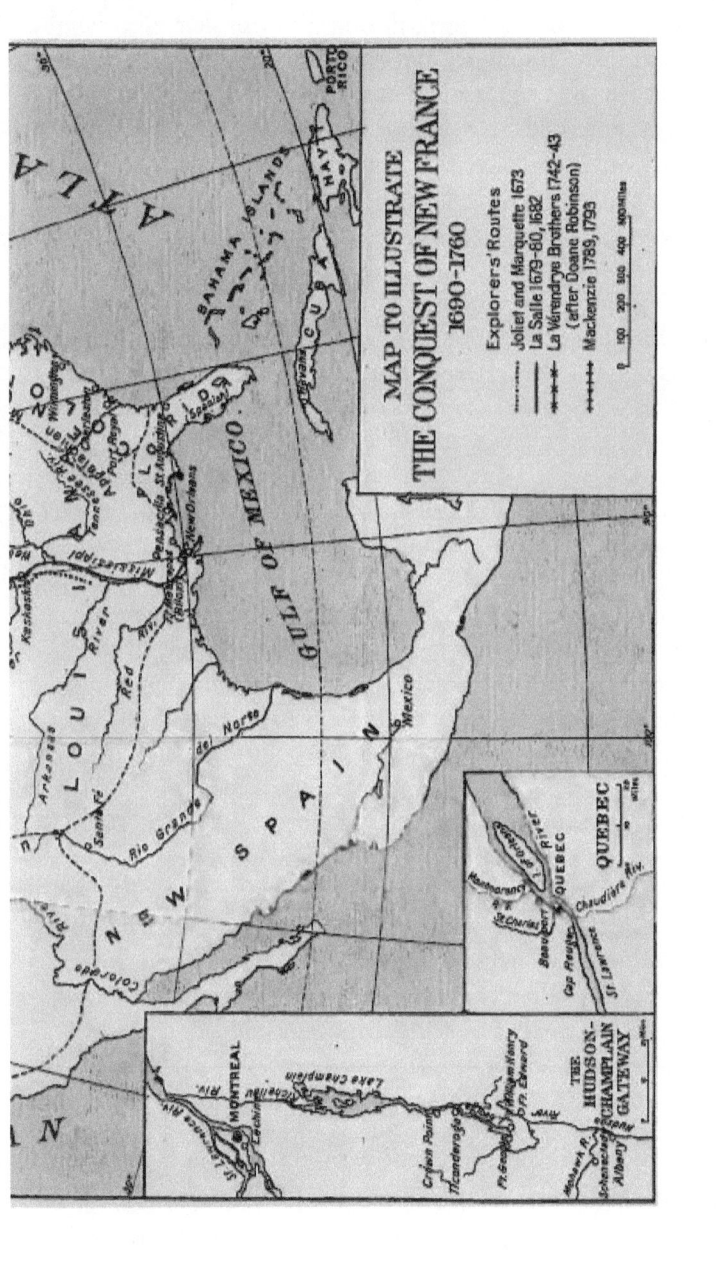

cent of their face value. It is a form of madness to which human greed is ever liable. Walpole's financial insight condemned from the first the wild outburst, and his common sense during the crisis helped to stem the tide of disaster. The South Sea Bubble burst partly because Spain stood sternly on her own rights and punished British smugglers. During many years the tension between the two nations grew. No doubt Spanish officials were harsh. Tales were repeated in England of their brutalities to British sailors who fell into their hands.

In 1739 the story of a certain Captain Jenkins that his ear had been cut off by Spanish captors and thrown in his face with an insulting message to his government brought matters to a climax. Events in other parts of Europe soon made the war general. When, in 1740, the young King of Prussia, Frederick II, came to the throne, his first act was to march an army into Silesia. To this province he had, he said, in the male line, a better claim than that of the woman, Maria Theresa, who had just inherited the Austrian crown. Frederick conquered Silesia and held it. In 1744 he was allied with Spain and France, while Britain allied herself with Austria, and thus Britain and France were again at war.

In America both sides had long seen that the war was inevitable. Never had French opinion been more arrogant in asserting France's right to North America than after the Treaty of Utrecht. At the dinner-table of the governor in Quebec there was incessant talk of Britain's incapacity, of the sheer luck by which she had blundered into the occupation of great areas, while in truth she was weak through lack of union and organisation. A natural antipathy, it was said, existed between her colonies and herself; she was a monarchy while they were really independent republics. France, on the other hand, had grown stronger since the last war. In 1713 she had retained the island of Cape Breton and now she had made it a new menace to British power. Boston, which had breathed more freely after the fall of Port Royal in 1710, soon had renewed cause for alarm in regard to its shipping.

On the southern coast of Cape Breton, there was a spacious harbour with a narrow entrance easily fortified, and here France began to build the fortress of Louisbourg. It was planned on the most approved military principles of the time. Through its strength, the boastful talk went, France should master North America. The king sent out cannon, undertook to build a hospital, to furnish chaplains for the service of the Church, to help education, and so on. Above all, he sent to Louisbourg soldiers. Reports of these wonderful things reached the English colonies and caused fears and misgivings. New England believed that Louisbourg reflected the pomp and wealth of Versailles.

The fortress was, in truth, slow in building and never more than a rather desolate outpost of France. It contained in all about four thousand people. During the thirty years of the long truce it became so strong that it was without a rival on the Atlantic coast. The excellent harbour was a haven for the fishermen of adjacent waters and a base for French privateers, who were a terror to all the near trade routes of the Atlantic. On the military side Louisbourg seemed a success. But the French failed in their effort to colonize the island of Cape Breton on which the fortress stood.

Today, (1918), this island has great iron and other industries. There are coal-mines near Louisbourg; and its harbour, long deserted after the fall of the power of France, has now an extensive commerce. The island was indeed fabulously rich in coals and minerals. To use these things, however, was to be the task of a new age of industry. The colonist of the eighteenth century—a merchant, a farmer, or a fur trader—thought that Cape Breton was bleak and infertile and refused to settle there. Louisbourg remained a compact fortress with a good harbour, free from ice during most of the year, but too much haunted by fog. It looked out on a much-travelled sea. But it remained set in the wilderness.

Even if Louisbourg made up for the loss of Port Royal, this did not, however, console France for the cession of Acadia. The fixed idea of those who shaped the policy of Canada was to recover Acadia and meanwhile to keep its French settlers loyal to France. The Acadians were not a promising people with whom to work. In Acadia, or Nova Scotia, as the English called it, these backward people had slowly gathered during a hundred years and had remained remote and neglected. They had cleared farms, built primitive houses, planted orchards, and reared cattle. In 1713 their number did not exceed two or three thousand, but already they were showing the amazing fertility of the French race in America. They were prosperous but ignorant. Almost none of them could read.

After the cession of their land to Britain in 1713 they had been guaranteed by treaty the free exercise of their religion and they were Catholics to a man. It seems as if history need hardly mention a people so feeble and obscure. Circumstances, however, made the role of the Acadians important. Their position was unique. The Treaty of Utrecht gave them the right to leave Acadia within a year, taking with them their personal effects. To this Queen Anne added the just privilege of selling their lands and houses. Neither the Acadians themselves, however, nor their new British masters were desirous that they should leave. The Acadians were content in their old homes; and the British did not wish them to help in building up the neighbouring French stronghold on Cape Breton.

It thus happened that the French officials could induce few of the Acadians to migrate and the English troubled them little. Having been resolute in acquiring Nova Scotia, Britain proceeded straightway to neglect it. She brought in few settlers. She kept there less than two hundred soldiers and even to these she paid so little attention that sometimes they had no uniforms. The Acadians prospered, multiplied, and quarrelled as to the boundaries of their lands. They rendered no military service, paid no taxes, and had the country to themselves as completely as if there had been no British conquest. They rarely saw a British official. If they asked the British Governor at Annapolis to settle for them some vexed question of rights or ownership he did so and they did not even pay a fee.

This is not, however, the whole story. England's neglect of the colony was France's opportunity. Perhaps the French court did not follow closely what was going on in Acadia. The successive French Governors of Canada at Quebec were, however, alert; and their policy was to incite the Abenaki Indians on the New England frontier to harass the English settlements, and to keep the Acadians an active factor in the support of French plans. The nature of French intrigue is best seen in the career of Sebastien Rale. He was a highly educated Jesuit priest. It was long a tradition among the Jesuits to send some of their best men as missionaries among the Indians. Rale spent nearly the whole of his life with the Abenakis at the mission station of Norridgewock on the Kennebec River. He knew the language and the customs of the Indians, attended their councils, and dominated them by his influence. He was a model missionary, earnest and scholarly.

But the Jesuit of that age was prone to be half spiritual zealot, half political intriguer. There is no doubt that the Indians had a genuine fear that the English, with danger from France apparently removed by the Treaty of Utrecht, would press claims to lands about the Kennebec River in what is now the State of Maine, and that they would ignore the claims of the Indians and drive them out. The governor at Quebec helped to arouse the savages against the arrogant intruders. English border ruffians stirred the Indians by their drunken outrages and gave them real cause for anger. The savages knew only one way of expressing political unrest. They began murdering women and children in raids on lonely log cabins on the frontier.

The inevitable result was that in 1721 Massachusetts began a war on them which dragged on for years. Rale, inspired from Quebec, was believed to control the Indians and, indeed, boasted that he did so. At last the English struck at the heart of the trouble. In 1724 some two hundred determined men made a silent advance through the forest to the mission village of Norridgewock where Rale lived, and Rale died fighting the assailants. In Europe a French Jesuit such as he would have worked among diplomats and at the luxurious courts of kings. In America he worked among savages under the hard conditions of frontier life. The methods and the aims in both cases were the same—by subtle and secret influence so to mould the actions of men that France should be exalted in power. In their high politics the French sometimes overreached themselves. To seize points of vantage, to intrigue for influence, are not in themselves creative. They must be supported by such practical efforts as will assure an economic reserve adequate in the hour of testing. France failed partly because she did not know how to lay sound industrial foundations which should give substance to the brilliant planning of her leaders.

To French influence of this kind the English opposed forces that were the outcome of their national character and institutions. They were keener traders than the French and had cheaper and better goods, with the exception perhaps of French gunpowder and of French brandy, which the Indians preferred to English rum. Though the English were less alert and less brilliant than the French, the work that they did was more enduring. Their settlements encroached ever more and more upon the forest. They found and tilled the good lands, traded and saved and gradually built up populous communities. The British colonies had twenty times the population of Canada. The tide of their power crept in slowly but it moved with the relentless force that has subsequently made nearly the whole of North America English in speech and modes of thought.

When, in 1744, open war between the two nations came at last in Europe, each prepared to spring at the other in America—and France sprang first. In Nova Scotia, on the narrow strait which separates the mainland from the island of Cape Breton, the British had a weak little fishing settlement called Canseau. Suddenly in May, 1744, when the British at Canseau had heard nothing of war, two armed vessels from

Louisbourg with six or seven hundred soldiers and sailors appeared before the poor little place and demanded its surrender. To this the eighty British defenders agreed on the condition that they should be sent to Boston which, as yet, had not heard of the war. Meanwhile they were taken to Louisbourg where they kept their eyes open. But the French continued in their offensive. The one vital place held by the British in Nova Scotia was Annapolis, at that time so neglected that the sandy ramparts had crumbled into the ditch supposed to protect them, and cows from the neighbouring fields walked up the slope and looked down into the fort.

It was Duvivier, the captor of Canseau, who attacked Annapolis. He had hoped much for help from the Indians and the Acadians, but, though both seemed eager, both failed him in action. Paul Mascarene, who defended Annapolis, was of Huguenot blood, which stimulated him to fight the better against the Catholic French. Boston sent him help, for that little capital was deeply moved, and so Annapolis did not fall, though it was harassed during the whole summer of 1744; and New England, in a fever at the new perils of war, prepared a mighty stroke against the French.

This expedition was to undertake nothing less than the capture of Louisbourg itself. The colonial troops had been so often reminded of their inferiority to regular troops as fighting forces that, with provincial docility, they had almost come to accept the estimate. It was well enough for them to fight irregular French and Indian bands, but to attack a fortress defended by a French garrison was something that only a few bold spirits among them could imagine. Such a spirit, however, was William Vaughan, a Maine trader, deeply involved m the fishing industry and confronted with ruin from hostile Louisbourg. Shirley, the Governor of Massachusetts, a man of eager ambition, took up the proposal and worked out an elaborate plan. The prisoners who had been captured at Canseau by the French and interned at Louisbourg now arrived at Boston and told of bad conditions in the fortress.

In January, 1745, Shirley called a session of the General Court, the little parliament of Massachusetts, and, having taken the unusual step of pledging the members to secrecy, he unfolded his plan. But it proved too bold for the prudent legislators, and they voted it down. Meanwhile New England trade was suffering from ships which used Louisbourg as a base. At length public opinion was aroused and, when Shirley again called the General Court, a bare majority endorsed his plan. Soon thereafter New England was aflame. Appeals for help were sent to England and, it is said, even to Jamaica. Shirley counted on aid from a British squadron, under Commodore Peter Warren, in American waters, but at first Warren had no instructions to help such a plan. This disappointment did not keep New England from going on alone. In the end Warren received instructions to give the necessary substantial aid, and he established a strict blockade which played a vital part in the siege of the French fortress.

In this hour of deadly peril Louisbourg was in not quite happy case. Some of the French officers, who would otherwise have starved on their low pay, were taking part in illicit trade and were neglecting their duties. Just after Christmas in 1744, there had been a mutiny over a petty question of butter and bacon. Here, as in all French colonies, there were cliques, with the suspicions and bitterness which they involve. The Governor Duchambon, though brave enough, was a man of poor judgment in a position that required both tact and talent. The English did not make the mistake of delaying their preparations. They were indeed so prompt that they arrived at Canseau early in April and had to wait for the ice to break up in Gabarus Bay, near Louisbourg, where they intended to land. Here, on April 30, the great fleet appeared. A watcher in Louisbourg counted ninety-six ships standing off shore. With little opposition from the French the amazing army landed at Freshwater Cove.

Then began an astonishing siege. The commander of the New England forces, William Pepperrell, was a Maine trader, who dealt in a little of everything, fish, groceries, lumber, ships, land. Though innocent of military science, he was firm and tactful. A British officer with strict military ideas could not, perhaps, have led that strange army with success. Pepperrell knew that he had good fighting material; he knew, too, how to handle it. In his army of some four thousand men there was probably not one officer with a regular training. Few of his force had proper equipment, but nearly all his men were handy on a ship as well as on land. In Louisbourg were about two thousand defenders, of whom only five or six hundred were French regulars. These professional soldiers watched with contempt not untouched with apprehension the breaches of military precedent in the operations of the besiegers. Men harnessed like horses dragged guns through morasses into position, exposed themselves recklessly, and showed the skill, initiative, and resolution which we have now come to consider the dominant qualities of the Yankee.

In time Warren arrived with a British squadron and then the

French were puzzled anew. They could not understand the relations between the fleet and the army, which seemed to them to belong to different nations. The New Englanders appeared to be under a governor who was something like an independent monarch. He had drawn up elaborate plans for his army, comical in their apparent disregard of the realities of war, naming the hour when the force should land "unobserved" before Louisbourg, instructing Pepperrell to surprise that place while everyone was asleep, and so on. Kindly Providence was expected even to give continuous good weather. "The English appear to have enlisted Heaven in their interests," said a despairing resident of the town; "so long as the expedition lasted they had the most beautiful weather in the world." There were no storms; the winds were favourable; fog, so common on that coast, did not creep in; and the sky was clear.

Among the French the opinion prevailed that the English colonists were ferocious pirates plotting eternally to destroy the power of France. Their liberty, however, it was well understood, had made them strong; and now they quickly became formidable soldiers. Their shooting, bad at first, was, in the end, superb. Sometimes in their excess of zeal they overcharged their cannon so that the guns burst. But they managed to hit practically every house in Louisbourg, and since most of the houses were of wood there was constant danger of fire. Some of the French fought well. Even children of ten and twelve helped to carry ammunition.

The Governor Duchambon tried to keep up the spirits of the garrison by absurd exaggeration of British losses. He was relying much on help from France, but only a single ship reached port. On May 19, 1745, the besieged saw approaching Louisbourg a great French ship of war, the *Vigilant*, long looked for, carrying 64 guns and 560 men. A northwest wind was blowing which would have brought her quickly into the harbour. The British fleet was two and a half leagues away to leeward. The great ship, thinking herself secure, did not even stop to communicate with Louisbourg but wantonly gave chase to a small British privateer which she encountered near the shore.

By skilful manoeuvring the smaller ship led the French frigate out to sea again, and then the British squadron came up. From five o'clock to ten in the evening anxious men in Louisbourg watched the fight and saw at last the *Vigilant* surrender after losing eighty men. This disaster broke the spirit of the defenders, who were already short of ammunition. When they knew that the British were preparing for a combined assault by land and sea, they made terms and surrendered on the 17th of June, after the siege had lasted for seven weeks. The garrison marched out with the honours of war, to be transported to France, together with such of the civilian population as wished to go.

The British squadron then sailed into the harbour. Pepperrell's strange army, ragged and war-worn after the long siege, entered the town by the south gate. They had fought as crusaders, for to many of them Catholic Louisbourg was a stronghold of Satan. Whitfield, the great English evangelist, then in New England, had given them a motto—*Nil desperandum Christo duce*. There is a story that one of the English chaplains, old Parson Moody, a man of about seventy, had brought with him from Boston an axe and was soon found using it to hew down the altar and images in the church at Louisbourg.

If the story is true, it does something to explain the belief of the French in the savagery of their opponents who would so treat things which their enemies held to be most sacred. The French had met this fanaticism with a savagery equally intense and directed not against things but against the flesh of men. An inhabitant of Louisbourg during the siege describes the dauntless bravery of the Indian allies of the French during the siege:

> Full of hatred for the English whose ferocity they abhor; they destroy all upon whom they can lay hands.

He does not have even a word of censure for the savages who tortured and killed in cold blood a party of some twenty English who had been induced to surrender on promise of life. The French declared that not they but the savages were responsible for such barbarities, and the English retorted that the French must control their allies. Feeling on such things was naturally bitter on both sides and did much to decide that the war between the two nations should be to the death.

The fall of Louisbourg brought great exultation to the English colonies. It was a unique event, the first prolonged and successful siege that had as yet taken place north of Mexico. An odd chance of war had decreed that untrained soldiers should win a success so prodigious. New England, it is true, had incurred a heavy expenditure, and her men, having done so much, naturally imagined that they had done everything, and talked as if the siege was wholly their triumph. They were, of course, greatly aided by the fleet under Warren, and the achievement was a joint triumph of army and navy. New England

SIR WILLIAM PEPPERRELL

alone, however, had the credit of conceiving and of arousing others to carry out a brilliant exploit.

Victory inspires to further victory. The British, exultant after Louisbourg, were resolved to make an end of French power in America. "*Delenda est Canada!*" cried Governor Shirley to the General Court of Massachusetts, and the response of the members was the voting of men and money on a scale that involved the bankruptcy of the Commonwealth. Other colonies, too, were eager for a cause which had won a success so dazzling, and some eight thousand men were promised for an attack on Canada, proud and valiant Massachusetts contributing nearly one-half of the total number. The old plan was to be followed. New York was to lead in an attack by way of Lake Champlain. New England was to collect its forces at Louisbourg. Here a British fleet should come, carrying eight battalions of British regulars, and, with Warren in command, the whole armada should proceed to Quebec. Nothing came of this elaborate scheme. Neither the promised troops nor the fleet arrived from England. British ministers broke faith with the colonists in the adventure with quite too light a heart.

Stories went abroad of disorder and dissension in Louisbourg under the English and of the weakness of the place. Disease broke out. Hundreds of New England soldiers died and their bones now lie in graves, unmarked and forgotten, on the seashore by the deserted fortress; at almost any time still their bones, washed down by the waves, may be picked up on the beach. There were sullen mutterings of discontent at Louisbourg. Soldiers grumbled over grievances which were sometimes fantastic. Rumour had been persistent in creating a legend that vast wealth, the accumulated plunder brought in by French privateers, was stored in the town. From this source a rich reward in booty was expected by the soldiers.

In fact, when Louisbourg was taken, all looting was forbidden and the soldiers were put on guard over houses which they had hoped to rob. For the soldiers there were no prizes. Louisbourg was poor. The sailors, on the other hand, Were fortunate. As a decoy Warren kept the French flag flying over the harbour, and French ships sailed in, one of them with a vast treasure of gold and silver coin and ingots from Peru valued at £600,000. One other prize was valued at £200,000 and a third at £140,000. Warren's own share of prize money amounted to £60,000, while Pepperrell, the unrewarded leader of the sister service, piled up a personal debt of £10,000. Quarrels occurred between soldiers and sailors, and in these the New Englanders soon proved by no means the cowards which complacent superiority in England considered them; rather, as an enlightened Briton said, "If they had pickaxe and spade they would dig a way to Hell itself and storm that stronghold."

Behind all difficulties was the question whether, having taken Louisbourg, the British could continue to hold it. France answered with a resolute "No." To retake it she fitted out a great fleet. Nearly half her navy gathered under the Duc d'Anville and put to sea on June 20, 1746. If in the previous summer God had helped the English with good weather, by a similar proof His face now appeared turned a second time against the French. In the great array there were more than sixty ships, which were to gather at Chebucto, now Halifax, harbour, and to be joined there by four great ships of war from the West Indies. Everything went wrong. On the voyage across the Atlantic there was a prolonged calm, followed by a heavy squall. Several ships were struck by lightning. A magazine on the *Mars* blew up, killing ten and wounding twenty-one men. Pestilence broke out.

As a crowning misfortune, the fleet was scattered by a terrific storm. After great delay d'Anville's ship reached Chebucto, then a wild and lonely spot. The expected fleet from the West Indies had indeed come, but had gone, since the ships from France, long overdue, had not arrived. D'Anville died suddenly—some said of apoplexy, others of poison self-administered. More ships arrived full of sick men and short of provisions. D'Estournel, who succeeded d'Anville in chief command, in despair at the outlook killed himself with his own sword after the experience of only a day or two in his post. La Jonquière, a competent officer, afterwards Governor of Canada, then led the expedition. The pestilence still raged, and from two to three thousand men died.

One day a Boston sloop boldly entered Chebucto harbour to find out what was going on. It is a wonder that the British did not descend upon the stricken French and destroy them. In October, La Jonquière, having pulled his force together, planned to win the small success of taking Annapolis, but again storms scattered his ships. At the end of October, he finally decided to return to France. But there were more heavy storms; and one French crew was so near starvation that only a chance meeting with a Portuguese ship kept them from killing and eating five English prisoners. Only a battered remnant of the fleet eventually reached home ports.

The disaster did not crush France. In May of the next spring, 1747, a new fleet under La Jonquière set out to retake Louisbourg. Near the coast of Europe, however. Admirals Anson and Warren met and completely destroyed it, taking prisoner La Jonquière himself. This disaster effected what was really the most important result of the war: it made the British fleet definitely superior to the French. During the struggle England had produced a new Drake, who attacked Spain in the spirit of the sea-dogs of Elizabeth. Anson had gone in 1740 into the Pacific, where he seized and plundered Spanish ships as Drake had done nearly two centuries earlier; and in 1744, when he had been given up for lost, he completed the great exploit of sailing round the world and bringing home rich booty. Such feats went far to give Britain that command of the sea on which her colonial Empire was to depend.

The issue of the war hung more on events that occurred in Europe than in America, and France had made gains as well as suffered losses. It was on the sea that she had sustained her chief defeats. In India she had gained by taking the English factory at Madras; and in the Low Countries she was still aggressive. Indeed, during the war England had been more hostile to Spain than to France. She had not taken very seriously her support of the colonies in their attack on Louisbourg and she had failed them utterly in their designs on Canada. It is true that in Europe England had grave problems to solve. Austria, with which she was allied, desired her to fight until Frederick of Prussia should give up the province of Silesia seized by him in 1740.

In this quarrel England had no vital interest. France had occupied the Austrian Netherlands and had refused to hand back to Austria this territory unless she received Cape Breton in return. Britain might have kept Cape Breton if she would have allowed France to keep Belgium. This, in loyalty to Austria, she would not do. Accordingly, peace was made at Aix-la-Chapelle in 1748 on the agreement that each side should restore to the other its conquests, not merely in Europe but also in America and Asia. Thus it happened that the British flag went up again at Madras while it came down at Louisbourg.

Boston was of course angry at the terms of the treaty. What sacrifices had Massachusetts not made! The least of them was the great burden of debt which she had piled up. Her sons had borne what Pepperrell called "almost incredible hardships." They had landed cannon on a lee shore when the great waves pounded to pieces their boats and when men wading breast high were crushed by the weight of iron. Harnessed two and three hundred to a gun, they had dragged the pieces one after the other over rocks and through bog and slime, and had then served them in the open under the fire of the enemy. New

Englanders had died like "rotten sheep" in Louisbourg. The graves of nearly a thousand of them lay on the bleak point outside the wall. What they had gained by this sacrifice must now be abandoned. A spirit of discontent with the mother country went abroad and, after this sacrifice of colonial interests, never wholly died out. It is not without interest to note in passing that Gridley, the engineer who drew the plan of the defences of Louisbourg, thirty years later drew those of Bunker Hill to protect men of the English race who fought against England.

Everyone knew that the peace of 1748 was only a truce and Britain began promptly new defences. Into the spacious harbour of Chebucto, which three years earlier had been the scene of the sorrows of d'Anville's fleet, there sailed in June, 1749, a considerable British squadron bent on a momentous errand. It carried some thousands of settlers, Edward Cornwallis, a governor clothed with adequate authority, and a force sufficient for the defence of the new foundation. Cornwallis was delighted with the prospect. "All the officers agree the harbour is the finest they have ever seen"—this, of Halifax harbour with the great Bedford Basin, opening beyond it, spacious enough to contain the fleets of the world.

> The country is one continuous wood, no clear spot to be seen or heard of. D'Anville's fleet . . . cleared no ground; they encamped their men on the beach.

The garrison was withdrawn from Louisbourg and soon arrived at Halifax, with a vast quantity of stores. A town was marked out; lots were drawn for sites; and everyone knew where he might build his house. There were prodigious digging, chopping, hammering. "I shall be able to get them all Houses before winter," wrote Cornwallis cheerily. Firm military discipline, indeed, did wonders. Before winter came, a town had been created, and with the town a fortress which from that time has remained the chief naval and military stronghold of Great Britain in North America. At Louisbourg some two hundred miles farther east on the coast.

France could re-establish her military strength, but now Louisbourg had a rival and each was resolved to yield nothing to the other. The founding of Halifax was in truth the symbol of the renewal of the struggle for a continent.

CHAPTER 5

The Great West

In days before the railway had made possible a bulky commerce by overland routes, rivers furnished the chief means of access to inland regions. The fame of the Ganges, the Euphrates, the Nile, and the Danube shows the part which great rivers have played in history. Of North America's four greatest river systems, the two in the far north have become known in times so recent that their place in history is not yet determined. One of them, the Mackenzie, a mighty stream some two thousand miles long, flows into the Arctic Ocean through what remains chiefly a wilderness. The waters of the other, the Saskatchewan, discharge into Hudson Bay more than a thousand miles from their source, flowing through rich prairie land which is still but scantily peopled. On the Saskatchewan, as on the remaining two systems, the St. Lawrence and the Mississippi, the French were the pioneers. Though today the regions drained by these four rivers are dominated by the rival race, the story which we now follow is one of romantic enterprise in which the honours are with France.

More perhaps by accident than by design had the French been the first to settle on the St. Lawrence. Fishing vessels had hovered round the entrance to the Gulf of St. Lawrence for years before, in 1535, the French sailor, Jacques Cartier, advanced up the river as far as the foot of the torrential rapids where now stands the city of Montreal. Cartier was seeking a route to the Far East. He half believed that this impressive waterway drained the plains of China and that around the next bend he might find the busy life of an oriental city. The time came when it was known that a great sea lay between America and Asia and the mystery of the pathway to this sea long fascinated the pioneers of the St. Lawrence. Canada was a colony, a trading-post, a mission, the favourite field of Jesuit activity, but it was also the land which offered by way of the St. Lawrence a route leading illimitably westward to the Far East.

One other route rivalled the St. Lawrence in promise, and that was the Mississippi. The two rivers are essentially different in their approaches and in type. The mouth of the St. Lawrence opens directly towards Europe and of all American rivers lies nearest to the seafaring peoples of Europe. Since it flows chiefly in a rocky bed, its course changes little; its waters are clear, and they become icy cold as they approach the sea and mingle with the tide which flows into the great Gulf of St. Lawrence from the Arctic regions. The Mississippi, on the other hand, is a turbid, warm stream, flowing through soft lands. Its shifting channel is divided at its mouth by deltas created from the vast quantity of soil which the river carries in its current. On the low-lying, forest-clad, northern shore of the Gulf of Mexico it was not easy to find the mouth of the Mississippi by approaching it from the sea. The voyage there from France was long and difficult; and, moreover, Spain claimed the lands bordering on the Gulf of Mexico and declared herself ready to drive out all intruders.

Nature, it is clear, dictated that, if France was to build up her power in the interior of the New World, it was the valley of the St. Lawrence which she should first occupy. Time has shown the riches of the lands drained by the St. Lawrence. On no other river system in the world is there now such a multitude of great cities. The modern traveller who advances by this route to the sources of the river beyond the Great Lakes surveys wonders ever more impressive. Before his view appear in succession Quebec, Montreal, Toronto, Buffalo, Cleveland, Detroit, Chicago, Duluth, and many other cities and towns, with millions in population and an aggregate of wealth so vast as to stagger the imagination.

Step by step had the French advanced from Quebec to the interior. Champlain was on Lake Huron in 1615, and there the Jesuits soon had a flourishing mission to the Huron Indians. They had only to follow the shore of Lake Huron to come to the St. Mary's River bearing towards the sea the chilly waters of Lake Superior. On this river, a much frequented fishing ground of the natives, they founded the mission of Sainte Marie du Saut. Farther to the south, on the narrow opening connecting Lake Huron and Lake Michigan, grew up the post known as Michilimackinac. It was then inevitable that explorers and missionaries should press on into both Lake Superior and Lake Michigan. By the time that Frontenac came first to Canada in 1672 the French had a post called St. Esprit on the south shore of Lake Superior near its western end and they had also passed westward from Lake Michigan and founded posts on both the Illinois and the Wisconsin Rivers which flow into the Mississippi.

France had placed on record her claim to the whole of the Great West. On a June morning in 1671 there had been a striking scene at Sainte Marie du Saut. The French had summoned a great throng of Indians to the spot. There, with impressive ceremony, Saint-Lusson, an officer from Canada, had set up a cedar post on which was a plate engraved with the royal arms, and proclaimed Louis XIV lord of all the Indian tribes and of all the lands, rivers, and lakes, discovered and to be discovered in the region stretching from the Atlantic to that other mysterious sea beyond the spreading lands of the West. Henceforth at their peril would the natives disobey the French king, or other states encroach upon these his lands.

A Jesuit priest followed Saint-Lusson with a description to the savages of their new lord, the King of France. He was master of all the other rulers of the world. At his word the earth trembled. He could set earth and sea on fire by the blaze of his cannon. The priest knew the temper of his savage audience and told of the king's warriors covered with the blood of his enemies, of the rivers of blood which flowed from their wounds, of the king's countless prisoners, of his riches and his power, so great that all the world obeyed him. The savages gave delighted shouts at the strange ceremony, but of its real meaning they knew nothing. What they understood was that the French seemed to be good friends who brought them muskets, hatchets, cloth, and especially the loved but destructive firewater which the savage palate ever craved.

The mystery of the Great Lakes once solved, there still remained that of the Western Sea. The St. Lawrence flowed eastward. Another river must therefore be found flowing westward. The French were eager listeners when the savages talked of a mighty river in the west flowing to the sea. They meant, as we now suppose, the Mississippi. There are vague stories of Frenchmen on the Mississippi at an earlier date; but, however this may be, it is certain that in the summer of 1673 Louis Joliet, the son of a wagon-maker of Quebec, and Jacques Marquette, a Jesuit priest, reached and descended the great river from the mouth of the Wisconsin to a point far past the mouth of the Ohio.

France thus planted herself on the Mississippi, though there her occupation was less complete and thorough than it was on the St.

Lawrence. Distance was an obstacle; it was a far cry from Quebec by land, and from France the voyage by sea through the Gulf of Mexico was hardly less difficult. The explorer La Salle tried both routes. In 1681-1682 he set out from Montreal, reached the Mississippi overland, and descended to its mouth. Two years later he sailed from France with four ships bound for the mouth of the river, there to establish a colony; but before achieving his aim he was murdered in a treacherous attack led by his own countrymen.

It was Pierre Le Moyne, Sieur d'Iberville, who first made good France's claim to the Mississippi. He reached the river by sea in 1699 and ascended to a point some eighty miles beyond the present city of New Orleans. Farther east, on Biloxi Bay, he built Fort Maurepas and planted his first colony. Spain disliked this intrusion; but Spain—soon to be herself ruled, as France then was, by a Bourbon king—did not prove irreconcilable and slowly France built up a colony in the south. It was in 1718 that Iberville's brother, Jean Baptiste Le Moyne, Sieur de Bienville, founded New Orleans, destined to become in time one of the great cities of North America. Its beginnings were not propitious. The historian Charlevoix describes it as being in 1721 a low-lying, malarious place, infested by snakes and alligators, and consisting of a hundred wretched hovels.

In spite of this dreary outlook, it was still true that France, planted at the mouth of the Mississippi, controlled the greatest waterway in the world. Soon she had scattered settlements stretching northward to the Ohio and the Missouri, the one river reaching eastward almost to the waters of the St. Lawrence system, the other flowing out of the western plains from its source in the Rocky Mountains. The old mystery, however, remained, for the Mississippi flowed into the Gulf of Mexico, into Atlantic waters already well known. The route to the Western Sea was still to be found.

It was easy enough for France to record a sweeping claim to the West, but to make good this claim she needed a chain of posts, which should also be forts, linking the Mississippi with the St. Lawrence and strong enough to impress the Indians whose country she had invaded. At first she had reached the interior by way of the Ottawa River and Lake Huron, and in that northern country her position was secure enough through her posts on the upper lakes. The route farther south by Lake Ontario and Lake Erie was more difficult. The Iroquois menaced Niagara and long refused to let France have a footing there to protect her pathway to Lake Erie and the Ohio Valley.

It was not until 1720, a period comparatively late, that the French managed to have a fort at the mouth of the Niagara. On the Detroit River, the next strategic point on the way westward, they were established earlier. Just after Frontenac died in 1698, La Mothe Cadillac urged that there should be built on this river a fort and town which might be made the centre of all the trading interests west of Lake Erie. End the folly, he urged, of going still farther afield among the Indians and teaching them the French language and French modes of thought. Leave the Indians to live their own type of life, to hunt and to fish. They need European trade and they have valuable furs to exchange. Encourage them to come to the French at Detroit and see that they go nowhere else by not allowing any other posts in the western country.

Cadillac was himself a keen if secret participant in the profits of the fur trade and hoped to be placed in command at Detroit and there to become independent of control from Quebec. Detroit was founded in 1701; and. though for a long time it did not thrive, the fact that on the site has grown up one of the great industrial cities of modern times shows that Cadillac had read aright the meaning of the geography of North America.

When France was secure at Niagara and at Detroit, two problems still remained unsolved. One was that of occupying the valley of the Ohio, the waters of which flow westward almost from the south shore of Lake Erie until they empty into the vaster flood of the Mississippi. Here there was a lion in the path, for the English claimed this region as naturally the hinterland of the colonies of Virginia and Pennsylvania. What happened on the Ohio we shall see in a later chapter. The other great problem, to be followed here, was to explore the regions which lay beyond the Mississippi. These spread into a remote unknown, unexplored by the white man, and might ultimately lead to the Western Sea. We might have supposed that France's farther adventure into the West would have been from the Mississippi up its great tributary the Missouri, which flows eastward from the eternal snows of the Rocky Mountains. Always, however, the uncertain temper of the many Indian tribes in this region made the advance difficult. The tribes inhabiting the west bank of the Mississippi were especially restless and savage. The Sioux, in particular, made life perilous for the French at their posts near the mouth of the Missouri.

It thus happened that the white man first reached the remoter West by way of regions farther north. It became easy enough to coast along the north and the south shore of Lake Superior, easy enough to find rivers which fed the great system of the St. Lawrence or of the Mississippi. These, however, would not solve the mystery. A river flowing westward was still to be sought. Thus, both in pursuit of the fur trade and in quest of the Western Sea, the French advanced westward from Lake Superior. Where now stands the city of Fort William there flows into Lake Superior the little stream called still by its Indian name of Kaministiquia. There the French had long maintained a trading-post from which they made adventurous journeys northward and westward.

The rugged regions still farther north had already been explored, at least in outline. There lay the great inland sea known as Hudson Bay. French and English had long disputed for its mastery. By 1670 the English had found trade to Hudson Bay so promising that they then created the Hudson's Bay Company, which remains one of the great trading corporations of the world. With the English on Hudson Bay, New France was between English on the north and English on the south and did not like it. On Hudson Bay the English showed the same characteristics which they had shown in New England. They were not stirred by vivid imaginings of what might be found westward beyond the low-lying coast of the great inland sea.

They came for trade, planted themselves at the mouths of the chief rivers, unpacked their goods, and waited for the natives to come to barter with them. For many years the natives came, since they must have the knives, hatchets, and firearms of Europe. To share this profitable trade, the French, now going overland to the north from Quebec, now sailing into Hudson Bay by the Straits, attacked the English; and on those dreary waters, long before the Great West was known, there had been many a naval battle, many a hand-to-hand fight for forts and their rich prize of furs.

The chief French hero in this struggle was that son of Charles Le Moyne of Montreal, Pierre Le Moyne d'Iberville, who ended his days in the task of founding the French colony of Louisiana. He was perhaps the most notable of all the adventurous leaders whom New France produced. He was first on Hudson Bay in the late summer of 1686, in a party of about a hundred men, led by the Chevalier de Troyes, who had marched overland from Quebec through the wilderness. The English on the Bay, with a charter from King Charles II, the friend of the French, and in a time of profound peace under his successor, thought themselves secure. They now had, however, a rude awakening. In the dead of night, the Frenchmen fell upon Fort Hayes, captured its dazed garrison, and looted the place. The same fate befell all the other English posts on the Bay. Iberville gained a rich store of furs as his share of the plunder and returned with it to Quebec in 1687, just at the time when La Salle, that other pioneer of France, was struck down in the distant south by a murderer's hand.

Iberville was, above all else, a sailor. The easiest route to Hudson Bay was by way of the sea. More than once after his first experience he led to the Bay a naval expedition. His exploits are still remembered with pride in French naval annals. In 1697 he sailed the *Pelican* through the ice-floes of Hudson Straits. He was attacked by three English merchantmen, with one hundred and twenty guns against his forty-four. One of the English ships escaped, one Iberville sank with all on board, one he captured. That autumn the hardy *corsair* was in France with a great booty from the furs which the English had laboriously gathered.

The triumph of the French on Hudson Bay was short-lived. Their exploits, though brilliant and daring, were more of the nature of raids than attempts to settle and explore. They did no more than the English to ascend the Nelson or other rivers to find what lay beyond; and in 1713, by the Treaty of Utrecht, as we have already seen, they gave up all claim to Hudson Bay and yielded that region to the English.

Pierre Gaultier de Varennes, Sieur de la Vérendrye, was a member of the Canadian *noblesse*, a son of the Governor of Three Rivers on the St. Lawrence. He was born in 1685 and had taken part in the border warfare of the days of Queen Anne. He was a member of the raiding party led against New England by Hertel de Rouville in 1704 and may have been one of those who burst in on the little town of Deerfield, Massachusetts, and either butchered or carried off as prisoners most of the inhabitants. Shortly afterwards we find him a participant in warfare of a less ignoble type. In 1706 he went to France and became an ensign in a regiment of grenadiers.

Those were the days when Marlborough was hammering and destroying the armies of Louis XIV. La Vérendrye took part in the last of the series of great battles, the bloody conflict at Malplaquet in 1709. He received a bullet wound through the body, was left for dead on the field, fell into the hands of the enemy, and for fifteen months was a captive. On his release he was too poor to maintain himself as an officer in France and soon returned to Canada, where he served as an officer in a colonial regiment until the peace of 1713. Then the ambitious young man, recently married, with a growing family and slight resources, had to work out a career suited to his genius.

His genius was that of an explorer; his task, which fully occupied his alert mind, was that of finding the long dreamed of passage to the Western Sea. The venture certainly offered fascinations. Noyon, a fellow-townsman of La Vérendrye at Three Rivers, had brought back from the distant Lake of the Woods, in 1716, a glowing account, told to him by the natives, of walled cities, of ships and cannon, and of white-bearded men who lived farther west.

In 1720 the Jesuit Charlevoix, already familiar with Canada, came out from France, went to the Mississippi country, and reported that an attempt to find the path to the Western Sea might be made either by way of the Missouri or farther north through the country of the Sioux west of Lake Superior. Both routes involved going among warlike native tribes engaged in incessant and bloody struggles with each other and not unlikely to turn on the white intruder. Memorial after memorial to the French court for assistance resulted at last in serious effort, but effort handicapped because the court thought that a monopoly of the fur trade was the only inducement required to promote the work of discovery.

La Vérendrye was more eager to reach the Western Sea than he was to trade. To outward seeming, however, he became just a fur trader and a successful one. We find him, in 1726, at the trading-post of Nipigon, not far from the lake of that name, near the north shore of Lake Superior. From this point it was not very difficult to reach the shore of one great sea, Hudson Bay, but that was not the Western Sea which fired his imagination. Incessantly he questioned the savages with whom he traded about what lay in the unknown West. His zeal was kindled anew by the talk of an Indian named Ochagach. This man said that he himself had been on a great lake lying; west of Lake Superior, that out of it flowed a river westward, that he had paddled down this river until he came to water which, as La Vérendrye understood, rose and fell like the tide.

Farther, to the actual mouth of the river, the savage had not gone, for fear of enemies, but he had been told that it emptied into a great body of salt water upon the shores of which lived many people. We may be sure that La Vérendrye read into the words of the savage the meaning which he himself desired and that in reality the Indian was describing only the waters which flow into Lake Winnipeg.

La Vérendrye was all eagerness. Soon we find him back at Quebec stirring by his own enthusiasm the zeal of the Marquis de Beauharnois, the Governor of Canada, and begging for help to pay and equip a hundred men for the great enterprise in the West. The governor did what he could but was unable to move the French court to give money. The sole help offered was a monopoly of the fur trade in the region to be explored, a doubtful gift, since it angered all the traders excluded from the monopoly. La Vérendrye, however, was able, by promising to hand over most of the profits, to persuade merchants in Montreal to equip him with the necessary men and merchandise.

There followed a period of high hopes and of heart-breaking failure. In 1731 La Vérendrye set out for the West with three sons, a nephew, a Jesuit priest, the Indian Ochagach as guide—a party numbering in all about fifty. He intended to build trading-posts as he went westward and to make the last post always a base from which to advance still farther. His difficulties read like those of Columbus. His men not only disliked the hard work which was inevitable but were haunted by superstitious fears of malignant fiends in the unknown land who were ready to punish the invaders of their secrets. The route lay across the rough country beyond Lake Superior. There were many long portages over which his men must carry the provisions and heavy stores for trade.

At length the party reached Rainy Lake, and out of Rainy Lake the waters flow westward. The country seemed delightful. Fish and game were abundant, and it was not hard to secure a rich store of furs. On the shore of the lake, in a charming meadow surrounded by oak trees. La Vérendrye built a trading-post on waters flowing to the west, naming it Fort St. Pierre.

The voyageurs could now travel westward with the current. It is certain that other Frenchmen had preceded them in that region, but this is the first voyage of discovery of which we have any details. Escorted by an imposing array of fifty canoes of Indians, La Vérendrye floated down Rainy River to the Lake of the Woods, and here, on a beautiful peninsula jutting out into the lake, he built another post, Fort St. Charles. It must have seemed imposing to the natives. On walls one hundred feet square were four bastions and a watchtower; evidence of the perennial need of alertness and strength in the Indian country. There were a chapel, houses for the commandant and the priest, a powder-magazine, a storehouse, and other buildings.

La Vérendrye cleared some land and planted wheat, and was thus the pioneer in the mighty wheat production of the West. Fish and game were abundant and the outlook was smiling. By this time the second winter of La Vérendrye's adventurous journeying was near, but even the cold of that hard region could not chill his eagerness. He himself waited at Fort St. Charles but his eldest son, Jean Baptiste, set out to explore still farther. We may follow with interest the little group of Frenchmen and Indian guides as they file on snowshoes along the surface of the frozen river or over the deep snow of the silent forest on, ever on, to the West. They are the first white men of whom we have certain knowledge to press beyond the Lake of the Woods into that great Northwest so full of meaning for the future.

The going was laborious and the distances seemed long, for on their return they reported that they had gone a hundred and fifty leagues, though in truth the distance was only a hundred and fifty miles. Then at last they stood on the shores of a vast body of water, ice-bound and forbidding as it lay in the grip of winter. It opened out illimitably westward. But it was not the Western Sea, for its waters were fresh. The shallow waters of Lake Winnipeg empty not into the Western Sea but into the Atlantic by way of Hudson Bay. Its shores then were deserted and desolate, and even to this day they are but scantily peopled. In that wild land there was no hint of the populous East of which La Vérendrye had dreamed.

At the mouth of the Winnipeg River, where it enters Lake Winnipeg, La Vérendrye built Fort Maurepas, named after the French minister who was in charge of the colonies and who was influential at court. The name no doubt expresses some clinging hope which La Vérendrye still cherished of obtaining help from the king. Already he was hard pressed for resources. Where were the means to come from for this costly work of building forts? From time to time he sent eastward canoes laden with furs which, after a long and difficult journey, reached Montreal. The traders to whom the furs were consigned sold them and kept the money as their own on account of their outlay. La Vérendrye in the far interior could not pay his men and would soon be without goods to trade with the Indians.

After having repeatedly begged for help but in vain, he made a rapid journey to Montreal and implored the governor to aid an enterprise which might change the outlook of the whole world. The governor was willing but without the consent of France could not give help. By promising the traders, who were now partners in his monopoly, profits of one hundred *per cent* on their outlay, La Vérendrye at last secured what he needed. His canoes were laden with goods, and soon brawny arms were driving once again the graceful craft westward. He had offered a new hostage to fortune by arranging that his fourth son, a lad of eighteen, should follow him in the next year.

La Vérendrye pressed on eagerly in advance of the heavy-laden canoes. Grim news met him soon after he reached Fort St. Charles on the Lake of the Woods. His nephew La Jemeraye, a born leader of men, who was at the most advanced station, Fort Maurepas on Lake Winnipeg, had broken down from exposure, anxiety, and overwork, and had been laid in a lonely grave in the wilderness. Nearly all pioneer work is a record of tragedy and its gloom lies heavy on the career of La Vérendrye. A little later came another sorrow-laden disaster. La Vérendrye sent his eldest son Jean back to Rainy Lake to hurry the canoes from Montreal which were bringing needed food. The party landed on a peninsula at the discharge of Rainy Lake into Rainy River, fell into an ambush of Sioux Indians, and were butchered to a man. This incident reveals the chief cause of the slow progress in discovery in the Great West: the temper of the savages was always uncertain.

There is no sign that La Vérendrye wavered in his great hope even when he realised that the Winnipeg River was not the river flowing westward which he sought. We know now that the northern regions of the American continent east of the Rocky Mountains are tilted towards the east and the north and that in all its vast spaces there is no great river which flows to the west. La Vérendrye, however, ignorant of this dictate of nature, longed to paddle with the stream towards the west. The Red River flows from the south into Lake Winnipeg at a point near the mouth of the Winnipeg River. Up the Red River went La Vérendrye and found a tributary, the Assiniboine, flowing into it from the west.

At the point of junction, where has grown up the city of Winnipeg, he built a tiny fort, called Fort Rouge, a name still preserved in a suburb of the modern Winnipeg. The explorers went southward on the Red River, and then went westward on the Assiniboine River only to find the waters persistently flowing against them and no definite news of other waters leading to the Western Sea. On the Assiniboine, near the site of the present town of Portage la Prairie in Manitoba, La Vérendrye built Fort La Reine. Its name is evidence still perhaps of hopes for aid through the queen if not through the King of France.

In 1737 La Vérendrye made once more the long journey to Montreal. His fourteen canoes laden with furs were an earnest of the riches of the wonderful West and so pleased his Montreal partners that again they fitted him out with adequate supplies. In the summer of 1738 we find him at Fort La Reine, rich for the moment in goods with which to trade, keen and competent as a trader, and having great influence with the natives. All through the West he found Indians who went to trade with the English on Hudson Bay, and he constantly urged them not to take the long journey but to depend upon the French who came into their own country. It was a policy well fitted to cause searching of heart among the English traders who seemed so secure in their snug quarters on the seashore waiting for the Indians to come to them.

La Vérendrye had now a fresh plan for penetrating farther on his alluring quest. He had heard of a river to the south to be reached by a journey overland. It was a new thing for him to abandon canoes and march on foot but this he now did and with winter approaching. On October 16, 1738, when the autumn winds were already chill, there was a striking little parade at Fort La Reine. The drummer beat the garrison to arms. What with soldiers brought from Canada, the voyageurs who had paddled the great canoes, and the Indians who dogged always the steps of the French traders, there was a muster at the fort of some scores of men. La Vérendrye reviewed the whole company and from them chose for his expedition twenty soldiers and voyageurs and about twenty Assiniboine Indians. As companions for himself he took François and Pierre, two of his three surviving sons, and two traders who were at the fort.

We can picture the little company setting out on the 18th of October on foot, with some semblance of military order, by a well-beaten trail leading across the high land which separates the Red River country from the regions to the southwest. La Vérendrye had heard much of a people, the Mandans, dwelling in well-ordered villages on the banks of a great river and cultivating the soil instead of living the wandering life of hunters. Such wonders of Mandan culture had been reported to La Vérendrye that he half expected to find them white men with a civilization equal to that of Europe. The river was in reality not an unknown stream, as La Vérendrye hoped, but the Missouri, a river already frequented by the French in its lower stretches where its waters join those of the Mississippi.

It was a long march over the prairie. La Vérendrye found that he could not hurry his Indian guides. They insisted on delays during days of glorious autumn weather when it would have been wise to press on and avoid the winter cold on the wind-swept prairie. They went out of their way to visit a village of their own Assiniboine tribe; and, when they resumed their journey, this whole village followed them. The prairie Indians had a more developed sense of order and discipline than the tribes of the forest. La Vérendrye admired the military regularity of the savages on the march. They divided the company of more than six hundred into three columns: in front, scouts to look out for an enemy and also for herds of buffalo; in the centre, well protected, the old and the lame, all those incapable of fighting; and, for a rear-guard, strong fighting men. When buffalo were seen, the most active of the fighters rushed to the front to aid in hemming in the game. Women and dogs carried the baggage, the men condescending to bear only their weapons.

Not until cold December had come did the party reach the chief Mandan village. It was in some sense imposing, for the Indian lodges were arranged neatly in streets and squares and the surrounding palisade was strong and well built. Around the fort was a ditch fifteen feet deep and of equal width, which made the village impregnable in Indian warfare. After saluting the village with three volleys of musket fire, La Vérendrye marched in with great ceremony, under the French flag, only to discover that the Mandans were not greatly unlike the Assiniboines and other Indians of the West whom he already knew. The men went about naked and the women nearly so. They were skilled in dressing leather. They were also cunning traders, for they duped La Vérendrye's friends, the Assiniboines, and cheated them out of their muskets, ammunition, kettles, and knives. Great eaters were the Mandans. They cultivated abundant crops and stored them in cave cellars. Every day they brought their visitors more than twenty dishes cooked in earthen pottery of their own handicraft.

There was incredible feasting, which La Vérendrye avoided but which his sons enjoyed. The Mandan language he could not understand and close questioning as to the route to the Western Sea was thus impossible. He learned enough to discredit the vague tales of white men in armour and peopled towns with which his lying guides had regaled him. In the end he decided for the time being to return to Fort La Reine and to leave two of his followers to learn the Mandan language so that in the future they might act as interpreters. When he left the Mandan village on the 13th of December, he was already ill and it is a wonder that he did not perish from the cold on the winter journey across hill and prairie. He says:

In all my life I have never endured such misery from illness and fatigue, as on that journey.

On the 11th of February he was back at Fort La Reine, worn out and broken in health but still undaunted and resolved never to abandon his search.

Abandon it he never did. We find him in Montreal in 1740 involved in what he had always held in horror—a lawsuit brought against him by some impatient creditor. The report had gone abroad that he was amassing great wealth, when, as he said, all that he had accumulated was a debt of forty thousand *livres*. In the autumn of 1741 he was back at Fort La Reine, where he welcomed his son Pierre from a fruitless journey to the Mandans.

The most famous of all the efforts of the family was now on foot. On April 29, 1742, a new expedition started from Fort La Reine, led by La Vérendrye's two sons, Pierre and François. They knew the nature of the task before them, its perils as well as its hopes. They took with them no imposing company as their father had done, but only two men. The party of four, too feeble to fight their way, had to trust to the peaceful disposition of the natives. When they started, the prairie was turning from brown to green and the rivers were still swollen from the spring thaw. In three weeks they reached a Mandan village on the upper Missouri and were well received.

It was after midsummer when they set out again and pressed on westward with a trend to the south. The country was bare and desolate. For twenty days they saw no human being. They had Mandan guides who promised to take them to the next tribe, the Handsome Men—*Beaux Hommes*—as the brothers called them, a tribe much feared by the Mandans. The travellers were now mounted; for the horse, brought first to America by the Spaniards, had run wild on the western plains where the European himself had not yet penetrated, and had become an indispensable aid to certain of the native tribes. Deer and buffalo were in abundance and they had no lack of food.

When they reached the tribe of *Beaux Hommes*, the Mandan guides fled homeward. Summer passed into bleak autumn with chill winds and long nights. By the end of October, they were among the Horse Indians who, they had been told, could guide them to the sea. These, however, now said that only the Bow Indians, farther on, could do this. Winter was near when they were among these Indians, probably a tribe of the Sioux, whom they found excitedly preparing for a raid on their neighbours farther west, the Snakes. They were going, they said, towards the mountains and there the Frenchmen could look out on the great sea. So the story goes on. The brothers advanced ever westward and the land became more rugged, for they were now climbing upward from the prairie country.

At last, on January 1, 1743, they saw what both cheered and discouraged them. In the distance were mountains. About them was the prairie, with game in abundance. It was a great host with which the brothers travelled for there were two thousand warriors with their families who made night vocal with songs and yells. On the 12th of January, nearly two weeks later, with an advance party of warriors, the La Vérendryes reached the foot of the mountains, "well wooded with timber of every kind and very high," Was it the Rocky Mountains which they saw? Had they reached that last mighty barrier of snow-capped peaks, rugged valleys, and torrential streams, beyond which lay the sea? That they had done so was long assumed and many conjectures have been offered as to the point in the Rockies near which they made their last camp.

Their further progress was checked by an unexpected crisis. One day they came upon an encampment of the dreaded Snake Indians which had been abandoned in great haste. This, the Bow Indians thought, could only mean that the Snakes had hurriedly left their camp in order to slip in behind the advance guard of the Bows and massacre the women and children left in the rear. Panic seized the Bows and they turned homeward in wild confusion. Their chief could not restrain them. "I was very much disappointed," writes one of the brothers, "that I could not climb the mountains"—those mountains from which he had been told that he might view the Western Sea.

There was nothing for it but to turn back through snowdrifts over the bleak prairie. The progress was slow for the snow was sometimes two feet deep. On the 1st of March the brothers parted with their Bow friends at their village and then headed for home. By the 20th they were encamped with a friendly tribe on the banks of the Missouri. Here, to assert that Louis XV was lord of all that country, they built on an eminence a pyramid of stones and in it they buried a tablet of lead with an inscription which recorded the name of Louis XV, their king, and of the Marquis de Beauharnois, Governor of Canada, and the date of the visit.

Truth is sometimes stranger than fiction. One hundred and seventy years later, on February 16, 1913, a schoolgirl strolling with some companions on a Sunday afternoon near the High School in the town of Pierre, South Dakota, stumbled upon a projecting corner of this tablet, which was in an excellent state of preservation. Thus we know exactly where the brothers La Vérendrye were on April 2, 1743, when they bade farewell to their Indian friends and set out on horseback for Fort La Reine.

Spring had turned to summer before the brothers reached their destination. On July 2, 1743, they relieved the anxiety of their waiting father after an absence of fifteen months. Moving slowly as they did, could they have travelled from the distant Rockies from the time in January when they turned back? It seems doubtful; and in spite of the long-cherished belief that the brothers reached the foothills of the Rocky Mountains, it may be that they had not penetrated beyond the barrier which we know as the Black Hills. The chance discovery of a forgotten plate by schoolchildren may in truth prove that, as late as in 1750, the Rocky Mountains had not yet been seen by white men and that the first vision of that mighty range was obtained much farther north in Canada.

After 1743 the French seem to have made no further efforts to reach the Western Sea by way of the Missouri. If in reality the brothers had not gone beyond the Black Hills in South Dakota, then their most important work appears to have been done within what is now Canada, as discoverers of the Saskatchewan, the mighty river which carries to far-distant Hudson Bay the waters melted on the eastern dopes of the Rocky Mountains. It was by this route up the Saskatchewan that fifty years later was solved the tough and haunting problem of going over the mountains to the Pacific Ocean.

La Vérendrye now ascended the Saskatchewan for some three hundred miles to the forks where it divides into two great branches. He was going deeper into debt but he hoped always for help from the king. It is pathetic to see today, on the map of that part of western Canada which he and his sons explored, a town, a lake, and a county called Dauphin, in honour of the heir to the throne of France. No doubt La Vérendrye had the thought that someday he might plead with the Dauphin when he had become King for help in his great task.

Before the year 1749 had ended La Vérendrye, who had returned to Montreal, was in his grave. His sons, partners in his work, expected to be charged with the task—to which the king, in 1749, had anew appointed their father—of continuing the work of discovery in the

West. François, for a time ill, wrote in 1750 from Montreal to La Jonquière, the governor at Quebec, that he hoped to take up the plans of his father. The governor's reply was that he had appointed another officer, Legardeur de Saint-Pierre, to lead in the search for the Western Sea. François hurried to Quebec.

The governor met him with a bland face and seemed friendly. François urged that he and his brothers claimed no pre-eminence and that they were ready to serve under the orders of Saint-Pierre. The governor was hesitant; but at last told François frankly that the new leader desired no help either from him or from his brothers. François was dismayed. He and his brothers were in debt. Already he had sent on stores and men to the West and the men were likely to starve if not followed by provisions. His chief property was in the West in the form of goods which would be plundered without his guardianship. To tide over the immediate future, he sold the one small piece of land in Montreal which he had inherited from his father and threw this slight sop to his urgent creditors.

Saint-Pierre, strong in his right of monopoly, insisted that the brothers should not even return to the West. François urged that to go was a matter of life and death. In some way he secured leave to set out with one laden canoe. When Saint-Pierre found that François had gone, he claimed damages for the intrusion on his monopoly and secured an order to pursue François and bring him back. He caught him at Michilimackinac. The meeting between the two men at that place involved explanations. Face to face with an injured man, Saint-Pierre admitted that he had been in the wrong, paid to François many compliments, and regretted that he had not joined hands with the brothers.

The mischief done was, however, irreparable. François, crippled by opposition, could not carry on his trade with success and in the end he returned to Montreal a ruined man overwhelmed with debt. He wrote to the French court a noble appeal for relief:

> I remain without friends and without patrimony ... a simple ensign of the second grade; my elder brother has only the same rank as myself; my younger brother is only a junior cadet. This is the result of all that my father, my brothers and myself have done.... There are in the hands of your Lordship resources of compensation and of consolation. I venture to appeal to you for relief. To find ourselves excluded from the West would mean to

be cruelly robbed of our heritage, to realise for ourselves all that is bitter and to see others secure all that is sweet.

The appeal fell on deaf ears. The brothers sank into obscurity. During Montcalm's campaigns from 1756 to 1759 Pierre and François seem to have been engaged in military service. François was killed in the siege of Quebec in 1759. After the final surrender of Canada, the *Auguste*, a ship laden for the most part with refugees returning to France, was wrecked on the St. Lawrence. Among those on board who perished was Pierre de la Vérendrye. He died amid the howling of the tempest and the cries of drowning men. Tragedy, unrelenting, had pursued him to the end.

Legardeur de Saint-Pierre, the choice of the Marquis de la Jonquière to take up the search for the Western Sea in succession to the elder La Vérendrye, himself went only as far as Fort La Reine. It was a subordinate, the Chevalier de Niverville, whom he sent farther west to find the great mountains and if possible the sea. The winter of 1750/51 had set in before Niverville was ready. He started apparently from Fort Maurepas, on snowshoes, his party dragging their supplies on toboggans. Before they reached Paskoya on the Saskatchewan (the modern Le Pas) they had nearly perished of hunger and were able to save their lives only by catching a few fish through the ice.

Niverville was ill. He sent forward ten men by canoe up the Saskatchewan. They travelled with such rapidity that on May 29, 1751, they had reached the Rockies. They built a good fort, which they named Fort La Jonquière, and stored it with a considerable quantity of provisions. If, as seems likely, the brothers La Vérendrye saw only the Black Hills, these ten unknown men were the discoverers of the Rocky Mountains.

Saint-Pierre braced himself to set out for the distant goal but he was easily discouraged. Niverville, he said, was ill; the Indians were at war among themselves; some of them were plotting what Saint-Pierre calls "treason" to the French and their "perfidy" surpassed anything in his lifelong experience. The hostile influence of the English he thought all-pervasive. Obviously these are excuses. He did not like the task and he turned back.

As it was, he tells a dramatic story of how Indians crowded into Fort La Reine in a threatening manner and how he saved the fort and himself only by rushing to the magazine with a lighted torch, knocking open a barrel of powder, and threatening to blow up everything and everybody if the savages did not withdraw at once. He was eager to leave the country. In 1752 he handed over the command to St. Luc de la Corne and, in August of that year, having experienced "much wretchedness" on his journeys, he was safely back in Montreal. The founding of Fort La Jonquière was, no doubt, a great feat. Where the fort stood we do not know. It may have been on the North Saskatchewan, near Edmonton, or on the south branch of the river near Calgary. In any case it was a far-flung outpost of France.

The English had always been more prosaic than the French. The traders on Hudson Bay worked, indeed, under a monopoly not less rigorous than that which Canada imposed. Without doubt, many an Englishman on the Bay was haunted by the hope and desire to reach the Western Sea. But the servants of the Company knew that to buy and sell at a profit was their chief aim. They had been on the whole content to wait for trade to come to them. By 1740 the Indians, who made the long journey to the Bay by the intricate waters which carried to the sea the flood of the Saskatchewan and Lake Winnipeg, were showing to the English articles supplied by the French at points far inland. It thus became evident that the French were tapping the traffic in furs near its source and cutting off the stream which had long flowed to Hudson Bay.

In June, 1754, Anthony Hendry, a young man in the service of the Company, left York factory on Hudson Bay to find out what the French were doing. We have a slight but carefully written diary of Hendry's journey. He does not fail to note that in the summer weather life was made almost intolerable by the "*musketoos*." Traveling by canoe he reached the Saskatchewan River and tells how, on the 22nd of July, he came to "a French house." It was Fort Paskoya. When Hendry paddled up to the river bank two Frenchmen met him and "in a very genteel manner" invited him into their house. With all courtesy they asked him, he says, if he had any letter from his master and where and on what design he was going inland. His answer was that he had been sent "to view the country" and that he intended to return to Hudson Bay in the spring.

The Frenchmen were sorry that their own master, who was apparently the well-known Canadian leader, St. Luc de la Corne, the successor of Saint-Pierre, had gone to Montreal with furs, and added their regrets that they must detain Hendry until this leader's return. At this Hendry's Indians grunted and said that the French dared not do so. Next day Hendry took breakfast and dinner at the fort, gave "two feet of tobacco" (at that time it was sold in long coils) to his hosts, and in return received some moose flesh. The confidence of his Indian guides that the French would not dare to detain him was justified. Next day Hendry paddled on up the river and advanced more than twenty miles, camping at night by "the largest Birch trees I have yet seen."

Hendry wished to see the country thoroughly and to come into touch with the natives. The best way to do this and to obtain food was to leave the river and go boldly overland. He accordingly left his canoes behind and advanced on foot. The party was starving. On a Sunday in July he walked twenty-six miles and says "neither bird nor beast to be seen,—so that we have nothing to eat." The next day he travelled twenty-four miles on an empty stomach and then, to his delight, found a supply of ripe strawberries, "the size of black currants and the finest I ever eat."

The next day his Indians killed two moose. He then met natives who, when he asked them to go to Hudson Bay to trade, replied that they could obtain all they needed from the French posts. The tact and skill of the French were such that, as Hendry admits, reluctantly enough, the Indians were already strongly attached to them. Day after day Hendry journeyed on over the rolling prairie in the warm summer days. He came to the south branch of the Saskatchewan near the point where now stands the city of Saskatoon and crossed the river on the 21st of August. Then on to the West, eager to take part in the hunting of the buffalo.

Hendry is almost certainly the first Englishman to see this region. In the end he reached the mountains. He makes no mention of having seen or heard anything of Fort La Jonquière, built three years earlier. He had aims different from those of La Vérendrye and other French explorers. Not the Western Sea but openings for trade was he seeking. His great aim was to reach the tribe called later the Blackfeet Indians, who were mighty hunters of the buffalo. Hendry was alive to the impressions of nature. The intense heat of August was followed in September by glorious weather, with the nights cool and the mosquitoes no longer troublesome. The climate was bracing. He complains only, from time to time, of swollen feet, and we need not wonder since his daily march occasionally went beyond twenty-five miles. Sometimes for days he saw no living creature.

At other times wild life was prolific: there were moose in great abundance, bears, including the dreaded grizzly—one of which killed an Indian of his company and badly mutilated another—beaver, wild horses, and, above all, the buffalo. "Saw many herds of buffalo grazing like English cattle," he says, on the 13th of September, and the next day he goes buffalo hunting. Guns and ammunition were costly. His Indians, who used only bows and arrows, on this day killed seven— "fine sport," says Hendry. Often the Indians took only the tongue, leaving the carcass for the wolves, who naturally abounded in such advantageous conditions. It is not easy now to imagine the part played by the buffalo in the life of the prairie. As Hendry advanced the herds were so dense as sometimes to retard his progress. Other writers tell of the vast numbers of these creatures.

Alexander Henry, the younger, writing on April 1, 1801, says that in a river swollen by spring floods, drowned buffalo floated past his camp in one continuous line for two days and two nights. In prairie fires thousands were blinded and would go tumbling down banks into streams or lie down to die. One morning the bellowing of buffaloes awakened Henry and he looked out to see the prairie black.

> The ground was covered at every point of the compass, as far as the eye could reach, and every animal was in motion.

Daily as Hendry advanced he saw smoke in the distance and his Indians told him that it came from the camp of the Blackfeet. He reached them on Monday the 14th of October. When four miles away he was stopped by mounted scouts who asked whether he came as a friend or as an enemy. He was taken to the camp of two hundred tents pitched in two rows, and was led through the long passage between the tents to the big tent of the chief of whom he had heard much. Not a word was spoken. The chief sat on a white buffalo skin. Pipes were passed round and each person was presented with boiled buffalo flesh. When talk began, Hendry told the chief that his great leader had sent him to invite them to come to trade at Hudson Bay where his people would get powder, shot, guns, cloth, beads, and other things. The chief said it was far away, and his people knew nothing of paddling. Such strangers to great waters were they that they would not even eat fish. They despised Hendry's tobacco. What they smoked was dried horse dung. In the end Hendry was dismissed and ordered to make his camp a quarter of a mile away from that of the Blackfeet.

It was close by the present site of Calgary and apparently in full view, on clear days, of the white peaks of the Rocky Mountains that Hendry visited the Blackfeet. He lingered in the far western country through the greater part of the winter. On a portion of his return journey he used a horse. When the spring thaw came, once more he took to the water in canoes. He complains of the idleness of his Indian companions who would remain in their huts all day and never stir to lay up a store of food even when game was abundant. Conjuring, dancing to the hideous pounding of drums, feasting and smoking, were their amusements.

On his way back Hendry revisited the French post on the Saskatchewan. The leader, no doubt St. Luc de la Corne, had returned from Montreal and now had with him nine men.

"The master," Hendry says, "invited me in to sup with him, and was very kind. He is dressed very genteel." He showed Hendry his stock of furs; "a brave parcel," the admiring rival thought. Hendry admits the superiority of the French as traders. They "talk several languages to perfection; they have the advantage of us in every shape." In the West, as in the East, France was recognised as a formidable rival of England for the mastery of North America.

When Hendry was making his peaceful visit to the French fort in 1755, the crisis of the struggle had just been reached. In that year the battle line from Acadia to the Ohio and the Mississippi was already forming, and the fate of France's eager efforts to hold the West was soon to be decided in the East. If Britain should conquer on the St. Lawrence, she would conquer also on the Saskatchewan and on the Mississippi.

Conquer she did, and thus it happened that it was Britain's sons who took up the later burdens of the discoverer. In the summer of 1789, just at the time when the great Revolution was beginning in France, Alexander Mackenzie, a Scotch trader from Montreal, starting from Lake Athabasca, north of the farthest point reached by Hendry, was pressing still onward into an unknown region to find a river which might lead to the sea. This river he found; we know it now as the Mackenzie. For two weeks he and his Indians and voyageurs paddled with the current down this mighty stream, and on July 14, 1789, the day of the fall of the Bastille, he saw whales sporting in Arctic waters.

The real goal which Mackenzie sought was that of La Vérendrye, a western and not a northern ocean. Three years later, after months of preparation, he attempted the great feat of crossing the Rocky Mountains to the sea. After nine months of rugged travel, across mountain streams and gorges, in peril daily from hostile savages, on July 22, 1793, he reached the shore of the Pacific Ocean, the first white man to go by land over the width of the continent from sea to sea. It was thus a Scotchman who achieved that of which La Vérendrye had so long dreamed; and with no aid from the state but with only the resources of a trading company.

Ten years later, when France sold to the United States her last remaining territory of Louisiana, the American Government equipped an expedition under Lewis and Clark to cross the Rocky Mountains by way of the Missouri, the route from which the La Vérendrye brothers had been obliged to turn back. The party began the ascent of the Missouri on May 14, 1804, and arrived in the Mandan country in the late autumn. Here they spent the winter of 1804-05. Not until November 15, 1805, had they completed the hard journey across the Rocky Mountains and reached the mouth of the Columbia River on the Pacific Ocean. Little did La Vérendrye, in his eager search for the Western Sea, imagine the difficulties to be encountered and the hardships to be endured by those who were destined, in later days, to realise his dream.

CHAPTER 6

The Valley of the Ohio

Almost at the moment in 1749 when British ships were lying at anchor in Halifax harbour and sending to shore hundreds of boatloads of dazed and expectant settlers for the new colony, there had set out from Montreal, in the interests of France, an expedition with designs so far-reaching that we wonder still at the stupendous issues involved in efforts which seem so petty. The purpose of France was now to make good her claim to the whole vast West. It was a picturesque company which pushed its canoes from the shore at Lachine on the 15th of June, six days before the British squadron reached Halifax. There was a procession of twenty-three great birch-bark canoes well filled, for in them were more than two hundred men, at least ten in each canoe, together with the necessary impedimenta for a long journey. There were twenty soldiers in uniform, a hundred and eighty Canadians skilled in paddling and in carrying canoes and freight over the portages, a band of Indians, and fourteen officers with Céloron de Blainville at their head.

The acting Governor of Canada at this time was a dwarf in physique, but a giant in intellect, the brilliant naval officer, the Marquis de la Galissonière, destined later to inflict upon the English in the Mediterranean the naval defeat which caused the execution of Admiral Byng as a coward. This remarkable man—planning, like his predecessor Frontenac, on a scale suited to world politics—saw that the peace of 1748 settled nothing, that in the balance now was the whole future of North America, and that victory would be to the alert and the strong.

He chose Céloron, the most capable of the hardy young Canadian *noblesse* whom he had at hand, a man accustomed to the life of the forest, and sent with him this large party to assert against the English the right of France to the valley of the Ohio. The English were now to be shut out definitely from advancing westward and to be confined to the strip of territory lying between the Atlantic coast and the Alleghany Mountains, a little more than that strip fifty miles wide talked about in Quebec as the maximum concession of France, but still not very much according to the ideas of the English, and even this not secure if France should ever grow strong enough to crowd them out.

At no time do we find more vivid the contrast in type between the two nations. Before a concrete fact the British take action. When they gave up Louisbourg they built Halifax. Their traders had pressed into the Ohio country, not directed under any grandiose idea of empire, but simply as individuals, to trade and reap for themselves what profit they could. When they were checked and menaced by the French, they saw that something must be done. How they did it we shall see presently. It was the weakness of the English colonies that they could not unite to work out a great plan.

If Virginia took steps to advance westward, Pennsylvania was jealous lest lands which she desired should go to a rival colony. France, on the other hand, had complete unity of design. Céloron spoke in the name of the King of France and he spoke in terms uncompromising enough. "The Ohio," said the King of France through his agent, "belongs to me." It is a French river. The lands bordering upon it are "my lands." The English intruders are foreign robbers and not one of them is to be left in the western country: "I will not endure the English on my land." The Indians, dwelling in that region, are "my children."

Scattered over the vast region about the Great Lakes were a good many French. At the lower end of Lake Ontario stood Fort Frontenac, a menace to the colony of New York, as the dwellers in the British post of Oswego on the opposite shore of the lake well knew. We have already seen that the French held a fort at Niagara guarding the route leading farther west to Lake Erie and to regions beyond Lake Erie, by way of the Ohio or the upper lakes, to the Mississippi. Near the mouth of the Mississippi, New Orleans was now becoming a considerable town with a governor independent of the governor at Quebec.

Along the Mississippi at strategic points stretching northward beyond the mouth of the Missouri were a few French settlements, ragged enough and with a shiftless population of fur traders and farmers, but adequate to assert France's possession of that mighty highway. The weak point in France's position was in her connection of the Mississippi with the St. Lawrence by way of the Ohio. This was the place of danger, for here English rivalry was strongest, and it was to cure this weakness that Céloron was now sent forth.

Céloron moved toilsomely over the portage which led past the great cataract of Niagara and launched his canoes on Lake Erie. From its south shore, during seven days of heart-breaking labour, the party dragged the canoes and supplies through dense forest and over steep hills until they reached Chautauqua Lake, the waters of which flow into the Allegheny River and by it to the Ohio. For many weary days they went with the current, stopping at Indian villages, treating with the savages, who were sometimes awed and sometimes menacing. They warned the Indians to have no dealings with the scheming English who would "infallibly prove to be robbers," and asserted as boldly as Céloron dared the lordship of the King of France and his love for his forest children.

Céloron realised that he was on an historic mission. At several points on the Ohio, with great ceremony, he buried leaden plates, as La Vérendrye had done a few years earlier in the far West, bearing an inscription declaring that, in the name of the King of France, he took possession of the country. On trees over these memorials of lead he nailed the arms of France, stamped on sheets of tin. Since that day at least three of the plates have been found.

Céloron's expedition went well enough. He advanced as far west on the Ohio as the mouth of the Great Miami River, then up that river, and by difficult portages back to Lake Erie. It was a remarkable journey; but in the late autumn he was back again in Montreal, not sure that he had achieved much. The natives of the country were, he thought, hostile to France and devoted to the English who had long traded with them. This opinion was in truth erroneous, for, when the time of testing came, the Indians of the West fought on the side of France. Montcalm had many hundreds of them under his banner. The expedition meant the definite and final throwing down of the gauntlet by France. With all due ceremony she had declared that the Ohio country was hers and that there she would allow no English to dwell.

Legardeur de Saint-Pierre could hardly have known, when he left the hard region of the Saskatchewan in 1752, that a year later he would be sent to protect another set of outposts of France in the West. In 1753 we find him in command of the French forces in the Ohio country. Céloron had been sent to Detroit. If Saint-Pierre had played his part feebly on the Saskatchewan, he was now made for a brief period one of the central figures in the opening act of a world drama.

It is with a touch of emotion that we see on the stage, as the opponent of this not great Frenchman, the momentous figure of George Washington.

The fight for North America was now rapidly approaching its final phase in the struggle which we know as the Seven Years' War. During forty years, commissioners of the two nations had been trying to reach some agreement as to boundaries. Each side, however, made impossible demands. France claimed all the lands drained by the St. Lawrence and the Great Lakes and by the Mississippi and its tributaries—a claim which, if made good, would have carried her into the very heart of the colony of New York and would have given her also the mastery of the Ohio and the regions beyond. Britain claimed all the lands ever occupied by the Iroquois Indians, who had been recognised as British subjects by the Treaty of Utrecht. As those Indians had overrun regions north of the St. Lawrence, the British thus would become masters of a good part of Canada. Neither side was prepared for reasonable compromise. The sword was to be the final arbiter.

Events moved rapidly towards war. In 1753 Duquesne, the new Governor of Canada, sent more than a thousand men to build Fort Le Boeuf, on upper waters flowing to the Ohio and within easy reach of support by way of Lake Erie. In the next year the French were swarming in the Ohio Valley, stirring up the Indians against the English and confident of success. They jeered at the divisions among the English and believed their own unity so strong that they could master the colonies one by one. The two colonies most affected were Pennsylvania and Virginia, either of them quite ready to see its own citizens advance into the Ohio country and possess the land, but neither of them willing to unite with the other in effective military action to protect the frontier.

It is at this crisis that there appears for the first time in history George Washington of Virginia. In December, 1753, in the dead of winter, he made a long, toilsome journey from Virginia to the north through snow and rain, by difficult forest trails, over two ranges of mountains, across streams sometimes frozen, sometimes dangerous from treacherous thaws. On the way he heard gossip from the Indians about the designs of the French. They boasted that they would come in numbers like the sands of the seashore; that the natives would be no more an obstacle to them than the flies and mosquitoes, which indeed they resembled; and that not the breadth of a finger-nail of land belonged to the Indians. Washington was told by one of the French that "It was their absolute design to take possession of the Ohio and, by ——, they would do it!" It was no matter that the French were outnumbered two to one by the English, for the English were dilatory and ineffective.

In the end, Washington arrived at Fort Le Boeuf and presented a letter from Dinwiddie, the Lieutenant-Governor of Virginia, pointing out that the British could not permit an armed force from Canada to invade their territory of the Ohio and requiring that the French should leave the country at once. Legardeur de Saint-Pierre, to whom this firm demand was delivered, "an elderly gentleman," says Washington, with "much the air of a soldier" gave, of course, a polite answer in the manner of his nation, but he intended, he said, to remain where he was as long as he had instructions so to do. Washington kept his eyes open and made careful observations of the plan of the fort, the number of men, and also of the canoes, of which he noted that there were more than two hundred ready and many others building. The French tried to entice away his Indians and he says, "I cannot say that ever in my life I suffered so much anxiety." On the journey back he nearly perished when he fell into an ice-cold stream and was obliged to spend the night on a tiny island in frozen clothing. He brought comfort as cold to the waiting Dinwiddie.

The French meanwhile were always a little ahead of the English in their planning. Early in April, 1754, a French force of five or six hundred men from Canada, which had set out while Quebec was still in the icy grip of winter, reached the upper waters of the Ohio. They attacked and destroyed a fort which the English had begun at the forks where now stands Pittsburgh, and, in its place, began a formidable one, called Fort Duquesne after the Governor of Canada. In vain was Washington sent with a few hundred men to take possession of this fort and to assert the claim of the English to the land. He fell in with a French scouting party under young Coulon de Jumonville, killed its leader and nine others, and took more than a score of prisoners—warfare bloody enough in a time of supposed peace.

But the French were now on the Ohio in greater numbers than the English. At a spot known as the Great Meadows, where Washington had hastily thrown up defences, which he called Port Necessity, he was forced to surrender, but was allowed to lead his force back to Virginia, defeated in the first military adventure of his career. The French took the view that his killing of the young officer Jumonville was assassination, since no state of war existed, and raised a fierce clamour

ROBERT DINWIDDIE

that Washington was a murderer—a strange contrast to his relations with France in the years to come.

What astonishes us in regard to these events is that Britain and France long remained nominally at peace while they were carrying on active hostilities in America and sending from Europe armies to fight. There were various reasons for this hesitation about plunging formally into war. Each side wished to delay until sure of its alliances in Europe. During the war ending in 1748 France had fought with Frederick of Prussia against Austria, and Britain had been Austria's ally. The war had been chiefly a land war, but France had been beaten on the sea. Now Britain and Prussia were drawing together and, if France fought them, it must be with Austria as an ally.

Such an alliance offered France but slight advantage. Austria, an inland power, could not help France against an adversary whose strength was on the sea; she could not aid the designs of France in America or in India, where the capable French leader Dupleix was in a fair way to build up a mighty oriental empire. Nor had France anything to gain in Europe from an Austrian alliance. The shoe was on the other foot. The supreme passion of Maria Theresa who ruled Austria was to recover the province of Silesia which had been seized in 1740 by Prussia and held—held to this day, (1918). Austria could do little for France but France could do much for Austria. So Austria worked for this alliance.

It is a story of intrigue. Usually in France the king carried on negotiations with foreign countries only through his ministers, who knew the real interests of France. Now the astute Austrian statesman, Kaunitz, went past the ministers of Louis XV to Louis himself. This was, the heyday of Madame de Pompadour, the king's mistress. Maria Theresa condescended to intrigue with this woman whom in her heart she despised. There is still much mystery in the affair. The king was flattered into thinking that personally he was swaying the affairs of Europe and took delight in deceiving his ministers and working behind their backs. While events in America were making war between France and Britain inevitable, France was being tied to an ally who could give her little aid. She must spend herself to fight Austria's battles on the land, while her real interests required that she should build up her fleet to fight on the sea the great adversary across the English Channel.

The destiny of North America might, indeed, well have been other than it is. A France strong on the sea, able to bring across to America great forces, might have held, at any rate, her place on the St. Lawrence

WILLIAM SHIRLEY

and occupied the valleys of the Ohio and the Mississippi. We can hardly doubt that the English colonies, united by a common deadly peril, could have held against France most of the Atlantic coast. But she might well have divided with them North America; and today the lands north of the Ohio and westward beyond the Ohio to the Pacific Ocean might have been French. The two nations on the brink of war in 1754 were playing for mighty stakes; and victory was to the power which had control of the sea. France had a great army, Britain a great fleet. In this contrast lay wrapped the secret of the future of North America.

As the crisis drew near the vital thought about the future of America was found, not in America, but in Europe. The English colonies were so accustomed to distrust each other that, when Virginia grew excited about French designs on the Ohio, Pennsylvania or North Carolina was as likely as not to say that it was the French who were in the right and a stupid, or excitable, or conceited, colonial governor who was in the wrong. In Paris and London, on the other hand, there were no illusions about affairs in America. In both capitals it was realised that a grim fight was on. During the winter of 1754-55 extensive preparations were being made on both sides.

France equipped an army under Baron Dieskau to go to Canada; Britain equipped one under General Braddock to go to Virginia. Each nation asked the other why it was sending troops to America and each gave the assurance of benevolent designs. But in the spring of 1755 a British fleet under Admiral Boscawen put to sea with instructions to capture any French vessels bound for North America. At the same time the two armies were on the way across the Atlantic. Dieskau went to Canada, Braddock to Virginia, each instructed to attack the other side, while in the meantime ambassadors at the two courts gave bland assurances that their only thought was to preserve peace.

The English colonists showed a political blindness that amounted to imbecility. Albany was the central point from which the dangers on all sides might best be surveyed. Here came together in the summer of 1754 delegates from seven of the colonies to consider the common peril. The French were busy in winning, as they did, the support of the many Indian tribes of the West; and the old allies of the English, the Iroquois, were nervous for their own safety. The delegates to Albany, tied and bound by instructions from their Assemblies, had to listen to plain words from the savages.

The one Englishman who, in dealing with the Indians, had tact and skill equal to that of Frontenac of old, was an Irishman, Sir William Johnson. To him the Iroquois made indignant protests that the English were as ready as the French to rob them of their lands. If we find a bear in a tree, they said, someone will spring up to claim that the tree belongs to him and keep us from shooting the bear. The French, they added, are at least men who are prepared to fight; you weak and unprepared English are like women and any day the French may turn you out. Benjamin Franklin told the delegates that they must unite to meet a common enemy. Unite, however, they would not. No one of them would surrender to a central body any authority through which the power of the king over them might be increased. The Congress—the word is full of omen for the future—failed to bring about the much-needed union.

In February, 1755, Braddock arrived in Virginia with his army, and early in May he was on his march across the mountains with regulars, militia, and Indians, to the number of nearly fifteen hundred men, to attack Fort Duquesne and to rid the Ohio Valley of the French. He knew little of forest warfare with its use of Indian scouts, its ambushes, its fighting from the cover of trees. On the 9th of July, on the Monongahela River, near Fort Duquesne, in a struggle in the forest against French and Indians he was defeated and killed.

George Washington was in the fight and had to report to Dinwiddie the dismal record of what had happened. The frontier was aflame; and nearly all the Indians of the West, seeing the rising star, went over to the French. The power of France was, for the time, supreme in the heart of the continent. At that moment even far away in the lone land about the Saskatchewan, the English trader, Hendry, had to admit that the French knew better than the English how to attract the support of the savage tribes.

Meanwhile Dieskau had arrived at Quebec. In the colony of New York Sir William Johnson, the rough and cheery Irishman, much loved of the Iroquois, was gathering forces to attack Canada. Early in July, 1755, Johnson had more than three thousand provincial troops at Albany, a motley horde of embattled farmers, most of them with no uniforms, dressed in their own homespun, carrying their own muskets, electing their own officers, and altogether, from the strict soldier's point of view, a rabble rather than an army. To meet this force and destroy it if he could, Dieskau took to the French fort at Crown Point, on Lake Champlain, and southward from there to Ticonderoga at the head of this lake, some three thousand five hundred men, including his French regulars, some Canadians and Indians. Johnson's force lay at Fort George, later Fort William Henry, the most southerly point on Lake George.

The names, given by Johnson himself, show how the dull Hanoverian kings and their offspring were held in honour by the Irish diplomat who was looking for favours at court. The two armies met on the shores of Lake George early in September and there was an all-day fight. Each side lost some two hundred men. Among those who perished on the French side was Legardeur de Saint-Pierre, who had escaped all the perils of the western wilderness to meet his fate in this border struggle. The honours of the day seem to have been with Johnson, for the French were driven off and Dieskau himself, badly wounded, was taken prisoner. That Johnson had great difficulty in keeping his savages from burning alive and then boiling and eating Dieskau and smoking his flesh in their pipes, in revenge for some of their chiefs killed in the fight, shows what an alliance with Indians meant.

There was small gain to the English from Johnson's success. He was too cautious to advance towards Canada; and, as winter came on, he broke up his camp and sent his men to their homes. The colonies had no permanent military equipment. Each autumn their forces were dissolved to be reorganised again in the following spring, a lame method of waging war.

For three years longer in the valley of the Ohio, as elsewhere, the star of France remained in the ascendant. It began to decline only when, farther east, on the Atlantic, superior forces sent out from England were able to check the French. During the summer of 1758, while Wolfe and Boscawen were pounding the walls of Louisbourg, seven thousand troops led by General Forbes, Colonel George Washington, and Colonel Henry Bouquet, pushed their way through the wilds beyond the Alleghanies and took possession of the Ohio. The French destroyed Fort Duquesne and fled. On the 25th of November the English occupied the place and named it "Pitts-Bourgh" in honour of their great war minister.

CHAPTER 7

The Expulsion of the Acadians

We have now to turn back over a number of years to see what has been happening in Acadia, that oldest and most easterly part of New France which in 1710 fell into British hands. Since the Treaty of Utrecht in 1713 the Acadians had been nominally British subjects. But the Frenchman, hardly less than the Jew, is difficult of absorption by other racial types. We have already noted the natural aim of France to recover what she had lost and her use of the priests to hold the Acadians to her interests. The Acadians were secure in the free exercise of their religion. They had no secular leaders and few, if any, clergy of their own. They were led chiefly by priests, subjects of France, who, though working in British territory, owned no alliance to Great Britain, and were directed by the Bishop of Quebec.

For forty years the question of the Acadians remained unsettled.

Under the Treaty of 1713 the Acadians might leave the country. If they remained a year they must become British subjects. When, however, in 1715, two years after the conclusion of the treaty, they were required to take the oath of allegiance to the new king, George I, they declared that they could not do so, since they were about to move to Cape Breton. When George II came to the throne in 1727, the oath was again demanded. Still, however, the Acadians were between two fires. Their Indian neighbours, influenced by the French, threatened them with massacre if they took the oath, while the British declared that they would forfeit their farms if they refused.

The truth is that the British did not wish to press the alternative. To drive out the Acadians would be to strengthen the neighbouring French colony of Cape Breton. To force on them the oath might even cause a rising which would overwhelm the few English in Nova Scotia. So the tradition, never formally accepted by the British, grew up that, while the Acadians owed obedience to George II, they would be neutral in case of war with France. A common name for them used by the British themselves was that of the Neutral French. In time of peace the Acadians could be left to themselves. When, however, war broke out between Britain and France the question of loyalty became acute. Such war there was in 1744.

Without doubt, some Acadians then helped the French—but it was, as they protested, only under compulsion and, as far as they could, they seem to have refused to aid either side. The British muttered threats that subjects of their king who would not fight for him had no right to protection under British law. Even then feeling was so high that there was talk of driving the Acadians from their farms and setting them adrift; and these poor people trembled for their own fate when the British victors at Louisbourg in 1745 removed the French population to France. Assurances came from the British government, however, that there was no thought of molesting the Acadians.

With the order "As you were" the dominant thought of the Treaty of Aix-la-Chapelle in 1748, the highly organised and efficient champions of French policy took every step to ensure that in the next struggle the interests of France should prevail. Peace had no sooner been signed than Versailles was working in Nova Scotia on the old policy. The French priests taught that eternal perdition awaited the Catholic Acadians who should accept the demands of the heretic English. The Indians continued their savage threats. Blood is thicker than water and no doubt the natural sympathies of the Acadians were with the French. But the British were now formidable.

For them the founding of Halifax in 1749 had made all the difference. They, too, had a menacing fortress at the door of the Acadians, and their tone grew sterner. As a result, the Acadians were told that if, by October 15, 1749, they had not taken an unconditional oath of allegiance to George II, they should forfeit their rights and their property, the treasured farms on which they and their ancestors had toiled. The Acadians were in acute distress. If they yielded to the English, not only would their bodies be destroyed by the savage Micmac Indians, but their immortal souls, they feared, would be in danger.

The Abbé Le Loutre was the parish priest of the Acadian village of Beaubassin on Chignecto Bay and also missionary to the Micmac Indians, whose chief village lay in British territory not many miles from Halifax. British officials of the time denounced him as a determined fanatic who did not stop short of murder. As in most men, there was in Le Loutre a mingling of qualities. He was arrogant, domineering, and intent on his own plans. He hated the English and their heresy, and he preached to his people against them with frantic invective. He incited his Indians to bloodshed. But he also knew pity. The custom of the Indians was to consider prisoners taken by them as their property, and on one occasion Le Loutre himself paid ransom to the Indians for thirty-seven English captives and returned them to Halifax. It is certain that the French government counted upon the influence of French priests to aid its political designs.

"My masters, God and the King" was a phrase of the Sulpician father Piquet working at this time on the St. Lawrence. Le Loutre could have echoed the words. He was an ardent politician and France supplied him with both money and arms to induce the Indians to attack the English. The savages haunted the outskirts of Halifax, waylaid and scalped unhappy settlers, and, in due course, were paid from Louisbourg according to the number of scalps which they produced. The deliberate intention was to make new English settlements impossible in Nova Scotia and so to discourage the English that they should abandon Halifax. All this intrigue occurred in 1749 and the years following the treaty of peace.

If the English suffered, so did the Acadians. Le Loutre told them that if once they became British subjects they would lose their priests and find their religion suppressed. Acadians who took the oath would, he said, be denied the sacraments of the Church. He would also turn loose on the offenders the murderous savages whom he controlled. If pressed by the English, the Acadians, rather than yield, must abandon their lands and remove into French territory.

At this point arises the question as to what were the limits of this French territory. In yielding Acadia in 1713, France had not defined its boundaries. The English claimed that it included the whole region stretching north-eastward to the Gulf of St. Lawrence from the frontier of New England. The French, however, said that Acadia meant only the peninsula of Nova Scotia ending at the isthmus between Baie Verte and the Bay of Chignecto; and for years a Canadian force stood there on guard, daring the British to put a foot on the north side of the little river Missaguash, which the French said was the international boundary.

There was much excitement among the Acadians in 1750, when an English force landed on the isthmus and proceeded to throw up defences on the south side of the river. This outpost, which in due time became Fort Lawrence, was placed on what even the French admitted to be British territory. Forthwith on a hill two or three miles away, on the other side of the supposed boundary, the French built Fort Beauséjour. Le Loutre was on the spot, blustering and menacing. He told his Acadian parishioners of the little village of Beaubassin, near Fort Lawrence and within the British area, that rather than accept English rule they must now abandon their lands and seek the protection of the French at Fort Beauséjour. With his own hands he set fire to the village church. The houses of the Acadians were also burned. A whole district was laid waste by fire. Women and children suffered fearful privations—but what did such things matter in view of the high politics of the priest and of France?

During four or five years the hostile forts confronted each other. In time of peace there was war. The French made Beauséjour a solid fort, for it still stands, little altered, though it has been abandoned for a century and a half. It was chiefly the Acadians, nominal British subjects, who built these thick walls.

The arrogant Micmacs demanded that the British should hand over to them the best half of Nova Scotia, and they emphasised their demand by treachery and massacre. One day a man, in the uniform of a French officer, followed by a small party, approached Fort Lawrence, waving a white flag. Captain Howe with a small force went out to meet him. As this party advanced, Indians concealed behind a dike fired and killed Howe and eight or ten others. Such ruses were well fitted to cause among the English a resolve to enforce severe measures. The fire burned slowly but in the end it flamed up in a cruel and relentless temper. French policy, too, showed no pity. The Governor of Canada and the colonial minister in France were alike insistent that the English should be given no peace and cared nothing for the sufferings of the unhappy Acadians between the upper and the nether millstone.

At last, in 1755, the English accomplished something decisive. They sent an army to Fort Lawrence, attacked Fort Beauséjour, forced its timid commander Vergor to surrender, mastered the whole surrounding country, and obliged Le Loutre himself to fly to Quebec. There he embarked for France. The English captured him on the sea, however, and the relentless and cruel priest spent many years in an English prison. His later years, when he reached France, do him some credit. By that time the Acadians had been driven from their homes. There were nearly a thousand exiles in England. Le Loutre tried to befriend these helpless people and obtained homes for some of them in the parish of Belle-Isle-en-Mer in France.

In the meantime, the price of Le Loutre's intrigues and of the outrages of the French and their Indian allies was now to be paid by the unhappy Acadians. During the spring and summer of 1755, the British decided that the question of allegiance should be settled at once, and that the Acadians must take the oath. There was need of urgency. The army at Fort Lawrence which had captured Fort Beauséjour was largely composed of men from New England, and these would wish to return to their homes for the winter. If the Acadians remained and were hostile, the country thus occupied at laborious cost might quickly revert to the French. Already many Acadians had fought on the side of the French and some of them, disguised as Indians, had joined in savage outrage. A French fleet and a French army were reported as likely to arrive before the winter.

In fact, France's naval power with its base at Louisbourg was still stronger than that of Britain with its base at Halifax. When the Acadians were told in plain terms that they must take the oath of allegiance, they firmly declined to do so without certain limitations involving guarantees that they should not be arrayed against France. The Governor at Halifax, Major Charles Lawrence, was a stern, relentless man, without pity, and his mind was made up. Shirley, Governor of Massachusetts, was in touch with Lawrence. The Acadians should be deported if they would not take the oath. This step, however, the government at London never ordered. On the contrary, as late as on August 13, 1755, Lawrence was counselled to act with caution, prudence, and tact in dealing with the "Neutrals," as the Acadians are called even in this official letter.

Meanwhile, without direct warrant from London, Lawrence and his council at Halifax had taken action. His reasoning was that of a direct soldier. The Acadians would not take the full oath of British citizenship. Very well. Quite obviously they could not be trusted. Already they had acted in a traitorous way. Prolonged war with France was imminent. Since Acadians who might be allied with the savages could attack British posts, they must be removed. To replace them, British settlers could in time be brought into the country.

The thing was done in the summer and autumn of 1755. Colonel Robert Monckton, a regular officer, son of an Irish peer, who always showed an ineffable superiority to provincial officers serving under him, was placed in charge of the work. He ordered the male inhabitants of the neighbourhood of Beauséjour to meet him there on the 10th of August. Only about one-third of them came—some four hundred. He told them that the government at Halifax now declared them rebels. Their lands and all other goods were forfeited; they themselves were to be kept in prison. Not yet, however, was made known to them the decision that they were to be treated as traitors of whom the province must be rid. No attempt was made anywhere to distinguish loyal from disloyal Acadians. Lawrence gave orders to the military officers to clear the country of all Acadians, to get them by any necessary means on board the transports which would carry them away, and to burn their houses and crops so that those not caught might perish or be forced to surrender during the coming winter. At the moment, the harvest had just been reaped or was ripening.

When the stern work was done at Grand Pré, at Pisiquid, now Windsor, at Annapolis, there were harrowing scenes. In command of the work at Grand Pré was Colonel Winslow, an officer from Massachusetts—some of whose relatives twenty-five years later were to be driven, because of their loyalty to the British king, from their own homes in Boston to this very land of Acadia. Winslow issued a summons in French to all the male inhabitants, down to lads of ten, to come to the church at Grand Pré on Friday, the 5th of September, to learn the orders he had to communicate. Those who did not appear were to forfeit their goods.

No doubt many Acadians did not understand the summons. Few of them could read and it hardly mattered to them that on one occasion a notice on the church door was posted upside down. Some four hundred anxious peasants appeared. Winslow read to them a proclamation to the effect that their houses and lands were forfeited and that they themselves and their families were to be deported. Five vessels from Boston lay at Grand Pré. In time more ships arrived, but chill October had come before Winslow was finally ready.

By this time the Acadians realised what was to happen. The men were joined by their families. As far as possible the people of the same village were kept together. They were forced to march to the transports, a sorrow-laden company, women carrying babes in their arms, old and decrepit people borne in carts, young and strong men dragging what belongings they could gather. Winslow's task, as he says, lay heavy on his heart and hands:

> It hurts me to hear their weeping and wailing and gnashing of teeth.

By the 1st of November he had embarked fifteen hundred unhappy people. His last shipload he sent off on the 13th of December. The suffering from cold must have been terrible.

In all, from Grand Pré and other places, more than six thousand Acadians were deported. They were scattered in the English colonies from Maine to Georgia and in both France and England. Many died; many, helpless in new surroundings, sank into decrepit pauperism. Some reached people of their own blood in the French colony of Louisiana and in Canada. A good many returned from their exile in the colonies to their former home after the Seven Years' War had ended. Today their descendants form an appreciable part of the population of Nova Scotia, New Brunswick, and Prince Edward Island. The cruel act did one thing effectively: it made Nova Scotia safe for the British cause in the attack that was about to be directed against Canada.

Chapter 8

The Victories of Montcalm

In France's last, most determined, and most tragic struggle for North America, the noblest aspect is typified in the figure of Montcalm.

The circle of the king and his mistress at Versailles does not tell the whole story of France at this time. No doubt Madame de Pompadour made and unmade ministers, but behind the ministers was the great administrative system of France, with servants alert and efficient, and now chiefly occupied with military plans to defeat the great Frederick of Prussia. At the same time the intellect of France was busy with problems of science and was soon to express itself in the massive volumes of Diderot's *Encyclopaedia*. The soldiers of France were preparing to fight on many battlefields. The best of them took little part in the debilitating pleasures of Versailles.

Louis Joseph, Marquis de Montcalm, was a member of the ancient nobility of Languedoc, in the south of France. He was a scholar, a soldier, and a landowner. He could write a Latin inscription, fight a battle, and manage a farm—all with excellence. His was a fruitful race. His wife had borne him ten children, of whom six had survived. He was sincerely religious, a family man, enjoying quiet evenings at home. In his career, as no doubt in that of many other French leaders of the time, we find no lurid lights, no gay scenes at court—nothing but simple and laborious devotion to duty. Though a *grand seigneur*, Montcalm was poor. His letters show that his mind was always much occupied with family affairs, the need of economy, the careers of his sons, his mill, his plantations. He showed the minute care in management which the French practise better than the English.

In 1756 he was forty-four years of age, a soldier who had campaigned in Germany, Bohemia, and Italy, had known victory and defeat, had been a prisoner in the hands of the Austrians, and had made a reputation as a man fit to lead. He lived far from court and went to Paris only rarely. It was this quiet man who, on January 31, 1756, was summoned to Paris to head the military force about to be sent to Canada. Dieskau was a captive in English hands, and Montcalm was to replace Dieskau.

Thus began that connection of Montcalm with Canada which was destined three or four years later to bring to him first victory and then defeat, death, and undying fame. On receiving his appointment, he went to Paris, thanked the king in person for the honour done him, and was delighted that his son, a mere boy, was given the rank and pay of a colonel, one of the few abuses of court favour which we find in his career. On March 26, 1756, Montcalm embarked at Brest with his staff. War had not yet been declared, but already Britain had captured some three hundred French merchant ships, had taken prisoner nearly ten thousand French sailors, and was sweeping from the sea the fleets of France.

Owing to the fear of British cruisers, the voyage of Montcalm had its excitements. As usual, however, France was earlier in the field than Britain, who had in April no force ready for America which could intercept Montcalm. The storms were heavy, and on Easter Day, when Mass was celebrated, a sailor firm on his feet had to hold the chalice for the officiating priest. On board there were daily prayers, and always the service ended with cries of "God save the King!" Some of the officers on board were destined to survive to a new era in France when there should be no more a king.

Montcalm had with him a capable staff and a goodly number of young officers, gay, debonair, thinking not of great political designs about America but chiefly of their own future careers in France, and facing death light-heartedly enough. Next to Montcalm in command was the Chevalier de Lévis, a member of a great French family and himself destined to attain the high rank of Marshal of France, and a capable though not a brilliant soldier, whose chief gift was tact and the art of managing men. Third in command was the Chevalier de Bourlamaque, a quiet, reserved man, with no striking social gifts and in consequence not likely at first to make a good impression, though Montcalm, who was at the beginning a little doubtful of his quality, came in the end to rely upon him fully.

The most brilliant man in all that company was the young Colonel de Bougainville, Montcalm's chief *aide-de-camp*. Though only twenty-seven years old he was already famous in the world of science and was destined to be still more famous as a great navigator, to live through the whole period of the French Revolution, and to die only on the eve of the fall of Napoleon. In 1756 he was too young and clever to be always prudent in speech. It is from his quick eye and eager pen that we learn much of the inner story of these last days of New France. Montcalm discusses frankly in his letters these and other officers, with whom he was on the whole well pleased. In his heart he could echo the words of Bougainville as he watched the brilliant spectacle of the embarkation at Brest:

> What a nation is ours! Happy is he who leads and is worthy of it.

It was in this spirit of confidence that Montcalm faced the struggle in America. For him sad days were to come and his sunny, vivacious, southern temperament caused him to suffer keenly. At first, however, all was full of brilliant promise. So eager was he that, when his ships lay becalmed in the St. Lawrence some thirty miles below Quebec, he landed and drove to the city. It is the most beautiful country in the world, he writes, highly cultivated, with many houses, the peasants living more like the lesser gentry of France than like peasants, and speaking excellent French. He found the hospitality in Quebec such that a Parisian would be surprised at the profusion of good things of every kind.

The city was, he thought, like the best type of the cities of France. The Canadian climate was health-giving, the sky clear, the summer not unlike that of Languedoc, but the winter trying, since the severe weather caused the inhabitants to remain too much indoors. He described the Canadian ladies as witty, lively, devout, those of Quebec amusing themselves at play, sometimes for high stakes; those of Montreal, with conversation and dancing. He confessed that one of them proved a little too fascinating for his own peace of mind. The intolerable thing was the need to meet and pay court to the Indians whom the governor, the Marquis de Vaudreuil, regarded as valuable allies.

These savages, brutal, changeable, exacting, Montcalm from the first despised. It filled him with disgust to see them swarming in the streets of Montreal, sometimes carrying bows and arrows, their coarse features worse disfigured by war-paint and a gaudy headdress of feathers, their heads shaven, with the exception of one long scalp-lock, their gleaming bodies nearly naked or draped with dirty buffalo or

Louis Joseph, Marquis de Montcalm

beaver skins. What allies for a refined *grand seigneur* of France! It was a costly burden to feed them. Sometimes they made howling demands for brandy and for *bouillon*, by which they meant human blood. Many of them were cannibals. Once Montcalm had to give some of them, at his own cost, a feast of three oxen roasted whole. To his disgust, they gorged themselves and danced round the room shouting their savage war-cries.

The Governor of Canada, Pierre de Rigaud, Marquis de Vaudreuil, belonged to one of the most ancient families of France, related to that of Lévis. He had been born in Canada where his father was governor for the long period of twenty-two years, from 1703 to 1725, and in his outlook and prejudices he was wholly of New France, with a passionate devotion to its people, and a deep resentment at any airs of superiority assumed by those who came from old France. A certain admiration is due to Vaudreuil for his championship of the Canadians and even of the savages of the land of his birth against officers of his own rank and caste who came from France. There was in Canada the eternal cleavage in outlook and manners between the Old World and the New, which is found in equal strength in New England, and which was one of the chief factors in causing the American Revolution.

Vaudreuil, born at Quebec in 1698, had climbed the official ladder step by step until, in 1742, he had been made Governor of Louisiana, a post he held for three years. He succeeded the Marquis Duquesne as Governor of Canada in the year before Montcalm arrived. He meant well but he was a vain man, always a leading figure in the small society about him, and obsessed by a fussy self-importance. He was not clever enough to see through flattery. The Intendant Bigot, next to the governor the most important man in Canada, an able and corrupt rascal, knew how to manage the governor and to impose his own will upon the weaker man. Vaudreuil and his wife between them had a swarm of needy relatives in Canada, and these and other Canadians who sought favours from the governor helped to sharpen his antagonism to the officers from France. Vaudreuil believed himself a military genius. It was he and not Montcalm who had the supreme military command, and he regarded as an unnecessary intruder this general officer sent out from France.

Now that Montcalm was come, Vaudreuil showed a malignant alertness, born of jealousy, to snub and check him. Outward courtesies were, of course, maintained. Vaudreuil could be bland and Montcalm restrained, in spite of his southern temperament, but their dispatches show the bitterness in their relations. The court of France encouraged not merely the leaders but even officers in subordinate posts to communicate to it their views. A voluble correspondence about affairs in Canada has been preserved. Vaudreuil himself must have tried the patience of the French ministers for he wrote at prodigious length, exalting his own achievements to the point of being ludicrous.

At the same time, he belittled everything done by Montcalm, complained that he was ruining the French cause in America, hinted that he was in league with corrupt elements in Canada, and in the end even went so far as to request his recall in order that the more pliant Lévis might be put in his place. The letters of Montcalm are more reserved. Unlike Vaudreuil, he never stooped to falsehood. He knew that he was under the orders of the governor and he accepted the situation. When operations were on hand, Vaudreuil would give Montcalm instructions so ambiguous that if he failed he would be sure to get the discredit, while, if he succeeded, to Vaudreuil would belong the glory.

War is, at best, a cruel business. In Europe its predatory barbarity was passing away and there the lives of prisoners and of women and children were now being respected. Montcalm had been reared under this more civilized code, and he and his officers were shocked by what Vaudreuil regarded as normal and proper warfare. In 1756 the French had a horde of about two thousand savages, who had flocked to Montreal from points as far distant as the great plains of the West. They numbered more than thirty separate tribes or nations, as in their pride they called themselves, and each nation had to be humoured and treated as an equal, for they were not in the service of France but were her allies. They expected to be consulted before plans of campaign were completed. The defeat of Braddock in 1755 had made them turn to the prosperous cause of France.

Vaudreuil gave them what they hardly required—encouragement to wage war in their own way. The more brutal and ruthless the war on the English, he said, the more quickly would their enemies desire the kind of peace that France must have. The result was that the western frontiers of the English colonies became a hell of ruthless massacre. The savages attacked English settlements whenever they found them undefended. A pioneer might go forth in the morning to his labour and return in the evening to find his house in ashes and his wife and children lying dead with the scalps torn from their heads as trophies of savage prowess.

For years, until the English gained the upper hand over the French, this awful massacre went on. Hundreds of women and children perished. Vaudreuil reported with pride to the French court the number of scalps taken, and in his annals such incidents were written down as victories. He warned Montcalm that he must not be too strict with the savages or someday they would take themselves off and possibly go over to the English and leave the French without indispensable allies. He complained of the lofty tone of the French regular officers towards both Indians and Canadians, and assured the French court that it was only his own tact which prevented an open breach.

Canada lay exposed to attack by three routes: by Lake Ontario, by Lake Champlain, and by the St. Lawrence and the sea. It was vital to control the route to the West by Lake Ontario, vital to keep the English from invading Canada by way of Lake Champlain, vital to guard the St. Lawrence and keep open communications with France.

Montcalm first directed his attention to Lake Ontario. Oswego, lying on the south shore, was a fort much prized by the English as a base from which they could attack the French Fort Frontenac on the north side of the lake and cut off Canada from the West. If the English could do this, they would redeem the failure of Braddock and possibly turn the Indians from a French to an English alliance.

The French, in turn, were resolved to capture and destroy Oswego. In the summer of 1756, they were busy drawing up papers and instructions for the attack. Montcalm wrote to his wife that he had never before worked so hard. He kept every one busy, his *aide-de-camp*, his staff, and his secretaries. No detail was too minute for his observation. He regulated the changes of clothes which the officers might carry with them. He inspected hospitals, stores, and food, and he even ordered an alteration in the method of making bread. He reorganised the Canadian battalions and in every quarter stirred up new activity. He was strict about granting leave of absence.

Sometimes his working day endured for twenty hours—to bed at midnight and up again at four o'clock in the morning. He went with Lévis to Lake Champlain to see with his own eyes what was going on there. Then he turned back to Montreal. The discipline among the Canadian troops was poor and he stiffened it, thereby naturally causing great offense to those who liked slack ways and hated to take trouble about sanitation and equipment. He held interminable conferences with his Indian allies. They were astonished to find that the great soldier of whom they had heard so much was so small in stature,

PIERRE DE RIGAUD, MARQUIS DE VAUDREUIL

but they noted the fire in his eye. He despised their methods of warfare and notes with a touch of irony that, while every other barbarity continues, the burning of prisoners at the stake has rather gone out of fashion, though the savages recently burned an English woman and her son merely to keep in practice.

Montcalm made his plans secretly and struck suddenly. In the middle of August, 1756, he surprised and captured Oswego and took more than sixteen hundred prisoners. Of these, in spite of all that he could do, his Indians murdered some. The blow was deadly. The English lost vast stores; and now the French controlled the whole region of the Great Lakes. The Indians were on the side of the rising power more heartily than ever, and the unhappy frontier of the English colonies was so harried that murderous savages ventured almost to the outskirts of Philadelphia. Montcalm caused a *Te Deum* to be sung on the scene of his victory at Oswego.

In August he was back in Montreal where again was sung another joyous *Te Deum*. He wrote letters in high praise of some of his officers, especially of Bourlamaque, Malartic, and La Pause, the last "*un homme divin.*" Some of the Canadian officers, praised by Vaudreuil, he had tried and found wanting. He wrote to Lévis:

"Don't forget that Mercier is a feeble ignoramus. Saint Luc a prattling boaster, Montigny excellent but a drunkard. The others are not worth speaking of, including my first lieutenant-general Rigaud."

This Rigaud was the brother of Vaudreuil. When the governor wrote to the minister, he, for his part, said that the success of the expedition was wholly due to his own vigilance and firmness, aided chiefly by this brother, "*mon frère*," and Le Mercier, both of whom Montcalm describes as inept. Vaudreuil adds that only his own tact kept the Indian allies from going home because Montcalm would not let them have the plunder which they desired.

Montcalm struck his next blow at the English on Lake Champlain. In July, 1757, he had eight thousand men at Ticonderoga, at the northern end of Lake George. Two thousand of these were savages drawn from more than forty different tribes—a lawless horde whom the French could not control. A Jesuit priest saw a party of them squatting round a fire in the French camp roasting meat on the end of sticks and found that the meat was the flesh of an Englishman. English prisoners, sick with horror, were forced to watch this feast. The priest's protest was dismissed with anger: the savages would follow their own customs; let the French follow theirs. The truth is that the French had been only too successful in drawing the savages to them as allies. They formed now one-quarter of the whole French army. They were of little use as fighters and probably, in the long run, the French would have been better off without them. If, however, Montcalm had caused them to go, Vaudreuil would have made frantic protests, so that Montcalm accepted the necessity of such allies.

Each success, however, brought some new horrors at the hands of the Indians. Montcalm captured Fort William Henry, at the southern end of Lake George, in August, a year after the taking of Oswego. Fort William Henry was the most advanced English post in the direction of Canada. The place had been left weak, for the Earl of Loudoun, Commander-in-Chief of the British forces in America, was using his resources for an expedition against Louisbourg, which wholly failed. Colonel Monro, the brave officer in command at Fort William Henry, made a strong defence, but was forced to surrender. The terms were that he should march out with his soldiers and the civilians of the place, and should be escorted in safety to Fort Edward, about eighteen miles to the south.

This time the savages surpassed themselves in treachery and savagery. They had formally approved of the terms of surrender, but they attacked the long line of defeated English as they set out on the march, butchered some of their wounded, and seized hundreds of others as prisoners. Montcalm did what he could and even risked his life to check the savages. But some fifty English lay dead and the whole savage horde decamped for Montreal carrying with them two hundred prisoners.

Montcalm burned Fort William Henry and withdrew to Ticonderoga at the north end of the lake. Why, asked Vaudreuil, had he not advanced further south into English territory, taken Fort Edward—weak, because the English were in a panic—menaced Albany itself, and advanced even to New York? Montcalm's answer was that Fort Edward was still strong, that he had no transport except the backs of his men to take cannon eighteen miles by land in order to batter its walls, and that his Indians had left him. Moreover, he had been instructed to hasten his operations and allow his Canadians to go home to gather the ripening harvest so that Canada might not starve during the coming winter. Vaudreuil pressed at the French court his charges against Montcalm and without doubt produced some effect.

French tact was never exhibited with more grace than in the letters which Montcalm received from his superiors in France, urging upon him with suave courtesy the need of considering the sensitive pride of the colonial forces and of guiding with a light rein the barbaric might of the Indian allies. It is hard to imagine an English Secretary of State administering a rebuke so gently and yet so unmistakably. Montcalm well understood what was meant. He knew that some intrigue had been working at court but he did not suspect that the governor himself, all blandness and compliments to his face, was writing to Paris voluminous attacks on his character and conduct.

In the next summer (1758) Montcalm won another great success. He lay with his forces at Ticonderoga. The English were determined to press into the heart of Canada by way of Lake Champlain. All through the winter, after the fall of Fort William Henry, they had been making preparations on a great scale at Albany. By this time Amherst and Wolfe were on the scene in America, and they spent this summer in an attack on Louisbourg which resulted in the fall of the fortress. On the old fighting ground of Lake Champlain and Lake George, the English were this year making military efforts such as the Canadian frontier had never before seen. William Pitt, who now directed the war from London, had demanded that the colonies should raise twenty thousand men, a number well fitted to dismay the timid legislators of New York and Pennsylvania. At Albany fifteen thousand men came marching in by detachments—a few of them regulars, but most of them colonial militia who, as soon as winter came on, would scatter to their homes. The leader was General Abercromby—a leader, needless to say, with good connections in England, but with no other qualification for high command.

On July 5, 1758, there was a sight on Lake George likely to cause a flutter of anxiety in the heart of Montcalm at Ticonderoga. In a line of boats, six miles long, the great English host came down the lake and, early on the morning of the sixth, landed before the fort which Montcalm was to defend. The soul of the army had been a brilliant young officer, Lord Howe, who shared the hardships of the men, washed his own linen at the brook, and was the real leader trusted by the inept Abercromby. It was a tragic disaster for the British that at the outset of the fight Howe was killed in a chance skirmish. Montcalm's chief defence of Ticonderoga consisted in a felled forest. He had cut down hundreds of trees and, on high ground in front of the fort, made a formidable *abbatis* across which the English must advance.

Abercromby had four men to one of Montcalm. Artillery would have knocked a passage through the trunks of the trees which formed the *abbatis*. Abercromby, however, did not wait to bring up artillery. He was confident that his huge force could beat down opposition by a rapid attack, and he made the attack with all courage and persistence. But the troops could not work through the thicket of fallen trunks and, as night came on, they had to withdraw baffled. Next day Lake George saw another strange spectacle—a British Army of thirteen thousand men, the finest ever seen hitherto in America, retreating in a panic, with no enemy in pursuit. Nearly two thousand English had fallen, while Montcalm's loss was less than four hundred. He planted a great cross on the scene of the fight with an inscription in Latin that it was God who had wrought the victory. All Canada had a brief period of rejoicing before the gloom of final defeat settled down upon the country.

CHAPTER 9

Montcalm at Quebec

The rejoicing in Canada was brief. Before the end of the year the British were victorious at both the eastern and western ends of the long battle-line. Louisbourg had fallen in July; Fort Duquesne, in November. Fort Frontenac—giving command of Lake Ontario and, with it, the West—had surrendered to Bradstreet in August just after Montcalm's victory at Ticonderoga. The Ohio was gone. The great fortress guarding the gateway to the Gulf was gone. The next English attack would fall on Quebec. Montcalm had told Vaudreuil in the autumn, with vigorous precision, that the period of petty warfare, for taking scalps and burning houses, was past. It was time now to defend the main trunk of the tree and not the outer branches. The best Canadians should be incorporated into and trained in the battalions of regulars. The militia regiments themselves should be clothed and drilled like regular soldiers. Interior posts, such as Detroit, should be held by the smallest possible number of men. This counsel enraged Vaudreuil. Montcalm, he wrote, was trying to upset everything. Vaudreuil was certain that the English would not attack Quebec.

There is a melancholy greatness in the last days of Montcalm. He was fighting against fearful odds. With only about three thousand trained regulars and perhaps four times as many untrained Canadians and savages, he was confronting Britain's might on sea and land which was now thrown against New France. From France itself Montcalm knew that he had nothing to hope. In the autumn of 1758 he sent Bougainville to Versailles. That brilliant and loyal helper managed to elude the vigilance of the British fleet, reached Versailles, and there spent some months in varied and resourceful attempts to secure aid for Canada. He saw ministers. He procured the aid of powerful connections of his own and of his fellow-officers in Canada. He went to what was at this time the fountainhead of authority at the French court, and it was not the king. Bougainville wrote:

> The king is nothing; the *marchioness* is all-powerful—prime minister.

Bougainville saw the *marchioness*, Madame de Pompadour, and read to her some of Montcalm's letters. She showed no surprise and said nothing—her habit, as Bougainville said. By this time the name of Montcalm was one to charm with in France. Bougainville wrote to him:

> I should have to include all France if I should attempt to give a list of those who love you and wish to see you Marshal of France. Even the little children know your name.

There had been a time when the court thought the recall of Montcalm would be wise in the interests of New France. Now it was Montcalm's day and the desire to help him was real. France, however, could do little. Ministers were courteous and sympathetic; but as Berryer, Minister of Marine, said to Bougainville, with the house on fire in France, they could not take much thought of the stable in Canada.

This Berryer was an inept person. He was blindly ignorant of naval affairs, coarse, obstinate, a placeman who owed his position to intrigue and favouritism. His only merit was that he tried to cut down expenditure, but in regard to the navy this policy was likely to be fatal. It is useless, said this guardian of France's marine, to try to rival Britain on the sea, and the wise thing to do is to save money by not spending it on ships. Berryer even sold to private persons stores which he had on hand for the use of the fleet. If the house was on fire he did not intend, it would seem, that much should be left to burn.

The old Duc de Belle-Isle, Minister of War, was of another type, a fine and efficient soldier. He explained the situation frankly in a letter to Montcalm. Austria was an exigent ally, and Frederick of Prussia a dangerous foe. France had to concentrate her strength in Europe. The British fleet, he admitted, paralyzed efforts overseas. There was no certainty, or even probability, that troops and supplies sent from France would ever reach Canada. France, the duke said guardedly, was not without resources. She had a plan to strike a deadly blow against England and, in doing so, would save Canada without sending overseas a great army. The plan was nothing less than the invasion of England and Scotland with a great force, the enterprise which, nearly half a century later. Napoleon conceived as his master stroke against the proud maritime state. During that winter and spring France was building a great number of small boats with which to make a sudden descent and to land an army in England.

If this plan succeeded, all else would succeed. Montcalm must just hold on, conduct a defensive campaign and, above all, retain some part of Canada since, as the duke said with prophetic foresight, if the British once held the whole of the country they would never give it up. Montcalm himself had laid before the court a plan of his own. He estimated that the British would have six men to his one. Rather than surrender to them, he would withdraw to the far interior and take his army by way of the Ohio to Louisiana. The design was a wild counsel of despair for he would be cut off from any base of supplies, but it shows the risks he was ready to take. In him now the court had complete confidence. Vaudreuil was instructed to take no military action without seeking the counsel of Montcalm. Belle-Isle wrote to Montcalm:

> The king relies upon your zeal, your courage and your resolution.

Some little help was sent. The British control of the sea was not complete; since more than twenty French ships eluded British vigilance, bringing military stores, food (for Canada was confronted by famine), four hundred soldiers, and Bougainville himself, with a list of honours for the leaders in Canada. Montcalm was given the rank of Lieutenant-General and, but for a technical difficulty, would have been made a Marshal of France.

All this reliance upon Montcalm was galling to Vaudreuil. This weak man was entirely in the hands of a corrupt circle who recognised in the strength and uprightness of Montcalm their deadly enemy. An incredible plundering was going on. Its strength was in the blindness of Vaudreuil. The secretary of Vaudreuil, Grasse de Saint-Sauder, an ignorant and greedy man, was a member of the ring and yet had the entire confidence of the governor. The scale of the robberies was enormous. Bigot, the *intendant*, was stealing millions of *francs*; Cadet, the head of the supplies department, was stealing even more. They were able men who knew how to show diligence in their official work.

More than once Montcalm praises the resourcefulness with which Bigot met his requirements. But it was all done at a fearful cost to the State. Under assumed names the ring sold to the king, of whose interests they were the guardians, supplies at a profit of a hundred or a hundred and fifty *per cent*. They made vast sums out of transport. They drew pay for feeding hundreds of men who were not in the king's service. They received money for great bills of merchandise never delivered and repeated the process over and over again. To keep the Indians friendly, the king sent presents of guns, ammunition, and blankets. These were stolen and sold. Even the bodies of Acadians were sold. They were hired out for their keep to a contractor who allowed them to die of cold and hunger. Hundreds of the poor exiles perished.

The nemesis of a despotic system is that, however well-intentioned it may be, its officials are not controlled by an alert public opinion and yet must be trusted by their master. France meant well by her colony but the colony, unlike the English colonies, was not taught to look after itself. While nearly everyone in Canada understood what was going on, it was another thing to inform those in control in France. La Porte, the secretary of the colonial minister, was in the service of the ring. He intercepted letters which should have made exposures. Until found out, he had the ear of the minister and echoed the tone of lofty patriotism which Bigot assumed in his letters to his superiors.

History has made Montcalm one of its heroes—and with justice. He was a remarkable man, who would have won fame as a. scholar had he not followed the long family tradition of a soldier's career. Bougainville once said that the highest literary distinction of a Frenchman, a chair in the Academy, might be within reach of Montcalm as well as the baton of a Marshal of France. He had a prodigious memory and had read widely. His letters, written amid the trying conditions of war, are nervous, direct, pregnant with meaning, the notes of a penetrating intelligence. He had deep family affection. "*Adieu*, my heart, I believe that I love you more than ever I did before"; these were the last words of what he did not know was to be his last letter to his wife.

In the midst of a gay scene at Montreal, in the spring of 1759, he writes to Bourlamaque, then at Lake Champlain, with acute longing for the south of France in the spring. For six or seven months in the year he could receive no letters and always the British command of the sea made their expected arrival uncertain.

> When shall I be again at the Château of Candiac, with my plantations, my oaks, my oil mill, my mulberry trees? O good God.

He lays bare his spirit especially to Bourlamaque, a quiet, efficient, thoughtful man, like himself, and enjoins him to bum the letters—

which he does not, happily for posterity. Scandal does not touch him but, like most Frenchmen, he is dependent on the society of women. He lived in a house on the ramparts of Quebec and visited constantly the *salons* of his neighbour in the Rue du Parloir, the beautiful and witty Madame de la Naudière. In two or three other households he was also intimate and the bishop was a sympathetic friend. His own tastes were those of the scholar, and more and more, during the long Canadian winters, he enjoyed evenings of quiet reading.

The elder Mirabeau, father of the revolutionary leader of 1789, had just published his *Ami des Hommes* and this we find Montcalm studying. But above all he reads the great encyclopaedia of Diderot. By 1759 seven of the huge volumes had been issued. They startled the intellectual world of the time and Montcalm set out to read them, omitting the articles which had no interest for him or which he could not understand. C is a copious letter in an encyclopaedia, and Montcalm found excellent the articles on Christianity, College, Comedy, Comet, Commerce, Council, and so on. Wolfe—soon to be his opponent—had the same taste for letters. The two men, unlike in body, for Wolfe was tall and Montcalm the opposite, were alike in spirit, painstaking students as well as men of action.

At first Montcalm had not realised what was the deepest shadow in the life of Canada. Perhaps chiefly because Vaudreuil was always at Montreal, Montcalm preferred Quebec and was surprised and charmed by the life of that city. It had, he said, the air of a real capital. There were fair women and brave men, sumptuous dinners with forty or fifty covers, brilliantly lighted *salons*, a vivid social life in which he was much courted. The Intendant Bigot was agreeable and efficient. Soon, however, Montcalm had misgivings. It was a gambling age, but he was staggered by the extent of the gambling at the house of the *intendant*. He did not wish to break with Bigot, and there was perhaps some weakness in his failure to denounce the orgies from which his conscience revolted. He warned his own officers but he could not control the colonial officers, and Vaudreuil was too weak to check a man like Bigot. Whence came the money?

In time, Montcalm understood well enough. He himself was poor. To discharge the duties of his position he was going into debt, and he had even to consider the possible selling of his establishment in France. He had to beg the court for some financial relief. At the same time, he saw about him a wild extravagance. There was famine in Canada. During the winter of 1758-59 the troops were put on short rations and, in spite of their bitter protests, had to eat horse flesh. Suffering and starvation bore heavily on the poor. Through lack of food people fell fainting in the streets.

But the circle of Bigot paid little heed and feasted, danced, and gambled. Montcalm pours out his soul to Bourlamaque. He spends, he says, sleepless nights, and his mind is almost disordered by what he sees. In his journal he notes his own fight with poverty and its contrast with the careless luxury of a crowd of worthless hangers-on making four or five hundred thousand francs a year and insulting decency by their lavish expenditure. One of the ring, a clerk with a petty salary, a base creature, spends more on carriages, horses, and harness than a foppish and reckless young member of the *nouveaux-riches* would spend in France. Corruption in Canada is protected by corruption in France. Montcalm cries out with a devotion which his sovereign hardly deserved, though it was due to France herself, "O King, worthy of better service, dear France, crushed by taxes to enrich greedy knaves!"

The weary winter of 1758-59 at length came to an end. In May the ships already mentioned arrived from France, bringing Bougainville and, among other things, the news that Pitt was sending great forces for a decisive attack on Canada. At that very moment, indeed, the British ships were entering the mouth of the St. Lawrence. Canada had already been cut off from France. Montcalm held many councils with his officers. The strategy decided upon was to stand at bay at Quebec, to strike the enemy if he should try to land, and to hold out until the approach of winter should force the retirement of the British fleet.

CHAPTER 10

The Strategy of Pitt

During four campaigns the British had suffered humiliating disasters. It is the old story in English history of caste privilege and deadly routine bringing to the top men inadequate in the day of trial. It has happened since, even in our own day, as it has happened so often before. It seems that imminent disaster alone will arouse the nation to its best military effort. In 1757, however, England was thoroughly aroused. Failure then on her own special element, the sea, touched her vitally. Admiral Byng—through sheer cowardice, as was charged—had failed to attack a French fleet aiding in the siege of the island of Minorca which was held by the English, and Minorca had fallen to the French.

Such was the popular clamour at this disaster that Byng was tried, condemned, and shot. There was also an upheaval in the government. At no time in English history were men more eager for the fruits of office; and now, even in a great crisis, the greed for spoils could not be shaken off. The nation demanded a conduct of the war which sought efficiency above all else. The politicians, however, insisted on government favours.

In the end a compromise was reached. At the head of the government was placed a politician, the Duke of Newcastle, who loved jobbery and patronage in politics and who doled out offices to his supporters. At the War Office was placed Pitt with a free hand to carry on military operations. He was the terrible comet of horse who had harried Walpole in the days when that minister was trying to keep out of war. He knew and even loved war; his fierce national pride had been stirred to passion by the many humiliations at the hand of France; and now he was resolved to organise, to spend, and to fight, until Britain trampled on France. He had the nation behind him. He bullied and frightened the House of Commons. Members trembled if Pitt turned on them. By his fiery energy, by making himself a terror to weakness and incompetence, he won for Britain the Seven Years' War.

Though Pitt became Secretary of State for War in June, 1757, not until 1758 did the tide begin to turn in America. But when it did turn, it flowed with resistless force. In little more than a year the doom of New France was certain. The first great French reverse was at a point where the naval and military power of Britain could unite in attack. Pitt well understood the need of united action by the two services. Halifax became the radiating centre of British activities. Here, in 1757, before Pitt was well in the saddle, a fleet and an army gathered to attack Louisbourg—an enterprise not carried out that year partly because France had a great fleet on the spot, and partly, too, on account of the bad quality of British leadership.

Only in the campaign of 1758 did Pitt's dominance become effective. With him counted one quality and one alone, efficiency. The old guard at the War Office were startled when men with rank, years, influence, and every other claim but competence for their tasks, were passed over, and young and obscure men were given high command. To America in the spring of 1758 were sent officers hitherto little known. Edward Boscawen, Commander of the Fleet, and veteran among these leaders, was a comparatively young man, only forty-seven; Jeffrey Amherst, just turned forty, was Commander-in-Chief on land. Next in command to Amherst was James Wolfe, aged thirty.

These young and vigorous men knew the value of promptness or they would not have been tolerated under Pitt. Before the end of May, 1758, Boscawen was in Halifax harbour with a fleet of some forty warships and a multitude of transports. On board were nearly twelve thousand soldiers, more than eleven thousand of them British regulars. The colonial forces now play a minor part in the struggle; Pitt was ready to send from England all the troops heeded. The array at Halifax, the greatest yet seen in America, numbered about twenty thousand men, including sailors. Before the first of June the fleet was on its way to Louisbourg. The defence was stubborn; and James Wolfe, who led the first landing party, had abundant opportunity to prove his courage and capacity. By the end of July, however, Louisbourg had fallen, and nearly six thousand prisoners were in the hands of the English. It was the beginning of the end.

In the autumn Wolfe was back in England, where he was quickly given command of the great expedition which was planned against

Quebec for the following year. Admiral Sir Charles Saunders, who seems almost old compared with Wolfe, for he was nearly fifty, was in chief command of the fleet. Amherst had remained in America as Commander-in-Chief, and was taking slow, deliberate, thorough measures for the last steps in the conquest of New France.

To be too late had been the usual fate of the many British expeditions against Canada. No one, however, dared to be late under Pitt. On February 17, 1759, the greatest fleet that had ever put out for America left Portsmouth. More than two hundred and fifty ships set their sails for the long voyage. There were forty-nine warships, carrying fourteen thousand sailors and marines, and two hundred other ships manned by perhaps seven thousand men in the merchant service, but ready to fight if occasion offered. Altogether nearly thirty thousand men now left the shores of England to attack Canada.

There is a touch of doom for France in the fact that its own lost fortress of Louisbourg was to be the rendezvous of the fleet. Saunders, however, arrived so early that the entrance to Louisbourg was still blocked with ice, and he went on to Halifax. In time he returned to Louisbourg, and from there the great fleet sailed for Quebec. The voyage was uneventful. We can picture the startled gaze of the Canadian peasants as they saw the stately array, many miles long, pass up the St. Lawrence. On the 26th of June, Wolfe and Saunders were in the basin before Quebec and the great siege had begun which was to mark one of the turning-points in history.

Nature had furnished a noble setting for the drama now to be enacted. Quebec stands on a bold semi-circular rock on the north shore of the St. Lawrence. At the foot of the rock sweeps the mighty river, here at the least breadth in its whole course, but still a flood nearly a mile wide, deep and strong. Its currents change ceaselessly with the ebb and flow of the tide which rises a dozen feet, though the open sea is eight hundred miles away. Behind the rock of Quebec, the small stream of the St. Charles furnishes a protection on the landward side. Below the fortress, the great river expands into a broad basin with the outflow divided by the Island of Orleans. In every direction there are cliffs and precipices and rising ground. From the north shore of the great basin the land slopes gradually into a remote blue of wooded mountains. The assailant of Quebec must land on low ground commanded everywhere from heights for seven or eight miles on the east and as many on the west. At both ends of this long front are further natural defences—at the east the gorge of the Montmorency River, at

Edward Boscawen

the west that of the Cap Rouge River.

Wolfe's desire was to land his army on the Beauport shore at some point between Quebec and Montmorency. But Montcalm's fortified posts, behind which lay his army, stretched along the shore for six miles, all the way from the Montmorency to the St. Charles. Wolfe had a great contempt for Montcalm's army—"five feeble French battalions mixed with undisciplined peasants." If only he could get to close quarters with the "wily and cautious old fox," as he called Montcalm! Already the British had done what the French had thought impossible. Without pilots they had steered their ships through treacherous channels in the river and through the dangerous "Traverse" near Cap Tourmente. Captain Cook, destined to be a famous navigator, was there to survey and mark the difficult places, and British skippers laughed at the forecasts of disaster made by the pilots whom they had captured on the river. The French were confident that the British would not dare to take their ships farther up the river past the cannonade of the guns in Quebec, though this the British accomplished almost without loss.

Wolfe landed a force upon the lower side of the gorge at Montmorency and another at the head of the Island of Orleans. He planted batteries at Point Lévis across the river from Quebec, and from there he battered the city. The pleasant houses in the Rue du Parloir which Montcalm knew so well were knocked into rubbish, and its fascinating ladies were driven desolate from the capital. But this bombardment brought Wolfe no nearer his goal. On the 31st of July he made a frontal attack on the flats at Beauport and failed disastrously with a loss of four hundred men. Time was fighting for Montcalm.

By the 1st of September Wolfe's one hope was in a surprise by which he could land an army above Quebec, the nearer to the fortress the better. Its feeble walls on the landward side could not hold out against artillery. But Bougainville guarded the high shore and marched his men incessantly up and down to meet threatened attacks. On the heights, the battalion of Guienne was encamped on the Plains of Abraham to guard the Foulon. This was a cove on the river bank from which there was a path, much used by the French for dragging up provisions, leading to the top of the cliff at a point little more than a mile from the walls of the city.

On the 6th of September the battalion of Guienne was sent back to the Beauport lines by order of Vaudreuil. Montcalm countermanded the order, but was not obeyed, and Wolfe saw his chance. For days he threatened a landing, above and below Quebec, now at one point, now at another, until the French were both mystified and worn out with incessant alarms. Then, early on the morning of the 13th of September, came Wolfe's master-stroke. His men embarked in boats from the war-ships lying some miles above Quebec, dropped silently down the river, dose to the north shore, made sentries believe that they were French boats carrying provisions to the Foulon, landed at the appointed spot, climbed up the cliff, and overpowered the sleeping guard.

A little after daylight Wolfe had nearly five thousand soldiers, a "thin red line," busy preparing a strong position on the Plains of Abraham, while the fleet was landing cannon to be dragged up the steep hill to bombard the fortress on its weakest side. Montcalm had spent many anxious days. He had been incessantly on the move, examining for himself over and over again every point, Cap Rouge, Beauport, Montmorency, reviewing the militia of which he felt uncertain, inspecting the artillery, the commissariat, everything that mattered. At three o'clock in the morning of one of these days he wrote to Bourlamaque, at Lake Champlain, noting the dark night, the rain, his men awake and dressed in their tents, everyone alert.

> I am booted and my horses are saddled, which is in truth my usual way of spending the night. I have not undressed since the twenty-third of June.

On the evening of the 12th of September the batteries at Point Lévis kept up a furious fire on Quebec. There was much activity on board the British war-ships lying below the town. Boats filled with men rowed towards Beauport as if to attempt a landing during the night. Here the danger seemed to lie. At midnight the British boats were still hovering off the shore. The French troops manned the entrenched lines and Montcalm was continually anxious. A heavy convoy of provisions was to come down to the Foulon that night, and orders had been given to the French posts on the north shore above Quebec to make no noise. The arrival of the convoy was vital, for the army was pressed for food. Montcalm was therefore anxious for its fate when at break of day he heard firing from the French cannon at Samos, above Quebec. Had the provisions then been taken by the English?

Near his camp all now seemed quiet. He gave orders for the troops to rest, drank some cups of tea with his *aide-de-camp* Johnstone, a Scotch Jacobite, and at about half-past six rode towards Quebec to the camp of Vaudreuil to learn why the artillery was firing at Samos. Immediately in front of the governor's house he learned the momentous news. The English were on the Plains of Abraham. Soon he had the evidence of his own eyes. On the distant heights across the valley he could see the redcoats. No doubt Montcalm had often pondered this possibility and had decided in such a case to attack at once before the enemy could entrench and bring up cannon. A rapid decision was now followed by rapid action. He had a moment's conversation with Vaudreuil. The French regiments on the right at Vaudreuil's camp, lying nearest to the city, were to march at once. To Johnstone he said, "The affair is serious," and then gave orders that all the French left, except a few men to guard the ravine at Montmorency, should follow quickly to the position between Quebec and the enemy, a mile away.

Off to this point he himself galloped. Already, by orders of officers on the spot, regiments were gathering between the walls of the city and the British. The regiments on the French right at Beauport were soon on the move towards the battlefield, but two thousand of the best troops still lay inactive beyond Beauport. Johnstone declares that Vaudreuil countermanded the order of Montcalm for these troops to come to his support and ordered that not one of them should budge. There was haste everywhere. By half-past nine Montcalm had some four thousand men drawn up between the British and the walls of Quebec. He hoped that Bougainville, advancing from Cap Rouge, would be able to assail the British rear: "Surely Bougainville understands that I must attack."

The crisis was over in fifteen minutes. Montcalm attacked at once. His line was disorderly. His centre was composed of regular troops, his wings of Canadians and Indians. These fired irregularly and lay down to reload, thus causing confusion. The French moved forward rapidly; the British were coming on more slowly. The French were only some forty yards away when there was an answering fire from the thin red line; for Wolfe had ordered his men to put two balls in their muskets and to hold their fire for one dread volley. Then the roar from Wolfe's centre was like that of a burst of artillery; and, when the smoke cleared, the French battalions were seen breaking in disorder from the shock, the front line cut down by the terrible fire.

A bayonet charge from the redcoats followed. Some five thousand trained British regulars bore down, working great slaughter on four thousand French, many of them colonials who had never before fought in the open. The rout of the French was complete. Some fled

JAMES WOLFE

to safety behind the walls of Quebec, others down the Côte Ste. Geneviève and across the St. Charles River, where they stopped pursuit by cutting the bridge. Both Wolfe and Montcalm were mortally wounded after the issue of the day was really decided, and both survived to be certain, the one of victory, the other of defeat. Wolfe died on the field of battle. Montcalm was taken into a house in Quebec and died early the next morning. It is perhaps the only incident in history of a decisive battle of world import followed by the death of both leaders, each made immortal by the tragedy of their common fate.

At two o'clock in the afternoon of the day of defeat, Vaudreuil held a tumultuous council of war. It was decided to abandon Quebec, where Montcalm lay dying and to retreat up the St. Lawrence to Montreal, to the defence of which Lévis had been sent before the fight. That night the whole French army fled in panic, leaving their tents standing and abandoning quantities of stores. Vaudreuil who had talked so bravely about death in the ruins of Canada, rather than surrender, gave orders to Ramezay, commanding in Quebec, to make terms and haul down his flag. On the third day after the battle, the surrender was arranged. On the fourth day the British marched into Quebec, where ever since their flag has floated.

Meanwhile, Amherst, the Commander-in-Chief of the British armies in America, was making a toilsome advance towards Montreal by way of Lake Champlain. He had occupied both Ticonderoga and Crown Point, which had been abandoned by the French. Across his path lay Bourlamaque at Isle aux Noix. Another British army, having captured Niagara, was advancing on Montreal down the St. Lawrence from Lake Ontario. Amherst, however, made little progress this year in his menace to Montreal and soon went into winter quarters, as did the other forces elsewhere. The British victory therefore was as yet incomplete.

The year 1759 proved dire for France. She was held fast by her treaty with Austria and at ruinous cost was ever sending more and more troops to help Austria against Prussia. The great plan of which Belle-Isle had written to Montcalm was the chief hope of her policy. England was to be invaded and London occupied. If this were done, all else would be right. It was not done. France could not parry Pitt's blows. In Africa, in the West Indies, in India, the British won successes which meant the ruin of French power in three continents. French admirals like Conflans and La Clue were no match for Boscawen, Hawke, and Rodney, all seamen of the first rank, and made the stronger because dominated by the fiery Pitt. They kept the French squadrons shut up in their own ports. When, at last, on November 20, 1759, Conflans came out of Brest and fought Hawke at Quiberon Bay, the French fleet was nearly destroyed, and the dream of taking London ended in complete disaster.

CHAPTER 11

The Fall of Canada

Though Quebec was in their hands, the position of the British during the winter of 1759-60 was dangerous. In October General Murray, who was left in command, saw with misgiving the great fleet sail away which had brought to Canada the conquering force of Wolfe and Saunders. Murray was left with some seven thousand men in the heart of a hostile country, and with a resourceful enemy, still unconquered, preparing to attack him. He was separated from other British forces by vast wastes of forest and river, and until spring should come no fleet could aid him. Three enemies of the English, the French said exultingly, would aid to retake Quebec: the ruthless savages who haunted the outskirts of the fortress and massacred many an incautious straggler; the French Army which could be recruited from the Canadian population; and, above all, the bitter cold of the Canadian winter.

To Murray, as to Napoleon long afterward in his rash invasion of Russia, General February was indeed the enemy. About the two or three British ships left at Quebec the ice froze in places a dozen feet thick, and snowdrifts were piled so high against the walls of Quebec that it looked sometimes as if the enemy might walk over them into the fortress. So solidly frozen was the surface of the river that Murray sent cannon to the south shore across the ice to repel a menace from that quarter. There was scarcity of firewood and of provisions. Scurvy broke out in the garrison. Many hundreds died so that by the spring Murray had barely three thousand men fit for active duty.

Throughout the winter Lévis, now in command of the French forces, made increasing preparations to destroy Murray in the spring. The headquarters of Lévis were at Montreal. Here Vaudreuil, the governor, kept his little court. He and Lévis worked harmoniously, for Lévis was conciliatory and tactful. For a time Vaudreuil treasured the thought of taking command in person to attack Quebec. In the end, however, he showed that he had learned something from the disasters of the previous year and did not interfere with the plans made by Lévis. So throughout the winter Montreal had its gayeties and vanities as of old. There were feasts and dances—but over all brooded the reality of famine in the present and the foreboding of disaster to come.

By April 20, 1760, the St. Lawrence was open and, though the shores were cumbered with masses of broken ice, the central channel was free for the boats which Lévis filled with his soldiers. It was a bleak experience to descend the turbulent river between banks clogged with ice. When Lévis was not far from Quebec, he learned that it was impossible to surprise Murray who was well on guard between Cap Rouge on the west and Beauport on the east. The one thing to do was to reach the Plains of Abraham in order to attack the feeble walls of Quebec from the landward side. Since Murray's alertness made impossible attack by way of the high cliffs which Wolfe had climbed in the night, Lévis had to reach Quebec by a circuitous route. He landed his army a little above Cap Rouge, marched inland over terrible roads in heavy rain, and climbed to the plateau of Quebec from the rear at Sainte Foy. On April 27, 1760, he drew up his army on the heights almost exactly as Wolfe had done in the previous September.

Murray followed the example of Montcalm. He had no trust in the feeble defences of Quebec and on the 28th marched out to fight on the open plain. The battle of Sainte Foy followed exactly the precedents of the previous year. The defenders of Quebec were driven off the field in overwhelming defeat. The difference was that Murray took his army back to Quebec and from behind its walls still defied his French assailant. Lévis had poor artillery, but he did what he could. He entrenched and poured his fire into Quebec. In the end it was sea power which balked him. On the 15th of May, when a British fleet appeared round the head of the Island of Orleans, Lévis withdrew in something like panic and Quebec was safe.

Lévis returned to Montreal; and to this point all the forces of France slowly retreated as they were pressed in by the overwhelming numbers of the British. At Oswego, the scene of Montcalm's first brilliant success four years earlier, Amherst had gathered during the summer of 1760 an army of about ten thousand men. From here he descended the St. Lawrence in boats to attack Montreal from the west. From the south, down Lake Champlain and the Richelieu River to the St. Lawrence, came another British force under Haviland also to attack Montreal. At Quebec Murray put his army on transports, left the city almost destitute of defence, and thus brought a third considerable force against Montreal.

There was little fighting. The French withdrew to the common objective as their enemy advanced. Early in September Lévis had gathered at Montreal all his available force, amounting now to scarcely more than two thousand men, for Canadians and Indians alike had deserted him. The British pressed in with the slow and inevitable rigor of a force of nature. On the 7th of September their united army was before the town and Amherst demanded instant surrender. The only thing for Vaudreuil to do was to make the best terms possible. On the next day he signed a capitulation which protected the liberties in property and religion of the Canadians but which yielded the whole of Canada to Great Britain. The struggle for North America had ended.

In the moment of triumph Amherst inflicted on the French army a deep humiliation to punish the outrages committed by their Indian allies. In the early days of the war Loudoun, the Commander-in-Chief in America, had vowed that the British would make the French "sick of such inhuman villainy" and teach them to respect "the laws of nature and humanity." Washington speaks of his "deadly sorrow" at the dreadful outrages which he saw, the ravishing of women, the scalping alive even of children. Philadelphians had seen the grim spectacle of a wagon-load of corpses brought by mourning friends and relatives of the dead and laid down at the door of the Assembly to show to pacifist legislators what was really happening.

The French regular officers as we have seen, had hated this kind of warfare. Bougainville says that his soul shuddered at the sights in Montreal, where the whole town turned out to see an English prisoner killed, boiled, and eaten by the savages. Worse still, captive mothers were obliged to eat the flesh of their own children. The French believed that they could not get on without the savage allies who committed these outrages, and they were not strong enough to coerce them. Amherst, on the other hand, held his Indians in check and rebuked outrage. Now he was stern to punish what the French had permitted. He could write proudly to a friend that the French were amazed at the order in which he kept his own Indians. Not a man, woman, or child, he said, had been hurt or a single atrocity committed. It was a vivid contrast with what had taken place after the British surrender to Montcalm at Fort William Henry. The day of retribution had come.

Sir Geoffrey Amherst

Because of such outrages, the French Army was denied the honours of war usually conceded to a brave and defeated foe. The French officers and men must not, Amherst insisted, serve again during the war. Lévis protested and begged Vaudreuil to be allowed to go on fighting rather than accept the terms, but in vain. The humiliation was rigorously imposed, and it was a sullen host which the British took captive.

France had lost an Empire. It was nearly three years still before peace was signed at Paris in 1763. To Britain France yielded everything east of the Mississippi except New Orleans, and to Spain she ceded New Orleans and everything else to which she had any claim. The *fleurs-de-lis* floated still over only two tiny fishing islands off the Newfoundland shore. All the glowing plans of France's leaders—of Richelieu, of Louis XIV, of Colbert, of Frontenac, of the heroic missionaries of the Jesuit Order—seemed to have come to nothing.

The fall of France did much to drag down her rival. Already was America restless under control from Europe. There was now no danger to the English in America from the French peril which had made insecure the borders of Massachusetts, of New York, of Pennsylvania, and Virginia, and had brought widespread desolation and sorrow. With the removal of the menace went the need of help and defences for the colonies from the motherland. The French belief that there was a natural antipathy between the English of the Old World and the English of the New was, in reality, based on the fact of a likeness so great that neither would accept control or patronage from the other. Towards the Englishman who assumed airs of superiority the antagonism of the colonists was always certain to be acute. Open strife came when the assumption of superiority took the form of levying taxes on the colonies without asking their leave. In no remote way the fall of French Canada, by removing a near menace to the English colonies, led to this new conflict and to the collapse of that older British Empire which had sprung from the England of the Stuarts.

When Montreal fell there were in the St. Lawrence many British ships which had been used for troops and supplies. Before the end of September, the French soldiers and also the officials from France who desired to go home were on board these ships bound for Europe. By the end of November most of the exiles had reached home. Varying receptions awaited them. Lévis, who took back the army, was soon again, by consent of the British government, in active service. Fortune smiled on him to the end. He died a great noble and Marshal of

France just before the Revolution of 1789; but in that awful upheaval his widow and his two daughters perished on the scaffold. Vaudreuil's shallow and vain incompetence did not go unpunished. He was put on trial, accused of a share in the black frauds which had helped to ruin Canada.

The trial was his punishment. He was acquitted of taking any share of the plunder and so drops out of history. Bigot and his gang, on the other hand, were found guilty of vast depredations. The former Intendant was for a time in the Bastille and in the end was banished from France, after being forced to repay great sums. We find echoes of the luxury of Quebec in the sale in France of the rich plate which the rascal had acquired. There were, however, other and even worse plunderers. They were tried and condemned chiefly to return what they had stolen. We rather wonder that no expiatory sacrifice on the scaffold was required of any of these knaves. Lally Tollendal, who, as the French leader in India, had only failed and not plundered, was sent to a cruel execution.

Under the terms of the surrender and of the final Treaty of Peace in 1763, civilians in Canada were given leave to return to France. Nearly the whole of the official class and many of the large landowners, the *seigneurs*, left the country. In Canada there remained a priesthood, largely native, but soon to be recruited from France by the upheaval of the Revolution, a few seigneurial families, natural leaders of their race, a peasantry, exhausted by the long war but clinging tenaciously to the soil, and a good many hardy pioneers of the forest, men skilled in hunting and in the use of the axe.

Out of these elements, amounting in 1763 to little more than sixty thousand people, has come that French-Canadian race in America now numbering perhaps three millions. The race has scattered far. It is found in the mills of Massachusetts, in the canebrakes of Louisiana, on the wide stretches of the prairie of the Canadian West, but it has always kept intact its strong citadel on the banks of the St. Lawrence. New France was, in reality, widely separated in spirit from old France, before the new master in Canada made the division permanent. The imagination of the Canadian peasant did not wander across the ocean to France. He knew only the scenes about his own hearth and in them alone were his thought and affections centred.

The one wider interest which the *habitant* treasured was love for the Catholic Church of his fathers and of his own spiritual hopes. It thus happened that when France in revolution assailed and for a time overthrew the Church within her borders, the heart of French Canada was not with France but with the persecuted Church; she hated the spirit of revolutionary France. *Te Deums* were sung at Quebec in thanksgiving for the defeats of Napoleon. In language and what literary culture they possessed, in traditions and tastes, the conquered people remained French, but they had no allegiance divided between Canada and France. To this day they are proud to be simply Canadians, rooted in the soil of Canada, with no debt of patriotic gratitude to the France from which they sprang or to the Britain which obtained political dominance over their ancestors after a long agony of war. To the British Crown many of them feel a certain attachment because of the liberty guaranteed to them to pursue their own ideals of happiness. In preserving their type of social life, their faith and language, they have shown a resolute tenacity. To this day they are as different in these things from their fellow-citizens of British origin in the rest of Canada as were their ancestors from the English colonies which lay on their borders.

The French in Canada are still a separate people. From time to time a nervous fear seizes them lest too many of their race may be lost to their old ideals in the Anglo-Saxon world surging about them. Then they listen readily to appeals to their racial unity and draw more sharply than ever the lines of division between themselves and the rest of North America. They remain a fragment of an older France, remote and isolated, still dreaming dreams like those of Frontenac of old of the dominance of their race in North America and asserting passionately their rights in the soil of Canada to which, first of Europeans, they came. At the mouth of the Mississippi in the Louisiana founded by Louis XIV, along the St. Lawrence in the Canada of Champlain and Frontenac, with a resolution more than half pathetic, and in a world that gives little heed, men of French race are still on guard to preserve in America the lineaments of that older France, long since decayed in Europe, which was above all the eldest daughter of the Church.

The Fall of Canada

Contents

Preface	139
The Fall of Quebec	141
Quebec During the Winter of 1759-60	171
Montreal During the Winter of 1759-60	203
The Battle of Sainte Foy	231
The Relief of Quebec by the Fleet	260
The Advance to Montreal	281
The Fall of New France	306

Preface

The present volume, *A Chapter in the History of the Seven Years' War*, covers only a year of history in a colony which contained at the time less than one hundred thousand Europeans. It would not be surprising if some reader were to ask whether a study in such detail was worthwhile. It may be said, however, that the Seven Years' War is one of the most important struggles in the history of mankind, and that the topic of the present volume, the transfer of Canada from French to British sovereignty, was a vital event in the history of the British Empire. If only a small population was directly affected, the issues were none the less far-reaching. The few French in North America in 1760 have now multiplied into nearly three million people, scattered over both Canada and the United States. Already in 1760 they had developed their own type of social life; they have since clung to it with great tenacity; and today it is one of the factors in the life of Canada which cannot be ignored. Such a study seemed a necessary beginning for investigations in the later history of Canada on which the author has been engaged.

Toronto,
July, 1914.

CHAPTER 1

The Fall of Quebec

Horace Walpole calls the year 1759 the 'great year', the 'wonderful year', because of the victories which it brought to his country. France and Britain were in the midst of the terrible Seven Years' War, which involved the loss of nearly a million lives. The outcome of the war was still uncertain. During the summer the English people had been uneasy. France was known to be making great preparations to invade Britain, and many a good citizen went to bed each night in dread lest the roar of the cannon of the invader might be in his ears before morning. Wolfe had just led a great expedition to Quebec, but already there were gloomy forebodings that his attempt would fail. News travelled slowly in those days, and it was not until the early autumn that good tidings arrived.

Word then came that at the end of July General Amherst had captured Ticonderoga, the fort which commanded the entrance to Canada by way of Lake Champlain, and that at the very same time Sir William Johnson had captured Fort Niagara, the key to the whole commerce of the region beyond Lake Ontario. England was exultant. Horace Walpole wrote on September 13, 1759, the date, though he did not yet know it, of another and greater victory in Canada: 'We have taken more places and ships in a week than would have set up such pedant nations as Greece and Rome to all futurity. If we did but call Sir William Johnson "*Gulielmus Johnsonus Niagaricus*" and Amherst "*Galfridus Amhersta Ticonderogicus*" we should be quoted a thousand years hence as the patterns of valour, virtue, and disinterestedness; for posterity always ascribes all manner of modesty and self-denial to those that take the most pains to perpetuate their own glory.'

The exultation caused by the fall of Ticonderoga and Niagara soon gave way to new fears. Word came from Wolfe that Amherst had failed to join him before Quebec and that he had little hope of capturing the fortress. This news was made public, and, of course, caused gloom and depression. Almost immediately after this came, however, the tidings that Wolfe had won a great victory and that Quebec had fallen. Walpole expresses the pride and joy of the time. He now jested at the fears of invasion and at the weakness of the French Navy: 'Can the lords of America', he asked, 'be afraid of half a dozen canoes?' The bells, he said, were being worn thin with ringing for victories, and one was forced to ask every morning what success there was for fear of missing one. He writes to his friend Montague, on October 21:

> I don't know a word of news less than the conquest of America; you shall hear from me again if we take Mexico or China before Christmas.

The English, he added, were like Alexander: they had no more worlds left to conquer. He affected to be bored by meeting so many people who had won military honours; it is 'very fatiguing: all the world is made knights or generals'. There was nothing in all history, he thought, to equal the victories of this year.

The simple-minded public, which received this joyful news, now assured itself that the struggle was over and that Canada had fallen. It dismissed America from its thoughts. The newspapers of the time make hardly any reference to the later campaign in that part of the world. Only when, seven months after the September day of Wolfe's victory, the British met with bloody defeat on the very ground where he had triumphed, did the nation realise that France still fought for the mastery of Canada. Walpole wrote in June 1760:

> Who the deuce was thinking of Quebec? America was like a book one has read and done with ... but here we are on a sudden reading our book backwards.

He mourns over the 'rueful slaughter' of brave men and concludes sadly that 'the year 1760 is not the year 1759'. During the year 1760, however, British arms were to achieve the final conquests in both India and Canada which the victories of 1759 had left still uncertain. In Canada, with which alone we are here concerned, the struggle carried on between September 1759 and September 1760 lays bare the condition to which France's great colony had been brought. We find in a survey of those last days of New France much that helps to explain the later history of the French race in Canada. We therefore take up the story from the moment on September 13, 1759, when Wolfe's musketry had shattered the French lines on the Plains of Abraham and when the fate of Quebec was still doubtful.

The game of war has never been played in surroundings more striking than those at Quebec. The mighty current of the St. Lawrence, contracted here to a breadth of about a thousand yards, washes the base of the high cliffs on which the stronghold stands and then broadens into a great basin four or five miles wide. On the east side of the basin the beautiful island of Orleans divides the river into two channels, a narrow and intricate one at the north, a broad one at the south. The deep blue of the silent, forest-clad mountains, the clear air, the rushing tide of the spacious river, are all elements in a scene of entrancing beauty. Quebec stands at the east end of a plateau seven or eight miles long and in places two or three miles wide. Though the fortifications were insignificant. Nature had made the place almost impregnable. At the north the River St. Charles flows into the St. Lawrence near the base of the high ground and constitutes a natural and difficult ditch for the assailant to cross. On the east and the south side, the plateau falls in steep cliffs to the strand of the St. Lawrence. On the west side the drop to the valley of the Cap Rouge River is not less sheer.

Wolfe's problem had been to reach Quebec on this plateau, and he had been almost baffled. Soon after his arrival he had taken possession of the Lévis shore and, across the mile of river, had battered many houses in Quebec to fragments with his cannon. Still the cliffs remained impregnable. To attack Quebec from the front promised destruction. On the French left flank, along the seven miles of the Beauport shore, lay entrenched the army of Montcalm, and here successful attack was impossible, as one attempt, repulsed with heavy loss, had made clear. At the other side of Quebec attack seemed equally hopeless. The high cliffs at Cap Rouge could be easily defended, and Colonel de Bougainville, one of the best officers in the French army, had been sent there with some two thousand men to watch every movement of the British and to concentrate his force rapidly at any threatened point.

In the end Wolfe had achieved what seemed impossible. By a secret movement at night he had landed an army at the base of the cliffs, had climbed the steep path at the Anse au Foulon, had overpowered the guard which had been left criminally weak, and at eight o'clock on September 13 had drawn up his thin red line on the Plains of Abraham a mile from the walls of Quebec, C Here Montcalm had attacked him promptly on the same morning and the battle had been fought which meant, in the long run, the ruin of French power in America.

This momentous battle of September 13 was especially fatal to the leaders on both sides. Not only was Wolfe killed; Monckton, his next in command, was shot through the body and disabled. On the French side, to the loss of the commander-in-chief, Montcalm, was added that of the realised on his death-bed that in his defeat was involved the loss of Quebec. One of the last acts of the dying leader was to write to Brigadier Townshend, for the time the British commander, to acknowledge that the surrender of the fortress must follow. Montcalm wrote:

> Obliged to cede Quebec to your arms, I have the honour to entreat your Excellency's kind offices for our sick and wounded.

Before the next day broke he was dead.

The Governor of Canada, the Marquis de Vaudreuil, in whom resided final military and civil authority, was with Montcalm before Quebec. Though vain and boastful, he was yet well-meaning and devoted to the interests of Canada, his native' country. To be a Canadian was in his view to be a member of a superior race; a single Canadian, he once wrote to the Home Government, was a match for from three to ten Englishmen. Vaudreuil did not lack a certain bombastic courage, but he inspired no confidence and was not the man to lead in a crisis. Montcalm's impulsive, but probably necessary, march to meet Wolfe on the Plains of Abraham had come so early on September 13 that the brief battle, little more than a skirmish, but big with great issues, had been lost and won before eleven o'clock in the morning.

Vaudreuil had followed the rapid march of Montcalm from the camp at Beauport. Before he could reach the field, so fatal to France, crowds of fugitives from the broken army revealed the ill fortune of the day. At first Vaudreuil would not believe that all was lost, and he talked wildly of rallying his Canadians and of marching up the steep Côe Ste Geneviève to dispute with the victors their possession of the Plains of Abraham. Some of the Canadians whom he sent forward apparently did useful work in checking the British pursuit of the beaten army. But, for the time, nothing more could be done. Cadet, one of the corrupt ring who were making vast fortunes by robbing New France, besought the governor not to risk a second battle.

Convinced at length of the folly of this plan, Vaudreuil took up his

PLAN OF QUEBEC
R. St. Charles
General Hospital
Lakes
Palace Gate
Hotel Dieu
St. John's Bastion
Jesuits Coll
The Seminary
Cathedral
Bishop's Palace
St. John's Gate
St. Ursula's Bastion
From Ste Foy
Ursulines
St. Louis Gate
Castle of St. Louis
UPPER TOWN
LOWER TOWN
From Sillery & Three Rivers
St. Louis Bastion
HEIGHTS OF ABRAHAM
Diamond Bastion
Diamond
R. St. Lawrence
Roads

ENVIRONS OF QUEBEC
Scale 0 5 10 Miles
St. Charles R.
Beauport
I. of Orleans
Charlesbourg
Old Lorette
Quebec
Pt. Levi
St. Joseph
Levis
Sillery
Cap Rouge R.
St. Foys
Cap Rouge
St. Augustin
Pt. aux Trembles
Jacques Cartier R.
Jacques Cartier Pt.
Lawrence
R. St.
Chaudière R.
Etchemin R.
Roads

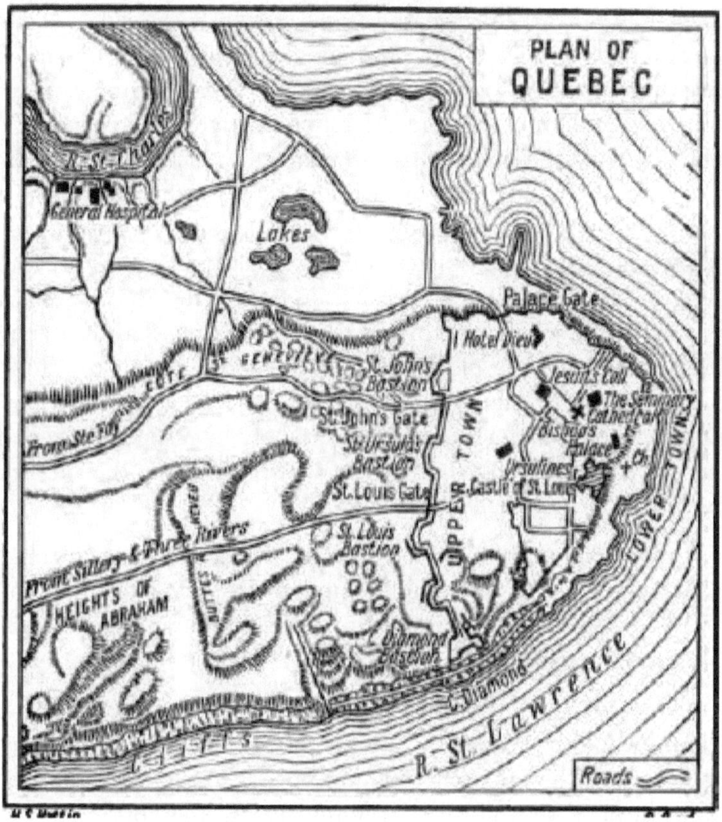

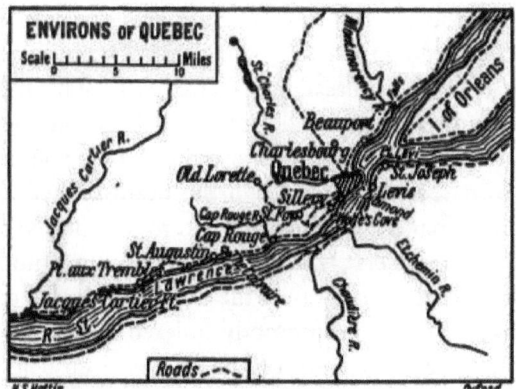

position in an extensive redoubt on the left bank of the St. Charles River. It was reached from the Quebec side by a bridge of boats which could be easily destroyed should the British advance so far. The route from Quebec was protected in some degree by the cannon of the town. A boom of logs had been stretched across the mouth of the St. Charles and the hulks of two dismantled French frigates lay there in shallow water. They were armed with cannon which swept the approaches by water to the bridge. To this bridge now came crowding the disorganised French soldiers, unable to take refuge in Quebec, because the gates were closed, and anxious to have the St. Charles River between them and the victorious foe. The fragments as they arrived Vaudreuil sent to their old positions at Beauport.

The Chevalier Johnstone, a Scots Jacobite serving with the French and a close friend of Montcalm, tells us how he made his way at this time to the redoubt. He found there at two o'clock in the afternoon, four hours after the defeat of Montcalm:

> An incredible confusion and disorder; a general panic and consternation; M. de Vaudreuil listening to everyone, and always to the advice of him who spoke to him last; not an order given with reflection or coolness.

Two captains of the regiment of Béarn were shouting out that the redoubt would be carried in an instant, that they should all be put to the sword, and that the only thing to do was to surrender the whole colony at once. Others were protesting against this course. An alarm was raised that the ships of the British fleet were edging in towards the shore. During the panic someone gave instructions to cut away the bridge of boats. At the time a considerable part of the French army was still crowding the road leading from Quebec and the Royal Roussillon regiment was already on that side of the bridge waiting to cross. Johnstone says that he and a colonial officer stopped the fatuous work of destroying the bridge and drove away the soldiers who had their axes raised to hew through the beams. When a council of war met in a house near the redoubt, Johnstone ventured to enter the room where seven officers sat with Vaudreuil, the governor, and Bigot, the *intendant*. The *intendant* was at the table, pen in hand. Johnstone heard nothing, for Vaudreuil promptly ordered him to be gone as he had no business there. He went off, he says, in deep dejection at the loss of Montcalm, and very tired, but not too tired to stir up some officers whom he met to protest against surrender.

Various courses were open to the French. They might stay where they were, rally their strength, and attack the foe before he could entrench himself or force Quebec to surrender. A second possibility was to retire beyond the Jacques Cartier River, thirty miles above Quebec, where the army would be in touch with the French ships which had ascended the St. Lawrence to escape from the British fleet. Here they might await the arrival of Montcalm's successor, the Chevalier de Lévis, absent at Montreal. Last of all, the French might accept counsels of despair and end the struggle by surrendering the colony. Before the Council met, Vaudreuil had sent a hurried request to Montcalm for advice and had received a message naming these three alternatives. Undoubtedly some of the French officers of the regular army favoured the surrender of the entire colony and talked openly before their men in this sense.

Vaudreuil declares that the Chevalier de Montreuil, who had had a long experience in Canada and was the senior officer present, insisted upon retreat to Jacques Cartier. This may well be: Montreuil was an officer who lacked insight and capacity. It seems that only the civilians present were for immediate fighting. The Intendant Bigot warned the officers that, with winter coming on, it was folly to think of a retreat that involved the abandonment of the tents and other needed supplies at Beauport, things which could not be replaced. He declares that he and Vaudreuil stood out for attacking the British forthwith, but that the officers were unanimous against this course.

In truth the soldiers had no confidence in Vaudreuil as a leader. During the absence of Lévis the young Colonel de Bougainville ranked next to Vaudreuil, but he was posted at Cap Rouge and no commander was present who could speak with authority. It is true that Bougainville was only a few miles away and that his opinion might have been secured without much delay. Some of the officers present were, however, jealous of this brilliant young friend of Montcalm. Most of them, while unwilling to fight, were also unwilling to surrender. Their great fear was lest the British should cut off the possibility of retreat up the river towards Montreal. To prevent this, it was quickly decided that immediately after nightfall the French army should withdraw to Jacques Cartier.

After the council Vaudreuil was full of bustling activity. He must have kept his secretaries busy. At half-past four in the afternoon he sent a dispatch to Lévis at Montreal urging him to join the defeated army at once. To M. de Ramezay, in command at Quebec, he sent elaborate instructions to surrender the town rather than to await its capture by assault, and enclosed a draft of the terms to ask. At six o'clock, with, as he said, grief in his heart at the decision to retreat, he sent to the stricken Montcalm in Quebec a report of what he had done, courteous regrets at Montcalm's misfortune, and hopes for his recovery. Thus, even in a moment of supreme excitement, Vaudreuil forgot none of the proprieties. But he hated Montcalm; he was glad now to be rid of him; and soon, to draw blame away from himself, he wrote a letter to the French Minister of War full of charges blackening the memory of the dead leader:

> If I had been sole master, Quebec would still have been in the king's hands.

About ten o'clock on the night of the battle, when Vaudreuil had already fled, Montcalm sent a message approving of what he had done and of the terms proposed for the surrender of Quebec. Both leaders thus agreed that the fortress must yield.

Vaudreuil and his officers now lost their heads in their deadly fear lest the British should occupy the lines of retreat towards Montreal and divide the French forces in Canada into two parts. The situation of the French was by no means hopeless. Between the Beauport camp and the victorious British lay a considerable river, fordable only at one place and at low tide; a little west of the Plains of Abraham, at Cap Rouge, was Bougainville with between two and three thousand men in an excellent position to attack the enemy in the rear; in Quebec itself were as many more men capable of bearing arms and of aiding the troops from Beauport to attack the British front. The French could, indeed, rally something like 10,000 men. But confidence in Vaudreuil as a soldier was impossible; no commanding personality was there to weld together the scattered fragments of this discouraged host; and, lacking direction, it fled.

Soon after nightfall the retreat from Beauport began. Orders were given that the army should break into three divisions and that each division should retire as silently as possible so that the British might not become aware of the retreat. There was grave mismanagement somewhere. Poulariez, the officer commanding the eastern wing of the army at Montmorency, was left without instructions. After long waiting, he sent to Vaudreuil's headquarters, only to find that the Governor had run away and that he himself was left to follow as best he could. The French marched by way of Charlesbourg and Old Lorette.

It unfortunately happened that brandy was served out to the soldiers, and this helped to destroy any semblance of order in the retreat. The Chevalier Johnstone says:

> This was not a retreat, but a flight the most abominable; a rout even a thousand times worse than that of the morning on the Heights of Abraham, and with so much confusion and disorder that, if the English had known it, it would not have required more than three hundred men to cut in pieces our whole army. Except the Royal Regiment of Roussillon, which M. Poulariez kept ... in order, I did not see thirty men of any one regiment together; all the troops mixed and interspersed and everyone running as fast as his legs could carry him as if the enemy were pursuing them close at their heels.

Daine, another French observer, says, (to the Minister of War, October 9, 1759):

> No rout was ever more complete than that of our army. Posterity will hardly believe it.

Not only the Canadian militia but even some of the regulars were so panic-stricken that, after calling for refreshments at the houses of the farmers, they rushed off, too fearful of pursuit to partake of what was brought. French Canadian peasants told the British at a later time that in the retreat Vaudreuil and the officers took no thought for their men, but went off in such haste that they 'flew through the air like a cannon ball'. Though a great part of the army was without food, Vaudreuil took good care that needed supplies and excellent cooks should accompany him on the retreat. Apart from a little ammunition and some tents and camp kettles, the French abandoned their cannon, munitions of war, provisions, and baggage. Since there were few, if any, wagons, not even a barrel of powder could be taken. Officers and men alike lost their personal effects.

At daybreak on the morning of the 14th, Bougainville, now at Lorette, was first made aware of the retreat of the French. By that time the whole host had swept past, panic-stricken and convinced that it would be safe only beyond the river at Jacques Cartier. That evening, after a long and weary march, the fugitives reached Pointe aux Trembles and there rested. By daybreak of the 15th they were again in motion. When they reached the Jacques Cartier River they found the bridge broken down. The army was intent on putting the river between itself and pursuit. It managed somehow to cross and that night the weary men were lodged in the barns on the right bank. They were now thirty miles from Quebec and, for the time at least, safe.

Meanwhile, neither in Quebec nor in the British Army had the retreat become known. Before leaving, the French had broken down the bridge across the St. Charles so that the British might not cross easily to the Beauport side. The tents at Beauport remained standing and the British thought that they were still occupied. The British were themselves busy in making sure of their own defences before Quebec. Two days after the battle a French officer visited the abandoned camp, found it undisturbed, and, to the alarm of the British, fired off some cannon that stood ready charged. Ramezay, shut up in Quebec, sadly needed the provisions left at Beauport and could easily have secured them; but he was not notified of the French retreat, and in the end the provisions were carried off by the starving *habitants* and by the Indians.

The French hopes now rested in the successor of Montcalm, the Chevalier de Lévis. This leader of a lost cause was a member of a French family so ancient that it claimed descent from the tribe of Levi and cousinship with the Virgin Mary. There was a picture in the Château of Lévis in which a member of the family was represented as addressing the Virgin as his cousin. The *chevalier* was himself destined to win new lustre for the family by the high position to which in later years he attained as Duke and Marshal of France. Montcalm had said of him that, while a man of routine and not very able, he was practical, sensible, and alert, with an admirable capacity to think for himself when thrown on his own resources. During many days while the French had steadily baffled. Wolfe's plans, Montcalm and Lévis had been constantly together, except when the tireless energy of Lévis had worn out Montcalm.

Later, with great regret, Montcalm had been obliged to part with Lévis and to send him to secure the approaches to Montreal from the south and the west. Thus Lévis had not fought in the memorable battle of September 13. But the evil tidings reached him quickly. At six o'clock on the morning of the 15th a courier arrived at Montreal with the news of the defeat. At nine o'clock Lévis was on his way to Quebec. He received on the road a letter from the Chevalier de Montreuil, an old companion in arms, begging him to use all diligence and saying that he alone could save the situation. In spite of a storm and of bad roads he made rapid progress. When he arrived at Jacques Cartier on September 17 there was joy in the French camp.

It was, however, with bitter rage that Lévis saw on all sides the evidence of incompetence. Panic had spread everywhere. Officers and men were alike disorganised. Lévis wrote:

> I never saw anything like it, absolutely everything—tents, kettles, and all their equipment, they had left behind at Beauport.

Many Canadians had deserted and, in disgust, the Indian allies of the French had already set out on the return journey to their villages. The task of Lévis was assuredly a grave one. He strongly condemned the retreat to Jacques Cartier. But Quebec still held out, and, at all hazards, he said, its loss must be prevented; rather than surrender the fortress to the English, the defenders should destroy it and thus leave the enemy no stronghold in which to pass the winter. The first task of the defeated army was thus to rescue Quebec, and Lévis gave orders at once that the march back should begin. Vaudreuil had always been on friendly terms with Lévis and now he was all acquiescence. He wrote on October 5 to the French Minister of War:

> As soon as the Chevalier de Lévis arrived, I conferred with him and was charmed to see him disposed to lead the army back towards Quebec.

Bougainville still kept a guard at Cap Rouge and Old Lorette; he had not joined the flight of Vaudreuil and now stood between him and pursuit. Lévis and Vaudreuil quickly sent messages to Quebec cancelling the instructions to surrender. Bigot, all energy in carrying out a plan of which he thoroughly approved, undertook to get supplies of food into Quebec. One plan was to send them down by way of the river. He had done this often before, in spite of the presence of the British fleet, and he could do it again. Moreover, a route by land was still open. The French had a depot of provisions at Charlesbourg, and, since the British had not yet occupied the camp at Beauport, the path to Quebec was clear. As a matter of fact, provisions reached Quebec on the evening of the 17th by both these routes.

All this time, however, the British were showing great vigour. Townshend, now in command, had made it his first duty to strengthen his own camp, and by five o'clock on the day of the battle he had entrenchments five feet high on the Plains of Abraham. Late that night he occupied the General Hospital on the banks of the St. Charles River, crowded now with from twelve hundred to fifteen hundred of the wounded of both sides. On the 14th both sides agreed to a short truce for the burial of the dead. The season was late; the fleet must soon depart or be caught in the ice; and the British well understood that not a moment was to be lost in taking Quebec. Admiral Holmes says:

> The utmost diligence was used and the greatest fatigue undergone, with spirit and cheerfulness by everybody, to bring the campaign soon to an end.

Two thousand men were already busy making fascines and gabions to protect an approach to the walls. By the evening of the 13th, many of the trees on the Plains of Abraham likely to protect an assailant had been cut down, and the houses near the British camp had all been fortified. On that night the British slept within a thousand yards of the walls of Quebec. In a few days most of the underwood within a mile of their flank and rear had been cleared away. For a day or two they were aided by fine weather. They used the steep road from the strand of the river up to the heights at the Anse au Foulon, henceforth to be called Wolfe's Cove, for drawing artillery and ammunition to the Plains of Abraham. This toilsome task was carried on with much energy. Sailors as well as soldiers showed great alacrity; in this work on land the word of command was given as on board ship: An eyewitness who saw the men toiling up the hill says:

> It was really diverting to hear the midshipmen cry out "Starboard, starboard, my brave boys".—Doughty, iv.; vi.

Tragedy meanwhile hovered over Quebec. Montcalm died early on the morning of the 14th, content, as he said, to leave the military command in the hands of Lévis, whose talents and capacity he had always valued. Vaudreuil had agreed that Quebec must surrender; so also had Montcalm; and its defenders could claim the warrant of both leaders for such an act. Naturally they now had deep searching of heart. For a day or two Ramezay kept up the appearance of a resolution to hold the place. His shot and shell greatly annoyed the British on the Plains of Abraham and forced them on the 15th to change their line of encampment; even after this, British batteries on the south side of the river, more than a mile away, were disturbed by Ramezay's ceaseless fire, as were also the boats carrying munitions of war from the Point of Levy to Wolfe's Cove.

There was, however, no heart in the defence of Quebec. Disorder and riot soon broke out. Those within the town had not realised at first that now they were left to their own devices. Across the basin they could see the white tents of the French at Beauport, and since, as they supposed, the French army was still there, rescue seemed not impossible. Disillusion came with the news of the headlong flight to Jacques Cartier and not unnaturally, it produced a panic.

The Chevalier de Ramezay, who commanded at Quebec, was a Canadian by birth and had spent his whole life in the service of the colony. He was the fifteenth child of Claude de Ramezay, who had been Governor of Montreal. Three of his brothers had perished in the service of the French king. As early as in 1720 Ramezay had attained the rank of ensign. Later he had seen almost every variety of service in the country. Since he was only a colonial officer he was rather despised by the officers from France. One of these, Joannès, town-major of Quebec, declares, for instance, that, as Ramezay had only known rough backwoods fighting, he had no conception of the proper way to defend a fortress.

The Governor, Vaudreuil, a fellow Canadian, did not like Ramezay and had mortified him by putting another officer, the Chevalier de Bernetz, in command of the Lower Town. The courage of Ramezay is not, however, to be doubted. Now, face to face with a difficult problem, he required both courage and wisdom. Even though Montcalm and Vaudreuil had admitted that the fortress must surrender and had outlined the terms to be demanded, it was for Ramezay himself to decide when the moment to yield should come. As Montcalm lay dying Ramezay went to him for orders. The stricken leader was, however, resolved to leave such decisions to those who should survive to see the future. His time was short, he said, and he had business to attend to of more moment than the affairs of a ruined colony.

As, a few months later, the British themselves found, to defend Quebec against assault would not be easy. The French Government had always shrunk from the great cost of proper fortifications, and the strength of Quebec was due less to what man had done than to natural position. It had been hitherto immune from assault only because of the difficulty of scaling the steep heights rising from the river, but now these heights had been gained by a triumphant foe. Montcalm himself had called ridiculous the defences on the landward side before which the British were entrenched. The wall, not yet really finished, which confronted the British encamped on the Plains of Abraham, was commanded by high ground only a few hundred yards away. It was better fitted for defence against muskets and bows and arrows than against artillery. For fear of shaking the rest of the fortifications, the French engineers had not used the necessary explosives to make excavations in the rock. There was thus no ditch. There were no outworks. The walls, if bombarded by the powerful batteries which the British were erecting, could probably not resist a cannonade for two hours. To meet attack from this side the defenders had not a single battery capable of action.

The town itself was a ruin. The Lower Town, curving for a mile or two along the strand of the river and inhabited by the traders and poorer classes, was a dismal sight. No less than five hundred and thirty-five houses had been burned, hardly a dozen remained standing, and some of the narrow streets were impassable owing to the debris caused by the British bombardment. The part of the city known as the Upper Town, where dwelt the governor, the bishop and other ecclesiastics, and the leading citizens, had fared somewhat better. Its principal buildings were, however, in ruins. The governor's residence—the Castle of St. Louis—the Bishop's palace, the Cathedral, the Jesuits' College, had all been in range of cannon on the opposite shore, and, of the first three, at least, the British batteries had left little but the walls. In the Seminary, a college for the training of priests, standing near the Cathedral, only the kitchen was left, and here the Curé of Quebec was living as best he could. Wolfe's guns had dismounted some batteries in the Upper Town and these were now filled with debris. Even walls six feet thick had not withstood his furious bombardment.

After the defeat of the 13th of September Ramezay had asked that a French engineer should be sent into Quebec to help him make the best of its shattered defences; but the disorganised leaders had not heeded the request. During the siege no stores of provisions had been kept in Quebec, because of the danger from the British fire. Supplies had been brought daily from the camp at Beauport and from the surrounding country. No doubt there was food in private houses, but most of it was now kept concealed by the owners. With supplies for only a few days in sight, Quebec seemed on the verge of starvation. There were a good many mouths to feed. Among the civilians were two thousand seven hundred women and children and a host of clerks, workmen, and domestic servants. The French, too, must feed their many invalids at the General Hospital. In addition to these were the forces in the town, numbering perhaps two thousand six hundred. About eleven hundred and fifty were regular soldiers; the rest were untrained militia—peasants, mechanics, and merchants.

As early as on the morning of the 14th the citizens of Quebec held a meeting to consider their position. Headed by the mayor, they then entreated Ramezay to surrender. They had been prepared, they said, to face the loss of their homes and their property. During the prolonged bombardment they had not murmured. Now, however, the British had won a signal victory. Quebec, face to face with famine, could no longer be defended. Under the rules of war, if Ramezay should wait till it was taken by assault, not only men but helpless women and children would be put to the sword. Some there were who opposed these views and declared that the citizens of Quebec seemed more anxious to save their goods than their country. But the wish to surrender was not confined to unarmed citizens.

Many of the Canadian militia, an amateur soldiery, were fearful that, if found fighting, they would be treated with the rigour meted out, under the rules of war, to civilians in arms; or that, if treated as soldiers, they would, upon surrender, be transported to France. They now declared that they would no longer serve and that they looked upon themselves as civilians only. When the drums beat for muster they refused to take their places, much to the wrath of the officers of the regular service. They abandoned even the exposed posts of which they had charge. A French officer, enraged, proposed to fall upon them sword in hand; but menaces, promises, even the experiment of serving out brandy, failed to inspire them with courage. They deserted in bands. Flight by way of Beauport was still possible. Within a day or two some nine hundred had gone off, a few to the British, but most of them to find refuge with the inhabitants of the surrounding country. The spirit of the men in the regular force was nearly as bad and it was soon apparent that even the officers were almost unanimous in desiring surrender.

What was Ramezay to do? On the 15th of September he called a council of war. By this time Vaudreuil's flight to Jacques Cartier had become known to all. At the council of war Ramezay read the instructions in regard to surrender which he had received from Vaudreuil; he made also a statement as to the famine imminent in the town. Then he asked each officer, with these naked facts before him, to give in writing his independent view of what should be done. Fifteen officers were present and we have still the record, solemnly made, of each man's opinion. For continuing the fight one officer alone stood out. The captain of the town artillery, M. Jacquot de Fiedmont, who had elsewhere shown conspicuous courage, wrote his advice 'to put the garrison on still shorter rations and push the defence to the last extremity'.

All the others, however, advised an opposite course, and the council of war decided that the best thing to be hoped for was an honourable surrender, and that, should there be delay, even this might not be possible. The hapless commander, with whom rested the final word, may well have been perplexed as to his duty. Ill health did not make his burden lighter. On the 15th he asked permission from the British to send the women and children past their lines, but the request met with a stern refusal. (Townshend Papers, Doughty, v. 269. Knox ii. says the permission was granted and that the women were sent over the St. Charles into the country. Knox, however, is often inaccurate). His foe would not allow him to be relieved even of this difficulty.

Scarcity of provisions caused the most serious problem. Since the French tents were still standing at Beauport, Ramezay sent thither, hoping to find provisions; but, as we have seen, the inhabitants and the Indians had already made help from this quarter impossible. What portion of the abandoned supplies they could not carry off they had wasted, and Ramezay's messengers found strewn about in the wildest disorder flour and other stores that might have saved Quebec. Just at this time came one gleam of hope.

News arrived from the defeated French Army. A letter from Vaudreuil, which must have been written during his wild retreat, reached Ramezay with the tidings that he was sending into Quebec both provisions and troops.

The hapless commander in Quebec had to ask himself what chance there was that such a promise could be fulfilled. He said nothing about the letter but, in order to get more light, sent out two officers, Joannès, of the French regular service, and Magnan, of the Canadian militia, to learn for themselves what the prospect of succour by the panic-stricken French Army really was, and, if possible, to see Vaudreuil in person. By this time, however, the governor was far away. Joannès pledged himself to go out and return in a single night, that of the 15th. He went some nine or ten miles towards Jacques Cartier; and then sent forward an urgent letter to Vaudreuil to say that there was a bad state of feeling in Quebec and that, if no word was received from him by ten o'clock on the morning of the 17th, negotiations for surrender would be opened.

What Joannès saw and heard, perhaps from Bougainville at Lorette, led him to believe that rescue was by no means impossible, and he returned to Quebec convinced that the defenders should hold out.

In this he was supported by the brave Fiedmont. But Ramezay was of stuff less stern. Lévis had not yet arrived at Jacques Cartier and a distressing account of the lack of discipline and order in the French army had reached Ramezay. Help from such a force was, he thought, hardly to be expected. By this time, indeed, he had decided to give up the fight. Vaudreuil charges that Ramezay reached this decision without having informed himself of the conditions in Quebec, and declares that there were cattle and horses in the town which would have prevented famine.

It must be said that Ramezay had no good reason to believe that the demoralised French Army could now render effective help. It is, of course, easy to suggest what he might have done, but from one urgent fact he could not escape—about him were women and children now in panic fear and clamorous for food. Vaudreuil had instructed him not to hold out until the British should assault Quebec. Now, because the foe had worked with fiery energy, this assault was imminent. By the morning of the 17th the British had a hundred and eighteen guns mounted in their batteries and were almost ready to open fire upon the feeble walls. Just at this time, too, the line-of-battle ships shifted to a position nearer the town and prepared for a bombardment. A renewed panic followed in Quebec. Ramezay himself describes his situation:

> It was no longer possible for me to hold any post securely. The batteries had been abandoned and the weak points were no longer guarded. I had not officers enough to carry out my orders; I could no longer count upon the militia officers since the request to surrender which they had made. My situation soon became only too clear. On the 17th ... there was an alarm, and I learned that an English force was coming in small boats to land in the lower town. At the same time, we saw all the warships get under sail to come nearer the shore. A strong English column advanced by land towards the palace gate where the entrance was unguarded. I ordered a general alarm and every man to take his place.
>
> While I was in the square with several officers, an officer whom I had sent to carry out my orders returned to tell me that none of the militia would fight. At the same moment the militia officers came to me. They said that they were in no temper to sustain an assault; that they well knew I had orders to the con-

trary; and that they intended to replace their weapons in the armoury, so that, when the enemy entered Quebec, the militia should be found without arms and should not be put to the sword. Henceforth, they said, they should regard themselves, not as soldiers but as civilians. If the army had not abandoned them they would have continued to show the same devotion that they had shown throughout the siege; now, however, with no further resources left, they did not feel obliged to face a useless massacre; such a sacrifice would not delay by one hour the taking of the town.

All this time the enemy drew nearer and my situation was cruel. I took the opinion of several officers near me, and, in particular, that of my second in command, the Chevalier de Bernetz. By their advice I raised the flag, according to the orders I had received, and sent to the enemy's camp M. de Joannès, *aide-major*, with the terms of capitulation which M. de Vaudreuil had sent to me.

Not only the militia had fallen into a state of abject terror. 'To my great regret', says the French officer, Bernetz, 'I saw this same unhappy spirit working in the hearts of the regular soldiers. I shed tears of grief over it.' He mourns, indeed, that he had not been killed earlier in the campaign, instead of living to see this final humiliation. At three o'clock on the afternoon of the 17th, in pouring rain, Joannès, despite his vigorous protests against surrender, was sent to the British general to ask for terms. Townshend and Admiral Saunders took counsel together, made moderate demands, and gave Ramezay the four hours from seven to eleven o'clock of that night for consideration. Joannès had secured as long a time as possible, in order to increase the chance of rescue, and now he and Fiedmont, on their knees even, entreated Ramezay not to yield. They begged him, if he could do no more, to evacuate the Lower Town and concentrate his force in the Upper Town, where he would be almost safe from the fire of the British ships.

It was too late; Ramezay's spirit was gone. His forces were utterly discouraged. Wholesale desertion was taking place and starvation seemed imminent. The heavy rain added to the discouragement, for it would retard any rescuing movement. Ramezay reasoned, moreover, that even if the British were in Quebec, they would still be as vulnerable there as in their fortified post on the Plains of Abraham. In fact, when seven months later the French attacked Quebec, the British preferred to fight on the open plain.

A little before eleven o'clock at night, Joannès was sent out again to the British camp with a final acceptance of the terms offered, terms, it should be noted, better than those which Vaudreuil had told Ramezay to accept. Each side was to take a hostage from the other in pledge of good faith. While this arrangement was being carried out a singular thing happened. Ere the dejected Joannès had left Quebec to return to the British headquarters with the final surrender, help reached Quebec. A force of fifty mounted men, under Captain de la Rochebeaucour, sent by Bougainville, entered the town from the side towards Beauport, and brought with them some sacks of provisions and the news that other supplies were coming by water and that rescue was near.

When Ramezay had signed the capitulation he had not been aware of La Rochebeaucour's arrival. This brave officer now went to Ramezay and, like others, begged on his knees for delay. Whether, had Ramezay known sooner of this succour, he would have drawn back, and whether within the next few days France and England would again have grappled in deadly strife on the Plains of Abraham, who can say? The help had come too late. Ramezay had already signed the capitulation and would not draw back. La Rochebeaucour rode off, carrying with him some of the provisions that he had brought for the relief of Quebec and bitterly angry at the conduct of Ramezay.

There is no doubt that, had the surrender been delayed even another day, the British would have been in a dangerous situation. Lévis was marching back to Quebec with an army that trusted him as a leader, and the British had good reason to be nervous about their position. They were thus eager to enter the town. The weather, which had been delightful for a day or two after the battle, was now cold and wet. Rain had made the roads so bad that only with difficulty could the troops drag up further artillery to the Plains of Abraham. It was desirable that the British should occupy Quebec before it was further injured by bombardment, for they might have to find winter quarters there.

Accordingly, they were ready to grant easy terms. On one thing only were they unbending: the garrison in Quebec should not serve longer in Canada. When Ramezay asked leave to join the French Army under Lévis, Townshend's answer was that all but the militia must be embarked at once for France. The British agreed that the garrison, bearing arms, with drums beating and matches lighted, should march to the ships with the honours of war; they agreed further to respect private property, to leave the inhabitants of Quebec undisturbed in their houses, and to permit the free exercise of the Roman Catholic faith, until this question should be finally determined by a treaty of peace.

These arrangements were completed on the 18th. Then the grenadiers, commanded by Lieutenant-Colonel Murray, took possession of the gates of the Upper Town. At the same time a naval force, under Captain, afterwards Sir Hugh, Palliser, occupied the Lower Town. On the Grand Parade, with all the pomp of war, Townshend himself received the keys of the fortress from its former masters and the British flag was raised over Quebec. The French garrison which marched out made a brave showing and left only a ruined city to their foes. Since the day of the battle the numbers in the French ranks had declined; now rather less than two thousand men, of whom more than nine hundred were militia, surrendered. All but the militia were to be taken at once to France.

The fatal intelligence of the surrender of Quebec reached Bougainville when he was less than two miles away. Lévis heard it near Cap Rouge, less than ten miles from Quebec, when his army had already covered the greater part of the return march. He writes:

> The news which rendered useless all that I had done, affected me infinitely. It is unheard of that a place should surrender which had been neither attacked nor invested.

Bourlamaque, in command at Isle aux Noix, wrote that the blow was incomprehensible, terrible. The fall of the fortress meant, indeed, as time was to show, the loss to France of an empire.

The surrender of Quebec caused in the French Army the natural and stern resolve that before spring came they would recapture the fortress. To this everything else must give way. Lévis would have wished to close in at once on Quebec and to harass the victors without delay. For this task, however, his resources were slender. He had no artillery and but little ammunition. Even food he could get only with great difficulty. Wolfe's cruel policy of desolating the parishes was now justified; the country about Quebec could not support an attacking army. Lévis soon resolved that for the moment a siege was impossible. To be safe from attack, he decided to return to Jacques Cartier, whither the French had fled so precipitately on the night of the 13th. With the river of that name as his frontal defence against a further

British advance, he could make plans in some security.

Once more, therefore, in bad weather and over roads heavy with recent rains, the discouraged and defeated French Army dragged itself away from Quebec. By the 24th of September the second retreat was completed and many of the French soldiers, turning their swords into pruning-hooks, were helping the Canadian farmers to reap the scanty harvest. A high bluff on the right bank of the Jacques Cartier River, where it joins the St. Lawrence, furnished a site little inferior to that of Quebec for a fort. The French leaders were quickly busy with plans. By September 26 engineers had begun to lay out new works. In the end, the works proved so strong that, as a matter of fact, Jacques Cartier was the last point on the St. Lawrence where the French flag was lowered.

For the time, however, little more could be done. The foraging parties could secure little, and famine was imminent. When, on October 4, some Canadians brought in twenty cattle which they had secured in the neighbourhood of Quebec, the rejoicing was great over what proved, after all, but a mouthful for so considerable an army. Lévis sent to the French frigates still lying in the river some distance above Quebec to ask for food, but his boats returned empty. By October 15 the army at Jacques Cartier had in sight provisions for only nine days. With such scant resources it was impossible to keep a great force at that point. The French quickly found that they could not hold together their Indian allies, unless they could supply them with food. Since this was impossible, the Indians soon scattered to their own villages. For the moment at least Quebec was safe in the possession of its new owners.

With the fall of Quebec, the outlook for France in North America was indeed gloomy. She had made magnificent claims to hold the vast region stretching from the mouth of the St. Lawrence to the mouth of the Mississippi. From the early days of discovery, the sons of France, more imaginative than their English rivals, had been haunted by the mystery of the interior. While the English had rarely ventured far from the sea-coast, the French pioneers had pressed inland. Champlain had reached the Great Lakes; La Salle had linked the St. Lawrence with the Mississippi in his dream of a far-reaching French Empire; La Vérendrye had gone still farther afield and had penetrated to the foothills of the Rocky Mountains. Fur-traders had followed the explorers.

To this day, in regions far remote, regions which have passed to another race, French geographical names and some lingering remnants of French speech often furnish a reminder of the far-reaching energies of the explorers and traders of New France. To assert her claim and to protect the richest fur-trade in the world, France had built forts at the chief points of vantage. At the forks of the Ohio, commanding the commerce of that river, the *fleurs-de-lis* had waved over Fort Duquesne. At Niagara, commanding the passage from Lake Ontario to Lake Erie, stood another French stronghold. Fort Frontenac commanded the point where Lake Ontario narrows into the River St. Lawrence. These were the chief forts, but at many other places, even in the far west on the Red River and beyond it, the energy of France was represented by posts, where her traders gathered the harvest of furs from half a continent.

Now, however, this fabric which France had reared was tumbling down. One by one the British had mastered the vantage points. The summer of 1758 had been disastrous to the outposts of France. With the fall of Louisbourg in July she was stripped of power east of Quebec. At the end of August in that year the British had captured Fort Frontenac at the head of the St. Lawrence and cut off communications between Quebec and the West. A little later, in bleak November, they had struck a vigorous blow on the Ohio, captured Fort Duquesne, and were now rearing in its place Fort Pitt, named after the great minister. Niagara had still held out defiantly, but in the summer of 1759 it too had fallen. Thus, except at a few scattered points where surrender must come whenever the British should demand it, the whole power of France in the interior had fallen. After the disaster at Quebec, only the central region about Montreal remained to her.

This place was now the point of danger. Vaudreuil, though vain and bombastic, was not a coward, and he soon resolved to take up his head-quarters in Montreal. Accordingly, on September 28, he issued a pompous ordinance placing Lévis in command on the lower river, and then set out from Jacques Cartier, On the first of October he arrived in Montreal, in company with the Bishop of Quebec, and was soon planning with feverish energy to meet the expected attack on this last foothold of France in Canada.

It seemed possible that Montreal might be won by the British before winter set in. It was menaced from the west and from the south. At Oswego, near the point where the St. Lawrence River flows out of Lake Ontario, General Gage had gathered an army to descend the river to Montreal. His path was not clear, for the French had a fort called La Galette at La Presentation, some seventy miles down the

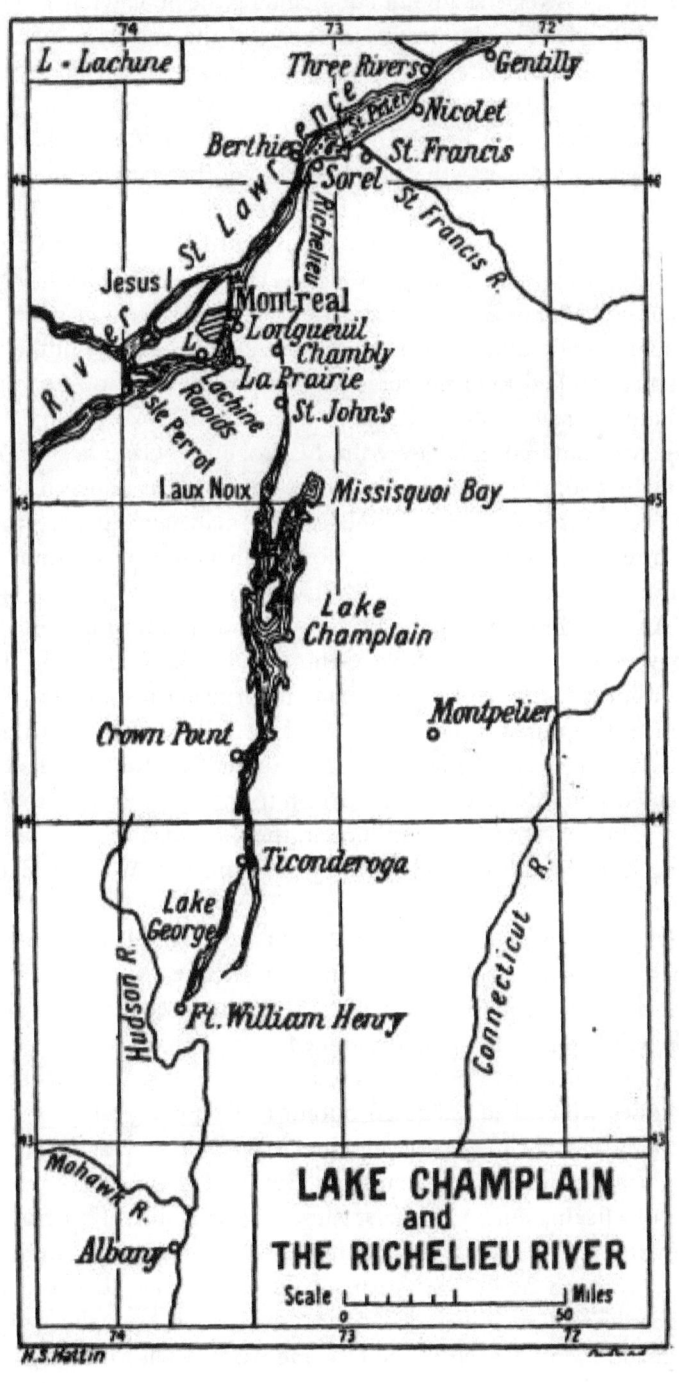

river from Oswego, at a point commanding the St. Lawrence and near the Mohawk Valley, leading to the heart of the colony of New York. The fort was a centre from which the Indians in alliance with the French had made numerous forays and caused much trouble.

Its defences were, however, weak and Gage could easily have overpowered it. It was not this problem but another which chiefly troubled him. If he descended to La Galette, could he winter his force there, in case it was impossible to advance to Montreal? If Gage had known what was happening at Quebec, he would probably have made a start for Montreal. Communications in this campaign were, however, extremely difficult. It is actually true that the news of the fall of Quebec reached England, three thousand miles away, on October 16 and did not reach General Amherst, who was on Lake Champlain, less than two hundred miles away, until October 18. Gage heard nothing of it for a long time, and in the end, 'to my great concern,' says his superior officer, Amherst, decided not to make any advance towards Montreal during that season. In slow deliberation he was more than a rival of his chief.

Amherst himself was approaching Montreal from the south along the war-worn route by Lake George and Lake Champlain. It had been hitherto a line of advance fatal to British arms. In 1757 Montcalm had captured a British army at Fort William Henry at the foot of Lake George. In the next year at Ticonderoga Montcalm had again inflicted a bloody defeat on the British trying to advance by this route into Canada. Now Amherst himself, the Commander-in-Chief, was using it for his advance. He had set out from Fort William Henry at the south end of the lake on July 21, 1759. The French did not try to check his progress up Lake George and Lake Champlain. Ticonderoga, where the British had been beaten with such heavy loss in the previous year, the French blew up at Amherst's advance; Crown Point, on Lake Champlain, they also abandoned.

All this had been done by August 1, and it was the news of these successes which had led to an outburst of rejoicing in England and to the humorous suggestion by Horace Walpole that Amherst should be given the title of Ticonderogicus. But, having done so much in the face of a fleeing enemy, Amherst paused to make sure of his ground. At Crown Point he found what he thought the best situation in America for a fort, and he decided to build there a massive structure which might defy the enemies of Britain for all time. Soon he had three thousand men engaged in the task. He worked with untiring energy and all that he did was good. But during these weeks after August 1 the crisis of Wolfe's attack on Quebec had come, and the appearance of Amherst on the St. Lawrence would have been of inestimable service to the despairing British leader. Help did not appear. What Wolfe achieved, he achieved alone; Amherst gave him no aid.

Without doubt Amherst was an efficient officer. General Yorke wrote, (*Life of Lord Chancellor Hardwicke*), of Amherst:

> There does not exist in this year, a worthier nor a more modest man than that nor a plainer or better soldier.....But, Wolfe has more fire.

And this difference really explains the slow policy of Amherst. He would run no risks. Even at the cost of much time, he must be secure in every step he took. To himself the reasons for not advancing at once from Crown Point were all-sufficient. His scouts reported that the French had three or four armed vessels on the lake. To take forward his army and its equipment by land was impossible because of bad roads and of the danger of ambush in the forest; and he could not take it by water in small boats unless he was able to drive off the armed ships of the French, He paused, accordingly, to build the necessary vessels and a floating battery.

The military task before him was formidable. Montcalm had sent one of his best officers, Bourlamaque, to guard this route. With Bourlamaque were now about thirty-five hundred men in a strong position. Lake Champlain discharges its waters into the Richelieu River. A few miles after leaving Lake Champlain this river is divided by an island which the French called Isle aux Noix. On this island they had built a strong fort. Its cannon swept the approaches by way of the river. To reach the St. Lawrence Amherst must pass this fort. If he attacked it from the water, the French cannon could demolish his small vessels. If he advanced to the attack with a land force, he would find the island fort protected on all sides by the river.

Amherst's problem had been made more difficult by lack of communication with the British before Quebec. Hardly any news trickled through the French lines. As early as August 7 Amherst had sent a letter to Wolfe by way of Nova Scotia and the Kennebec River. Since it would be long in arriving, he had made next day a more direct attempt. He sent Captain Kennedy, a kinsman of General Murray, with some companions to go through the forest to the St. Lawrence by way of the Indian settlements on the south shore. If Kennedy encountered

Indians he was to promise them a liberal reward for bringing him to General Wolfe. Kennedy encountered the Indians of St. Francis, but, instead of honouring his flag of truce and acting as friendly guides, they treated him and his party as spies, put them in irons, and carried them to the French. The first news that reached Amherst came on September 10 in the form of a letter from Montcalm saying that they were his prisoners.

The conduct of the St. Francis Indians to Captain Kennedy brought to a head the resolve of the British to punish these savages. There was not only this but an older score to settle with them. For well-nigh a century they had been a terror to the people of New England and had carried on murderous warfare against the helpless frontier settlements. Amherst now authorized a party of two hundred and twenty picked men, called in frontier warfare 'Rangers', under a well-known leader, Major Rogers, to go by forest pathways to the headquarters of the savages and inflict on them summary punishment.

The expedition set out on September 13, the very day of Wolfe's great victory. Amherst wrote:

> Take your revenge, but don't forget that though these villains have dastardly and promiscuously murdered the women and children of all ages, it is my orders that no women or children are killed or hurt.

We have Rogers's own account of what he did. In some way the intrepid ranger managed to get past the French armed vessels patrolling Lake Champlain, He hid his boats on the shores of its northern inlet, Mississquoi Bay, left two friendly Indians on watch, and then began a long and painful march through the forest. His goal, St. Francis, was distant a march of many days. When Rogers had been out two days, friendly Indians warned him that a strong party of the enemy had found his boats and was pursuing him. Bourlamaque, at Isle aux Noix, had in fact discerned the purpose of the expedition and had sent a warning to the priest at St. Francis—a warning apparently not heeded. Rogers pushed forward, hoping to outdistance his pursuers, who moved leisurely, since they thought they should catch him on his return journey.

On the tenth day of a toilsome progress through wet spruce bog, where the water was usually about a foot deep and where the men could be dry at night only by swinging themselves in hammocks made of the branches of trees, he reached the River St. Francis about fifteen miles above the village. Since the village lay on the opposite bank of the river, it was necessary to cross. At the ford the water was five feet deep and the current very swift. Rogers put the tallest of his men up stream and, by holding on to each other, they crossed over with the loss of only a few muskets. The force had now good dry ground on which to march and it crept towards the village. When three miles distant, Rogers halted his party and climbed a tree, to take his bearings. Then, in the early evening, he and Lieutenant Turner and Ensign Avery went farther forward to reconnoitre.

They found the Indians engaged in a dance. Rogers drew his force nearer to the village until, at three o'clock in the morning, he was distant but five hundred yards. By this time the noisy festivities were over and the quiet of night and of sleep had settled down upon the savages. At half an hour before sunrise the signal for attack was given. The savages had no time to take arms in defence and an appalling massacre followed. With the exception of three houses, where was stored corn which Rogers reserved for the use of his party, all the houses were soon on fire. Many Indians who had concealed themselves in the cellars and lofts of their houses were burned to death. Others who tried to get away in canoes were either shot or died by drowning. Among those who thus perished was the priest.

By seven o'clock in the morning the grim work was completed. Some two hundred Indians had been killed, including, it should seem, a good many women, in spite of the instructions of Amherst to the contrary. Rogers himself had lost but one man, an Indian from New England. The church, a fine one for the time, was burned and a rich collection of manuscripts relating to Indian life was destroyed. One ornament, a silver statue, was carried off by the victors to New England.

There is no doubt that the massacre was looked upon by the British as a righteous judgement. Rogers say:

> These savages were notoriously attached to the French and had for nearly a century past harassed the frontiers of New England, killing people of all ages and sexes in a most barbarous manner ... and to my own knowledge in six years' time, carried into captivity and killed on the before-mentioned frontiers, four hundred persons. We found in the town hanging on poles over their doors, &c., about six hundred scalps, mostly English.

Rogers set out for home by a circuitous route. He met with terrible hardships. Some of his men starved to death, others found on their route corpses of their own countrymen scalped and horribly mangled by the enemy, and were obliged to eat this ghastly food. Ten, it is said, were taken and carried back to St. Francis, where they were tortured to death by furious Indian women, whose lives they had probably spared. For some time, haggard and worn men continued to drift into the various French and English posts half dead with exhaustion. Rogers himself returned in the end to Crown Point and made his triumphant report to Amherst.

The savage exploit of Rogers was only side-play. It was still Amherst's intention to be master of Montreal before winter. He was now confronted by a discouraged enemy. The news of the death of Montcalm had reached Bourlamaque at Isle aux Noix on September 18. He managed to keep it from the English and for some days he tried to keep it even from his own men. But rumours of what had happened began to be whispered about. When, a little later, to the news of the death of Montcalm was added that of the fall of Quebec, there was general consternation. Bourlamaque tried to restore confidence by saying that the British, few in number and with winter coming on, were themselves in an untenable position and could take no further aggressive action. He says that the return of Vaudreuil to Montreal was a new discouragement to the French Army; we are left to conjecture whether it was the impending presence of the volatile governor or the fact that he was obliged to fall back from Quebec which caused this feeling.

Bourlamaque's health was bad; he was worn out by the fatigues of the campaign of the summer and had been ill for months with fever, asthma, and other ailments. Now he hardly undressed to go to bed, and an old wound kept him from sound sleep. During each night he made four or five rounds of inspection. The tone of his letters is naturally despondent. But he writes:

> We shall fight to our utmost, come what can.

The Canadians were now discontented and unwilling to serve. When enrolled, they deserted by hundreds; a force of five hundred men which Lévis sent to Bourlamaque numbered on its arrival only one hundred and twenty. The Indians were no better. They had little taste for the operations of regular war and went off to their homes regardless of the fate impending over New France. Bourlamaque says that even the offer of a keg of brandy would not tempt them to do scouting work for him.

The autumn proved stormy and the gales stirred up heavy seas on Lake Champlain. The season was at its worst when, at last, Amherst began his advance in force. On October 13, he embarked his army in whale-boats and, defended by a miniature navy consisting of a brig, a sloop, and a floating battery, well-armed, he advanced down Lake Champlain. The array of about seventy boats was striking enough to have attracted attention; yet, owing to what must have been glaring incompetence, M. de Laubara, the naval officer in command of the French ships on the lake, was not aware of the approach of the enemy until his own retreat by the river to Isle aux Noix was cut off.

In face of the overwhelming superiority of the English he fled down Mississquoi Bay and, when night came on, sank two of his vessels, stranded a third, landed his force, and took to the woods. The party was without food and, in the end, the men were reduced to eating their own shoes. The sailors proved helpless on shore and the refugees would probably have perished in the wilds had it not been for some Scottish prisoners whom they had with them. These men, at home in the forest, led the party safely to Montreal. The fourth vessel of Laubara's squadron ultimately reached Isle aux Noix, but the loss of the ships took from the French any possibility of action by way of the water.

Had Amherst now pressed in on Isle aux Noix it would probably have yielded. His foe was delighted at his inactivity. Bourlamaque wrote:

> In spite of my belief that he risks his head by doing nothing, I begin to think that he will make no movement during this campaign.

In fact, Amherst had delayed too long. Gales made the lake no longer navigable to his whale-boats loaded down with men. He was forced to land on the west shore, there to wait for better weather. Just at this time news reached him of the fall of Quebec. It might well have furnished an added inducement to press forward. But he did not see it in this way. Certain now that Canada must yield, in any case, he turned back to Crown Point, in order to spare his men the perils of a needless campaign. It was a thoughtfulness for which they were not grateful, for it robbed them of the glory of the final conquest of Canada. Bourlamaque wrote to Lévis concerning Amherst:

> I do not know how he will be able to save his head, assuredly

he is making a stupid campaign.

Yet he had done something. The French ships on the lake had been destroyed or captured and the English could no longer be kept from pressing in when they liked on the feeble defences at Isle aux Noix. Active campaigning was now suspended by the approach of winter. The best that each army expected to do was to hold its own during that season and to be ready for effective work in the early spring.

CHAPTER 2

Quebec During the Winter of 1759-60

At Quebec the British now prepared for a long and stern winter. They were full of joy and thanksgiving for their great success. Quartermaster-Sergeant Johnson wrote:

> Let us now sing unto the Lord a new song, for he has done marvellous things for us this day: his right hand, and his holy arm hath gotten us the victory.... Let us look through the annals of antiquity—let us search the records of former ages, and see whether we can find so great a conquest in so short a time, by so small a number of men.

On the 23rd the field of battle was the scene of a thanksgiving service. On the 27th the Ursuline Chapel, the only one left intact in Quebec, was used for a similar purpose. A naval chaplain, the Rev. Elie Dawson, preached a sermon which shows how the glory of Wolfe was already regarded.

> Ye mountains of Abraham, decorated with his trophies, tell how plainly ye opposed him when he mounted your lofty heights with the strength and swiftness of an eagle: Stand fixed upon your rocky base, and speak his Name and Glory to all future generations!

Again, a week later, when the town had been regularly occupied, the victors offered in the same chapel renewed thanksgivings. With fine impartiality some of the French inhabitants attended this service. The good nuns of the Ursuline Convent must have been shocked at the desecration by heretics of their house of prayer; but, during the winter, Protestant and Roman Catholic services continued to be held in the same structure. In England a special form of prayer and thanksgiving was issued for use in the churches with the petition that the 'haughty adversaries' might 'confess and amend the injurious behaviour of which they have been guilty'. 'The Lord God of Israel fought for Israel,' said a preacher, Mr. Townley, at St. Paul's. To him the enemies of England were assuredly the enemies of the Lord. (Pamphlets in the Canadian Archives).

Delighted as were the victors with their conquest, they still had doubts whether it would not be wise to destroy Quebec. To defend, without the aid of a fleet, a ruined fortress, in a hostile country, and in face of the rigours of a Canadian winter, was assuredly no light task. The generals and the admirals debated the matter in a council of war and reached the conclusion to defend to the last what Wolfe had so laboriously won. There was a great extent of wall to be protected and for such a task it would be necessary to leave at Quebec every available soldier. On September 24 the British muster roll showed an army of 8,504 men, all told, but of these only 5,707 were, at the moment, fit for duty. In the end only a few grenadiers, rangers, and artillery men were sent away, and Quebec was left with 7,313 defenders of all ranks to face the winter and the enemy.

******

The regiments left at Quebec were the 15th, 28th, 35th, 43rd, 47th, 48th, 58th, 60th, and 78th. In addition, there were the men of the Royal Artillery. The 60th Regiment contained two battalions of colonial troops (Royal Americans); there were besides 100 Colonial Rangers.

******

The town once occupied, not a moment was lost in getting ready for the winter. The British evacuated the posts at the Point of Levy and the Island of Orleans, which Wolfe had used as his bases. On the night of the 18th, not without difficulty, they put a force across the St. Charles and occupied the redoubt where a few days before the Chevalier Johnstone had found such confusion in the French counsels. It was taken with the exchange of only a few shots. The victors lost no time in sending home the French troops who had surrendered. They were embarked promptly in four ships and, a few days after the fall of Quebec, they set sail for France, no doubt much to their joy. To some of them, because of their sin of failure, the mother country gave a stern welcome. Ramezay, in particular, had to meet bitter attacks and to endure shame and poverty for the loss of Quebec, Vaudreuil, who had instructed him to surrender the fortress, sent home an official letter blaming him for carrying out these instructions.

Since there seemed to be no anchorage in the river where, during the winter, large ships would be safe from destruction by ice. Admiral Saunders made ready to sail away with his whole fleet. Before departing the transports unloaded vast quantities of stores. In the Lower Town the Intendant's Palace, a stately building which greatly impressed the victors, became the chief depot for supplies, while in the Upper Town the large Jesuits' College was used in part for a similar purpose. The Jesuits remaining in the place were few in number. At first the British took three-fourths of the building and a little later they took it all. The task of unloading the stores involved heavy labour. There were almost no horses in Quebec, and to reach the Upper Town the men had to drag the casks and bags up a very steep hill. In addition, since the cannon found at Quebec were worn out and almost useless, the victors had to disembark artillery and place it in proper position. Some of the streets were so nearly impassable from the debris of fallen houses that it was a heavy preliminary labour to clear them for traffic. General Murray writes:

> There was not a man but was constantly employed.

Until the preliminary work was done the army remained on the Plains of Abraham. On September 29, however, the troops marched into Quebec. The officers drew lots for quarters in the ruined houses and the accommodation was primitive enough. Captain Knox tells us that to him fell a shed used as a cart-house and stable; for ceiling he had only a few loose boards and above him was a hay-loft; but a little carpentry wrought wonders, and with a good stove he was able, as winter advanced, to fight the cold successfully. He thought, however, that he would have been more comfortable in a tent.

Captain John Montresor secured a roofless house and at first had not a single board for the needed repairs. But he could look after himself; he took what timber he needed from a house too far gone to be lived in, and a couple of carpenters soon gave him a roof over his head. If officers were lodged so ill the lot of the private soldier was hard indeed. His quarters were bad; so also was his bedding; and for food he soon had little but salted provisions. Moreover, since the government had failed to send out money with which to pay the army, the private soldier had no means to purchase small additions to his comfort. For him, as chill winter drew on, the outlook was grim and the result was to prove tragic.

QUEBEC IN 1760

Monckton, disabled by his wound, was ordered to a milder climate; Townshend went home; and the command at Quebec devolved on Brigadier-General Murray, with Colonel Burton as his second in command. In the early days of October, the preparations for the sailing of the fleet were completed. When, on the 10th, a portion of it was ready, the departing ships saluted the garrison with twenty-one guns, return courtesies boomed out from the batteries on the shore, and the squadron proceeded on its homeward way. The other ships soon followed. A part of the fleet was to remain at Halifax under Lord Colville for the winter. Two sloops of war, the *Racehorse* and the *Porcupine*, and three small armed vessels remained at Quebec, puny evidence of Britain's might upon the sea.

For the time the naval strength of France on the St. Lawrence was greater than that of Britain. The few French frigates, which had reached Canada in the spring early enough to avoid the British fleet, had gone up the river beyond Quebec. Saunders, to his great regret, had been unable to reach them and they remained a source of considerable anxiety to the British. It was no doubt with many misgivings that Murray saw the British ships disappear behind the Island of Orleans. Colville was to come back at the first possible moment in the spring, but for six months Murray would be cut off from succour by the sea. Between him and any chance of aid by land from England's American colonies lay many miles of well-nigh virgin forest, the water pathways of which would soon be held in the iron grasp of winter.

James Murray, the officer now left to defend Quebec, was the fifth and youngest son of a Scottish peer, the fourth Lord Elibank. The first bearer of the title had held to Charles I during the Civil War and the Scottish peerage of Elibank was his reward. A few years later this ancestor had been one of the Scottish peers who opposed the surrender of Charles by the Scots to the English Parliament. The loyalty of the Murrays to the Stuarts in the seventeenth century was continued in the eighteenth. Long after the defeat of the second Pretender the family was supposed to be tainted with Jacobitism, and Horace Walpole declared that if a Stuart could have displaced George III in England the then Lord Elibank would have won prompt recognition for services in a second Restoration.

Perhaps the knowledge of this suspicion helped to make James Murray especially zealous. The date of his birth is uncertain, but he was now about forty years old. His father had wished him to be an advocate, but he had run away from home and had enlisted in the Scots-

Dutch brigade in Holland. For the time his family lost sight of him. It happened, however, a few years later, that a friend of the family, who saw the changing of the guard at Bergen-op-Zoom, was astonished when he recognised in a smart-looking young non-commissioned officer the missing member of the house of Murray. He soon returned to England and entered the army, this time as an officer. When, long after, he reached the rank of general, he was able to say that he had served in every degree in the army but that of drummer. In spite of his own complaints to the contrary, he had made a fairly rapid advance. Wolfe, under whom he had served as a brigadier, was, however, his junior in years. Murray was keen—too keen as the event proved—to win by daring service fame like that which made Wolfe's name for ever glorious.

In Murray's family there was both wit and resolution. The resolution was mingled sometimes with the bravado that gained for them the nickname of 'The Windy Murrays '. James Murray's brother Patrick, Lord Elibank, transformed, by a fortunate marriage, from a poor into a rich Scottish peer, was among those who welcomed Dr. Johnson on his famous Scottish journey. To Johnson's insolent note in his dictionary that oats is 'a grain, which in England is generally given to horses, but in Scotland supports the people', Elibank made the well-known retort: 'And where will you find such men and such horses?' Elibank moved in the literary society of the time at Edinburgh; he was the patron of the historian Robertson and of the poet Home, and was regarded as a choice spirit by men like David Hume, Adam Smith, and Adam Fergusson. Johnson once said, 'I never was in Lord Elibank's company without learning something'.

At the 'Select Society' in Edinburgh he met in debate on equal terms the brilliant Charles Townshend, brother of Townshend, the general who commanded at Quebec after Wolfe's fall. Alexander Murray, another brother, took up the role of a political agitator and, having attacked the government in the spirit that, a little later, made John Wilkes famous, was ordered in 1751, by the House of Commons, to kneel at the bar to receive censure for inciting to riot in London. He answered defiantly, 'I beg to be excused; I never kneel but to God.' When the Speaker pressed him, he answered firmly, 'Sir, I am sorry I cannot comply with your request. I would do anything else.' For his inflexible pride in defying the House he was committed to Newgate, and, though his physician declared that the confinement imperilled his life, he refused to accept the partial release of going out in the custody of the sergeant-at-arms; his brother, who had petitioned for his freedom, he declared to be a mean and paltry puppy. Alexander Murray's tough nature survived the poisonous air of Newgate, and when, on the adjournment of the House, the Sheriffs of London released him, he was escorted by a great concourse of people through the streets under a banner inscribed, 'Murray and Liberty', The House pursued him still and he spent many years in exile. Amid the heated passions of the time such an obstreperous and defiant brother can have done no good to the military prospects of the commander at Quebec.

James Murray was, however, well able to take care of himself. In 1759 he was a tried soldier, who had seen service in Europe, in the West Indies, and, with distinction, in the previous year at Louisbourg. He was ardent, high-spirited, and fearless; he had a thorough knowledge of the art of war and the ability and good sense to use his knowledge well. He possessed a fine courtesy of manner. The French officers, his foes, thought him an agreeable companion; 'although he is our enemy, I am unable to speak too well of him,' wrote Malartic, a French officer, to his leader Lévis. Murray was always paying gracious compliments to the courage of his opponents.

For the hardships of his own troops he showed a manly sympathy, and the Canadians found the stern resolution of the soldier in harrying their villages tempered by the humane regret of the man who felt for their sufferings. His 'military talents, added to his intrepid courage and resolution, made him both feared and admired', wrote Johnson, one of his non-commissioned officers. Murray was impatient of opposition and quick-tempered, but quick also to regret the hasty action or words of a moment of anger. While an impulsive generosity was one of his most striking characteristics, the thirst to emulate the glory of Wolfe was one of his chief failings. There were no chances that he would not take to win fame. He possessed, says Lieutenant Malcolm Fraser, one of his officers, all the military virtues except prudence.

Murray tried to draw the French into making a truce for the winter, but against this they were firm. (Monckton wrote to Pitt on October 8, 1759, that the French wished a truce, but this must have been a mistake). To consent to such an agreement, with the British in possession of the strongest position in the country, would have enabled this enemy to draw support from the inhabitants, and would have been regarded by the world at large as only preliminary to final surrender. The defeated army hoped, not without reason, that isolation in a hostile country, the rigour of the coming winter, disease, and the absence of a fleet would so weaken the British as to make their destruction possible before reinforcements should come in the spring.

The French counted upon their Indian allies to help make life a burden to the British. Some French officers still had high hopes of success. Letters sent to Quebec on the chance that they might in some way be forwarded to France were intercepted by Murray, and one evening at dinner, much to the chagrin of a French officer who was present, he read aloud one of these epistles.

> Quebec has indeed fallen, but we have excellent means for re-taking it this winter—the cold, the Canadians, and the Indians.

It seemed probable that if the French campaign should resolve itself into a siege of Quebec the fortress would fall. It was in no condition to withstand a vigorous attack. Wolfe had, indeed, found to his cost that Quebec was strong on the side of the river. To try to scale the heights, in face of a defending force, was, as Major Mackellar, the chief of the engineer corps, had proved to Wolfe, to invite destruction, for the ascent of the cliff could easily be so guarded that probably not a single assailant would escape. None the less, Quebec was really weak; but the danger came from the landward side. Long after, when Murray had had the experience of three years in defending Quebec, he declared that it was badly placed, that the situation never could be strong, and that the attempt to make it so would cost an immense sum. (Murray's *Report, 1762*, printed in Authorities, No. 5.)

A high ridge on the adjacent Plains of Abraham swept the whole line of defence. A thin wall, built for protection against attack by Indians, stretched inward from Cape Diamond, the cliff overlooking the St. Lawrence, to the suburb of St. Roch. This wall, as we have seen, was too weak to withstand a vigorous cannonade. Already there were many breaches in the feeble defences. Montcalm had preferred to fight in front of rather than behind the walls. Murray now repaired the breaches, opened embrasures, and mounted some guns. His men were soon busy erecting a row of block-houses at the distance of a musket-shot outside the walls, both to keep an enemy from occupying the high ground which commanded them and to prevent surprise.

But Murray had no confidence in these defences except as against light field artillery and musketry. Major Mackellar indeed advised him to throw up entrenchments on the Plains of Abraham and to trust to them rather than to the walls until reinforcements should arrive in the spring. It was Murray's fixed resolve, if a French force should attack Quebec, to carry out this policy, and not to stay behind the walls. Nothing could indicate more clearly his conviction that Quebec was really weak.

When the British were once securely in Quebec the Canadians accepted the inevitable with cheerfulness. On September 21, in obedience to a military order, the farmers and other inhabitants within a radius of nine miles of the fortress flocked to the town to take an oath to be faithful to King George, and not to arm against him or to be a party to anything that might injure him. On the next day, September 22, Murray issued a manifesto telling the inhabitants that the British had come not to ruin them but to give them mild and just government. They should be secure, he promised, in their property and in the exercise of their religion. As far as possible he disarmed the inhabitants of the parishes. So docile were they that they seemed to him pleased with the change of rulers. Lévis wrote in his journal with a touch of bitterness:

> The inhabitants of the Government of Quebec appear to accommodate themselves to the English.

Murray reported on January 30, 1760, that six thousand Canadians had taken the oath of fidelity and brought in their arms. As there were only about sixty or seventy thousand Canadians of all ages and of both sexes in the country, these six thousand must have included nearly the whole adult male population in the district of Quebec. Murray employed some of them with their horses and sleighs to bring in wood; others he employed as artificers. All were paid for their work.

Though some of the Canadians near Quebec were in a half-starving condition, they still had fresh vegetables; the English, on the other hand, had an abundance of biscuit and of salt meat; and exchanges were effected with mutual advantage. The British soldiers were soon on friendly terms with the habitants, and shared their provisions and even their slender allowance of rum with their new friends. It was the season of the harvest, and Captain Knox writes that on one day he saw more than twenty soldiers assisting the French in the labours of the harvest-field near Quebec. The work was done with no thought of reward; when asked what pay was expected, one of the soldiers said! 'It would be rank murder to take anything from the poor devils, for they have lost enough already.' This pitying attitude softened the asperities of war. As a military measure the British had ruthlessly destroyed houses and villages in the territory which they held; and, not without reason, the Canadians had been taught to look upon them as barbarians. Now they found generous traits in the newcomers who were to remain the masters of Canada.

All the British soldiers, it is true, were not conspicuous for humanity and generosity. On the day of the surrender of Quebec reports of outrages on the Canadians reached Townshend. He promptly offered a reward of five guineas for the discovery of the offenders. A few days later, when some women at the Point of Levy complained of robbery and outrage by soldiers encamped there, the several detachments were paraded that the women might identify the offenders. They declared that it was not those wearing the ordinary military dress, but *les gens sans culottes* who were guilty. This pointed to the Highlanders, and the offenders were promptly detected and punished. The incident was unusual; during the operations in Canada the Highlanders had been remarkable for humanity and steadiness. Their strange appearance and dress, however, frightened the French, who nicknamed them *les sauvages d'Écosse*—the Scotch savages.

Murray soon found that to make an effective defence he must do more than hold Quebec. To ensure the health of his troops he required access to the supplies of fresh provisions in the neighbouring villages. Moreover, a large quantity of fire-wood would be necessary during the winter and, in consequence, the British must control some areas of forest. Above all, the Canadians and also the Indians must be kept as far from Quebec as possible, for they were dangerous neighbours. When the British first occupied the town the French sent in hostile scouting parties, which made the roads unsafe. Bands of savages, disguised sometimes as wild animals, came up almost to the walls, and committed numerous outrages. To ensure safety the British found it necessary to occupy all the approaches to Quebec.

Murray planned, indeed, to extend his outposts so as to keep the French Army beyond the River Jacques Cartier. He was forced, however, to adopt a course less ambitious, and to place his farthest outpost at Lorette, not on the plateau but in the valley, some eight miles to the west. There he fortified the church, and by holding this place he cut off the enemy from the most important road to Quebec, the one which led through Charlesbourg. The church at Ste Foy, on the plateau some five miles from Quebec, and commanding a more southerly road from the west, he also fortified. At both Lorette and Ste Foy he stationed fieldpieces, and he surrounded the positions with entrenchments and stout picket-work. He held himself ready also to place a force at Cap Rouge. These posts meant the control of the parishes in the immediate neighbourhood of Quebec, and he provided for the administration of justice in these parishes by appointing a Canadian magistrate.

It was desirable also to control the south side of the St. Lawrence. For some time, Murray was unable to throw a force across the river; on November 30, however, he sent one Captain Leslie, with a detachment of two hundred men to disarm the inhabitants. Not until three weeks later, on Christmas Day, did Captain Leslie return. Then he reported that every officer and soldier in his party had been frostbitten. Though he had achieved less than he had hoped, he had disarmed the inhabitants in a considerable area and had taken from them an oath of fidelity. Murray, in summing up his work in the last days of 1759, could say that the sway of George II was recognised everywhere eastward of Cap Rouge on the northern bank of the St. Lawrence and eastward of the River Chaudière on the southern bank.

The British complained bitterly that the French did not play the game of war as it was played in Europe. The savage allies of the French insisted on fighting in their own way. Should a soldier be missing it was as likely as not that his body would be found outside the walls, scalped and mutilated. The Indians, indeed, scalped not only the dead but the wounded. Similar outrages there had been in the course of the war on the British side. Malcolm Fraser, a Highland officer, describes his horror at the brutal savagery of the Colonial Rangers.

But these methods were firmly checked by the leaders when present. Generals like Amherst restrained sternly their Indian allies, always restlessly eager for massacre and scalps. Without doubt the French leaders, though they disliked the methods of the Indians, had shown, in this respect, less strength than the British. They had, it is true, urged moderation on the savages, and to save prisoners from torture they had sometimes paid ransoms to their Indian captors. They did not, however—perhaps they dared not with their weaker forces—punish, as Amherst punished, those who were guilty of outrage.

Now the outrages were nearly all on the French side, and the belief sank deeply into the hearts of the British forces that it was a regular French practice to permit Indians to scalp and murder the wounded left on the battle-field. It was stated and believed that even Montcalm, after entertaining a British officer at his table, had then permitted the savages to torture him. The Canadians, it was said, were now told to make no prisoners, but to bring in scalps as trophies of their prowess and to receive a handsome reward. Lévis was not chiefly blamed for this conduct. He was looked upon as an honourable soldier.

It was against Vaudreuil that the rage of the British turned. He told the Canadians that the British did not keep faith and that, in turn, no promises made to them were binding; thus, he said, the inhabitants might ignore the solemn oath of neutrality which they had given to the British victor. Bernier, the French commissary, sent to Quebec after the surrender, reported to Lévis:

> It is impossible to describe the impression which the English have of M. de Vaudreuil or of the council which controls him, prudence and modesty forbid my repeating what they say. They consider him as bloodthirsty, deceitful, a wanton liar, who wishes the ruin of the country.

Many horrors attributed to Vaudreuil were described in England—a country, says Bernier, 'where everything is printed' (*dans un pays où tout s'imprime*)—and made a great impression. Horace Walpole echoes the general sentiment:

> Had he fallen into our hands our men were determined to scalp him, he having been the chief and blackest author of the cruelties exercised on our countrymen.

Though happily this stern vengeance found no place, the time was to come when, on account of such practices, a deep humiliation should be exacted from the defeated French Army.

Since the French had a few frigates and other ships in the river above Quebec, the British were always on the watch lest these should pass down and get away to France. It was, indeed, vital to the French that they should escape, for only by them could Vaudreuil send home a statement of his needs and a request for prompt help in the early spring. On November 22 the French fleet dropped down the river and anchored above Quebec off Sillery. Voices of those on board reached the shore and the British were convinced from the continual chattering that the ships were crowded with families returning to France. The intention of the French was to pass Quebec that night when it was dark. The wind, however, failed them, and when the British opened fire the French ships retired out of range.

A day or two later they had better luck. On a very dark night and with a fresh and favourable wind they repeated the attempt to get away. The British gunners fired a vast quantity of shot and shell at the passing ships, silent and dim in the gloom. The fire was not entirely effective. Some of the ships sailed past and continued their voyage. It was found, however, when morning broke, that, owing less to the British fire than to bad seamanship, five of the ships had run aground. Four were set on fire by their crews; one lay stranded and abandoned on the south shore. A tragedy followed. Without Murray's knowledge Captain Miller of the sloop *Racehorse*, left at Quebec for the winter, went in a schooner to survey the wrecks.

Accompanied by a lieutenant and thirty or forty men he boarded the stranded ship lying near the mouth of the River Etchemin. The French, whether by accident or design, had left powder lying about loose. Unhappily someone lighted a fire and there was a terrible explosion. Most of the British were killed outright; those not killed were left so deplorably injured that no one of them could help the others.

The schooner in which they had crossed the river was soon boarded by crews which had escaped from the French ships and it was taken after a sharp fight. The victors hurried away; but, a little later, a Canadian ventured to board the stranded ship in search of plunder. To his horror he found many dead bodies; he also found Captain Miller, the lieutenant, and two seamen still alive but dreadfully burned and in great agony. He cared for them as best he could and in the end they were taken for treatment to the Ursuline Convent at Quebec. To the great grief of the garrison. Miller and the lieutenant died within a few days and Murray had to deplore the useless loss of brave men. The ship-carpenters taken prisoners in the schooner by the French could be ill-spared. Murray was building flat-bottomed boats for the river campaign of the coming summer and was sorely in need of men skilled to do this work.

When it was evident that Quebec must be prepared to stand a siege, Murray gave permission to the French inhabitants to withdraw if they wished to do so. The cost of living in a besieged city would be great, he pointed out, and he asked those to go away who had not adequate means. Many families, even the Bishop of Quebec himself, removed to Montreal. Some of the inhabitants went only as far as Three Rivers or to neighbouring villages, while still others departed to live in the woods in Indian style. Those, however, who wished to do so had the right under the capitulation to remain in their own houses, and this a good many of the obscurer sort did. The English found that these humble people did not hesitate to call down maledictions upon Vaudreuil for their misfortunes. The women were specially vehement;

their bitter invectives involved the wish 'that he may be brought to as miserable and barbarous an exit as ever a European suffered under savages.'

When Captain Knox heard these imprecations he slyly suggested that they should ask for an exit as barbarous 'as ever an Englishman suffered under savages by his orders'. The revilers of Vaudreuil assented to this, though in calmer moments they would deny that any of the French leaders had approved of such outrages. This was not true. At this very time Vaudreuil was inciting the savages to commit outrages on the Canadians who accepted British rule. At last, in November, Murray issued a proclamation denouncing the governor's conduct and in turn menacing the Canadians with all the rigours that the rules of war would allow, if they should prove unfaithful to their new oath of allegiance.

Over the French who remained in Quebec Murray established a 'stern but just' rule. They were guaranteed, for the time being, the full rights of their religion. During the winter, multitudes thronged to the Ursuline Chapel, and Captain Knox describes how he was 'agreeably entertained' at this chapel by high mass celebrated with great pomp of vestments. But his Protestant soul was vexed by another ceremony and one that it is not now easy to identify. He writes in December:

> I cannot omit taking notice of an incident that happened here yesterday. Passing in the evening through one of the streets, before it was dark, I met a crowd of French people, of both sexes, with staves and lanthorns, and seemingly in great haste; upon inquiry I found that it was one of the Popish ceremonies. These deluded creatures were going in quest of Barrabbas, the robber, who was released at the crucifixion of the Saviour of the world; and, having, after a long search, discovered a man who was to personate him, being concealed for that purpose, they bound him like a thief, and whipped him before them, with shouts and menaces, until they arrived at one of their churches, where it was pretended he was to suffer as Christ did, in commemoration of His passion.

In spite of Protestant critics like Knox, Murray ordered that 'the compliment of the hat' should be paid by the officers to religious processions as they passed through the streets; any one whose conscience would be compromised by such recognition was asked to go out of his way to avoid meeting processions. Some of the corner houses in Quebec had niches in the walls, with statues, as large as life, of St. Joseph, Ste Ursule, and other saints. From the first days of the occupation any injury to such property was strictly forbidden and plundering was to meet with the penalty of death. Though religious gatherings were permitted, all other meetings were forbidden. Lights in the houses must be put out at ten. The inhabitants must give up their arms. They must report promptly to the authorities any persons newly arrived whom they sheltered. If they went out after dark they must carry lanterns to show that their errand was legitimate and that they were not trying to conceal it. British soldiers might not intermarry with the French or work for them. On penalty of death the Canadians might not, unknown to Murray, enter into correspondence with people of the adjoining country. It is necessary to add that, in spite of such precautions, the French leaders at Montreal were kept well informed as to what was happening at Quebec.

Murray enforced his regulations with considerable rigour. For being out after dark without a lantern two citizens of Quebec were flogged. When a former inhabitant of the city arrived from Montreal and did not at once report his coming to the governor, both he and the friend in whose house he was concealed were thrown into prison. A prominent citizen, accused of corresponding with the enemy, was arrested, confronted with two intercepted letters directed to him, and threatened that if he did not confess he should receive a hundred lashes and be drummed out of the town with a halter round his neck. The man protested his innocence so earnestly that punishment was postponed.

Then it was found that he was the victim of a malicious trick. It had become known that he had taken the oath of fidelity to the sovereign of Great Britain and, in resentment at this desertion of the French cause, a former business partner had sent the letters from Montreal, knowing that they would fall into the hands of the British. In November a similar outburst of resentment overtook a Canadian who was bringing provisions from the Point of Levy to Quebec. Some French light horse seized and plundered him, beat him inhumanly, wounded him with their sabres, and then sent him over to Quebec with the message:

> Now go and tell your fine English Governor how we have treated you, and we hope soon to serve him, and his valiant troops, in the same manner.

It was of the priests and especially of the Jesuits that the British were the most suspicious. We know, indeed, that the French Army counted upon these allies for help against Quebec, (Lévis MSS., x.) Murray learned that some priests, taking advantage of the hardships endured by his soldiers, had incited them to discontent and desertion. He banished a priest whom he found in the act of giving what may well have been innocent instruction to some of his men laid up in hospital. A soldier who had been condemned to death for desertion Murray pardoned, when it became known that the man had been incited by a priest to commit the offence. At first Murray had left to the Jesuits, now few in number, a part of their fine building, taking the rest as a depot for provisions.

Everywhere at that time Jesuits were under a cloud of suspicion, a state of opinion that led a few years later to the abolition of the order by the Pope. Rumours of intrigue by the Jesuits reached Murray. He welcomed this excuse, since he wished to use the remainder of their building, and on October 26 he gave them notice that they must leave Quebec as soon as possible. Shortly after this a barrel of gunpowder and a cask of 15,000 cartridges were found to have been 'artfully concealed' by a Jesuit's valet. He and his master were arrested and confined separately. When the valet admitted his guilt, the Jesuit pleaded that his servant was an idiot whose testimony should not be heeded.

To this the retort was that it would have been an act of folly if the powder had been concealed a little earlier when the weather was so damp as to destroy it, but that the offender had waited until there had been a hard frost; and, in short, 'if the fellow is an idiot his abettors and accomplices are no fools.' Murray turned the Jesuits out of their building, in spite of murmurs from some of the inhabitants, who claimed that to dispossess the Jesuits of their property was to violate the conditions of surrender.

A few of the priests and Jesuits most suspected Murray kept in confinement. Naturally some of the suspicions proved unjust. Captain Knox was sent to arrest a suspected priest. He writes:

> I found him in his house, and arrested him in the name of his Britannic Majesty; the poor old man was greatly terrified, and entreated me earnestly to tell him his crime: but I made no other delay than to post a sentinel, whom I had taken with me, in the apartment with this ancient father.

It turned out that the priest had been quite guiltless of what was suspected.

Among his own people Murray had difficult problems of government. The British private soldier of the time was, in any case, too often ignorant, degraded, and drunken. The recent desolation of the surrounding country had involved a kind of plundering warfare which had debauched the soldiers and, at first, great rigour was necessary to restore good habits. There was much theft, robbery, and desertion, the last offence being caused, no doubt, by the desire to escape from possible punishment for the other crimes. To check this the sentence of death was often passed. On October 28 a soldier was shot on the Grand Parade for desertion. A fortnight later a soldier of the 48th regiment was executed for robbing a Quebec citizen.

At the same time an inhabitant, formerly a drummer in the French service, who was caught in the act of enticing some soldiers of the Royal American regiment to desert, was hanged. When, at another time, a court martial condemned two men to death for robbery, Murray decided that the death of one would suffice to teach the needed lesson and ordered lots to be cast as to which should die. We can picture the torrent of emotions linked with such a cast, but the man who made the fortunate throw showed outwardly no satisfaction, while, says Captain Knox, 'the other poor fellow was instantly executed, and behaved quite undaunted, though with great decency.'

With similar vigour Murray checked the vice of drunkenness. He ordered that no liquor should be sold, so that the men might have only the allowance served out regularly. Then, any soldier found drunk was to receive twenty lashes a day until he should tell where he had secured the liquor and his allowance of rum was to be stopped for six weeks. Others than soldiers met with similar severity. More than once women were whipped through the streets for the offence of selling rum.

In the Orders of the day we get an excellent picture of the military discipline of the time, and it commands admiration for its efficiency. As so often in the subsequent history of the army, some of the younger officers were prone to a contented ignorance in regard to their duty. Men of this type Murray took sharply to task. He ruled with something like iron rigour. The sentences of a single court martial show how stern was the discipline enforced. 'One soldier was sentenced to receive a thousand lashes, for absenting his duty (*sic*), and using expressions tending to excite *mutiny and desertion*. A second, for being disguised, with an intention to desert, and being out of his quarters at an undue time of night,—to receive three hundred. A third, for an intention to desert,—one thousand. And a fourth, for desertion, and endeavouring to inveigle others to desert,—*to suffer death.*'

In spite of occasional blackguardism the spirit of the men was excellent. For the most part they were cheerful and ready for hard service. They were always quick to volunteer for any difficult duty and in this respect were better than their officers; in November, when officers and men were invited to volunteer for a special scouting service, no officer came forward though the men were ready. Officers and men, alike, however, were prepared for any service to which they were ordered. The tasks before the defenders of Quebec were heavy. They had to repair a great number of houses within the walls, to build the line of block-houses as outer defences of the walls, to strengthen the walls themselves, to open embrasures, to drag cannon into position, to store away an inconceivable quantity of ammunition, to cut and put into magazines thousands of fascines, and to perform a hundred other exhausting labours. In their tasks the men took the cheery humorous view of life that has helped to carry the British arms through so many crises. Captain Knox writes:

> Their daily allowance of rum contributes not a little to exhilarate them under their present harrowing circumstances.

For the hardships of even the lower animals they showed sympathy. The Canadians used dogs as beasts of burden to haul wood and water, and these beasts sometimes dragged great loads on the light sleighs to which they were harnessed. One day a band of soldiers, straining in the street at their own load of wood, met a peasant and two dogs dragging a similar burden. The men instantly hailed the dogs as fellow-workers, called them comrade and yoke-mate, and invited both the man and his animals to share their scanty meal. When Murray heard the story 'he expressed himself like a tender parent towards his brave soldiers for their immense yet unavoidable hardships' and laughed at the humour with which they bore the stern exigencies of war.

The effect of this spirit was that every soldier tried to outdo his fellows in zeal. Murray had no money with which to pay them, for the *Hunter* sloop of war, sent from Halifax with £20,000 on board, had set out too late in the season to reach Quebec and had turned back. The result was that the pay of the troops remained in arrears from October 24, 1759. Murray declined to issue a paper currency and he forbade the circulation of the discredited French paper money with which the

Canadians, to their sorrow, were so familiar. The officers of the fleet, before going away, had collected £4,000, which they lent to the army. When this supply was exhausted, Murray issued his own and Colonel Burton's notes at six months for £8,000 and asked the garrison to volunteer advances of cash on the security thus offered. The sum was promptly made up, the sober and frugal men of Fraser's Highlanders contributing no less than £2,000. Murray complains of the 'villainy' of the English traders who, unlike the soldiers, hoarded all the specie paid in to them.

In Quebec were three communities of women, the Ursuline Nuns, devoted chiefly to education, the Nuns of the General Hospital, whose special task was the care of the old and the indigent, and the Nuns of the Hôtel Dieu, whose work was to nurse the sick. For these nuns, helpless women as they were, the conquerors showed every consideration. It was necessary to use their extensive houses as hospitals, and, in consequence, they themselves were huddled into rather narrow quarters. The Ursuline Nuns were obliged to give up two of the three floors of their fine building to wounded officers and soldiers.

In the wing of the Holy Family, Murray held meetings of his council; even the chapel, as we have seen, was used twice a week for Protestant services. The nuns lived in the top flat and were carefully protected. The British repaired their building, which had suffered during the siege. A sentry stood night and day before the door of the convent; the nuns drew daily supplies from the commissariat department established in the neighbouring Jesuits' College; and convalescent soldiers cut wood, carried water, and cleared the paths of snow for them.

In return for this special protection the ladies were unsparing of courtesies to the British. They furnished delicacies for the wounded. Even in those troubled days they found leisure for fine needlework, and on St. Andrew's Day, in compliment to Murray's Scottish nationality, they presented to him and some other officers a set of crosses of St. Andrew curiously worked:

> In a corner of the field of each cross was wrought an emblematical heart expressive of that attachment and affection which every good man naturally bears to his native country.

For Scots of humbler rank the kind-hearted nuns were not less solicitous. The bare legs of the men in kilts aroused their special compassion in the severe weather, and they worked long woollen hose 'to cover the limbs of the poor strangers'. Murray marked the doors in the Ursuline Convent beyond which no soldier might pass. From their quarters in the top flat the nuns descended at regular intervals for prayers in the chapel, where, as a cloistered community, they were strictly guarded from intrusion. But one evening a sister descending to ring the angelus bell saw a soldier in the chapel. She cried out, the sentry came running in to seek the cause of the noise, and the man was seized. He protested that he had wished only to see the procession of nuns file past to their prayers, but he was haled before a court martial which pronounced a heavy sentence. Then the venerable mother-superior, now seventy-five years old, wrote a touching letter to Murray, asking pardon for the offender, and the general could not refuse the humane request.

Since Wolfe's victory the General Hospital at Quebec, lying outside the walls across the meadows near the bank of the St. Charles River, had been a centre of great interest for the victors. At its head was Madame Sainte-Claude, the sister of Ramezay, the last French defender of Quebec. Before the surrender of the fortress the convents in the town had found their position dangerous from the incessant bombardment and, in the end, their inmates had decided to take refuge in the General Hospital, which lay beyond the range of the British fire. Here they proved of great service in helping to nurse the sick. It was the mother-superior of the Hôtel Dieu and her nuns who had first wended their way to this refuge.

The next day the nuns of the Ursuline Convent, flying from the bombs and bullets which were piercing the walls of their house, had found safety across the meadows in the same haven. A good many refugees from the suburbs of Quebec sought there, too, a temporary abiding place, and the ladies of the Hospital had their hands full. On the memorable 13th of September the trembling nuns had looked out from the windows on dire slaughter; and soon the wounded were being brought to them until between twelve and fifteen hundred had been laid on the beds and floors of the large building.

Late that night, when as many members of the three communities as could be spared were prostrate before the altar to implore the mercy of God amid these troubled scenes, their fears had been aroused anew by repeated and violent knocking at the outer doors. A British officer, said, probably incorrectly, to have been General Townshend himself, with a guard of two hundred men, had come to take possession. The officer reassured the nuns and they received every courtesy from the British. After the British occupation most of the Ursulines and the nuns of the Hôtel Dieu returned to their convents in Quebec, where they showed great devotion in nursing the sick. The British had urged that the French army should furnish support to their own wounded in the Hospital, but this Vaudreuil protested the French were unable to do. When the limited resources of the nuns of the General Hospital became exhausted, Murray ordered the inhabitants of the surrounding villages to bring them supplies.

During the hard winter in Quebec the pity of the nuns of the General Hospital knew no distinctions of race. In going about their duties among officers and men, Captain Knox says:

> They were exceedingly humane and tender.... When our poor fellows were ill, and ordered to be removed from their own odious regimental hospitals to this general receptacle, they were indeed rendered inexpressibly happy; each patient had his bed with curtains allotted to him and a nurse to attend him; sometimes she will take two, three, or more, under her care, according to the number of sick or wounded in the house.... Every officer has an apartment to himself, and is attended by one of those religious sisters, who, in general, are young, handsome, and fair; courteous, rigidly reserved, and very respectful.... Their office of nursing the sick furnishes them with opportunities of taking great latitudes, if they are so disposed; but I never heard any of them charged with the least levity.

Thirty years earlier, in 1733, some Canadian nuns had been less demure and a French Minister of State, M. de Maurepas, had sent out a letter to rebuke them for their worldly conduct in going out into society and attending dinners and suppers. The minister intended that the standard for Canada, if not for France, should be austere. (Smith, *History of Canada,* i.)

At the General Hospital were gathered a considerable number of French officers, most of them convalescent. Under the terms of the Cartel agreed to by the belligerents, they were not prisoners and they had their own table as in the days before the capitulation. The French commissary in Quebec, M. Bernier, did not think highly of these gentlemen.

> Their pretensions are so extravagant in all things that it is impossible to satisfy them.

Because he had been placed in charge of the arrangements affect-

THE GENERAL HOSPITAL, QUEBEC

ing them they looked upon him as a valet at their beck and call. But he makes allowances; they are ill and idle and, he says sententiously, 'Idleness is a great vice and illness makes us fretful.' Captain Knox saw much of these officers. He spent a week in command of the small garrison which held the hospital and, compared with the stable which constituted his quarters in Quebec, he found it an oasis in the desert. The General Hospital still exists, little changed from what it was when Knox thought it a 'very stately building', having 'two great wings, one fronting the north, and the other the south', with a 'superb church' in the south wing and 'a very neat chapel' in the other. He says:

> I have lived here at the French king's table, with an agreeable polite society. . . . Some of the gentlemen were married, and their ladies honoured us with their company; they were generally cheerful, except when we discoursed upon the late revolution, and the affairs of the campaign; then they seemingly gave way to grief uttered by profound sighs, and followed by an "O, mon Dieu".

The men seemed less depressed. In fine weather Knox sometimes walked with, them in the garden; at other times he played picquet. When the French officers discovered that he understood French better than he could speak it, they would, in defiance of manners, converse among themselves in Latin. We may believe that its range was limited and Knox knew that language better than his French companions. Their phrases usually wound up with a rapturous and theatrically spoken declamation from Virgil in regard to their own hardships:

> *Per mare, per terras, per tot discrimina rerum*

and:

> *Nos patriam fugimus, nos dulcia linquimus arva.*

✶✶✶✶✶✶

The lines, very incorrectly quoted from Book I of the *Aeneid*, may be rendered: On sea and land, in many crises of events, we have left behind our country and relinquished her pleasant pastures.

✶✶✶✶✶✶

Knox racked his brains for an appropriate rebuke and at length hit upon a neat citation, also from Virgil, which summed up the British point of view:

O Meliboee, Deus nobis haec otia fecit,
(O Meliboeus, it is God who has given to us these tranquil days).

After this there was no more spouting of tragic phrases. He says:

> We dined, every day between eleven and twelve, and afterwards were respectively served with a cup of laced coffee (coffee with spirits added); our dinners were generally indifferent but our suppers (what they called their *grand repas*, or best meal) were plentiful and elegant. I was at a loss, the first day, as every person was obliged to use his own knife and wine, there being only a spoon and a four-pronged fork laid with each napkin and plate. ... Each person here produces an ordinary clasped knife from his pocket, which serves him for every use; and, when they have dined or supped, they wipe and return it: the one I had, before I was provided with my own, was lent me by the Frenchman who stood. at my chair, and it gave my meat a strong flavour of tobacco, which, though it might have supplied the want of garlic to the owner, or his countrymen, was so exceedingly disgustful to me, that I was obliged to change my plate, and it was with difficulty I could eat any more.

Dining so early Knox did not trouble about breakfast, but, after he had been at the hospital two or three days, a nun brought him a polite note from Madame Sainte-Claude inviting him to an English breakfast. He found her surrounded by nuns engaged in needlework. On a table in the middle of the room was a plentiful supply of tea, milk, and slices of bread an inch thick 'covered with a profusion of butter'. A beverage black as ink was offered to Knox, the hostess assuring him that, to suit the supposed English taste, half a pint of tea had been put in the pot and then well boiled with the water. To the good lady's obvious distress, Knox declared that he preferred milk; 'she had heard the English always preferred tea for breakfast.' Conversation did not flag and Knox says that he 'passed near two hours most agreeably, in the society of this ancient lady and her virginal sisters'.

The ancient lady, who was of great stature, proved less innocent than she seemed. As the winter wore on Murray found that rumours of British defeats and of the conclusion of a peace favourable to France were emanating from the General Hospital. They were circulated in the hope of discouraging the British soldiers. Murray, though usually friendly to the nuns, is said by Knox to have sent an officer to reproach

Madame Sainte-Claude for conduct unfitting one who had turned from the world, and to say that:

> If she is tired of living out of the world, and will change her habit for that of a man, she being of a proper stature, his Excellency will enrol her as a grenadier and upon her good behaviour, will duly promote, and grant her every farther indulgence in his power.

Murray found that another community of nuns, those of the Hôtel Dieu, also sent to the French army news of what was taking place in Quebec. At the intercession of the Duchess d'Aiguillon Pitt had written to ask for special care of these nuns. Murray, however, had at length to warn them that if they did not mend their ways their house would be converted into a barracks for troops and they themselves would be banished from Quebec. The nuns showed so strenuous a zeal for the conversion of the heretics to whom they ministered that the Bishop of Quebec, Mgr. Pontbriand, a saintly man, quietly told them that their own piety and modesty rather than their words were likely to touch the hearts of their patients. He told them, too, that they had a duty to the conqueror, since 'according to the teaching of St. Paul', they owed obedience to the King of England, for the time the ruler of Quebec. (Letters to Mother St. Helen, Montreal, October 28 and December 31, 1759—Canadian Archives).

Until the late autumn, the serene atmosphere and the bright sky at Quebec were very agreeable, but 'hoary winter 'soon appeared, as Knox says, 'with hasty strides.' The cold was to prove the great enemy. The rigours of a Canadian winter are not really difficult to combat, but the British in Quebec were wholly without experience in fighting them. This winter of 1759-60 appears to have been unusually severe; by February, even spirits stored in cellars were found frozen. Adequate clothing had not been provided for the soldiers, and the Highlanders in particular, with their bare legs, suffered severely until, with the assistance of the good nuns and by other strenuous efforts, most, if not all, of them had been furnished with trousers or with long knit hose.

Sentries at their posts were often severely frost-bitten. In the Orders the men were warned when this happened to avoid going near a fire and to rub the frost-bitten part with snow. Sentries on duty in the open air were sometimes quickly deprived by the cold of the power of speech. The guard was changed in severe weather every half-hour or even oftener. Men who underwent the prolonged exposure of winter expeditions suffered terribly; much farther south than Quebec, at Crown Point, during this winter a British surgeon amputated in a single day no less than one hundred toes, frozen in a march from Ticonderoga.

For protection from the cold the men at Quebec cut up blankets to make socks and gloves. In order to replenish the supply, Murray seized blankets from the Canadians, with the promise to pay for them on the arrival of the ships in the spring. The soldiers wore anything they could get which promised warmth, even the French uniforms found in the stores at Quebec. *Moccasins* proved warmer than boots and were less likely to cause slipping. Accordingly, the soldiers appeared on parade in *moccasins*. Knox says:

> Our guards, on the Grande Parade made a most grotesque appearance in their different dresses; and our inventions to guard us against the extreme rigour of this climate are various beyond imagination: the uniformity, as well as the nicety, of the clean methodical soldier, is buried in the rough fur-wrought garb of the frozen Laplander; and we rather resemble a masquerade than a body of regular troops; insomuch that I have frequently been accosted by my acquaintances, who, though familiar their voices were to me, I could not discover or conceive who they were; besides, every man seems to be in a continual hurry; for, instead of walking soberly through the streets, we are obliged to observe a running or trotting pace.

When the weather was cold no one stirred out unless absolutely obliged to do so. Persons going out covered everything but the eyes. The appreciation of the attractions of a Canadian winter, now so general, is apparently the result of education.

Sometimes the snow was so deep that it blocked the streets. It lodged in such a mass under the walls of Quebec that assailants could almost have walked into the town over the snow banks. To avert this danger, after each snowfall the British soldiers dug the snow away from the wall and piled it so as to form a second outer defence. A line of barrels filled with snow frozen into solid ice helped to make a glacis of this outer defence and a kind of ditch separated it from the stone wall. Even when snow did not block the streets of Quebec there was another difficulty, for ice often made them extremely slippery.

Mountain Street, the descent of the steep cliff separating the Upper from the Lower Town, became a sheet of ice, and soldiers found it safer to sit down and slide to the bottom than to try to walk. 'Creepers' to make the footing secure were in great demand, as also, when snow had fallen, were snow-shoes. Taught by some of the Rangers from New England, the light infantry practised walking on snow-shoes and, though the practice was at first fatiguing, it was not difficult to learn. So useful did the snow-shoes prove that Murray required the people of the surrounding country and of Quebec to hand over the snow-shoes which they possessed. In mid-winter, soldiers mounting guard were ordered always to bring snow-shoes with them in order that, if necessary, they might be able to pursue the enemy over the snow.

The St. Lawrence, when first frozen over, was, for a time, without a covering of snow and furnished a great expanse of smooth ice. One day a French prisoner saw his opportunity. Going with a soldier to bring a bucket of water from the river, he slipped off his shoes and ran away in his stockings on the ice. The soldier, armed with a bayonet only, and wearing boots without 'creepers', cut a ridiculous figure as he slipped on the ice in his vain efforts to pursue the fugitive. The British, always athletic, could not resist the temptation to skate on this sea of glass which lay before Quebec, and a French officer, writing in February, notes grimly that this practice gave the hostile Indians great pleasure and that they had already captured six of the defenders of Quebec.

The visitors had been in Quebec only a few days when they saw that one of their chief problems would be to secure fire-wood. The supply from ruined houses and old fences was soon exhausted. Not less than twenty thousand cords of wood were needed and only about a thousand cords were on hand. At first, on chill nights, the soldiers upon guard had been permitted to have fires in the open air, but this was soon forbidden, in order to save wood. A few days after the surrender two frigates were sent about four miles up the river to procure some wood which the Canadians had piled on the heights. A body of Rangers kept off assailants while the wood was thrown over the precipice and secured by the sailors.

By order of Lévis the French burned all the firewood which they could find on the south bank of the river as far as the Point of Levy, so that it might not fall into Murray's hands. The British were soon repenting bitterly that, in the course of their siege of Quebec, they had destroyed quantities of wood. Murray ordered the Canadians to bring in wood, and offered them five shillings for each cord. But they supplied it only slowly and reluctantly. As the winter advanced, he was obliged to seize what sleighs he could and to require the service from his own men, paying them, however, the price he had offered to the Canadians.

This cutting of wood proved the most severe task of the army. For a time, fuel was brought by water from Isle Madame and the Island of Orleans, but, on account both of the distance and of the difficulty in winter of navigating the river, filled with floes of ice, Murray was obliged to look for his chief supply to the forests at Ste Foy, five miles away.

From two hundred and fifty to three hundred men were kept busy at this work. It was especially trying because of the inexperience of the men in handling the axe. They also suffered terribly from frost-bites. Since almost no horses were available in Quebec the soldiers had to do the work of horses. In teams of eight, yoked in couples like beasts of burden, and with a ninth man to guide the sleigh, they dragged wood four or five miles to the town, through snow so deep, at times, that it was necessary to mark the road by beacons. The service was dangerous as well as difficult; Indians were lurking in the neighbourhood to cut off stragglers, and to be captured meant death by scalping and also barbarous mutilation. The sleighing parties were obliged to carry arms and ammunition, and by practice the men were able so to carry their weapons that they could get at them easily even while drawing the sleighs. It was this service more than anything else which wore down the strength of the troops in the course of the winter.

Unsalted food was always a pressing need. There was an abundance of fish in the river, and the soldiers learned from the Canadians how to take fish through holes in the ice. The garrison was ready either to buy outright from the Canadians fresh meat and vegetables or to give in exchange for them wine, biscuits, and salted provisions, while these things lasted. Extravagant prices were sometimes asked by the Canadians. At length, on the request of the British and French traders in Quebec, a maximum price for bread and meat was fixed by Colonel Young, whom Murray had appointed to act as a magistrate in civil affairs, with the aid of some of the principal inhabitants. All butchers must have licences and they were not to charge more than 6*d*. a pound for mutton and 5*d*. for beef. When the men grumbled about the food, Murray ordered that anyone complaining of his allowance should be brought to trial for sedition.

Though the exchange of provisions with the Canadians had been brisk for a time, the supplies, on both sides, were soon exhausted and there remained little to exchange. Murray levied a contribution of three hundred cattle on the inhabitants of the subdued country, but this resource was not adequate. Even salted provisions became in time scarce. It had been supposed that supplies for a year had been left at Quebec by the fleet, but, towards the spring, the garrison found itself face to face with famine. The unfortunate Canadians remaining in Quebec were then, of course, even worse off than the soldiers. Murray at last ordered that in each week the provisions for one day allotted to the officers and men should be handed over to the inhabitants. The soldiers accepted this plan without a murmur, though they themselves were being reduced to mere skeletons from lack of food.

Disease aided famine in Quebec. Almost from the first the health of the troops suffered. Since there was a suspicion that this might be due to the poisoning of the wells with dead dogs and cats, the men were ordered to drink only the water from the river. But the real tragedy was caused by a deadly outbreak of scurvy, which was believed to follow upon an exclusive diet of salted meat and upon the absence of vegetables. Knox wrote as early as November;

> Our brave soldiers are growing sickly, their disorders are chiefly scorbutic, with fevers and dysenteries.

Every available remedy was tried. In the barrack-rooms regulations were posted for the preserving of health against. scurvy. The men were ordered to boil their pork in fresh water, and in no case to eat uncooked meat. Murray had found a good supply of wine in the French stores, and, since it was deemed a cure for scurvy, he encouraged the men to buy it out of their scanty resources. Ginger and vinegar, tar-water, and other remedies were tried. Perhaps the best one was a liquor made from the spruce tree, and Murray gave orders that every day the men should drink some of this mixed with their allowance of rum.

Yet hundreds died. Daily, as the winter wore on, there were not less than two or three funerals, and sometimes there were half a dozen. Knox wrote in January:

> The men grow more unhealthy as the winter advances, and scarce a day passes without two or three funerals.

In February he repeats:

> Our soldiers grow more sickly, and many of them are daily carried off by the inveteracy of their disorders.

And in March:

> Our forces are now reduced to three thousand fit for duty; our sick, lame, and convalescents amount to nineteen hundred.

In April the troops were stricken with the disease at the rate of two hundred a week, and most of the men had become little more than skeletons, hobbling about with the aid of crutches. Before the end of April two thousand men were unfit for any service and about a thousand had died. The ground was so hard frozen that final burial was impossible, and the bodies of many hundreds of British soldiers were laid away in the snow, to be preserved by the intense cold until spring should, permit their committal to mother earth. There were in Quebec five hundred and sixty-seven women camp-followers, the invariable and usually disreputable accompaniment of the armies of the time. While disease was carrying off its sadly numerous victims, these women remained perfectly healthy, and they rendered useful service in nursing the sick soldiers and in washing and mending.

The Canadian inhabitants were not as fortunate as the women; though they suffered less than the soldiers, about a hundred and twenty died during the winter. No doubt the Canadians were the more liable to disease because they were underfed. What money they had was the paper money issued in Canada by the French, and this the English traders in Quebec would not accept.

Behind everything was the great military problem of defending the fortress. Gossip was always busy as to the designs and the successes of the enemy. Towards the end of November, it was rumoured in Quebec that a ship from France had passed up unobserved, in the night, and had brought news that the French had destroyed Halifax, had retaken Louisbourg, and had put two-thirds of the garrisons to the sword. It was added that a fleet carrying troops would arrive in the early spring from France to perform similar feats at Quebec. Later came a rumour that the French had destroyed the greatest fleet which had ever sailed from the shores of England; that they had conquered Ireland, and had massacred troops and natives alike when found in arms; and that they would soon make a triumphant peace and re-occupy Quebec. Usually, the day of vengeance was not postponed so indefinitely.

At first rumour said that Lévis was resolved to spend Christmas in Quebec; he would set its roofs on fire by a shower of hot arrows and, in the confusion, carry the place by storm. It was this threatened assault before Christmas which led Murray, always nervous about the strength of his walls, to build the block-houses on the side towards the Plains of Abraham and to drill his men in the use of snow-shoes, apparently with the intention of fighting on the snow outside the walls. Christmas passed, and then it was in February that dire things were to happen. At one time the French general, in sporting humour, wrote to propose a wager with Murray that help from France would arrive before the British could receive aid from England. Murray's answer was spirited and prophetic:

> I have not the least inclination to win your money, for, I am very certain, I shall have the honour to embark your Excellency and the remains of your half-starved army, for Europe, in British bottoms, before the expiration of the ensuing summer.

The fulfilment of this prophecy was to become a grim reality for the French.

Other rumours pointed to a British success. With some truth the French army was reported by deserters to be half starved. It was said that the Canadians had grown anxious for final surrender to the British. The Indian allies of the French were also reported to be discontented and arrogant; to have threatened to stone Vaudreuil to death for his incompetence; and to have refused to fight unless given permission to scalp the dead and wounded on the field. There was a report of a great British success near Chambly, and of the cutting to pieces at that point of the French Regiment de la Reine. Someone had seen great fires near Montreal and had taken it as evidence of a British camp in that neighbourhood.

On one occasion a French deserter who had spread such rumours was brought before Murray. A French officer, a prisoner on parole, was present. The deserter declared that the French army was in such distress and disorganisation that it had become a mere rabble. Murray handed the man a silver dollar. In Canada, discredited paper money had long been almost the only currency. The man looked at the dollar: 'This is no French money!' he said, and then added:

> A few of these properly applied would induce even the officers, as well as soldiers, of the miserable French Army to follow my example.

At this the French officer flew into a rage so violent that Murray threatened him with imprisonment.

When Murray's soldiers were discouraged by rumours of reverses in the outside world he resorted to a stratagem to counteract these reports. On April 3, after long waiting for news, he sent a sergeant and four rangers across the river with instructions to come in on the British outpost at the Point of Levy as if they were an express from General Amherst. Of course, only good news could come by such means, and, without saying anything definite, Murray was able greatly to encourage the garrison. He adds that the device 'visibly affected the French inhabitants' who, however, were well able to keep their own counsel. Captain Knox says that they showed no concern or discomposure at unacceptable news, but only the more sedulously whispered reports of French victories.

Chapter 3

Montreal During the Winter of 1759-60

The distresses of the British in Quebec during this winter were surpassed by those of the French in Montreal. In this little town, which was almost the extreme outpost in New France of European civilization, the defenders had gathered for the final rally against the invaders. Usually the town contained from eight to nine thousand inhabitants; now, however, its population was greatly increased by refugees from all parts of Canada. Many of these refugees had come because they feared not only the British but also their own Indians, likely at any time to go over to the enemy and to commit brutal outrages against their former friends. The savages were, it was said, particularly incensed against Vaudreuil, as the cause of the misfortunes in which they found themselves included, and threatened to kill him.

Leading citizens from Quebec were now in Montreal, and the Bishop of Quebec ruled his church from that place. In Montreal was also what remained in Canada of a Court, which once had imitated Versailles. An appearance of old-world luxury marked this town on the edge of the wilderness. Captain Knox, who saw the place in the autumn of 1760 says:

> From the number of silk robes, laced coats, and powdered heads of both sexes, and almost of all ages, that are perambulating the streets from morning till night, a stranger would be induced to believe that Montreal is entirely inhabited by people of independent and plentiful fortunes.

Some years earlier, the Swedish traveller Kalm had described the inhabitants of Montreal as 'well-bred and courteous, with an innocent and becoming freedom'; to Knox, who saw them under the shadow of defeat, they appeared cheerful and sprightly. Their town stretched in a thin line for two and a half miles along the river front, 'For delight fullness of situation,' says Knox, 'I think I never saw any town to equal it.' Its few streets were regular, though narrow, and its houses were well constructed. Knox could find it in his heart to describe the public buildings as beautiful and commodious, and one of them at least as 'extremely magnificent'. He thought Montreal 'infinitely preferable to Quebec'. Quebec, however, was now associated in his mind with pestilence and famine. The Chevalier Johnstone, who served on the defeated side, thought Montreal a dismal place.

The picture that we get of the social life of the colony at this time is not edifying. In New England Puritanism was still a living force, manners were grave, life was simple, and the tone of society was pure and restrained. In New France, on the other hand, reckless extravagance, corruption in business methods and immoral licence in social life had long been characteristics of the upper class of society. The men who held office in Canada were nominees of the French Court, and some of them reflected in the distant colony the abandoned tone of the worst circles at Versailles. In Canada, as in France, there were not wanting voices of protest.

The Roman Catholic Church in Canada had always stood for an austere view of life, and, with hardly an exception, her priests had supported it by their example and by their discipline over their flocks. At Montreal the priests of the Sulpitian Seminary were a powerful corporation, lords of the whole island under feudal tenure, and they showed a desire to keep up a censorship of morals. A hostile critic says that they asserted a right to supervise what was done in private houses, and that even the French generals trembled under their authority for fear of reports which might be sent to France. (*Mémoires sur le Canada*, 1749-60).

The Bishop of Quebec, Monsignor Pontbriand, now living at Montreal, was a high-minded and holy man. In this crisis he exhorted Canadian society to consider its misfortunes as a call to prayer and to repentance for its sins. There is, however, no evidence that the call to greater seriousness was heeded. In time of disaster men are as likely to fall into reckless licence as to reform themselves. Montreal during this winter of 1759-60 had the same surface gaiety, the display, and, beneath all, the ugly self-seeking and corruption which were gnawing at the heart the older society and leading to revolution.

The real business man in the administration of Canada was the *intendant*, François Bigot. Under the system which had developed in France, each French province had two high officials, the governor and the *intendant*, the governor representing the dignity and the military power of the Crown, the *intendant* discharging the sober details of civil business. A similar system prevailed in Canada. The dozen or so *intendants* who had held the office had been on the whole competent and honest men; Bigot, the last of them, was surpassed by none in competence but he was wholly wanting in conscience, and his career in Canada was marked by unscrupulous pillage of the king, his master, and by lavish expenditure, on a scale that seems hardly credible when we consider the poverty of the colony.

Bigot had attractive qualities. He was able and assiduous in the discharge of his official duties, and during this winter, when, in some degree, he was forced to make bricks without straw, he performed wonders in securing provisions for the army. Lévis once wrote to him:

> No one shows more foresight and ingenuity than you to find resources.

But while a keen man of business he had also the tastes and ambitions of a man of fashion, and he made both Quebec and Montreal scenes of social dissipation, more suited to the life of a European capital than to that of a town in a poverty-stricken colony. He belonged to a family of Guienne, not, it is true, ranking among the nobility of France, but conspicuous in what had almost become another nobility, the men of the robe, the class from which the judges, the lawyers, and officials like the *intendants* were drawn. He had at court powerful relations who held high official position—the Marquis de Puysieux, the Maréchal d'Estrées, and apparently, too, the Comte de Maurepas, a former Minister of Marine.

He loved pomp and it had been his ambition to retire to France to live in luxury and ease for the remainder of his life. Already he had bought land; he had grand ideas of the style in which he should live, and had purchased furnishings for his house and table on a lavish scale. When misfortune overtook him and his effects in France were seized by the king, great nobles like the Maréchal de Richelieu were eager to become possessors of the plate and other articles in which he had invested some of his ill-gotten gains. (Papers in *Report on Canadian Archives*, 1905, i.)

In physique nature had not fitted Bigot for the role of social leader which he aspired to fill. He was small and fat, with reddish hair and a pimply skin. On the other hand, he had charming manners and he showed a marked capacity for making himself agreeable. This social tact was one of his chief gifts. He took little part in the personal quarrels that had raged in the colony between Vaudreuil and Montcalm; with some success, indeed, he had played the part of a mediator who invariably showed shrewd common sense in trying to smooth over differences and in advising friendly co-operation. The villain in the tragedy of the declining years of New France Bigot undoubtedly is; but villains would hardly be dangerous did they not possess some semblance of virtue. Bigot was loyal and devoted to those who shared in his pursuits. A contemporary writes:

> He had great wit and penetration, he was generous and benevolent and capable of filling a more eminent position than he occupied; when he had once given his confidence and his protection it was not easily that he drew back. . . . His manner of life was unaffected and full of consideration for those who attended upon or paid court to him. His table was richly furnished and he relieved the unfortunate with a generosity that approached munificence. His love of pleasure did not keep him from attention to his duty. He was extremely jealous of his authority and supported too keenly those who had his confidence and who unhappily were neither honest nor deserving. To them only would he listen; their counsels alone would he follow, and they made him commit stupendous faults. (*Mémoires sur le Canada,* 1749-60. The writer is a severe critic of the dying regime in Canada, but he is well informed and apparently accurate).

Some of the associates of Bigot were, one should suppose, conspicuously unfit to shine in that social world which it was his ambition to adorn. Hardly an ornament for high social circles was Cadet, the son of a butcher, and himself, in early years, first a cowherd at Charlesbourg and then a butcher at Quebec. His early advance was due to his striking, if unscrupulous, business capacity. In the early stages of the war there had been difficulties in the commissariat department and the French Court had then decided that, to provide adequate control, a single official should be given the contract and be made responsible for furnishing supplies to the army. Cadet's abilities qualified him to fill this office, and on January 1, 1757, he entered upon its duties with the title of Munitioner-General. From that time, he had full control. Canadian society was astonished that the butcher-knife should have given place so quickly to the sword which it appears his new office entitled him to wear. No one, however, could sneer at his capacity. In spite of his coarse manners he was generous and kindly and so prodigal in expenditure that he made many friends. In the end the complaisant Vaudreuil recommended him for a patent of nobility, and members of his family married into some of the most ancient families in France.

Corruption was an old story in Canada. The French Court paid meagre salaries to civil and military officers and it was a common practice, hardly censured in high quarters, for these men to engage in trading operations in order to eke out a livelihood. Since the system of government in Canada was completely despotic, officials could easily be placed in a privileged position in regard to some branches of commerce. Licences to trade in the interior, for instance, were issued by the government at its discretion.

The government also exercised the right to name the price of wheat and other staple commodities. Under a man like Bigot a system with possibilities of fraud was sure to receive its fullest development. His secretary, Deschenaux, was the son of a shoemaker at Quebec. In some way he made himself indispensable to the *intendant*. Bigot gave him his confidence and clung with great tenacity to this vain, ambitious, and arrogant parvenu. So greedy was he for gain that he declared he would rob even the altar itself. As secretary to the *intendant*, and to such an Intendant, Deschenaux could easily secure official sanction for his many plans to defraud the government and the people. He and Cadet worked together, and their rascalities were almost incredible.

A third person was joined with Cadet and Deschenaux in the leadership of a ring which planned boldly to master for its profit the whole resources of the colony. This third person was Major Péan, a Canadian by birth, the son of a military officer and himself an officer. In his case no personal quality secured the favour of the *intendant*. His merit consisted in the charms of his wife. Bigot had shown openly his admiration for some of the handsome ladies whom he entertained so prodigally, but he found his admiration discouraged either by them or by their husbands. Madame Péan was not beautiful but she was young, lively, and witty. When she received the *intendant's* advances, he vowed to make her the envy of the other women in Canada. In the end the pleasure-loving *intendant* became her slave. We are told, (*Mémoires sur le Canada,* 1749-60):

> He went regularly to spend his evenings with her, and she formed a little court of persons of her own stamp who gained her protection by their deference and, since the *intendant* could refuse her nothing, made fortunes. This went so far that those who had need of promotion or employment could get what they desired only through her. Domestics, lackeys, and other persons of no account became storekeepers at the posts. Ignorance and depravity proved no obstacle. Employments were, in brief, given to those she named, without discrimination, and her recommendation was worth as much as the greatest merit.

It would not be easy to find, though the scale is smaller, a more exact parallel of Madame de Pompadour at the Court of Louis XV than this of Madame Péan at the Court of Bigot on the confines of the Canadian wilderness. There is the difference, however, that the great lady in the Old World had little part in vulgar corruption and showed sometimes a sense of responsibility in the use of power which her copy in the New World lacked. Péan profited by his own complaisance. Cadet and Deschenaux found it wise to make him the third member of the triumvirate, which existed for the sake of plunder. Among other things Péan was given a commission to buy grain for the king's service. Bigot lent him the money for this enterprise. Péan bought the grain at a low price for ready money. A little later, Bigot, using his authority, issued a regulation which named a high price for grain, and when Péan sold his supply he made a great profit.

In the early days it was Bigot who led in the frauds. At that time, he and one Bréard, the Controller of Marine at Quebec, had worked together in systematic plunder. They imported goods from France and then sold them to the government at a very extravagant price. Bigot thus used his official position to rob the king whom he served. At first Cadet was Bigot's pupil, but he proved to be a pupil so apt that he soon became the master. It may be that Bigot drew back from this distorted image of himself. At any rate the two men quarrelled. Bigot poured contempt on Cadet as base-born and at last denounced him as a criminal. Certainly Cadet plundered on a colossal scale and Bigot's achievements in fraud pale before his. When both men were found guilty, Cadet was ordered to pay back from his spoils four times as much as was required of Bigot.

If Vaudreuil was not in collusion with the thieves he was certainly very blind. There was, at times, a reckless candour in Bigot. Himself corrupt, he invited corruption in others. Vergor, an army captain, bad in manners as well as in character, dull and uneducated, became the friend of Bigot, probably by sharing some of his vices. Bigot had secured for him the command at Fort Beauséjour, and this is the style in which the man next to the governor in authority wrote, on leaving for France in 1754, to an officer in a position of trust. Bigot wrote:

> Profit, my dear Vergor by your place; trim, lop off; all power is in your hands; do it so that you may be able soon to come and join me in France and buy an estate near mine.

Villainy is not often as refreshingly frank and reckless as this; we almost admire Bigot for his occasional candour. To Vaudreuil, however, he professed to be a model of virtue. It seems certain that Vaudreuil himself was more a fool than a knave. His secretary, St. Sauveur, was, however, a rascal. When secretary to an earlier governor, St. Sauveur had begun to amass a fortune by securing a monopoly of the brandy trade with the Indians. Murray spoke of him as a swindler and traitor, who abused his master's confidence, and wondered that Vaudreuil could be so blind. Vaudreuil was, indeed, precisely the kind of man whom a schemer like St. Sauveur could manage.

Whatever the limits to Vaudreuil's blame, he was, no more than Bigot, a check to corruption in Canada. He must at least have seen his own relations profiting by fraud. It is specifically charged that he made a large fortune, but his acquittal, when tried in France after the fall of Canada, leaves the door open to the belief that he was innocent of anything but incompetence.

It is not now possible to fix the share in the frauds of each of the persons concerned. Towards the end, as we have seen. Bigot was less active in plunder than Cadet, but he must have known what Cadet was doing. There were other great thieves and lesser thieves. Some members of the ring formed a society that carried on extensive trade. They had a great warehouse at Quebec; there was a similar warehouse at Montreal; and in both places the people came, in the end, to understand what these warehouses stood for and named each of them 'La Friponne', the swindle. One of the *intendant's* special friends was Varin, a vicious libertine, tiny in stature, insignificant in appearance, but perversely ingenious to secure dishonest gain. He was an official in the government service at Montreal and the chief leader in fraud at that place.

The ring had friends and accomplices in France. Some of these could meet and perhaps silence complaints made to the Court, others could assist in trading operations and in sending out supplies. They did some swindling on their own account. Bigot himself complains of the inferior quality of goods which they sent out from France.

One chief source of Cadet's profits sprang from the supply of rations for the troops. As the war went on the number of regular soldiers in the service tended to decline. No considerable reinforcements arrived from France, and owing to death, illness, and, above all, desertion, the troops decreased in number by nearly one-half. Yet Cadet continued to take payment for rations for the original number. When there were only eight thousand men in actual service he was paid for rations for thirteen thousand. Moreover, rations charged as containing two pounds of food contained only a pound and a half.

As long ago as the time when the Romans conquered and plundered Britain a favourite device of extortion had been to secure control of the food supply of the people, then to enhance the price, and finally to sell the needed grain at a great profit. The *triumivirs* bought up as much grain as they could and placed it in great storehouses on Péan's *seigniory* of St. Michel on the river a few leagues below Quebec. To make sure of scarcity they shipped some of their stores to other countries. When grain was already becoming scarce. Cadet secured from Bigot an order to make a levy on the farmers of grain for the king's posts. Bigot fixed the amount to be levied, but the ring went beyond this and took all the grain they could find. An army of Cadet's *employés* would descend upon the parishes in turn. They made each *habitant* surrender what they chose to take of his grain or cattle with no regard whatever to his own needs.

For the grain he would receive the low price named by the *intendant*. For the cattle he received nothing at the time. The clerks merely made a note of what they took and the munitioner fixed the price later, usually at not more than one-third of what it would cost to replace the animals. Sometimes the clerks failed to make a note of all they had taken and the habitant found redress practically impossible. If he went to Quebec to make a direct appeal to the *intendant*—upon whose kind heart his distress would probably have had some effect— he would find it impossible to see Bigot or to reach him in any way with the story of his wrongs. A too persistent complainant might find himself helpless in prison. When, by such methods, all the available supplies had been secured and the cry of scarcity had begun, the *in-*

tendant would come forward as the champion of the needy. He would issue an ordinance, apparently preventing extortion by naming a price for wheat, but fixing a price much higher than that paid by those who now held the grain. At this price the government would buy what it required; the wretched inhabitants would be obliged to do the same; and the conspirators would make a great profit.

Another type of fraud worked equally well. Under official pressure the import trade of the colony was easily concentrated in the hands of members of the ring. By Bigot's influence they imported their goods free of duty, on the ground that they were for the king's service. It was Bigot's custom each year to send to France requisitions for the supplies of the army and of the civil government in Canada. The *intendant* took good care to order less than was needed, and when the inevitable deficiency in supplies appeared the government was obliged to buy heavily from the swindlers, and it bought, of course, at a great advance in price.

But this was not all. The king not merely paid high prices; he paid for what he did not get. Corrupt officials certified accounts for goods which were never delivered, and these accounts were paid in the regular way. The king paid, too, for goods which were delivered but which could not possibly be required for his service. Expensive silks and velvets, mirrors mounted upon morocco, and similar articles were included in the commodities said to be necessary at the posts in the far interior. They were sold to the king by the corrupt ring, and if furnished at all were no doubt used by the plunderers or their mistresses at no cost to themselves.

The fur trade was the backbone of the commercial life of Canada and its profits were very large. Step by step, the French traders had penetrated farther and farther into the interior until, about twenty-five years before the fall of Canada, the Canadian brothers La Vérendrye had actually reached the foot-hills of the Rocky Mountains. The fur-traders needed military protection, and to provide this France had built forts and trading posts on the chief rivers and on the Great Lakes as centres of trade with the Indians. The forts were in command of military officers and were of course a part of the military equipment of Canada, supported by the government. To them supplies were carried at the king's expense; to them also presents were sent for the Indians, in order to keep them friendly.

Obviously such a situation furnished the opportunity to plunder. The route to the interior was at best difficult and exposed to accident.

The transport was by canoes, and those who set out from Montreal even early in the spring would be unlikely to make the long journey and to return to Montreal before the autumn. The rivers and lakes were often stormy. Heavy sacks had to be carried across portages on men's backs. On such journeys, even with an honest accounting, the king's stores were likely to suffer. But there was not an honest accounting. What was easier than that kegs of brandy should become more than half water on the long journey? What was more simple than to sell a keg of the king's brandy or a package of the king's goods to some trader met by the way and then to report that it had been thrown overboard to save the canoe while crossing a stormy lake? In the hands of Cadet and his friends it was sure to be the king's goods that suffered by such mishaps.

The pillage in connexion with the forts and posts in the interior was so rich that positions of influence at these places came to be much coveted. An unscrupulous man could make requisitions and certify bills for many times the amount of the goods he received, and he and the officials at Montreal and Quebec would share in the profits of the robbery. The so-called presents for the Indians were in reality sometimes sold to them. Goods sent as supplies for the king's troops were also sold. Furs bought with the king's money and worth great sums were appropriated by dishonest officials and sold for their own benefit. It is clear that some of the military officers at the forts took part in this plunder.

But the officers who fell were, for the most part, in the colonial service and long resident in the colony; few officers of the regular army who served in the regiments of Montcalm and Lévis were involved. Courage and honour were not passports for securing or holding a position at a fort or trading post. Those who would not lend themselves to the plans of the leaders were likely to be turned out of their places. It happened that men too persistently honest were imprisoned on some trumped-up charge. A year or two in the interior gave time for amassing a considerable fortune. Another opportunity for fraud was found in the contracts for transporting supplies to the forts in the far interior or from Quebec and Montreal to adjacent points.

We have details of what happened in connexion with transport from Montreal to St. Johns and Chambly, forts not many miles away, on the Richelieu River. In the name of persons who, in reality, had only a slight interest in the contract, Péan and others undertook this work. The king furnished the boats; they were taken to the mouth of

MONTREAL IN 1760

the Richelieu River at Sorel by the king's soldiers, and from there up the river to their destination by *habitants* impressed in the king's name, under what was known as a *corvée*. For such service the contractors paid out almost nothing, but they charged the king a high price. In addition to this their accounts against the king were sometimes paid more than once.

The plunderers made profit even out of the misfortunes of the Acadians, people of their own blood. These had been driven from their homes in what is now Nova Scotia, partly by the policy of the French, who did not wish them to remain and accept British rule, but more completely by the British, who expelled them from their farms because they would not take the oath of allegiance. Those who, helpless and poor, found refuge within the frontier of Canada, were in an especial degree the wards of the King of France. The court was ready to help them and at great cost sent food and supplies for this purpose. Here was an unexpected opening for fraud. These supplies were forwarded to the Acadians from Quebec, and from Louisbourg, before it fell. The king paid for good food for them; but they were fed with bad food or not fed at all. Some goods disappeared entirely on the way.

With what seems to us grim humour these starving Acadians were supposed to need for their comfort damasks, satins, and other articles of luxury. These were accordingly bought for the king at heavy cost, and were then sent at great cost to points far remote, there to be sold at a low price to the Acadians in order to help them. Not the Acadians, however, but representatives of the corrupt ring bought them, for almost nothing, and sent them back to Quebec to be sold at their real value. It was, we are told, 'a pretty woman' (*une jolie femme*), to whom Bigot could refuse nothing, who managed this fraud. Many of the unhappy Acadians were brought to Quebec in the year after their expulsion. It was a time of scarcity. They were denied bread and were fed on horse-flesh. Many of them died.

These homeless people were not allowed to go to the places in Canada which offered the best chance of success. Those who were willing to settle near Quebec on Madame Péan's *seigniory* and also on Vaudreuil's *seigniory* were given the adequate help denied to others. Misfortune was no protection against the cruelty of the plunderers. When the Acadians presented paper money at Quebec, Bigot's secretary, by delay in redeeming it, forced them in the end to accept one-half of one-third of its face value. Later he himself received from the government the full amount.

It must not be supposed that no voices of protest were raised against this system. Montcalm had seen what was going on. Some of the officers in the French service were, he said, 'stealing like *mandarins*', and the pettiest ensign was growing rich. The mode of living in Canada in Bigot's circle attracted attention, for it became extravagant beyond measure. In a country chiefly remarkable for the poverty and want of its people, men were building large houses, driving expensive equipages, and gambling for excessive sums. Cases of the rapid accumulation of a fortune were much talked of. A certain Pillet at Lachine made 600,000 *livres* in a single year by transporting the king's goods. Another inhabitant of Lachine made a fortune out of charges for storing the king's goods in his house; needless to say, the king's goods placed in his custody were plundered.

The Church, to her credit, spoke out against the scandals. The author of the most scathing account of these evils, (*Mémoires sur le Canada*, 1749-60), tells us that he was himself present in a parish church when a priest described and attacked the frauds. He called those who received the stolen goods thieves, blamed the *intendant* and the governor for what was going on, and demanded restitution to those who had suffered. A whole battalion of troops was present to hear this sermon, as were also many of the inhabitants. The fact that those who shared in the frauds were either natives of the colony or had been resident in it for some time is best explained when we remember that its life had long been corrupted by this system and that permanent residents in the country were in a better position than were new-comers to share in the plunder.

Very little gold or silver was in circulation in Canada and business was carried on with the medium of paper money. A part of this was in the form of cards issued by the authority of the French Court. But, since the total amount of the card money was only one million *francs*, this was not enough to carry on the business of the country, and the *intendant* had supplemented it by a system of his own. As occasion arose he issued what were called ordinances. These were the equivalent of the modern banknotes and ranged in amount from one *franc* to a hundred *francs*. They were accepted everywhere for purchases by the government and they formed the chief currency of the colony. If a holder wished to have his ordinances redeemed, all he had to do was to present them in October at the government offices. In return he received drafts on the royal Treasury in France which were duly honoured. As long as the credit of France was good and it was certain that the drafts would be met, all went well. Until the autumn of 1759 the ordinances seem to have been accepted everywhere without much question.

But now the system was breaking down. In October 1759 France herself suspended payment for a time on no less than eleven descriptions of stock, and Horace Walpole says that on the list of bankrupts drawn up in all seriousness in England was the French king, under the name of 'Louis le Petit, of the city of Paris, peace broker, dealer, and chapman'

The drafts from Canada, due in this year, were not paid, and the government announced that none would be paid until the peace. This of itself would have discredited the ordinances. But there were other causes of unrest. For some years the French Court had protested against the excessive amount of the drafts of Bigot. Repeated charges of corruption had already been made against him, and an official, M. Querdisien-Trema.is, was now in Canada to inquire into Canadian finance. Matters had gone beyond the *intendant's* control. M. Querdisien-Tremais wrote to the minister on September 22, 1759, only a few days after the fall of Quebec. He says that he has found it difficult to get information. The greatest disorder exists. Every kind of officer from the highest to the lowest engages in trade, and the greed for gain is insatiable. Discipline in the army is relaxed and the common soldiers are given the greatest licence. (Manuscript in Canadian Archives).

Bigot was in the power of those who had aided him in rearing the stupendous fabric of fraud, and they now showed increased eagerness to lay hands on all they could get before the final collapse. From the fall of Quebec to that of Montreal the only thought was of brigandage. There was a torrent of corruption. When Bigot could no longer gratify his partners in dishonesty they began to abuse him. His generosity had made for him not friends but ingrates. To keep them quiet, the *intendant* was obliged to let them do what they liked, and he found their demands insatiable. In this autumn of 1759 new plunderers were sent to the interior posts to make what they could while yet there was time. Soon staggering demands came in from the posts—accounts with the proper amount multiplied by five or six.

Lévis, new to the supreme command, received invoices amounting to great sums for supplies for the king's service. He was in no position to verify them and he let them pass. He moved freely, too freely some of his friends thought, in the society that profited by fraud. His relations indeed with the wife of one of the chief swindlers were such as to cause scandal. The demands upon the Treasury became ever more excessive, the volume of outstanding ordinances was greatly increased, and it was more than doubtful whether the court could or would honour the drafts now to be made upon it to redeem the ordinances.

Bigot, who, after the fall of Quebec, made his headquarters at Montreal, was in a desperate position. It was October, the month when he must redeem the ordinances and issue the drafts on France for sums that would startle the court. With the British fleet in command of the river it was very doubtful whether any communication with France was possible. Early in October, using what was, in the circumstances, not an invalid excuse for haste, the *intendant* sent a crier through the streets of Montreal to announce that only three days would be allowed for presenting the ordinances at the government offices and securing drafts on France. Of course those who did not present them within that time must keep them for at least another year, and, with Quebec in the hands of the English, another year would probably see the entire ruin of the colony. The *intendant's* plan caused commotion.

Many of the ordinances were held outside of Montreal and it was impossible to present them during the limited time that had been named. After some days Bigot's house was assailed by those who had brought their paper money, only to find that the days allowed by him had expired. Vehement were the curses upon the *intendant*. His course meant ruin for nearly everyone and especially for those who held these ordinances as their only pay for supplies sold to the government. It was double robbery to have their goods taken at a low price and to be paid in money now rendered worthless.

But Bigot persisted; a precipice was before him, a wolf behind; if he failed to take up the ordinances in Canada the Canadians would be against him; but if he took them up by heavy drafts on France the court would be more alarmed than ever and might repudiate him entirely. His action in demanding the sudden presentation of the ordinances made worthless those that remained, and speculators were soon able to buy them at about one-fifth of their face value. A cynic might say, indeed, that this collapse hardly mattered, for the complete ruin of the colony was imminent in any case. The government's credit was gone. Since no one would take the paper money, Lévis, when he needed resources, was obliged to borrow what gold and silver his officers and men possessed. This left them in a pitiable plight. Some of the officers sold even their clothes to supply their wants.

In such a situation it is obvious that at Montreal in the winter of

1759-60 the Gallic gaiety was subjected to some strain. Vaudreuil was already there when Lévis arrived in person to make it the centre of his plans against Quebec. Reports reached the British that Montreal was facing its tasks cheerfully. Dim echoes of the gossip of the time reach us. Vaudreuil's personal conduct appears to have been immaculate; in regard to him and his devout wife scandal is silent. Lévis, on the other hand, was no better, and probably no worse, than the average courtier of his age. His favourite saying that 'one must be on good terms with everyone', shows that he could adjust himself to his surroundings. With his conspicuous graces of person, he made himself agreeable to the ladies of Montreal.

In spite of the shadows hanging over this society, it managed to amuse itself. The *intendant*, the officers, and the ladies all alike gambled with a passion and on a scale startling even to those familiar with gambling scenes in France. They danced: Montreal was as gay as Versailles. We hear sometimes of bitterly cold weather, but, since no opposing army was near to cut off access to the forests, Montreal was not in the same distressing straits for firewood as Quebec. Prices were, however, high. A cord of wood, which usually cost as little as six *livres*, was now sold for from eighty to a hundred *livres*. Provisions were so scarce that even persons who had money found it difficult to buy what they needed. When Lent drew near there was unconscious humour in the bishop's permission to omit the usual Lenten abstinence. He commanded instead prayers for a happy issue from adversity and for a speedy and enduring peace between the two crowns.

Perhaps to inspire his followers Lévis professed no misgivings about the future; he talked as if he had only to present himself before Quebec to ensure its falling into his hands. In words the French could hardly have been more certain had Quebec already fallen. Anyone expressing misgivings was denounced as 'English'. An amusing comment upon this gasconade was furnished when Montreal fell into a panic in March at reported traces in the adjacent forest of an English camp. The alarm was needless. What had been discovered was an old camp abandoned by the French. Sometimes Lévis spoke of a wild scheme, which Montcalm had also cherished, of leaving Canada to its fate and of leading his forces farther into the interior, past Lake Ontario and Lake Erie and down the Ohio and the Mississippi to Louisiana. This was, however, in his darker moments. What he really hoped for was to keep up the fight until, at an early date, as he expected, peace should be concluded. Meanwhile he faced his tasks cheerfully enough.

There were disagreements with the British over the effects which the French officers had left in Quebec, The British had agreed that these should be returned to their owners. Vaudreuil sent some schooners down to Quebec bearing his own *maître d'hôtel*, Bigot's valet, and other servants to recover and bring back the numerous trunks and packages. On the plea that these servants might be officers in disguise, who would take military notes, the British refused to allow them to go about freely in the town. The garrison sent to France had been allowed only one day to claim their belongings, and the British at first insisted that only this time could now be allowed for the later claimants. The effects must, they said, be collected in the morning and examined and sealed and shipped the same afternoon.

M. Bernier, the commissioner, was in despair. There were not fifteen carters in the whole town. 'One might as well try to seize the moon with one's teeth,' he said, as to do what was required. He had, lost his horse and had worn himself out going on foot from the General Hospital to the town. In the end the British relaxed the conditions somewhat. A crier went through the town to order those who had effects to embark to get them ready. A good many people had requested M. Bernier to claim their property for them. In some cases, these belongings had been moved to other places. It happened, too, that owners had given inadequate directions. 'I should have needed a thousand legs if I had done all that was asked of me,' Bernier says.

Two British officers accompanied him from eight o'clock in the morning until five in the evening. 'I did nothing but run from the Upper to the Lower Town with the two examiners, going from house to house.' He put his seal on not less than three hundred trunks and felt, he declares, like an excise officer. He admits that some of the trunks thus sealed contained merchandise on which their owners expected to make a profit of 300 or 400 *per cent*, when it was sold at Montreal and other points.

Vaudreuil was fussily busy during these last days of his rule. He must have kept occupied a small army of secretaries, for he wrote interminable letters and memoirs full of petty comments upon events from day to day, of boastful promises as to what he should still do to save the colony, and of efforts to prove to his correspondents his own competence. He was ignoble enough to attack in a scurrilous way the memory of the dead Montcalm. So jealous was he of his rival that he did not shrink from planning to examine his private papers—a proposal which Lévis, in whose custody they had been left, checked by a stern letter. Even after this Vaudreuil did not hold his hand. On October 30, 1759, he wrote a long letter to the minister piling up grave charges.

> From the moment of M. de Montcalm's coming to the colony until his death he did not cease to sacrifice everything to his boundless ambition.... He tolerated among the soldiers every kind of outrageous talk against the government and allied himself with the most disreputable persons.... Upon the people he or his regular troops laid a terrible yoke. He abused those who were honest, supported insubordination, and shut his eyes to the pillage which the soldiers carried on; he even allowed them to sell before his face the provisions and cattle which they had stolen from the *habitants*. I am in despair, *Monseigneur*, to be obliged to paint such a portrait of the dead Marquis de Montcalm, but it contains only the exact truth. I should have said nothing had I remembered only his personal hate to myself, but I am too deeply grieved by the fall of Quebec to conceal from you the cause which is generally recognised by the public.

At Montreal Lévis had taken up his residence in the house formerly occupied by Montcalm. The officers who surrounded him were not a happy family. Adversity had not brought them to sink minor differences. Vaudreuil reports to the minister on November 9 a case in which officers came to blows. There were keen jealousies. Vaudreuil's brother, M. Rigaud, who held the post of Governor of Montreal, was bitterly incensed because Lévis had been placed over him in authority. He declared that it had been done by Vaudreuil because Lévis, unlike himself, would shut his eyes to Cadet's frauds. This was a pretty family quarrel and, in the end, Rigaud refused any longer to remain under the same roof with Vaudreuil and sought quarters elsewhere. We hear echoes of spiteful talk about the liaisons of Lévis; he boasted that his family was related to the Virgin Mary, and he relied more upon that, it was said, than upon attention to his religious duties.

It was an old story that Bougainville's rapid advancement was attributed to the favour of Madame de Pompadour; and Vaudreuil's pompous ways and interminable flow of words come in for some guarded satire. Many of the officers were, like Vaudreuil, inveterate letter-writers, and their correspondence shows how keen were their discords. Few of them had any interest in or cared about Canada. To them the 'wretched colony 'as they often called it, meant nothing.

On the whole, however, these officers were brave men willing to do a soldier's duty wherever they were placed. Their letters are dignified and we have from them no real complaints. But promotion in France is what they were always aiming at. To secure it they prepared interminable petitions. One of the chief anxieties of Lévis himself was to secure not merely decorations as distinguished as those of Montcalm but something beyond this—the *cordon bleu*—and his keenest hopes at this time are, he says, not for a money reward but for this honour. Talk as he might, he had little real hope that the colony could be saved by anything but peace. He could only strive that he and the other officers should win glory even from disaster.

Upon the *intendant* fell the responsibility of provisioning the army in Canada, and he gave orders to Cadet for supplies which that clever person, now at war with Bigot, declared he could not possibly fill. It was at best a difficult task to feed the army and it would have been more difficult had all the troops been kept at Montreal. They were accordingly distributed to different points and a good many of them were quartered on the inhabitants. These were to be paid fifteen *livres* a month for each soldier whom they received. Cadet, while paying this price, drew from the government much larger sums than he paid and was thus able to reap a corrupt profit for his comfort in a time of adversity. Sometimes with pay, but also sometimes without it, the unfortunate inhabitants were obliged to furnish whatever they had that the army desired.

Lévis, who admits that he took nearly all their cattle, at the same time urged his men to treat them with gentleness. M. Querdisien-Tremais declares, however, that the French soldiers treated the Canadians with great brutality, devastating in the most deplorable way the fields in which their crops were ripening, robbing them of vegetables, poultry, and cattle, with a waste that was pitiable in view of the impending famine. The Chevalier Johnstone says that the Canadians were 'devoured by rapacious vultures', who fattened while their victims starved. 'The gentlemen and officers are very devils at taking the cattle of the inhabitants,' Bigot wrote. Plundering was not the less unwelcome to the *habitants* because it was done by nominal friends. When their cattle were carried off in the name of the king, the owners received so poor a price that the seizure amounted to confiscation.

On the other hand, when the people who received so little wished to buy, they found prices excessive; a pound of butter cost from twelve to fifteen *livres* (the *livre* being substantially the equivalent of the modern *franc*), a pound of mutton three *livres*, a hen twelve *livres*, a pair of woollen socks sixty *livres*, a pair of shoes thirty *livres*, and so on.

In time the Canadians must have learned, in some districts, at least, to conceal their cattle from the plunderers, for the British found an adequate supply in the country in the autumn of 1760. Murray says, indeed, that horse-flesh was served to the troops in Canada when cattle were not scarce, because the supposed famine would justify the charging to the king of great sums for provisions. At Quebec, compared with Montreal, provisions seemed abundant and cheap. Murray was quite willing that Lévis and his officers should be supplied with wines, coffee, sugar, and other luxuries from Quebec.

Matters went, however, far beyond this. Johnstone says that French officers at Montreal, 'whom one would have taken for merchants rather than for military', managed, during the winter, to carry on an extensive trade with the British at Quebec. These officers brought provisions to Montreal and sold them there at such prices as to make fortunes. Murray remarked that their conduct gave him a poor opinion of their characters. The French officer, Malartic, even declared that, in spite of famine at Montreal, provisions were sent down the river from that place in exchange for large quantities of wine and brandy. So heavy was this traffic that, while food remained dear, wine and spirits fell in Montreal to one-fourth of their former price. Careful soldiers saw danger to French interests in the visits of traders to Quebec. They would divulge the French plans, wrote Colonel Dumas, since the terror which General Murray inspired would make the best-intentioned tell everything. (Lévis MSS., xi.)

It is not easy to determine what were the wishes and hopes of the inhabitants of the country as a whole. Already there was a deep cleavage between the colony and the motherland, and probably the majority of the Canadians would have seen gladly the end of the war, even at the cost of conquest by the British. As soon as Quebec fell the unwillingness of the Canadians to serve longer became very marked. Nor need we wonder at their attitude. About four thousand of their houses had already been burned by the British enemy. Now a more savage enemy threatened them, for, as long as the war endured, every village had a haunting dread of the Indians. The French leaders had never checked with sufficient rigour these uneasy allies and now in the days of France's adversity they were likely to commit bloody excesses.

A few outrages did occur. The losses which they caused were, however, trifling compared with the exactions and privations which the Canadians had to bear at the hands of their own defenders. The Chevalier Johnstone wondered indeed at the brave endurance of the people who suffered their oppressors without a murmur Vaudreuil could still speak of their goodwill and zeal. Yet many served sullenly enough. Most of the Canadians had returned to their homes for the winter, and now when summoned for any special service they employed every device to escape the unwelcome duty. The frequent excuse was that they were ill. If these answers represent the truth, we must conclude that during the winter whole villages were stricken simultaneously with some malady.

'All the world is ill,' wrote Bigot of the Canadians. Famine was indeed a universal cause of illness. The Chevalier Johnstone describes the wan and starving appearance of villagers, whose supplies of food were carried off without payment to the owners. At the military centres it was noticeable that the Canadian soldiers were more subject to illness than the French, owing, no doubt, to inadequate nourishment and want of proper clothing to meet the severe weather. The civilian population suffered fearfully. Those who dwelt in Montreal were hardly better off than the farmers in the outlying villages. Commerce was ruined, and the daily auction sales of personal effects showed either the pressing need of money or the desire to get rid of encumbrances and to quit the distressful land as soon as possible.

In spite, however, of discouragements we still find in this demoralised community the supreme desire to retake Quebec. Everyone had a plan, including, as the Chevalier Johnstone says contemptuously, 'women, priests, and ignoramuses.' Long memoirs on the all-important subject were prepared and submitted to the leaders. Even the Bishop of Quebec joined in showing how Quebec could be taken. One memoir suggests that, since exact information of what is being done in Quebec is needed, the Jesuits should be asked to furnish spies.

> They are able to inspire the necessary zeal to risk even life in a task to which the motive of religion may properly be related.

All the plans agreed on the main points that a large force—not less than 8,000 men—would be required and that the army must take with it a supply of ladders to aid in scaling the walls of Quebec. The writers discuss such small details as that the ladders must be sharp at the bottom in order to hold in the frozen ground, and that they must have hooks at the top so as to rest firmly on the walls; their exact length is also to be prescribed. Some hoped that with the aid of spies Quebec could be surprised; others, with more reason, despaired of this and thought that the only way would be to attack it openly, to tire out the garrison by repeated alarms until they surrendered, or until, with the aid possibly of a snow-storm, the town could be carried by assault. Should this happen, the garrison must be put to the sword since there were not provisions to feed them; the French could then live on the supplies of the British and await in security the arrival of succour from France.

The engineer Pontleroy criticized adversely these plans for attack. He thought them certain to fail. After this failure would come famine more acute, the discouragement, perhaps the revolt, of the Canadians, and desertion among the regular troops. The British, on the other hand, with their confidence revived, would be more aggressive than ever. Moreover, if peace came, as he expected, during the winter, the generals would have vain regrets over the futile sacrifice of brave men. But even Pontleroy saw that the British must be kept in fear of imminent attack. Vaudreuil, full of bombastic courage, was reported to have said that if Lévis would not undertake the attack, he would himself execute it 'at the head of his brave Canadians'. Reckless self-confidence led some to offer a practical demonstration of the way to take Quebec.

In one district, where a supply of ladders had been secured, practice in escalade was made on a neighbouring church. People flocked from the parishes to see the gallant performance. But the would-be assailants of Quebec were too impetuous. They rushed headlong to the mock attack; some ladders slipped, others gave way, and broken heads, broken arms, and broken legs were numerous. Captain Knox writes:

> These accidents so effectually chilled the enterprising natives, who were the first promoters of this Quixotic undertaking, that they positively refused, upon the ladders being replaced, to make further trial, concluding it would be impracticable to recover the town by insult or *escalade*.

The French outposts near Quebec had some trying experiences. At Jacques Cartier the officer whom Lévis had placed in command. Colonel Dumas, a competent man, but timid about taking responsibility, spent the winter in deadly fear that Murray would advance and overwhelm him. The inhabitants of the neighbourhood circulated wild rumours which changed from day to day. When he called upon the people for service he found that everyone was ill. So uncertain was he of his own men that he lived in daily dread lest the British should bribe some of them to burn the fort. In March 1760, a fire did break out in the bakery, by accident it should seem, and it was little short of a miracle that the flames did not reach and explode the magazine.

When Dumas tried to muster the inhabitants for an attack on Quebec, only four came from a village which had been expected to furnish fifteen. To his comfort, however, the four brought with them provisions to last ten days. When he brought in the few cattle that his district furnished the poor creatures were so lean that it was hardly worthwhile to kill them for food. A remnant of the Indians of St. Francis, who, owing to absence with the French, had escaped the massacre by Rogers, deserted the south side of the river and, crossing to the north, reached Dumas at Jacques Cartier. When he rebuked them for having abandoned M. Hertel, who was trying to organise the French forces in their own district, they went off in a rage, killing some of the wretched inhabitants as they went. The incident is characteristic of the slight control which the French had maintained over their savage allies throughout the war. (Letters of Vaudreuil, Lévis, and Dumas, *Report on Canadian Archives*, 1905).

We have seen Bourlamaque's efforts at Isle aux Noix to check any English advance from the south. Far up on the St. Lawrence, near the head of the rapids, the French still held the mission station known as La Présentation. No longer did they rely, however, upon its weak defences. During the autumn and winter they built a new fort on an island a few miles below the place which Gage had feared to attack in the autumn of 1759. This fort was named Fort Lévis, in honour of that general. The officer in command at Fort Lévis found it almost impossible to get work done on the defences.

By the end of October, 140 men of his small force had deserted, and after this others continued to go off with impunity. Demoralisation was general. The workmen, ready to do everything but their proper tasks, spent the time in providing for their own comfort and amusement rather than in building the fort. Chimneys built with great labour, but without proper mortar or other material, came clattering down when a fire was built, and there was the imminent prospect that the barracks would be without heat during the severe winter.

Desandroüins, the engineer in charge, was so inconsolable at this disaster that, for a time, he would take no food and seemed likely to fall ill. A great need of the builders was sawn planks. A Jesuit at a neighbouring Indian settlement, St. Regis, said that if men and supplies of food were given him he would furnish the needed planks. When seven men were sent the Jesuit used their labour for his own purposes and sent them back empty-handed. Later he had the temerity to plead that twenty men were really necessary, but were not supplied. A French officer writes in disgust, (Lévis MSS., x.):

> We have always been the dupes of the Church, now we must be on our guard against her seductions.

In the end, owing to scarcity of provisions, Lévis was forced in January to withdraw two-thirds of the men whom he had sent to build the new fort.

In the end the French centred their hopes in two designs: they would attack Quebec while the frost was still in the ground and Murray could not throw up defences on the Plains of Abraham; and, once in Quebec, they would await the succour from France without which every plan must fail. Upon this aid from France all hopes centred. After the fall of Quebec Vaudreuil had sent Le Mercier, the chief of the Colonial Artillery, as an envoy to France. He succeeded in getting away in one of the French ships which were able to leave Canada after the departure of the British fleet. Twenty years earlier this man had gone to Canada as a private soldier. He was suspected of sharing Bigot's frauds; certainly he had secured both riches and promotion in Canada, and he was not likely to encourage adverse inquiries into a system by which he had greatly profited.

He must have carried with him a heavy packet of dispatches, for those that remain to us are voluminous. He took, of course, the apologia of Vaudreuil for what he had done. Both the governor and Lévis wrote that the prime need was food and that the sheer force of famine, more dangerous than the enemy, must compel them to surrender by May if help were not forthcoming. In any case the king would lose some of his subjects by starvation during the winter. The fleet for Canada should set out not later than in February, so that it might be waiting at the mouth of the St. Lawrence to ascend the river at the first moment possible after the breaking up of the ice. Ten thousand men, provisioned for two years, and a full equipment for aggressive war would be necessary to save the colony; but, with such aid, Lévis said he could retake Quebec. He now based his plans on the expectation that Le Mercier would succeed and that, at the proper time, the required help from France would be forthcoming.

France, however, showed no resolve to aid her perishing colony.

The nation was engaged in a titanic struggle in Europe not only against the genius of Frederick the Great, but also against the wise recklessness of Pitt. There was bitter irony in the remark of 'Junius', that England owed more to Pitt than she could ever repay, 'for to him we owe the greatest part of our national debt, and that I am sure we can never repay.' (Letter XI.)

In order to humble France Pitt spent money with appalling profusion; in 1760 alone he demanded votes for £16,000,000. Lord Anson, the first Lord of the Admiralty, is one of the ablest organisers in the whole history of the British Navy. To Pitt's impatience, however, he often seemed slow and, on one occasion, Pitt had threatened to impeach him if his action was not more rapid. With Pitt driving Anson something was certain to be done. The display of naval force in America was to be overwhelming. Commodore Lord Colville remained at Halifax during the winter with five ships of the line and four frigates. In the early spring these were to join in the St. Lawrence a squadron of equal strength under Commodore Swanton sailing from England, while, at the same time, Captain Byron was to take five warships to Louisbourg. Such vast outlay and energy France could not rival.

French policy was, moreover, becoming adverse to adventures over the sea. The disastrous defeats of 1759 in both Europe and America, together with impending defeat in India, may well have led France to conclude that she was fighting her foes on too extended a front. Powerful voices like that of Voltaire were raised for the abandonment of Canada. The colony, it was claimed, cost France large sums and took from her, to plant amid harsh conditions and in a severe climate, people whom she needed at home. Canada would be ever at the mercy of the enemy. England, with a large population in her colonies in America, could always seize Canada and exact from France sacrifices in Europe in order that she might get back her possessions in America.

It was said, moreover, that in the vast spaces of Canada republics, not monarchies, would ultimately be formed and these would prove a menace to the monarchy in France. On the other side, the devout urged that if France let Canada go the Protestant heresy would prevail everywhere in North America and many souls would be lost. Moreover, the English would take not only Canada; they would become undisputed masters of the sea; they would expel France from the chief nursery of her navy, the cod fisheries; they would drive her from the West Indies. And it was not merely France that they would check; they would seize the possessions of Spain and Portugal. In a word, if

France lost her footing in Canada the whole world would be handed over to the Anglo-Saxon, and America in particular to Republicanism and to heresy. ('*Est-il important de conserver le Canada?*'—Manuscript in Canadian Archives).

Such arguments, fervid and ingenious as they were, proved of little weight to secure effective help. At the ministry of war was the Duc de Belle-Isle, Marshal of France. Born in 1684, he was a veteran who had frequented the court and had served in the wars of Louis XIV. Though a man of ability and decision, he was now seventy-six years of age, weary of the tasks from which death was soon to call him, and ineffective compared with an adversary possessing the fiery energy of Pitt. A year earlier, in February 1759, Belle-Isle had written to Montcalm to show that France was on the horns of a dilemma which made help impossible. If she sent aid the British would either capture it *en route* or they would be incited by France's efforts to greater efforts of their own. So Montcalm was told to shift for himself.

Lévis now fared a little better. On February 9, 1760, Belle-Isle wrote to say that the king had been much touched by the death of Montcalm but that the cause of France was in good hands with Lévis in command. Rescue, in the shape of food, munitions of war, and men, would be sent so that Lévis should be in a position to dispute Canada foot by foot with the English.

The event proved, however, that France could do little or nothing which involved the power to cross the sea. From the first her policy in this war had been fatal to her best interests. Her reasons for taking so fatuous a course will probably always remain something of a mystery. At a time when, on the continent of Europe, she was menaced by no dangers, but when, across the sea, she was in vital danger of losing all her possessions, she had chosen so to embroil herself in a land war in Europe that she could not build up her navy.

Sometimes the weak and inefficient Louis XV, out of a mere love of secrecy, would himself carry on important negotiations without the knowledge of his ministers. Perhaps it is chiefly to this that we owe the inept policy of France. Austrian policy was at this time directed by an able minister, Kaunitz, and in some way he had lured France from her real interests. For generations France and Austria had been enemies. Suddenly, with nothing to gain by her course, France had abandoned her old alliances and had joined Austria in an attack on Prussia ruled by the greatest soldier of the age, Frederick the Great.

Austria had demanded ever new sacrifices from her ally, and France, facing eastward to help Austria, failed to meet the attacks of her one dangerous enemy, Britain. During this war Britain kept France in a state of alarm similar to that of an earlier age when the hardy Norsemen had perpetually threatened the same coasts. Over and over again the British landed in France and wrought havoc. At last the French were goaded to make one supreme effort. They would land a force in Essex, march on London, and dictate terms of peace before the British capital. It was this plan which had kept the Londoner uneasy during the summer of 1759. But his peace of mind was to return to him.

At Quiberon Bay, in November, Hawke shattered the power of the French fleet at the very moment when Saunders was arriving in England from the triumph of Quebec. It is true that even after Quiberon, in February 1760, the French privateer Thurot landed near Belfast in Ireland and made that city pay an indemnity. This was, however, merely a flash in the pan. After Quiberon France could do almost nothing on the sea.

It is thus clear that the hopes of Lévis for rescue by a fleet in the spring of 1760 were hardly, in any case, justified. They were rendered less likely of fulfilment by the character of Berryer, the Secretary of the Navy in France. French naval policy had long been indecisive in character. There were five secretaries between 1749 and 1759, each with a policy of his own. Under Machault (1754-7) the navy was directed with vigour and success. La Galissonnière defeated Byng in the Mediterranean in 1756 and, as a result, the French took Minorca. But Machault was so incautious as to say unflattering things about Madame de Pompadour and he was dismissed in 1757. In 1759 that lady was able to put one of her friends in charge of the navy. Berryer had been a Lieutenant of Police and knew nothing about naval matters.

The Chevalier de Mirabeau, vigorous in expression after the manner of his famous family, once declared in a rage that Berryer was the enemy of all that was honest and as black in soul as he was in skin. The words call up a physical as well as a moral image and are probably not too just. Certainly, however, Berryer was coarse, brutal, and incapable. Belle-Isle, competent even in his extreme old age to plan for the army, hoped to find Berryer an effective colleague in the navy. He supported his appointment but soon learned his mistake.

Berryer would take no advice and was too strong in favour at Court to be dismissed. His one idea of naval policy was to reduce expenditure. Since Britain, with her life dependent on sea power, would use her whole resources to maintain her fleet, France, said Berryer, could not rival her and need not try to keep up a navy. He sold to private shipping interests some of the naval stores in the arsenals. His taste for detail was such that we find him inquiring why twelve *sous* are charged a day for feeding cats to kill rats in the arsenal at Toulon. Since money would be saved he saw no reason, he said, why officials who had served even as long as thirty years should not be summarily dismissed without a pension. Though we are tempted to admire anyone who practised economy in these extravagant days at the French Court, the economy of Berryer was misplaced. He reduced expenditure on the navy with such effect that the navy almost ceased to exist. (Lacour-Gayet, *La Marine militaire de la France sous le règne de Louis XV*, Paris, 1902).

When, therefore, early in 1760, Berryer wrote to Lévis words of pious exhortation we know that Lévis had not much to expect that would be effective. The king, said Berryer, counted on the courage, zeal, and experience of Lévis, and was sure he would do his best. This was less encouraging than the positive promises now made by Belle-Isle. The words of Berryer were written six months before Lévis received them, but they show that he was justified in expecting adequate and prompt help. Yet, in reality, while Pitt was moving Heaven and earth to make sure that his next blow should be final, France did very little, and this little came too late.

Berryer was so indifferent to the real nature of the crisis that the scale of his preparations was ludicrously inadequate. We see to what depths France's naval power had fallen when we learn that she had no frigate of her own to send to Canada and that she was obliged to purchase one from a private owner. The frigate was the *Machault* (it had, at least, a good name), the private owner was Cadet, the high priest of corruption in Canada; and we may be reasonably certain that not the king but Cadet profited by the deal. Some legal obstacles were put in the way of securing the services of a crew for the frigate, and. there was interminable delay.

As late as on April 4, 1760, long after Pitt had the fleet for Canada at sea, the President of the Navy Board is pained to hear that the *Machault* with the unarmed ships that were to accompany her has not yet sailed. On April 25 he learns that the convoy had left Bordeaux some days earlier. Two English frigates encountered the *Machault*. In the end she escaped from them. But before she could arrive at her destination three powerful British squadrons were already in Canadian waters and were joyfully looking for the arrival of the French squadron as their prey.

CHAPTER 4

The Battle of Sainte Foy

Rumours of the plans cherished at Montreal reached Quebec, and Murray was nervously awaiting events. Throughout the winter occasional courtesies passed between the leaders. In November, when there was an exchange of prisoners with Amherst at New York, and the French who had been released brought European newspapers to Montreal, Lévis sent some of them to Murray with a courteous note. But each side watched the other closely. The St. Lawrence was later than usual in forming its covering of ice, and until the ice formed it was not easy to cross the wintry flood from Quebec to the south shore. The French took advantage of this to send a captain named St. Martin to occupy the Point of Levy, opposite Quebec. He harassed Murray when he could and drew from the surrounding country provisions for the use of the needy garrisons in the interior. He established his force in the church and in the priest's house at the Point of Levy.

Fancying himself secure, St. Martin indulged in bravado by sending defiant messages across the river to Murray. One day a peasant made his way across the icy current to bring the written message that if the British wished to have their hair dressed and would honour the French at the Point of Levy with their company a corps of experts would be at their service. This was the threat of scalping which the Indians, if not the French, in St. Martin's force were quite ready to carry out. Murray answered it in a way that St. Martin little expected. It was now the early days of February, and one morning the British found to their joy that the surface of the river was frozen. This soon made passage to the south shore easy and gave an opening to punish the gasconade of St. Martin.

On February 13, in the darkness of the early morning, Major Dalling led some light infantry across the river on the ice. His cannon cleared the way and then, with his men on snow-shoes, he advanced to storm the church. St. Martin kept up a vigorous fire. The British were aided by the deep snow which enabled them to fire down on their foes through the windows of the church. They drove the French out and came away, after leaving a small garrison at the Point of Levy. The French, still aggressive, thought they could dislodge this weak force from the church. On February 24 St. Martin returned to the attack. Then, to rescue the garrison, Murray led four regiments across the river on the ice. The French again retired, and considerable stores of bread, meat, flour, and cheese which they had collected at the Point of Levy remained in Murray's hands.

Some Canadians who had taken the oath of allegiance had joined St. Martin, and this led Murray to chastise the inhabitants living on the south side of the river. On February 26 Major Eliot of the 43rd Regiment, with 300 soldiers and a body of sailors, began at the west side of the River Etchemin and burnt every house between that point and the River Chaudière, a distance of four or five miles. The helpless Canadians were driven from their homes in the severe winter. Murray issued a proclamation, expressing regret at the necessity of the step, and again warning the Canadians of what they must expect if they violated their oath to do nothing against King George. He now constructed two block-houses near the Point of Levy, one to command a landing-place opposite Cape Diamond, the other a little inland. In the end the homeless people were allowed to take possession of the quarters the British had occupied in the church.

To the British soldier this was, indeed, strange warfare in which artillery was used on the ice and soldiers marched on snow-shoes. In such conditions the French were quite at home and the British were not. This did not keep the British from making enterprising attacks. Having driven the French from the Point of Levy, they decided to attack the most advanced French outpost west of Quebec. At break of day on March 20 Captain McDonald of Fraser's Highlanders, guided by a French deserter, led five hundred men from Old Lorette in a rapid foray on the entrenched French camp at the Calvaire, near St. Augustin, a few miles beyond Cap Rouge. It was protected by an abattis of felled trees about three hundred yards wide. Through this the British pushed, firing briskly, only to find, on reaching the works, that the defenders had fled in panic.

The officer in command, M. Herbin, must have gone off very hurriedly, for he left behind his watch, his hat and feather, and also the mistress whom he had with him. The British captured some eighty prisoners. That the French were well off for luxuries was proved by a cask of wine and a small trunk of liqueurs which formed part of M. Herbin's equipment, and proved welcome to the victors in the bitter weather. So severe was the cold on this expedition that nearly a hundred of the Highlanders were badly frost-bitten and their companions had to drag them back to Quebec on sleighs; it was these sons of the north who suffered specially from the cold.

At the Calvaire the British had burned mills, granaries, and houses, property belonging to the nuns of the Hôtel Dieu at Quebec, and Murray sent an officer to these ladies to say that they were justly punished, since they had been sending intelligence of British movements to the French. A few days after this fight at the Calvaire, Captain Hazen, the leader of the Rangers recruited in the American colonies, was attacked near Lorette by a large body of French sent out probably to avenge the defeat at the Calvaire. The Colonials were eager to show themselves as effective as the regulars from Europe who had won the success at the Calvaire, and fought with such spirit that they drove off their assailants with considerable loss.

These skirmishes were only preliminary to the renewed struggle for Canada of which Quebec was destined again to be the centre. The opposing forces really knew very little of each other's doings. Lévis, however, owing to the friendly offices of the Canadian peasantry, was kept better informed than Murray about his enemy. When April came the British knew that the long expected attack on Quebec was near. Murray was in a position of dangerous isolation with no news from the outside world and no prospect of help until May. At Christmastime, Lieutenant Butler, of the Rangers, had tried to get through from Quebec to New York. He was, however, closely followed by a body of Indians. Only a friendly fall of snow, which covered his tracks, enabled him to elude his pursuers and to return to Quebec.

A little later Captain Montresor was more successful. He left Quebec on the 26th of January with an escort of twelve Rangers. He went by the wilderness route along the Chaudière, a route made famous sixteen years later by Benedict Arnold's terrible march through its remote regions to attack Quebec. One of Montresor's men perished from the cold. Twelve days before he reached the first New England settlement his supply of provisions gave out, and his men survived only by eating the spare leather of their shoes and equipment. The hardships of this terrible journey show that it was a far cry indeed from Quebec to the nearest English colony. The leaders could not communicate with each other so as to make concerted action effective, and Murray had to depend on himself alone.

As the spring approached, a persistent rumour that Amherst had taken and burnt Chambly, near Montreal, and was likely to capture Montreal, led Murray to hope that he himself might soon advance up the river from Quebec to aid in the final conquest. In reality this rumour was false, like many others; Murray's real task was to cling to what he already held. His enemy was only waiting for the time when the breaking-up of the ice should make possible a descent upon Quebec with a force superior to any which the defenders could rally.

It thus happened that in April everyone, both at Quebec and at Montreal, was watching the river. Much depended, of course, upon the weather. Early in April there were violent winds which promised the speedy breaking-up of the ice. The winter had been unusually severe and the frozen surface which linked Quebec with the Point of Levy still seemed very solid. For a long time, it withstood wind and storm. By April 10, however, a change came. From a few miles above Quebec, at the mouth of the Chaudière River, all the way to Montreal the ice was now breaking; the swollen river was dotted with scattered floes. It seemed that the ice opposite Quebec must soon give way. Not, however, for nearly two weeks did it yield.

At length, on April 23, it broke up. The river was now open and great sheets of ice floated down past Quebec and up again with the tide. It was a wild scene, and the navigation of the angry waters was a task not lightly to be undertaken. But, though the danger to small boats was extreme, this stormy highway was the readiest means of approach to Quebec, and Murray knew that now at any moment he might be assailed by way of the river.

He was ignorant of the plans of his foes, and could only keep watch with all possible alertness. He armed even the English traders at Quebec and their servants, placing Lieutenant Grant, of the 58th, in command of the hundred men thus secured. In order to avoid the necessity of watching a foe within as well as without the walls, he thought it wise to expel the French inhabitants, and on April 21, while assuring them that their exile would not be long, he ordered them to leave the town within three days. Only the nuns were allowed to remain for the task of nursing the sick. To turn out helpless civilians in the raw April weather was a stern measure of war that caused, of course, great confusion and discontent.

Perhaps, however, it was not as cruel as it seemed, for famine and death might await civilians in a beleaguered town. The men bore their fate in becoming silence. The women, however, protested loudly that the terms of the capitulation, which guaranteed to them the use of their property, had been violated; they had often heard, they said, that the English were a faithless nation, and now they saw for themselves how true this was. Some added, what they probably knew to be false, that there was not the smallest danger of an attack by Lévis. Murray made the expulsion as lenient as possible. He allowed the people to carry away what property they could and to store their remaining movables at the monastery of the Récollets, in the custody of the friars and of two of the inhabitants. Since other calls on the energies of the army made it difficult still to bring wood from Ste Foy, he used as fuel the timber of some of the abandoned houses.

Murray, without a fleet, was helpless on the water, and he heard, therefore, with concern that the French frigates in the upper river would attack him as soon as the ice was gone. He prepared some floating batteries to protect the town on the side of the river. The *Racehorse* and the *Porcupine* had been drawn in to shore for the winter. When, on April 9, Murray gave orders to cut them out he found the ice round their hulks no less than fourteen feet thick. By the 17th the two ships were ready for service, and, as soon as the ice in the river gave way, they were anchored before Quebec.

At the same time Murray made ready a schooner to send down the river to meet the expected fleet under Lord Colville, who had wintered at Halifax. She carried pilots for his ships and was instructed to urge prompt help for Quebec. By April 20 she was ready, and soon, amid floes of ice and between banks still white with snow, she was speeding on her errand.

With the spring thaw the roads about Quebec became quagmires. To move artillery over them was a nearly impossible task. The difficulty, which Murray himself experienced, would be worse for an army marching on Quebec, and this made him the more certain that his real danger lay in an advance of Lévis by the river. There was a persistent report that Lévis would try to land his artillery at Cap Rouge, the bold cape at the west end of the great plateau on which Quebec stands. If Murray could protect the cape and the shore between Cap Rouge and Quebec, a distance of eight or nine miles, Lévis would be forced to disembark above Cap Rouge. He would have to march inland, cross the River of Cap Rouge some miles from the cape itself, and approach Quebec from the north by way of Lorette and Ste Foy.

It was important, therefore, to make sure of Cap Rouge, and Murray decided to entrench a force there. On April 18 he sent a detachment of light infantry to Cap Rouge and quartered them in the houses of the inhabitants. The ground was so hard frozen that the men could do almost nothing in the way of throwing up defences, and the post proved strong only in its natural position. Its occupation by Murray exercised, however, a decisive influence, as we shall see.

Lorette also Murray made strong, as it was a menaced position. On April 19 and 20 his men were busy dragging thither, over roads clogged with mud and half-melted snow, two heavy fieldpieces. Without horses it would have been killing work at any time, but it was specially so when almost every one of the men was weakened by scurvy. 'I was obliged', says Murray, 'to use them with the greatest tenderness.' After all, he found that Lorette was too remote to be safe, and he decided to abandon it. Accordingly, on the night of April 25, he issued an order that the Lorette garrison should retire and that all the bridges over the Cap Rouge River should be destroyed to impede the enemy's march.

The feeble troops had then the weary task of hauling the guns back across a marsh and up a steep hill to Ste Foy. Murray still hoped to retain his outpost at Ste Foy. He had no thought of remaining behind the walls of Quebec. Should it be attacked, he was assured by the engineers that a force could fight with more effect entrenched in front of the fortress than behind its crazy walls. On April 26 the engineers marked the lines on the Plains of Abraham where the British intended to face their foe.

The French descent upon Quebec so long talked of was now really imminent. Lévis could carry down his ammunition and supplies only by means of the river, and he was therefore obliged to wait until the ice should break up. To delay longer than this, would, he thought, be dangerous, for he ought to arrive at Quebec before a thaw should enable Murray to throw up entrenchments outside the walls. Lévis expected to surprise the English by rapid action, as Wolfe had surprised the French themselves. Though Amherst was in New York for the winter, Lévis knew that he would move at as early a date as possible. Quebec must, therefore, fall quickly, so that the French, with their expected reinforcements, could turn back to meet Amherst's advance.

Early in March preparations were going on busily at Montreal. Criers went through the streets summoning the merchants to turn in their supplies to the royal magazines. The Canadians were asked to send muskets, camp kettles, and clothing, in order to replenish the military stores. So scarce was ammunition that the people were ordered to bring what powder they had to the magazines, where they should be paid for it at the rate of three *livres* a pound. Under threat of the lash, Lévis ordered his men not to dispose of any of the supplies furnished by the king or of any part of their equipment, no matter how worn it might seem. Vaudreuil instructed the householders to keep constantly on hand provisions for six weeks for themselves and for the soldiers quartered in their houses. He declares that the inhabitants showed great willingness to aid his plans.

With bad ammunition, but little artillery, and a distressing scarcity of provisions, the French general had no easy task in equipping his army. To remedy the lack of bayonets he collected all the butcher's knives to be found and fitted them with handles that could be fastened to the muskets. Some of the officers were without swords. Coats, trousers, and warm underclothing were lacking in the stores. Lévis withdrew what artillery he dared to take from the posts at Isle aux Noix and St. Johns, but even then he had a pitiable equipment for battering down the walls of a fortress. He took for his cavalry all the horses in Montreal capable of service. The work went on cheerily. In spite of bad equipment his forces were eager for the fight. Colonel Dumas at Jacques Cartier wrote to Vaudreuil:

> Ah, how I long to be on the way to Quebec. I am anxious about the passage of the army at this point; the least thing may delay it here, and the worry this causes me is inexpressible; but still I flatter myself that, in such a case, you and the Chevalier de Lévis will do me the justice to believe that I have done my very best.

The army of Lévis was composed of varied elements. Conditions had not favoured good organisation. Many of the men, scattered for the winter in the villages and living in the houses of the French-Canadian farmers, had grown slack in the sense of discipline. Lévis had tried to place an officer at each centre to look after the men, but the control by such an officer must have been slight. The backbone of the army of Lévis consisted of the regulars from France. These *troupes de terre* were now tried veterans in Canadian warfare, for most of them had come out with Montcalm in 1756. There were eight battalions: La Reine, Languedoc, La Sarre, Béarn, Royal Roussillon Guienne, and two battalions of Berry.

Though numbers were now depleted, Lévis still had about five thousand of these regular troops in Canada, and of these three thousand were available for the attack on Quebec. There was another small force of regulars in Canada known as the *troupes de la marine*. The marine department performed the duties which, under the British system, would now pertain to the Colonial Office, and it recruited a small force for service in the colonies. It was expected that the men would become settlers when their term of service had expired. These colonial regulars, having served long in Canada, knew the country better than the French regulars. They were an efficient force, but they numbered rather less than a thousand. Lévis took them all with him on the expedition to Quebec. On the French ships which had wintered at the mouth of the Richelieu River were a few hundred sailors under the lead of a competent commander, Vauquelain. The ships were to accompany the expedition, and proved of great service; but they added nothing to the fighting forces on land.

The Canadian militia played a considerable part throughout the war, and still had some fighting zeal, in spite of the hard treatment of the Canadians by the French, which has been already described. Montcalm had said that, at most, 7,000 Canadians could be mustered. Their situation as a people was isolated. Unused to comparing themselves with others, they were apt to swagger and to boast that one Canadian was equal to three Englishmen. This gasconade had no justification in fact. The Canadians were, in some respects, bad soldiers. They were badly armed, because the discarded arms in the king's arsenals had been sent to Canada. They were badly drilled; even some of their best officers, among them Ramezay, the defender of Quebec, could not give the orders usual in the French Army. Their discipline was so bad that they freely went off to their homes without leave.

This practice exasperated Lévis, and he threatened to hang deserters of this kind. Vaudreuil, however, himself born in Canada, was always the protector and champion of the Canadians. He restrained Lévis and said that the effect of severity would be to lose what help the Canadians might give, for they could easily manage not to be found in their villages when wanted. In their own way the Canadians were not ineffective soldiers, if tactfully led and treated with firmness and justice. Bourlamaque, himself an admirable soldier, said that Canada possessed a greater number of naturally brave men than any other country. He added, however, that the Canadian was the enemy of constraint, and that he was better in guerrilla warfare than in regular operations and pitched battles.

Lévis mustered in his force a few hundred Indians. During the war both sides employed these allies, but it is doubtful whether they were of much use. They may have rendered some service as scouts, but the reports they brought in were often vague and exaggerated. Scouting work requires a hard critical faculty, the power not merely to observe trifles, but to judge accurately their meaning. The Indian, the prey of childish superstition and alarms, gave heed to every wild rumour. What he loved best was the ignoble warfare now known as sniping. He prowled about the outskirts of Quebec, for instance, and killed and scalped many an incautious wayfarer. He was always an uncertain ally. Lurking in his mind was the sense that North America belonged to him and not to either of the intruding European races, and he was suspicious of both of them. The only motive certain to hold him in obedience was fear. As the French cause declined, this motive was wanting in relation to them, but it operated with increasing force in relation to the British as their superiority over their enemy became more manifest. From Amherst the Indians received curt, sharp words of command when they seemed restless, and stern punishment when they failed to obey. Though they grumbled and threatened, they were awed and they submitted.

Vaudreuil, on the other hand, had always seemed more afraid of the Indians than they were of him. He inherited from his father, who had been Governor of Canada in the early days when the Indians were many and the white men few, the belief that these allies were indispensable and must be allowed to follow their own customs. 'Your taste is French, mine is Indian; this is good food for me,' said an Indian to a French priest, who rebuked a party of savages sitting about a fire roasting on sticks the flesh of an Englishman. This was Vaudreuil's point of view; such practices were regrettable, but it was the way of the savages, and what could one do? An eyewitness says:

> He let them (the Indians) do what they liked, one saw them running about in Montreal, knife in hand, threatening and often insulting those they met. When complaints were made the governor said nothing. Indeed, after the incident, instead of reproaching and punishing the Indians, he loaded them with presents, believing that in this way their cruelty would be softened.—*Mémoires sur le Canada,* 1749-60.

Unhappily their licence tended rather to grow with indulgence. Though they were now but a weak factor in the French army they caused incessant anxiety, for they were ready to commit barbarous outrages on friend and foe alike.

Lévis drew up on April 17 the lists of troops for his expedition. (Lévis MSS., Journal of Lévis). In round numbers he had 3,600 regulars, including those of the colonial service, 2,800 Canadians, and 300 Indians. His fighting force thus numbered rather less than 7,000. 350 non-combatants were to accompany the expedition. Of these most were personal servants, and among them were 33 negroes. Only 16 surgeons were available. The numbers stated by Lévis include apparently the troops that he expected to take from the garrisons between Montreal and Quebec. It was likely that more Indians would join him, especially if he had an early success. He also counted upon help from the Canadians who lived in the district of Quebec.

This was under Murray's control and the inhabitants had declared on oath that they would take no part in hostile operations against the British. It is true that Vaudreuil issued a pontifical pronouncement releasing them from their oath, but this Murray declared was in violation of the law of nations. The unhappy people were certainly on the horns of a dilemma. On April 20, 1760, Lévis ordered a certain Captain Nadeau in the Quebec district to join him with his militia on pain of death. At a later time, Murray hanged this captain because he obeyed the order. As a rule Lévis required from those who had taken the oath only the service of helping to bring up supplies.

Vaudreuil sent his secretary to make a tour of the parishes and to warn the militia to be ready. He issued special letters to the captains of militia in the Quebec district, reminding them of the cruel and unjust treatment which they had received from Murray.

> You know too well by experience the aversion of the English for everything Canadian. You have had the saddest proof of the rigour of their government..... Now you are approaching the moment of triumph over this enemy. He must succumb to the efforts of our army.

A condition of success in war is to hate the enemy, and the Canadian pulpits were to be tuned so as to arouse this hate; Vaudreuil ordered the *curés* to tell the Canadians that they were fighting for their religion and the salvation of their country; upon the issue depended the question whether they should be free men or slaves in bondage to the hard and exacting English. He added that powerful aid was certain to come from France to make deliverance sure. In the certainty of this aid Vaudreuil himself believed. He sent pilots to points on the river below Quebec that they might aid the ascent of the expected fleet, and he issued elaborate instructions for the prompt forwarding overland of dispatches which it might bring. He still showed a naive belief in the zeal of the French Court and was apparently as eagerly expectant as a child.

On the 10th of March all the officers were ordered to join their regiments, and Lévis gave warning that the army might move at any time. The rendezvous was to be Pointe aux Trembles, a little farther down the river than the French fortified position at Jacques Cartier, and the various regiments were to make their way to this place. To do so by land in the spring-time over the roads sodden with melted snow would be a slow task; by water the advance would be rapid when the ice had once broken up. Bourlamaque, with La Pause, a capable and painstaking officer, was to go down the river in advance of the main army to make needed preparations. Bougainville was sent to command at Isle aux Noix, a danger-point which required a strong man. He disliked the service, for he would have preferred to be in the thick of the fight before Quebec. He wrote to Lévis:

> *Ah, mon général,* you have not willed that I should be with you. It is to me a mortal grief.

He had with him the competent engineer Lotbinière.

One great question remained: Who should lead the expedition? For a time Vaudreuil, though he was without real military experience, seems to have had the thought of commanding in person, and in April, when a start was almost momentarily expected, it was still uncertain whether he would go. Lévis, of course, wished himself to command. Gossip was busy and the ladies were on the side of the gallant *chevalier*. He, they said, was sure to succeed. In the end, certainly to the relief of everyone, Vaudreuil named Lévis to the supreme command. He announced:

> I have assembled an army for the siege of Quebec, and I have put the Chevalier de Lévis, major-general, in command of the expedition with authority the same as if I myself were in person at the head of the army.
> Nothing can equal the ardour of the troops, of the Canadians, and of the different Indian tribes, whom I have assigned to this expedition.

Lévis was instructed to grant easy terms to Quebec. The English were to be well treated if they would only yield.

When all were eager to start, the ice, as Malartic says, 'did not respond to their desires'; the river was still held in its frozen fetters. By April 4, however, there were signs that the ice was breaking, and then the excitement and expectancy were great. The army was to be carried in some four hundred open boats. The two French frigates, the *Atalante* and the *Pomone*, which had remained at the mouth of. the Richelieu River during the winter, were to accompany the expedition. There were ten or twelve transports laden with artillery, with supplies of ammunition and provisions, and with quantities of fascines to assist in the task of throwing up entrenchments before Quebec. To get ready the ships it was necessary to hew them out of the ice, still very thick.

On the 16th of April the ice began to break up and soon there was an open channel in the middle of the river at Montreal. To this the small boats were dragged over the ice. The embarking of stores, horses, and men, in these conditions, was dangerous work, for the ice was rotting and furnished at best an insecure footing. There were accidents, and Montegrou, a guerrilla leader, was drowned. But the affair was on the whole ably managed and speaks well for the competence of the French officers.

By the 20th of April the last man was embarked. Then the numerous flotilla, with the frigates and the transports under sail, and the hundreds of small boats propelled, for the most part, by oars, was on its way to attack Murray. Heavy banks of ice still lined the shores and made navigation and landing difficult and dangerous. The cold spring winds must have chilled the men to the bone, for they were not only ill-fed but also in many cases ill-clad. At night the boats were dragged, with great labour, over the ice to the shore, and the men rested as best they could in the cottages of the inhabitants.

Some part of the army, probably the companies quartered in places not far distant from the rendezvous, marched to this point by land over terrible roads. Each soldier carried with him provisions for eight days, and elaborate instructions had been given to those in the boats that this precious supply should be stored in a dry place. Cleanliness, too, was not forgotten. Each man might have half a pound of soap if he could pay for it. Lévis had warned the officers that when a force thus equipped set out officers and men should have the same rations. All must share alike on what was recognised as a desperate venture.

The shivering men in the boats, the weary men marching heavily by land, were blind and dumb creatures of a relentless fate. The French soldier cared nothing for Canada and the Canadian soldier by this time cared little for France. Yet, we are told, not a word of complaint was heard; the victims of war usually make their deep sacrifices willingly. Vaudreuil, Bigot, Bishop Pontbriand, and others remained at Montreal, to watch and wait and some of them to pray. the governor wrote to Lévis:

> Madame de Vaudreuil is continually in prayer and nothing can equal her solicitude until we have news. I cannot tell you how much you are in my mind.... *Madame* neither thinks nor speaks of anyone but you; accept from her a thousand and again a thousand tender things;.... in her ceaseless prayers she is thinking only of you.

At another time she is with the bishop joining her prayers to his. In the churches too, by order of the bishop, prayers were offered for the success of the expedition. (*Mandements des Évêques de Québec, ii.*)

For some time, all communications with Quebec had been cut off, since a cardinal part of the plan was that the place should be surprised. To prevent a threatening movement of the English by way of Lake Champlain it was necessary that the secret should also be kept on the frontier guarded by Bougainville, and elaborate precautions to effect this were taken. The efforts at secrecy had a measure of success. Direct information of what the French were doing did not reach Murray until the foe was almost upon him.

The army arrived at Pointe aux Trembles on April 25. Landing from the boats proved difficult. Only a channel in the centre of the river was open, and the ice, now rotted by the spring sun, was in places piled high, one floe upon another. The great highway by land from Montreal led straight through Pointe aux Trembles to the gates of Quebec over the high promontory at Cap Rouge.

If this point was undefended, Lévis might reach the Plains of Abraham by a rapid night march. At the same time a part of his force could drop down the river in boats, land near Sillery, as Wolfe had done, and climb to the Heights. Lévis expected to cut off the outposts of Murray at Ste Foy and Lorette, and to surprise and take Quebec by a sudden attack. Murray knew that a force was gathering at Pointe aux Trembles, but he could learn few details. He was, however, so on his guard that the scouts of Lévis reported discouraging news. There was a strong guard at Cap Rouge so that advance by the direct road was impossible.

Moreover, the heights between Cap Rouge and Quebec seemed well defended. The news made inevitable a change in the plans of Lévis, and he paused for a day at Pointe aux Trembles to mature another design. This was to land at St. Augustin, a little above Cap Rouge, and march rapidly inland. He could then cross the Cap Rouge River a few miles above its mouth and reach the road which led from Lorette up to Ste Foy, five miles from the city on the north side of the great plateau of Quebec. From Ste Foy to Quebec was an easy march and he might still be able to surprise Murray and cut off the outpost at Cap Rouge.

The 26th of April was a raw day with a north-east wind. At eight o'clock in the morning the army embarked at Pointe aux Trembles, and at ten it was at St. Augustin. Once more the men dragged the boats over the ice to the shore and also disembarked three cannon to be hauled, with incredible labour, for many miles, up steep hills and over roads deep with melting snow and mire. Lévis sent Bourlamaque in advance of the main army with some Indians and grenadiers to clear the way, to reconstruct the bridges across the Cap Rouge River which Murray had destroyed, and to advance by Old Lorette to a point as near Quebec as was consistent with safety. When Bourlamaque reached Old Lorette he found that the English had abandoned that place.

Between it and Ste Foy stretched a marshy plain called La Suette, across which was a road of wooden logs, the 'corduroy' road so familiar in pioneer days in Canada. Had the British torn up this road it would at least have retarded the advance of the French; but the road had been left intact. The British, still ignorant apparently of the approach of the enemy, did nothing to harass Bourlamaque as he approached Ste Foy. He promptly sent his Indians to occupy the end of the road near that place, and on the night of the 26th the advance guard of the French army lay in some houses so near Ste Foy that there was only a curtain of forest between them and that outpost. It looked as if their army could easily get in between Quebec and Cap Rouge.

But Nature did not favour France. The worn army, toiling slowly after Bourlamaque's scouting party, was overtaken by a terrific tempest with thunder, lightning, wind, and rain, more violent than anything seen in the country for years. The storm helped, in a singular way, to warn the British at Quebec. With the wind fierce and with the river full of great floes of ice, the small boats carrying the French troops were in imminent danger. At St. Augustin great floes of ice crushed and sank one of the boats laden with artillery. Some of the artillerymen were drowned, but one, after struggling for some time in the icy water, managed with great difficulty to climb out half dead upon a piece of ice large enough to support him. It drifted rapidly down with the tide past Quebec towards the Island of Orleans, bearing its human burden, and, on the turn of the tide, floated back again up the river. Though frozen almost into unconsciousness, the man still groaned loudly.

Knox tells us that shortly after midnight on the morning of the 27th the watch on board the *Racehorse*, one of the two British ships anchored before Quebec, with his senses alert for the slightest sound, heard the groans of the artilleryman. He raised an alarm, a boat was lowered, and the man was found and taken to shore. The British made every effort to revive him and so far succeeded that he recovered consciousness. Though in a half-dazed condition and astonished to find himself among the British, he was able to tell them who he was—one of a force of, as he thought, 12,000 or 15,000 men, only a few leagues from Quebec and now advancing by land to attack it. At first the British would not believe that Lévis was so near. The man was carried in a hammock up the steep ascent from the Lower to the Upper Town and about three o'clock in the morning was brought to Murray. The alarmed general credited the tale. He now realised that a powerful French army was almost at his door. In addition, as the man said, Lévis was confident that a fleet and an army from France were near and would soon join in the attack on Quebec.

The news aroused Murray to a new alertness. The great danger was to his outposts. The guard at Lorette had already been withdrawn, and he ordered the one at Cap Rouge to retire. He himself prepared to march out to Ste Foy with a considerable force. It was not safe even to hold the post on the south side of the river at the Point of Levy, and he sent orders to burn the block-houses there. This work was done so promptly that, with the provisions destroyed, the guns spiked, and the block-houses on fire, the garrison crossed to Quebec a few hours after the news of the advance of Lévis reached Murray. Quietly and almost without loss he had now concentrated in or near Quebec all his forces. The Chevalier Johnstone says:

What a remarkable and visible instance of fortune fighting for the English, had it not been for this unaccountable accident to the artilleryman, to all appearance M. de Lévis would have captured all the English advanced posts which were said to amount to fifteen hundred men.

※※※※※※

The truth of the story of the dying artilleryman has been doubted (Kingsford, *History of Canada, iv.*), but Knox and Fraser, officers in Quebec, tell the story, and Murray mentions that he was aroused at three o'clock in the morning. On the French side the story is also told by the Chevalier Johnstone, by Lévis, by Malartic, by Bigot, by a nun of the General Hospital, and in the anonymous *Relation de l'Expedition de Québec* (Lévis MSS., xi.). It is hardly to be doubted that the first alarm reached Quebec in the general sense indicated.

※※※※※※

Meanwhile Lévis was marching on Ste Foy with his main army. As we have seen, he had landed at St. Augustin a little before noon on the morning of the 26th. There he had rested and fed his men and at three in the afternoon he had set out on his march. Bourlamaque sent back word that he had made ready two bridges across the Cap Rouge River. At five the advancing column was overtaken by the frightful storm of wind and rain, thunder and lightning, which helped to give Murray warning. Some of the French reached Lorette before dark and quartered themselves in the houses of the inhabitants. But the greater part were overtaken by night and marched in the darkness, knee-deep in snow and mud, with a tempest raging about them, and soaked to the skin by a cold rain. Lévis says:

> It was a most frightful night, the storm and the cold were alike terrible, and the army suffered greatly. . . , Since the bridges were broken down the men had to wade in the water. It was so dark that the workmen could do but little in the way of repairs. Had it not been for the flashes of lightning we should have been forced by the darkness to halt.

The men marched in single file and not until far into the night did they reach Lorette. Before the day broke the force of Lévis was scattered in the adjoining houses of the inhabitants to get dry and warm and to prepare their arms for the coming struggle. Lévis himself had gone across the marshy La Suette to join Bourlamaque and to gauge the prospects of seizing Ste Foy and of cutting off the British outpost at Cap Rouge.

On the morning of April 27 cold rain was still falling. The terrible weather and the broken bridges had delayed the bringing up of the three cannon. Lévis waited, since he wished to use them for the attack on the fortified church at Ste Foy. It was now clear that Murray had been aroused and that the delay caused by the tempest had ruined any chance of taking Quebec by surprise. Not until ten o'clock in the morning was the main body of the French Army ready to leave Lorette. In heavy rain and under a dark and threatening sky the army advanced in single column along the narrow road across the marsh. The officers marched on foot with their men, and in places the water was up to their knees. Progress was slow, but by noon they had passed the trees which lined their route and were in sight of the church at Ste Foy.

The day was Sunday, but there was no mass at Ste Foy; not devout Catholics engaged in their worship, but British soldiers busy with grim war filled the church. It crowned the height known as the Côte d'Abraham, which extends to Quebec from the Cap Rouge River. The British had built a block-house at the point where the road reaches the top of the hill and had turned the church itself into a fortress. It was admirably situated for this purpose, for it commanded the single road by which Quebec could be reached along the edge of the height. As the column of wet and weary men appeared in the open near the top of the hill, the British opened fire upon them with their cannon and did some execution.

Once at the top, the French force deployed among the trees at their right, where they could watch in safety the operations of the foe. To bring up the three French cannon along the road, in face of the British fire, was impossible, and Lévis hastily decided to wait, if necessary, for the cover of night. Then he would turn the English left, get in between Ste Foy and Quebec, and cut off the garrison in this outpost if it had not already retired.

He was not obliged to wait so long. From the first, Murray understood the danger at Ste Foy, and he decided to withdraw this outpost too. Early in the morning of the 27th, in pelting rain, he drew up his force in Quebec and, taking those most fit for service, passed out through the St. John Gate for the march of five miles to Ste Foy. The regiments which remained in Quebec stood ready to advance in his support should this prove necessary. Murray was prepared to fight his foe wherever he should meet him. He found that Bourlamaque held already the head of the road leading across the marsh and, with something like dismay, he watched the French working round to his left through the trees.

On this morning of surprises, he had a further cause of disquiet. There had been a persistent rumour, and the dying artilleryman had confirmed it, that French ships had been seen coming up the river. It was even said that they were already at the *Traverse*, the lower end of the Island of Orleans, and Murray feared that, at any moment he might be attacked by water as well as by land. He was thus anxious to bring on an action at once. Lévis was, however, too wary to attack at a disadvantage. He sent to Murray a message that he would not fight that day, but that, on the next day, he should be ready for the English as early as they liked.

In view of the possible arrival of the French ships and of the danger lest he should be outflanked on his left, Murray decided to retire. At two o'clock in the afternoon the British at Ste Foy startled the French assailants watching them from the cover of the forest. There was a flash and a roar and then the French saw that the roof of the church had been blown off. Since the roads were very heavy and Murray besides had no wagons, he was unable to take away the provisions and ammunition stored in the church. He disabled two eighteen-pounders, which he left behind, but withdrew the rest of his artillery and, having set fire to the building, marched out. The rain which soaked his men to the skin helped to put out the fire. The French, agreeably surprised at Murray's retreat, attempted to harass his march. Lévis pushed forward his mounted men and grenadiers. They shouted at and fired upon the retiring British, but with little effect, for, in the march to Quebec, Murray's only casualties were the slight wounding of two men.

That night the French Army, thoroughly worn out by the wet and toilsome marches of the previous two days, slept in comparative comfort in the houses which stretched from Ste Foy towards Quebec. The British still held Dumont's mill, about a mile and a half from the walls of Quebec, but this was now their farthest outpost. After the fatigues of a long and miserable day, Murray gave his men a little added comfort by serving out an extra gill of rum. In order to dry their clothing, they tore down and burnt some old houses at St. Roch. Each army was doing what it could to fit itself for the morrow.

In spite of the challenge to Murray, Lévis did not expect that there would be a pitched battle on the next day. He had forced the British to withdraw into Quebec and he thought that they would stay there until attacked. He was now situated almost exactly as Wolfe himself had been situated a few months before. There was no barrier between him and the walls of Quebec. His boats, with the artillery and provisions brought from Montreal, were now free to use the landing which Wolfe had used at the Anse au Foulon. He was fortunate in having horses as well as men to do the work of dragging supplies to the heights which Wolfe had climbed. There he could entrench himself and either await the arrival of a French fleet or assault the feeble walls of Quebec at his discretion. He expected to spend the 28th in bringing up his forces and in giving his men the food and the rest which they sorely needed. He had promptly ordered the Canadian militia in the district of Quebec to join him and it would take a day at least for them to come in. On the 29th he would attack Quebec.

His enemy, however, did not wait upon his plans. Early on the morning of the 28th Lévis was abroad with Bourlamaque, riding over the ground which he intended to occupy. He found that the British had thought better of trying to hold even Dumont's mill, and that they had withdrawn from that outpost during the night. At break of day the mill was occupied by five companies of French grenadiers, and it gave Lévis an excellent rallying point on his extreme left. Far away to his right, near the edge of the ascent up which Wolfe's force had climbed so laboriously on the memorable September night of the previous autumn, were two redoubts.

These also the British had abandoned, and in the grey of the early morning Lévis sent a few dismounted men to occupy them. The forest of Sillery stretched almost from the Anse au Foulon across to the Ste Foy Road, so that the French could bring up their forces from Ste Foy and form them under the cover of the trees; these trees would also prove an excellent protection should the French be obliged to retreat. The undulating plain stretching across to the walls of Quebec was dotted with a few bushes left uncut by the British Army which had lain there for two weeks in the previous September.

While the trained eye of Lévis was surveying the chief features of the position, he saw, to his amazement, as he looked across to Quebec, less than two miles distant, that Murray's columns, instead of doing what the French had expected, and waiting behind the walls, were marching out with the obvious intention of meeting him in the open. He was all unprepared for such an attack. His next in command, Bourlamaque, was, it is true, well placed, with his grenadiers holding Dumont's mill on the extreme left. But the great mass of the French troops was coming up only leisurely and the English might be upon them before they had formed their line. Lévis rode back quickly to hasten the preparations and to give directions for meeting the new situation.

In Quebec the night had been full of activity and excitement. Should Murray await attack from Lévis? Seven months earlier, when Montcalm had realised that the British were about to attack Quebec from the Plains of Abraham, he had hurried up from Beauport to meet them outside the gates and had not relied upon the weak defences. Murray had always intended, as we have seen, to adopt a similar course, but he had hoped that the arrival of Lévis might be delayed until, with the snow gone and the frost out of the ground, he could entrench himself outside the walls. The line he had chosen was on the Heights of Abraham, at a point known as the Buttes à Neveu, about eight hundred yards from the walls.

These Heights commanded the walls. An enemy who occupied them might quickly batter down the defences of Quebec. On the other hand, a defender holding the Buttes à Neveu could prevent a nearer approach to Quebec. But now Lévis had arrived before Murray could fortify the Heights, and the problem for the British was whether to go out and still try to entrench themselves or to stay in Quebec behind their walls. Disease had sorely crippled Murray's force. It is not easy to make out the exact numbers, but nearly one thousand men had died of scurvy and two thousand three hundred were unfit for duty. Murray, with hardly more than three thousand men ready for action, believed himself greatly outnumbered by the French. Quartermaster-Sergeant Johnson declares that Lévis had not less than twenty-five thousand men—an absurd exaggeration—but even Murray himself thought that the disproportion was as four to one.

No wonder therefore that some thought he should not take the risk of meeting the enemy in the open. Murray, however, feared what Montcalm had feared, that he might be caught between an army on the one side and a fleet on the other, and he did not now change the opinion, formed months earlier, that it would be better to fight behind entrenchments on the Heights of Abraham than behind the walls of Quebec. He had unbounded confidence in his men; they had beaten the French often, he said. Above all, he wished to emulate Wolfe, and, like that hero, to win undying glory. Even the French understood that he had a passionate desire to become the final conqueror of Canada without help from other generals.

The Hon. Lieut-General James Murray

Accordingly, Murray now resolved to march out in the early morning, to take with him a large supply of entrenching tools, to fight the French if they would fight, but, in any case, to throw up entrenchments and make impossible the enemy's nearer approach to Quebec. With the ground still frozen and with, in some places, but a scanty soil covering the surface of the hard rock, entrenchments would be nearly impossible, and it was assuredly a difficult task that Murray set for his men. Johnson says that his general was too full of 'mad enthusiastic zeal'. None the less, the men were as eager as their leader to go out to meet the enemy.

In the dark of the early morning of April 28 the force began to muster in Quebec, and shortly after daybreak the army was ready to march. Each man carried, in addition to his weapons, a pick-axe or a spade. The array was sorry enough. Soldiers who had long been crippled in the hospital now threw aside their crutches and begged for a place in the ranks. One-third of Murray's army was composed of men really unfit for duty. Johnson says:

> Any man who was the least acquainted with the duty we were going on would have shuddered at the sight . . . such a poor pitiful handful of half-starved scorbutic skeletons; . . . but they went out . . . determined to a man to conquer or die.

Some of those who were not allowed to fall in dragged themselves after the advancing regiments and took their places when the army halted and the line of battle was formed. There were 3,866 men in Murray's whole force.

Murray's army marched out at half-past six in two columns; one by the St. John gate along the Ste Foy road, the other by the St. Louis gate along the road to Sillery. The rain of the previous day had ceased and the spring air was mild and pleasant. On the slopes exposed to the sun the brown earth was bare of snow, but there were still heavy drifts and these made passage difficult. The water lay deep in the hollows, for the frozen ground prevented proper drainage. Knowing that the French could as yet bring up few, if any, cannon, Murray trusted much to his artillery and took with him twenty field-pieces and two howitzers. Only a few horses were to be found in Quebec. In consequence, the cannon were hauled by men, themselves weak and sickly. When most needed, their strength was to prove unequal to the task of bringing up ammunition and of dragging heavy cannon through marshy ground cumbered with drifts of snow.

At seven o'clock Bourlamaque, looking out from the extreme left of the French position, saw that Murray's force had already covered the short distance to the Buttes à Neveu and was drawing up in line at that point in an advantageous position. To him, as to Lévis, Murray's advance was a complete surprise. Bourlamaque wrote:

> No one believed that the enemy would dare to advance, and the army was resting. . . . We were all worn out and wet. We had no thought of moving forward until daybreak on the next morning when we should have boats at the Anse au Foulon to support our advance guard on the right.—Bourlamaque to Bougainville, May 3, 1760; Kerallain.

It thus happened that Murray's march out of Quebec, rash as to some it appeared, might easily have proved disastrous to the French. To make his scanty force seem the more formidable he drew it up, as Wolfe had done, in a line only two deep. His artillery was soon sending bombs against the French, and, for a time at least, this caused dismay and something like confusion. Bourlamaque sent forward support for the advance guard in Dumont's mill and he hastily drew up three brigades in line. Meanwhile Lévis was trying to hurry forward the other brigades. This seemed to Murray to be his opportunity. A critical officer declares that his leader's passion for glory now got the better of his reason. He had intended to entrench his force on the Buttes a Neveu and await attack; now, however, he saw a chance to take the French unprepared, and he jumped at it with his usual impulsiveness, asking no advice from any one.

It is not clear that, by his advance, he could have struck a vital blow, for, at best, he could only have driven the French back to the edge of the wood. Knox says:

> Upon coming to our ground, we descried the enemy's van on the eminences of the woods of Sillery, and the bulk of their army to the right marching along the road of Ste Foy, inclining, as they advanced, in order to conceal themselves. Upon this discovery, and our line being already formed, the troops were ordered to throw down their entrenching tools and march forward, this being deemed the decisive moment to attack them, in hopes of reaping every advantage that could be expected over an army not yet thoroughly arranged. . . . Our forces advanced with great alacrity. . . . Our fieldpieces were exceedingly well served, and did amazing execution.

Murray would have been well advised had he stayed where he was. There he could make his position secure, and batter the advancing foe with his artillery, while keeping open a safe retreat to the town if necessary. But he pushed forward, and for the moment with apparent success. If we may credit Bourlamaque, Lévis was stricken with something like panic at this movement. Believing that his troops would not have time to form to meet Murray's attack, he gave orders to retire from Dumont's mill to a point less advanced, the house known as La Fontaine. As Bourlamaque himself rode forward to carry out this order, the British light infantry advanced upon the mill and poured in a fire so deadly that in drawing off the grenadiers Bourlamaque had his horse, or rather Bougainville's, for he had borrowed it from that friend, killed under him and was wounded by a bullet in the calf of the leg. The British occupied the mill and drove back the grenadiers with great loss.

Meanwhile, on the right, Lévis saw that until more troops arrived his men could not support their advanced position. He therefore ordered them back to the edge of the wood. The British took this for a general retreat. They pressed in, recaptured the redoubts occupied by Lévis in the early morning, and poured a heavy fire of cannon and musketry upon the retreating French. It looked as if the British had won the day.

They were, however, too confident. The main French force was now coming up rapidly, and, in spite of the severe British fire, the columns deployed into line at the edge of the wood. Lévis rode along in front of his army, a position greatly exposed, and ordered his men to prepare to charge. By word and gesture he cheered them on. He trusted much to his superiority of numbers, and hoped by using this superiority to outflank the British and to get between them and Quebec. Meanwhile the British were in trouble. When they pressed forward from the height on which their line had been drawn up, they soon found themselves in low and marshy ground where they had to fight standing knee-deep in snow and water. Their cannon stuck in the snowdrifts and there was no strength in the enfeebled men to draw them out.

It was impossible even to bring up supplies of ammunition, for as soon as the ammunition wagons had passed through the gates of Quebec they had stuck in deep pits of snow. The inevitable result followed. The artillery fire of the British gradually slackened. In time it ceased entirely and they could not answer the effective fire of the three guns

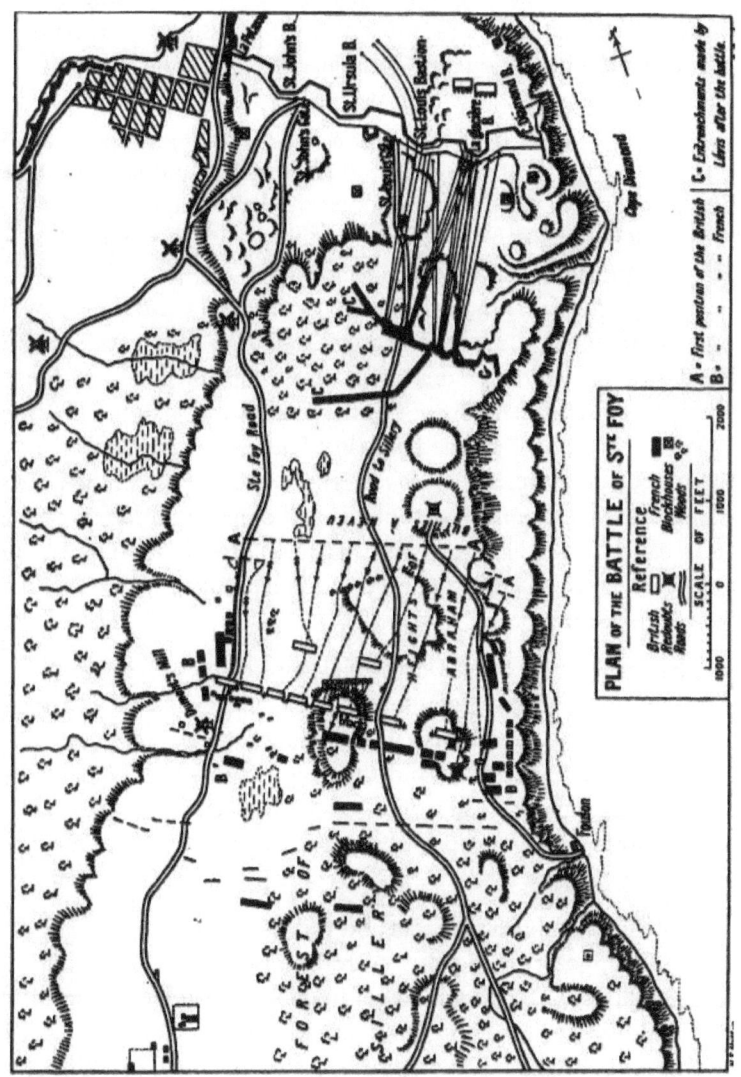

which Lévis had brought up with such great labour.

It was for this reason that the tide of battle now turned. The attention of Lévis was chiefly concentrated on his right. On the left Bourlamaque was wounded,—a serious loss to the French side, for so much was he the life and spirit of his troops that his loss earlier in the day, it was said, would have brought a complete victory to the British. In the confusion after his loss, the brigades on the left were without orders. They became impatient of standing in the wood in marshy land with snow and water rising sometimes to their waists, and they advanced on their own account. When they met the British light infantry pursuing the grenadiers driven from Dumont's mill, they pressed them back with great loss and reoccupied the mill.

At about the same time the French right charged on the two redoubts from which the British had driven them earlier in the day. The redoubts were no longer defended by artillery fire and the French quickly recaptured them. After this the battle went against the British. They fought with determined courage. They even recaptured the two redoubts. Once more, too, on their right they drove the French out of Dumont's mill. Here, indeed, took place the most murderous conflict of the day. It was a hand-to-hand struggle between the Highlanders and the French grenadiers. The Highlanders fought with their dirks. The Chevalier Johnstone says:

> These two antagonists, worthy the one of the other, were no sooner out by the windows, than they returned to the charge, and broke open the doors. . . . The grenadiers were reduced to forty men per company, and there would not have remained either Highlander or grenadier of the two armies, if they had not, as by tacit and reciprocal agreement, abandoned the desire of occupying the fort.

Outflanked on both the right and the left, the British were now in imminent danger of being cut off from the town. If Murray did not retire quickly the French would get in behind his force and surround it. He had time to spike his guns before the order was at length given to the troops to fall back, 'a command', says Captain Knox, 'they were hitherto unacquainted with.'

'Damn it, what is falling back but retreating?' some of the men cried out in protest. Retreat indeed was the word, and it was necessary to act quickly.

The French 'advanced . . . like a hasty torrent from a lofty precipice', says Quartermaster-Sergeant Johnson. The British left cannon, entrenching tools, and apparently everything that could be dropped. The wounded and dead remained lying on the field. The Chevalier Johnstone on the French side, says:

> Our army pursued them hotly, and if the cry had not been raised among our forces to stop, it would have possibly happened that we should have entered the city of Quebec pellmell with them, not being at any distance from the gates.

In fact it was only the blockhouses and a strong redoubt outside the walls that kept the French from cutting off the rear of the retreating British. It was fortunate for the defeated side that the French force was worn out by its previous fatigues. The weary men who had been exposed to rain and snow for days were in some cases so weak that they had little strength to use their bayonets when they overtook the British. The losses on both sides were heavy. Murray's casualties were about 1,200—one-third of his force, but the number killed was only about 300. The French had about 200 killed and more than 600 wounded. Lévis says that he had 5,000 men on the field, but that only 3,600 came into action. It was the most severely contested struggle of the whole war, and the last battle fought between French and British for Canada.

When Lévis saw that he had won the day, his first care was to occupy the General Hospital, lying on the banks of the St. Charles outside the walls of Quebec. His haste was due to his need of the ministrations of the nuns for the wounded, but also in part to the fear that his Indian allies, whom he had not kept well in hand, might make a dash upon the place and butcher the helpless, occupants. To avoid the rough and almost impassable roads, some of the wounded were sent in boats past Quebec and round to the St. Charles River where the hospital stands. Much to the indignation of Lévis, a boat carrying the wounded was fired on from Quebec by mistake and one man was killed. At the hospital itself there were ghastly scenes. A nun writes:

> Another pen than mine would be necessary to paint the horrors of sight and sound during the twenty-four hours in which the wounded were being brought in.—*Relation de ce qui s'est passé au Siège de Québec, par une Religieuse de l'Hôpital Général.*

The nuns prepared five hundred beds, but these were not enough. Then they filled their stables and barns with the wounded. Of seventy-two officers brought in thirty-three died.

> We saw nothing but torn arms and legs, and to add to the woe of the occasion the supply of linen gave out, so that we were obliged to use our sheets and our chemises.

No aid from the sister nuns of Quebec was to be expected, for they were pressed into the service of the needy British.

Horrors more grim than those of civilized war found place after the battle. The Indians serving with the French had behaved badly throughout the day. They had taken no part in the fighting but had skulked in the woods at the rear. They had even pillaged the haversacks and other equipment which the French had left behind. When their friends were masters of the field these dangerous allies came forth for their own savage work, and they were not checked. The battlefield was strewn with the dead and wounded. For the Indians to have scalped the dead would have been bad enough. They did this, but they did more. Officers and men, sometimes only slightly wounded but unable to join the British retreat, fell victims to the ruthless savages. Knox says, with pardonable warmth:

> Of the immense number of wounded men who were unavoidably left on the field of battle, twenty-eight only were sent to the hospital, the rest being given up as victims to glut the rage of the savage allies (of the French) and to prevent their forsaking them.

We are told in another account:

> All the wounded men, and several of the wounded officers who could not get off the field was (*sic*) as usual every one scalped for the entertainment of the conqueror.

Malartic says that the Indians scalped even some of the French. It is incredible that, as the British charge, the French officers encouraged such barbarities, but there is no doubt that they showed too little vigour in checking the savages. (Knox, ii.; note to Mackellar's Plan of the Battle of Ste Foy, *Report on Canadian Archives*, 1905, vol. ii; Malartic).

The bad news caused dismay in England. Pitt saw in it the danger of final failure to the work of years. He wrote on June 20 to Amherst trusting that, 'in the Providence of God' no fatal catastrophe might happen. Horace Walpole wrote to his friend Conway on June 21:

> I wish you *sorrow* of the Battle of Quebec. I thought as much

of losing the duchies of Aquitaine and Normandy as Canada.

Negotiations for peace were going on and the British reverse stiffened the terms of the French. A letter of an English statesman of the time sums up the prospect as the British saw it:

> We all here blame Mr. Murray, and are not at all satisfied with the reason he assigns for leaving the town to attack the enemy. He says, as I hear, that if the enemy got possession of the Heights of Abraham, the town was not defensible; but we wonder then, why he did not entrench himself there, and defend it by the force of his artillery, with which he was very well supplied and the French very ill; so that we cannot conceive, as long as our force was complete, how they could have any hopes of taking the town. As it is, however, I understand that there are no expectations that it can be saved, and, indeed, I am told that Murray himself gives little reason to hope it. The relief from Amherst is certainly impossible, and I do not think that he has ever shown activity enough to make one hope that he would make an attempt vigorous enough, even if there was a mere chance of success. How unexpected and unfortunate all this is! and how it has marred all our schemes of peace.—Jenkinson to Grenville, London, June 19, 1760: *Grenville Papers*, i.

CHAPTER 5

The Relief of Quebec by the Fleet

It was natural that the survivors in Quebec after the Battle of Ste Foy should be dejected and disorganised. One-third of those who had gone forth with such elation had been killed or wounded. The defeated army now expected every moment that Lévis would press the attack, take Quebec by assault, and put its defenders to the sword. Panic and despair found vent in reckless lawlessness. Then, as always, drink was the snare of the British soldier, and to get drink the men broke into stores and dwelling-houses. In such conditions an assault upon Quebec immediately after the battle might well have proved successful. The English thought that Lévis lacked, at this crisis, the insight and promptness of a great leader. Deserters who now came into the British camp declared, indeed, that the success of the French was due to the confidence of the army, not in Lévis, but in Bourlamaque, who, they said, was the life and spirit of the troops. The British undoubtedly expected a prompt assault on Quebec, and a day or two later, when it had not taken place. Captain Knox wrote:

> They have let slip a golden opportunity; had they followed their blow ... before the soldiers re-collected themselves, I am strongly inclined to think ... Quebec would have reverted to its old masters.

Lévis, however, delayed and hesitated. He wrote on the second day after the battle:

> The enemy is unmasking many embrasures; this shows that they can keep up a considerable fire. All this would be nothing if we had the artillery and the ammunition to answer them. We can only hope that some aid will come for us from France.

In spite of his victory he was not as strong as his enemy supposed. His labours were incessant, and he spoke of being worn out. A rare leader, such as Napoleon, would probably have followed up victory at once, and would have mastered Quebec even at the cost of dire slaughter. In the end, however, Quebec would fall to the power which could place in its basin the stronger fleet. Lévis paused to think of tomorrow, and perhaps he was wise. Certainly Vaudreuil and Bigot at Montreal believed that he was the sole hope of France. Their letters breathe an unwavering confidence in his skill which can hardly have been aroused except by really strong qualities.

The panic in Quebec did not last long. To check drunkenness Murray promptly ordered all the spirits in the Lower Town other than those of the king to be spilled. He also weakened with water the daily allowance of rum. Lawlessness he discouraged by promptly hanging a man found breaking into a house. Stragglers and marauders were warned that a similar fate awaited them. In the crisis Murray showed great capacity. His redoubt and blockhouses without the walls remained active. Lévis held the Buttes à Neveu not more than nine hundred yards from the walls. The British expected that he would begin a bombardment, but he could not do so at once.

His only cannon, for a time, were the three field-pieces which he had so laboriously brought with him over hills and through snow and mud from St. Augustin. He would, of course, turn the abandoned British cannon against their former owners, but it was not easy to bring up either these or his own cannon at the Anse au Foulon. Moreover, he had little ammunition, and what he had was of bad quality. Murray gave orders that the first cannon-ball which the French fired into Quebec should be brought to him, and we are told that the inspection gave him pleasure, for it proved the inferior quality of their powder. (Malartic).

Murray had thought of trying to take his army in boats to the island of Orleans, there to await the arrival of a British fleet, but he promptly abandoned this plan and resolved to hold Quebec. When the first panic was over, he kept up a vigorous fire at the French whenever they appeared at the high points which commanded the walls. 'The best we could do was to endeavour to knock their works to pieces before they could mount their cannon,' he wrote in his diary on the day after the battle, and he carried on this work with untiring energy. A dash by the enemy on the walls of Quebec under cover of darkness was possible. But it is more than doubtful whether it would have succeeded.

Superior in numbers though the French were, the British would have had a great advantage in fighting behind walls to meet an assault. The scaling-ladders prepared so laboriously during the winter would have been of great service to the French. But they had little stomach for such an enterprise, and with some justice. Their regulars now numbered only about three thousand; their Canadian allies had had no experience of this type of warfare; and for such an attempt the Indians were useless. In truth, Lévis had lost a great opportunity in not striking the British when they were in a panic after the battle. A similar opening did not recur.

Murray's men were soon confident and cheerful. Captain Knox wrote on May 2:

> We no longer harbour a thought of visiting France or England, or of falling a sacrifice to a merciless scalping-knife. We are roused from our lethargy; we have recovered our good humour.

The men boasted that if the French tried to storm the walls they would catch a Tartar, and they expressed their resolution in the words with which the English soldier of an earlier time is said to have awaited the French foe at Crecy:

> Damn them, if they do come, there is enough of them to fight, enough to be killed, and enough to run away.

On the second night after the battle Ensign Maw led twenty-two men in a sortie in the hope of taking a prisoner who could be forced to tell what the enemy was doing. The design failed, and six men were killed. The incident served to prove that the spirit of the men was even better than that of the officers. When, on May 1, Murray asked for volunteers to make a second sortie, some non-commissioned officers and men came forward, but not a single officer.

Murray tried to give his men some ground for good cheer. Late on the night of his defeat he issued to the army an order deploring the misfortunes of the day but promising ultimate success.

> The 28th of April has been unfortunate to the British arms, but affairs are not so desperate as to be irretrievable . . . The fleet may be hourly expected, reinforcements are at hand; and shall we lose, in one moment, the fruits of so much blood and treasure? Both officers and men are exhorted patiently to undergo the fatigues they must suffer, and to expose themselves

cheerfully to some dangers; a duty they own to their king, their country, and themselves.

There was heavy work to do, and, when order was once restored, Murray allowed the men a double supply of food and also of rum. Any of the French who still remained in Quebec were sent away. Murray named 'alarm posts' where the different regiments should be stationed. The men lived in what tents could be procured. This enabled them to be always on hand at the point of danger, and it also avoided the peril of being in houses which might be knocked to pieces by the cannon of the enemy. Except when on duty no officer or man was allowed to stir from these posts; for days Quebec had an army as much on the alert as if drawn up in line of battle face to face with the enemy. To prevent the secret approach of assailants, companies of rangers lay all night outside the walls, halfway between the town and the blockhouses. The hour just before daybreak was the most likely time for an assault, and each morning at this time the garrison was drawn up under arms until daylight. There was much engineering work to do, and it was all the more difficult because Major Mackellar, the chief of the engineering staff, had been dangerously wounded in the battle of April 28.

Within the walls, the British made batteries to enfilade the roads leading to the Lower Town, and they threw up barricades in different parts of the city. From dark until daybreak two hundred men worked outside the St. Louis gate, constructing defences that should protect that gate from attack. On Cape Diamond, Murray caused an observation tower to be built. It cost much labour, but from this high point within the walls he could survey the enemy's works and throw shot and shell into the vulnerable parts of their trenches. Nor while thus alert did Murray forget to urge the speedy coming of outside help. On the 30th the French on the heights saw the sloop of war *Racehorse* draw away from Quebec and hasten on her way down the river. They flattered themselves that the ship carried off the French deserters, so that, after the expected fall of the town, these traitors should not suffer the shameful execution which Lévis had promised if he caught them; but, in fact, she was speeding away to meet the expected British squadron and to hasten its arrival.

During the time of waiting, everyone in Quebec was obliged to work; even the women had their daily labour, by no means light. Those who could do nothing else made wads for the guns; and a day's task of 100 was required from each of the convalescents. The British opened embrasures in the walls, and they covered the parapet wall towards the enemy with bundles of wood, and rammed down earth between this lining and the wall of masonry; then the wall could not be shattered by cannon-balls. They planted artillery not only upon every bastion but upon the rather flimsy wall. The heaviest labour was that of dragging up the cannon from the Lower Town to replace what Murray had lost in the battle, and to strengthen the defences. Murray aimed to use one hundred and forty cannon, and he stripped the Lower Town of guns, planks, and platforms. The officers toiled with the men. Quartermaster-Sergeant Johnson writes:

> None but those who were present on the spot can imagine the grief of heart the soldiers felt, to see their officers doing the common labour of the soldier, equal with themselves; to see them yoked in the harness dragging up cannon from the lower town ... and at work at the batteries, with the barrow, pickaxe, and spade, with the same ardour as themselves.

At all hours of the night Murray and the Lieutenant-Governor, Colonel Burton, paid surprise visits to the various posts to make sure that nothing was neglected. Even with the best vigilance accidents sometimes happened. On May 3 a fire broke out near the Intendant's Palace and caused some destruction. The French supposed that the English were purposely destroying the town before the coming evacuation. Far away at Montreal, Vaudreuil, always fluent and often foolish, wrote to Lévis complaining of British barbarity in thus destroying Quebec!

The victory of Ste Foy had sent a thrill of pride and pleasure throughout New France. 'The jubilation here is unparalleled,' wrote Bougainville from Isle aux Noix. Vaudreuil and Bigot saw in it the beginning of the end of their sorrow. From Montreal, almost daily, Vaudreuil poured forth glowing letters full of hope. It was almost unnecessary, he wrote on May 4, to send Lévis a further supply of powder, for he would, of course, have taken Quebec. On May 5, in another mood, he says that he should regard the capture of Quebec as uncertain if anyone but Lévis was besieging the place, 'but with you there I am tranquil concerning the outcome.'

The next day, when a north-east wind is blowing, he rejoices, for it will be bringing nearer to Quebec the French vessels which he is sure are in the river. He bursts into praises of the part which the French-

Canadians took in the Battle of Ste Foy, though the French engineer Desandroüins says that three hundred of them deserted during the day. Even Bigot, a man of a colder temper, writes to tell Lévis that he must occupy the choicest room in the *intendant's* palace at Quebec, while he himself will be content with a little bed in a smaller chamber. Bigot has misgivings on May 9 when the north-east wind blows:

If, as seems likely, this continues, we have everything to fear.

Obviously he, unlike Vaudreuil, believed that it was a British and not a French fleet which such a wind would bring up the river.

Not long, however, after the Battle of Ste Foy, all in the French camp who were not irresponsible optimists had begun to realise the almost hopeless nature of their task. With a storm of shot and shell sweeping the Buttes à Neveu, Lévis found that he could not retain his camp as near Quebec as he had hoped, and he lost much time in moving it about a mile further back and in taking the necessary precautions for safety. The British fire plunged behind the Buttes a Neveu and made the ground look like a ploughed field for two miles from the walls. What Lévis aimed at was to get his guns soon in position and then to batter the walls and make breaches. This done, he thought he could either force Quebec to surrender or carry it by assault. Always he hoped to be aided by the expected fleet from France.

The plan of Lévis was not easy to carry out. The French could approach the exposed positions only by trenches, and to make these in the frozen ground was killing work. At some points where they wished to plant batteries they found only about six inches of earth covering the hard rock. The French had to carry much material needed for entrenchments in sacks for long distances over heavy roads and also to pass along narrow trenches to the exposed places. They brought their artillery in boats to the Anse au Foulon, and had to drag it up the steep height. Then they had to take the guns to the batteries through melting snow and through mud, in face of the plunging British fire on the Plains of Abraham. In the same way they had to carry with heavy labour fascines and gabions—bundles of wood and buckets to hold the earth in place in the entrenchments—to their positions.

The men who worked in the trenches were exposed to the biting cold at night and often to a terrific fire. Sometimes the British brought sixty guns to bear on a single point, and Knox declares that the enemy could never before have experienced so vigorous a bombardment. It is no wonder that while, on the British side, there were only thirty casualties during the siege, there were two hundred and six on the French side, and of these seventy-three were deaths. Daily three or four men were killed and half a dozen wounded; on one occasion a single shot from Quebec killed six French soldiers at work. These experiences were trying and the work went on but slowly. In answer to complaints Lévis gave vigorous and menacing orders to the engineers to get the artillery in place more quickly.

The work carried out before Quebec was done at needless cost. Corruption was as active as ever in the French administration. Cadet, its high priest, was in the French camp, busy, efficient, doing wonders in the way of securing supplies, but always robbing the king, his master. He went about now, followed by a staff befitting the rank of a general, and carrying himself as the equal of Lévis. He was treated with much deference by the General. Lévis declares that Cadet had gone beyond all expectations in furnishing provisions for his force, and that he was zealous and entirely devoted to the service. This was not inconsistent, however, with the pillage which he and others carried on. For every piece of cannon brought up from the Foulon to the trenches the sum of 1,800 *livres* was paid, and the same account was often rendered twice over. In the name of a clerk Cadet sent in great bills for supplies which in some cases were not required and in others were not delivered. Though Bigot had now broken with Cadet, he was in no position to check the brigandage which he himself had brought into being.

The preparations to bombard Quebec occupied a fortnight, and during that time the fire of the defenders met with no reply from the French camp. The British, looking out from Cape Diamond, could see horses and men dragging up guns and supplies. They could follow the movements in the trenches and make targets of the human occupants. Deserters who came into Quebec said that the French were keeping quiet until they could open simultaneously a battery of forty pieces on Quebec. Sometimes courtesies passed between the two armies. Murray sent to ask Lévis for spruce as medicine for his men sick of the scurvy, for now the British had no access to the neighbouring forests.

At first Lévis refused to send what might help to turn invalid enemies into combatants, but he sent Murray a supply for himself. In return Murray sent a Cheshire cheese and some casks of wine for the use of the sick in the General Hospital. Then Lévis sent a present of partridges and snipe.

The keenest hopes of each side were for succour from Europe.

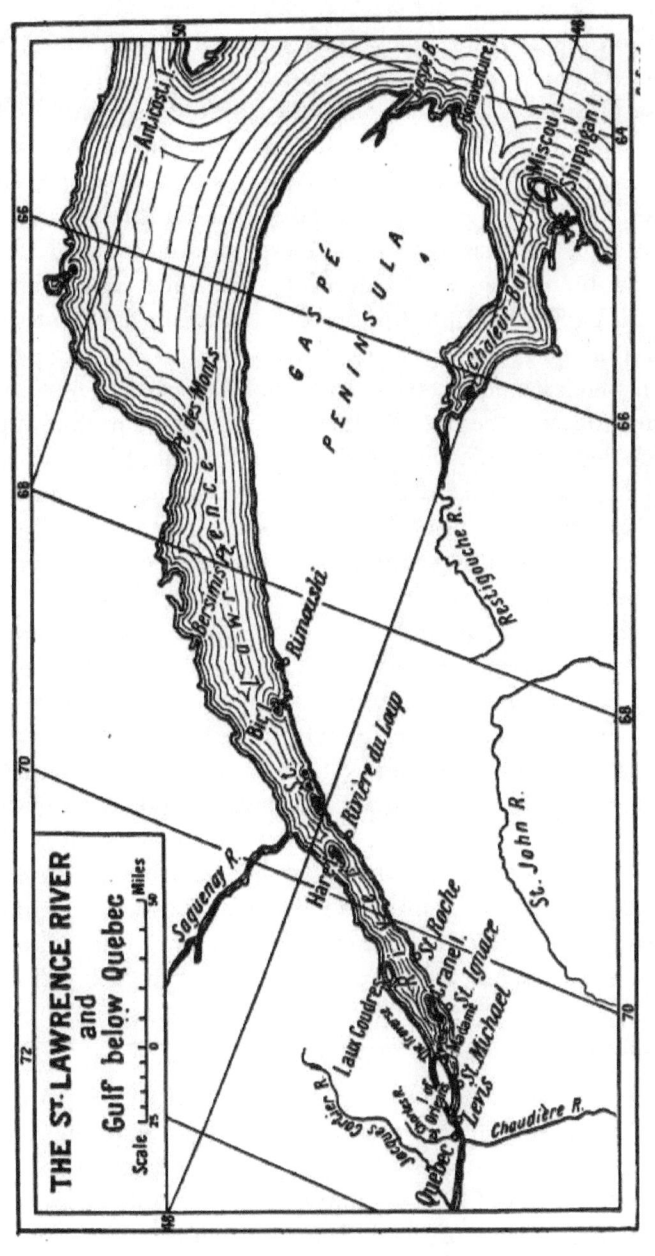

They watched the river. They watched the weather and were dismayed by every adverse wind which might delay the arrival of vessels under sail. The ship which Murray had sent down the river after his defeat on the 28th was followed by a French ship on May 4. When she passed Quebec its guns were turned on her, but she went on her course unharmed. Four days later, however, on the night of the 8th, when what Knox calls 'a delightful gale' was blowing from the east-south-east, a wind well fitted to speed ships up the river, she was seen on her way back. Her return was taken to mean that she had met a British force and was hurrying to escape from it. The defenders did not now fire as she passed Quebec, but an officer called out to her from the citadel on Cape Diamond to ask 'why she did not stay below to pilot up the French armada'.

All were aroused by this incident, and the next day every eye was strained to watch the river. Lévis had good reasons for misgivings. If a French fleet was near, word of its approach would have reached him by land as Vaudreuil had arranged; and he had heard nothing. At eleven o'clock on the morning of the 9th the watchers in Quebec and in the French camp saw a ship appear round the Point of Levy. 'For a moment we hoped she was French,' writes Malartic, and in the French camp the news that a ship was in sight received welcoming shouts of '*Vive le Roi.*' Among the British in Quebec all eyes were fixed upon the ship, every mind was in suspense.

To check the premature joy which they saw about them, some said that she could not possibly be British. But when she dropped anchor not far from the Point of Levy, and, in response to signals from Quebec, hoisted the British colours and fired a salute of twenty-one guns, her identity was no longer doubtful; she was the British frigate *Lowestoffe*. Quebec went mad with joy. Officers and soldiers mounted the parapets which looked out towards the French camp, threw their hats in the air, and shouted in the face of the enemy for well-nigh an hour. To show their glee the gunners fired off their cannon repeatedly. Knox writes:

> The general satisfaction is not to be conceived, and to form a lively idea of it is impossible, except by a person who had suffered the extremities of a siege, and been destined, with his brave friends and valiant countrymen, to the scalping knives of a faithless conqueror and his barbarous allies.

Some of those in Quebec gave utterance to devout praise. Quartermaster-Sergeant Johnson said:

> Let us turn ourselves and with the deepest humiliation and reverence adore that All-Seeing Providence whose Piercing Eye Saw our distresses, and in the needful time of our trouble sent us comfort.

The arrival of a single ship did not, however, necessarily mean deliverance for Quebec. Good news for the British she indeed brought. She was one of a considerable fleet under Commodore Swanton which had left England in March. She had been separated from the fleet at sea, and her commander, Captain Deane, confident in his ship, had decided to go on alone to Quebec. Off Newfoundland he met the British fleet from Halifax under Lord Colville on the way to the rendezvous at the island of Bic, in the St. Lawrence, about one hundred and sixty miles below Quebec, where Colville was to meet Swanton. It would, however, be some time still before the combined squadrons could reach Quebec, and meanwhile there was danger that the imminence of relief might induce Lévis to make a desperate assault.

Murray received word that such was his intention, and the night of the 9th, after the arrival of the *Lowestoffe*, was one of alarm in Quebec. All through the dark hours Murray kept half of the garrison on the ramparts. As soon as he could, he sent a sloop down the river to warn the approaching ships of the acute danger and of the need of haste. He found time to extend a courtesy to Lévis and sent him European newspapers which the *Lowestoffe* had brought. There was a half-malicious pleasure in the attention, for the journals contained the news of the overwhelming defeat of the French fleet at Quiberon Bay in November 1759; of the landing of the privateer Thurot in Ireland in February 1760; and of his subsequent defeat and death. The newspapers said nothing, however, about the contending armies in America. That campaign Europe seemed to have forgotten, something which Lévis did not fail to note, with misgivings, only too well founded, that his own country would pay but little heed to the needs of her half-strangled colony.

Murray's fear of an assault on the 9th proved unfounded. The night of the 10th was rainy, but again all was quiet in the French camp. In truth, before attempting an assault, Lévis wished first to batter the walls of Quebec with his guns, and these were not ready until the nth. On that day the long labours of the French were crowned with a measure of success, for at noon Lévis unmasked four batteries and began firing with great spirit. Every mortar and gun in the French lines was active without intermission; Lévis declares that the most experienced of his foes could never before have undergone such a fire.

'Our French, in despair of losing us, fired on us like very devils,' says a nun of the Ursuline convent in Quebec.

This fire produced a considerable effect; within a short time, the French had dismounted or disabled five of Murray's guns. The British fear that, under artillery fire, the walls of Quebec would prove rotten and easily breached was fully justified. Murray was dismayed at the havoc wrought by the bombardment. It added to his concern that his men were soon worn out with the hardships of remaining under arms night and day. By the evening of the 12th four had been killed and nine wounded by the French fire. '*Carcases*'—iron shells filled with inflammable material, and intended to set fire to the houses in Quebec—and shot and shell made at Three Rivers during the winter poured into Quebec. In fear lest the magazine at the Jesuit barracks should be blown up, Murray scattered his supplies to various parts of the town.

An assault under cover of so vigorous a fire seemed imminent. But Lévis could not keep up a strong attack. For only a day or two was he able to make his fire superior to that of the British. To his great disappointment, his cannon, which he knew to be weak in calibre, proved also poor in quality. Owing to lack of proper care by the artillerymen, some of them burst. His ammunition, too, was bad, the powder especially having suffered by exposure to the damp; the supply also was small. In consequence of these defects the French attack soon slackened. The order was given that each gun should fire but twenty times in twenty-four hours. The bad equipment was emphasized by the policy of the French engineer Pontleroy. Vaudreuil declares that he was capricious and self-willed. At any rate he had placed the batteries so far from the walls of Quebec, no doubt to save his men from the deadly English fire, that many of the guns were quite ineffective.

It was not long before Lévis had concluded that the attack on Quebec could not be pressed. Talk of raising the siege was soon heard. On the 13th the French leaders held a council at Bourlamaque's quarters. Failure must always find a scapegoat. There were now some who called the whole attempt against Quebec 'the folly of Lévis', while others laid all the blame on Pontleroy. To make a breach seemed hopeless, as did also a successful assault; and the discouraged officers decided that the only thing to do was to hold the British in check and await succour from France. Lévis tried to believe that such succour was possible, and he declares in his journal that Quebec would go to the side whose fleet arrived first. He did not know that succour left France only on April 12, more than a month after the British fleet had set out, and that even then France had sent help so slight that it was totally inadequate to meet the great naval force which Pitt had provided to ensure the conquest of Canada.

Again, as in the earlier days of the siege of Quebec, every one watched the weather. Lévis wrote to Bigot on May 15:

> Our situation is most disquieting, I fear that France has abandoned us; . . . nothing comes. . . . We have done and are doing what we can. If no help comes the colony is hopelessly lost. We trust that peace may be made in the interval. We can only prolong the conflict. To aid this you ought to use every means to collect all the grain to be had, since, if we are forced to raise the siege of Quebec, we must expect that the Canadians will wholly abandon us and their bad feeling will be such that we shall get nothing except by the use of force. . . . . It is no fault of ours; it appears that God has abandoned this wretched colony.

The despair of Lévis was justified. Far down the river at this time many British ships were threading their way, sometimes among floes of ice, to bring rescue to Quebec. Two great squadrons were converging on this point. The squadron under Commodore Swanton had set out from England in March. The other squadron under Lord Colville had wintered at Halifax. Though Colville had been anxious for an early start he was unable to get out of Halifax Harbour until April 22. Even then heavy fog and great fields of ice made progress difficult. Colville, sailing near the shores of the Gulf of St. Lawrence, had to face more dangers than Swanton on the open sea.

Off Cape Ray and St. Paul's Island he was delayed for twelve days by gales, fog, and ice. He had a number of transports in his convoy, and he notes in his diary his special fear lest he should lose sight of one of the most precious of them—that laden with clothing for the needy garrison of Quebec. (Manuscript diary of Colville lent to Colonel William Wood of Quebec by the present—1914—Lord Colville). Colville arrived at the rendezvous at the island of Bic on May 16, only to find that Swanton had come on May 14 and had gone on without a moment's delay because of an urgent summons from Murray to hasten to his rescue.

A similar message awaited Colville, and he followed in the race for Quebec. This ascent of the river by a squadron in the spring is the earliest on record. The channel was difficult and there were no pilots. In the previous year, however, British seamen had made careful observations, and now a long line of ships of war and transports, stretched out for miles in a river full of shoals and, at times, tempestuous like the sea, went on its way in confidence. The word was to make haste. Yet the ships were guided with such skill that not a serious accident occurred.

At Quebec, meanwhile, both sides were longing for the help which could come only by the river. At seven o'clock on the evening of May 15 a strong north-east wind was blowing, a wind that would speed ships on their way to Quebec. It was this wind which fixed the moment of the final crisis in the struggle for Canada. In the early evening the French, looking out from their camp, saw three ships come round the head of the island of Orleans. Men cling tenaciously to what they like to believe. Lévis, who had been despondent, now felt a delighted certainty that the ships were French. He clung to this faith even when the ships answered signals from Quebec and anchored in the basin near the Lower Town.

Late that night, however, some Indians brought to him an English prisoner whom they had taken while prowling near the walls of Quebec. Only when Lévis questioned this man did he believe the unwelcome truth. The ships were British. Swanton himself had arrived in the *Vanguard*, and a whole fleet was following him. It was a bitter moment for the French leader. He now saw that his most cherished hopes were vain, and that there would be no rescue from France. The next day he ordered the withdrawal of the artillery from the trenches. The whole army was to prepare to retire. The siege of Quebec was to be raised.

The British were determined to strike hard and at once. Between the departure of Saunders in the previous year and the arrival of Swanton, the French fleet in the St. Lawrence had been stronger than the British, and a source of incessant anxiety to Murray. Until it was destroyed the British could not use the water route to Montreal. In charge of this small fleet was Vauquelain, a seaman of great capacity. He was not a regular naval officer. His father had been a 'sea wolf' in the merchant service and he himself had been brought up to that calling. When the Seven Years' War broke out, good officers had been sorely needed in the French Navy, and M. de Moras, who was Secretary of the Navy in 1757, gave commands to officers in the merchant service.

This course met, however, with determined resistance from the regular naval officers. They were all of noble descent; it was a tradition that only men of noble birth should become officers in the royal navy; and they refused to co-operate with plebeians brought in from the merchant service. M, de Moras urged that France could not do, without such men, that heroes in French naval history like Du Quay-Trouin and Jean Bart had come from this class. This did not soften the bitterness of the opposition. Officers from the merchant service continued, however, to serve during the war, chiefly as privateers, and inflicted very great damage on British shipping. Vauquelain had come into prominence during the siege of Louisbourg, in 1758. He had managed during a fog to sail his ship past the blockading British fleet and to getaway to France to beg for help. The next year, 1759, he was sent to the St. Lawrence with the few ships that France could equip.

Nothing illustrates the spirit of the old regime in France better than the savage hostility with which men like Vauquelain were regarded. Regular naval officers would not take orders from them and went so far as to refuse to give them needed help in naval engagements; patriotism was sacrificed to pride. In spite of Vauquelain's brilliant service he was met in Canada by this class prejudice even among the army officers, and was not received in their society. From the letters of Montcalm, Lévis, Bourlamaque and others we should hardly gather that such a person existed. Vaudreuil, to whose orders he was subject, treated him coldly and gave the corrupt and intriguing Cadet such authority in respect to the ships that Vauquelain protested with warmth. Cadet, true to the spirit of the *parvenu*, strutted and swaggered, and spoke of 'my fleet', 'my ships', and 'my captains'. He did what he liked and reaped from the navy as he reaped from the army the rewards of far-reaching corruption.

Vauquelain had played a useful part in the attack on Quebec. By noon of the day of the battle of Ste Foy he had landed supplies at the Foulon. A little later Vaudreuil had ordered him to take his two frigates, the *Atalante* and the *Pomone*, down the river and to attack any British ships which should arrive. The difficulty of getting past the guns of Quebec had discouraged this enterprise, and the frigates anchored near the historic spot where Wolfe had landed at night. Here Vauquelain could help Lévis, and here he would remain while the siege went on. It was certain, however, that he would retire up the river the moment he was free to do so. When he had done this in the previous year, even Saunders, though he had a great fleet, had been unable to touch him. If now, he did it again he might defy another British fleet and help to keep Montreal secure from its approach. To prevent this a sudden and overwhelming blow must be struck at once. Accordingly, the moment Captain Swanton in the *Vanguard* dropped anchor in the basin of Quebec, Murray urged prompt action, and Swanton decided to go up the river and attack the French ships with the first turn of the tide.

The night of the 15th was stormy and the strong northeast wind aided the British plan of sailing up the river. There were two French frigates, and in all six ships. Vauquelain in the *Atalante* was prompt to see his danger. On the evening of the 15th he sent an officer ashore to ask Lévis for instructions. The storm raged throughout the night. Vauquelain watched and waited in vain for the return of his messenger. At four o'clock in the morning, though it was still dark, he could see far down the river between Quebec and the island of Orleans the shadowy forms of two of the ships which had arrived on the previous day. The wind was still strong, the sky was dark and clouded, and there were troublesome waves on the broad river.

Even in the darkness Vauquelain observed that the ships were making preparations to sail. He signalled to his own vessels to hoist their sails. Only when day was breaking did his messenger to Lévis return. He had been kept at the general's quarters until after midnight, and had then been delayed in putting off from shore, apparently because he had found his boat injured. He now brought instructions that if Vauquelain saw any movement on the part of the British to ascend the river, he should get away as soon as possible.

Not a moment was to be lost. The British ships were already moving. The other French frigate, the *Pomone*, cut her cable and set sail, and the transports did the same. With one of the British frigates already bearing down on him in the *Atalante*, Vauquelain had no time to raise his own anchor. So he, too, cut his cable and headed up the river. In the strong wind navigation was not easy, and disaster quickly overtook the *Potnone*. She could not clear the point of the Anse au Foulon and was soon aground. Vauquelain held on to protect the transports. But it became clear that they were not fast enough to escape the pursuer. Five or six miles above the Anse au Foulon the Cap Rouge River enters the St. Lawrence. Vauquelain now signalled to the transports to make for the mouth of this river and there run aground. He was sure that the British frigates would continue to pursue him up the river, and hoped that at least the stores in the transports might be saved.

What Vauquelain had hoped for took place. When the transports grounded, the *Diana* and the *Lowestoffe* held on in pursuit of the *Atalante*, Vauquelain soon perceived that they were overhauling him, and he then made the desperate resolve of running his ship also on shore. When he did this at Pointe aux Trembles, his two pursuers anchored within short range and began a furious bombardment. Vauquelain answered with vigour. To keep up his fire he had to cut away his main-mast, which was causing the ship to heel over too much. From half-past seven to half-past nine in the morning the fight went on, and Vauquelain, though outclassed, inflicted heavy damage on the British ships.

The falling of the tide caused the British, fearful of running aground, to draw off a little and to slacken their fire for a time. This gave the French some chance to escape to the shore. Vauquelain, however, had lost all his small boats. There were people on the shore within calling distance, and he cried out to them to send off a boat. Naturally, in view of the British fire, there was no prompt reply to this request. In the end, however, a boat came off. Vauquelain was especially anxious to send off his wounded. He put as many as possible into the boat and sent it to the shore. To bring the boat back without endangering lives, he attached to it a long rope by which it could be drawn to the ship. But the men who took the boat to the shore treacherously cast off the rope and ran away. Then the French on the ship had to rig up a clumsy raft with which they reached the shore and secured the boat.

By this time the powder of the French was wet and their ship had heeled over so that the guns were, in any case, useless. The work of landing the men went on. At half-past one in the afternoon only a boat-load remained. But, with the French fire silenced, the British now rowed in to board the enemy. When the boarding party called out to Vauquelain to lower his flag, he replied fiercely that they must come and haul it down, for he would not. He was himself wounded and so were most of the five officers and the six men still with him. The boarding party found them lying almost helpless.

Of the original ship's company, in spite of the escape of some to land, Vauquelain lost about fifty, probably one-third of the whole number, either killed or severely wounded. The British had one man killed and five wounded. Vauquelain had won their respect, and Murray loaded him with attentions and gave him quarters at the General Hospital. It is not without interest that Lévis, in describing the naval battle in his journal, does not even mention the name of Vauquelain.

This yawning gulf between the classes represented by the high-born *chevalier* and the plebeian sailor was not to be bridged. It helps to explain the bitter hatreds of the revolution which was drawing so near in France.

******

The heroism of Vauquelain has been a favourite topic with some French writers. Alfred de Vigny wrote a spirited poem on the subject. The statement is made that Vauquelain nailed his flag to the mast and threw his sword overboard, but I am not aware of any original authority for it. His own narrative is in the Lévis MSS., vol. xi.

******

On this disastrous day the French ships were nearly all destroyed. The French themselves set the *Pomone* on fire as she lay stranded off the Foulon. They were able to remove the equipment from the transports which ran ashore in the Cap Rouge River, and when this had been done they burned the ships. The British burned the *Atalante*. Of all the French ships, only one, a small sloop of war, the *Marie*, escaped. As she was laden with wounded officers and men, she had thrown her guns overboard and hastened up the river without waiting to take part in the fight. Nor did the British themselves wholly avoid disaster. Their ignorance of the river above Quebec was still great, and the *Lowestoffe*, the arrival of which on May 9 had caused such cheering on the ramparts of Quebec, ran aground on May 19 and became a total wreck.

This disaster, however, hardly marred the complete triumph of the British. Up to this time the difficult navigation of the St. Lawrence and the menace from the French ships which lay there had kept the British from advancing for more than a few miles above Quebec. Now the power of France on the sea in America was wholly shattered. She still had, indeed, one or two vessels far up on Lake Ontario, but to destroy them was to prove no hard task. In truth, on that stormy spring day of 1760, France's long naval record in Canada ended in final disaster. It was French seamen, Cartier and Champlain, who had first told Europe about the great river. In the days of Jean Bart, France had held both the St. Lawrence and the Mississippi, Iberville had humbled the English even on Hudson Bay. It was the white flag of France that Vauquelain had refused to pull down. Now it disappeared almost entirely from the river, and the rival power that was to become mistress of the seas at Trafalgar was already mistress of the St. Lawrence.

On the 16th, while the poor remains of the French Navy were being destroyed in the river, Lévis was preparing to withdraw the army which lay on the Heights before Quebec. All through the day he had troublesome evidence of Britain's sea-power. The *Vanguard*, a powerful ship of war, still continued to hover about the Anse au Foulon and bombarded the French positions within range. When night came the retreat of the French began. Lévis issued orders that the army should march at ten o'clock with La Pause in charge. The men were to march in silence, no weapons were to be discharged, no fires were to be made. One of the critics of Lévis says that he lost his head, and, dazed by his position, gave contradictory orders. Once more we see that he lacked the striking vigour and decision in a time of crisis which are indispensable to a great leader. When officers came to him for directions he would look at them blankly without saying a word. (*Mémoires sur le Canada*, 1749-60).

There was much confusion. The Indians, always troublesome, were now completely out of hand. In search of pillage and mad for drink they attacked the quarters of the officers and killed a grenadier on guard. One of them was in turn killed by another grenadier whom he tried to strangle. The Indians were soon drunk with the liquor thus secured, and some French soldiers also got drunk on stolen spirits. Bourlamaque wrote to Bougainville that everything fell into disorder. Lévis could not take away all his artillery, and most of it he frankly abandoned. He dragged some heavy guns to the edge of the cliff at the Foulon and threw them down to the strand below, in the hope that the French might be able to get them away in the boats. Some light artillery and field-pieces he sent up the river by land. He tried to load his small boats at the Foulon, but most of these were either sunk by the *Vanguard* or abandoned by their crews. In them were the personal effects of some of the French officers, now, of course, lost.

Under cover of night Lévis marched his army to Cap Rouge and by daybreak of the 17th he was comparatively safe beyond the river of Cap Rouge. It was here that the French transports had run aground. They were laden with provisions, and Lévis spent the 17th in trying to withdraw from them supplies which he sorely needed. Bourlamaque declares that the whole affair was badly managed. He himself, disabled by his wound, had been brought in a litter from the General Hospital. Now, surrounded chiefly by men also wounded, he tried to get something done.

At Cap Rouge lay one hundred and twenty boats, but the oars

had been left behind at the Foulon, and all day long Bourlamaque attempted in vain to have the oars brought up. He induced thirty Canadians to help him. Something was done, but, if we may believe the chief lieutenant of Lévis, there was a conspicuous lack of competent leadership in the French Army. On the 18th the army marched as far as Pointe aux Trembles, where, with something like dismay, they learned that more British ships had arrived at Quebec. This produced new fears and the resolve to press on farther to a safer place.

The next day the army reached the Jacques Cartier River. To cross was not easy, for there were no bridges or pontoons, and the clumsy *bateaux* were of little use in the swollen spring floods. Not until far into the night of the 19th was the task accomplished. Then the French army had the swift river between them and possible pursuit by land from Quebec. At this point eight months earlier Lévis had taken command of the army of Vaudreuil, worn out after a panic-stricken flight from Quebec. It must have been with bitterness of heart that he now found the experience of panic and flight repeated, and, this time, under his own leadership.

Meanwhile the French camp lay almost deserted. It was not long, however, before some inkling reached Quebec of what was happening. Deserters came in to say that the Canadian militia had been ordered by Lévis to return to their parishes. They had come in readily after the victory of Ste Foy, even from the parishes east of Quebec. Now from the walls the British could see large parties of Canadians filing off towards Charlesbourg and Beauport. Others managed to cross the river and were seen going to the south country. A few of them, however, still stayed in the trenches, by command of Lévis, to check any sally from Quebec. The British kept up a fierce artillery fire. Knox writes on May 16:

> I believe I may venture to advance, that there never was such tremendous firing heard ... as our artillery displayed this evening for near two hours.

Only slowly the British learned what had really taken place. Early on the morning of the 17th the Canadian soldiers left in the French entrenchments fired a volley of musketry in order to keep up the appearance of an active defence. After this they all retired. They had deceived the British, however, for it was not until the evening of the 17th—nearly a whole day after Lévis had begun his retreat—that a scouting party found the trenches abandoned. Murray pushed forward light infantry and grenadiers in the hope of overtaking the French army. But Lévis was well away, and the British, in high spirits, could only take possession of his abandoned camp. They found evidence that his retreat had been precipitate, for not only heavy articles such as cannon and mortars, but tents, baggage, fire-arms, and ammunition were left behind.

Captain Knox calls the retreat of Lévis a 'shameful flight', and he could explain it only by panic fear that the French Army might be caught between two forces. In spite of his haste Lévis left a letter recommending to Murray's care those lying wounded in the neighbouring houses and in the General Hospital. He also assured Murray that he had not required from the French-Canadians who had taken the oath to George II any military service, though he had made them work for his army, a course quite proper under the laws of war. Some things in the French camp filled the British with rage. Their officers and men who had been killed in the battle of the 28th had not been buried; perhaps with the scanty and frozen soil and the hard rock of the Plains of Abraham this would have been impossible. But the British now found that the dead had been treated with great indignity. The bodies had been scalped and mangled, and had then been thrown clear of the camp and left for ravenous birds and wild beasts. Hanging on the bushes the victors found a great many scalps of their countrymen, a sight that filled them with fury.

The flight of Lévis made the end of the long struggle hardly doubtful and relieved a tension that the British had found very real. Captain Knox wrote:

> If a French fleet had appeared first in the river, the place must inevitably have fallen.

His words reflect the opinion in Quebec; but he adds that, rather than surrender, the officers had resolved to die with arms in their hands, and that the men would follow their example. Lévis himself wrote to Belle-Isle, the French Minister of War, and to Berryer, the Minister of Marine, who were doing so little to help him, that 'a single frigate would have involved the surrender of Quebec and assured us the possession of Canada for another year.' This was a common saying on the French side—that a single ship would have saved Canada. But even the recapture of Quebec would have only delayed the final climax.

France was making no preparations that could cope with the

might of Britain in America. While the French Ministry was doing little or nothing for Canada, and was supinely hoping that something favourable might happen, Pitt, with vast resources, had been toiling for months to make victory certain. On May 19 Lord Colville's fleet from Halifax, composed of six ships of the line and seven frigates and sloops of war, arrived at Quebec; and after that date ships came up on every tide laden with stores and provisions. The puny efforts of France stand in vivid contrast with Pitt's far-reaching plans. At that moment a single frigate with a convoy of transports was coming from France to the rescue of Canada. She, like Canada, was only hastening to her doom. France had no master mind to rival Pitt.

CHAPTER 6

The Advance to Montreal

If the British supposed that an overwhelming naval force at Quebec would cause the French to lay down their arms at once they were mistaken. Lévis could retreat safely to the interior, and he believed that the difficult navigation of the St. Lawrence would protect Montreal from attack by the fleet. Since the incoming ships brought no strong addition to the land forces, Lévis was quite able to cope with the army at Quebec. Only when the fleet should move would he be in real danger. He found it impossible, however, to keep his army together at one point, for scarcity of provisions followed by desertion would then be inevitable.

Accordingly, he distributed his battalions even more completely than they had been distributed during the previous winter. He kept a force of 400 men at Pointe aux Trembles to watch the English, 300 at Jacques Cartier, and 1,100 farther up the river at Deschambault. Bougainville remained at Isle aux Noix to check a British advance on Montreal by way of the Richelieu River. Far above Montreal on the St. Lawrence, Fort Lévis would, it was hoped, block the advance of the British down the river should they try to come by that route.

In the losing battle now to be fought Lévis was at his best. He had not the slightest hope of succour. His own military reputation, however, and his chances of promotion in Europe depended on his holding out as long as possible. The army was only half-fed and not half-equipped. Assuredly no one who had seen its panic flight on May 17 would have supposed that it could hold out for nearly four months still. The officers bore, without much complaint and with the greatest courage, the terrible fatigues and the starvation which the campaign involved. Their only hope was that peace might be made before they should be obliged to lay down their arms. It was almost a matter of life and death to them that this should be the course of events. If they surrendered, the conqueror would undoubtedly insist that they should not serve again during the war. This might mean that they would be idle for years, lose all chance of promotion, and starve on the slender half-pay, or perhaps less, which they would receive from the Court of France.

Accordingly, the French longed for peace and made themselves believe that it was near. Malartic, the French officer who remained in charge of the French sick at Quebec after the retreat of Lévis, offered to bet Murray that peace would be made by August. On the British side there were no illusions as to the imminence of peace, and Murray told Malartic that he would lose, since peace was not to be hoped for that year. The British general knew something of the resolve of Pitt to bring France low before he treated with her. But the French leaders thought with Malartic. Their letters at this period are full of assurances that peace is near. Those of Vaudreuil glow with an abounding optimism based chiefly upon his own predictions. Writing on May 24, 1760, only a few days after the French flight from Quebec, he declares that the bearing of the British shows depression of spirits, and that this must be due to some disaster to their cause in Europe which they are concealing. Still whistling to keep up his own courage, he wrote on June 1 to Colonel Dumas:

> Canada is drawing near to the close of her suffering and misfortunes, so everything calls us to increase our efforts that we may not lose the fruit of the negotiations which are certainly under way to effect peace.

On June 3, to make public these cheering hopes, he issued a proclamation to the Canadians describing recent, but imaginary, French successes in Europe, and adding that, as a consequence of the French victory at Ste Foy:

> The King of England cannot possibly avoid acquiescing in such terms as our monarch shall prescribe to him; . . . the colony is nearing the conclusion of its distress and difficulties.

Even Bigot, a keen man of business, tried to explain the absence of help from France as wise economy; so assured was an early peace that the French Ministry had found it really unnecessary to send new forces to Canada. Lévis himself felt certain that the news of the defeat of April 28 would convince the British that Quebec had fallen and would lead them to conclude peace at once. Little did the French understand either the character or the resources of those they were fighting.

If the French leaders were still optimists, some of their men were not. Lévis, indeed, says that the men who remained with his force showed a cheerful courage; but there were many who did not remain. Some of the regulars had married in Canada, intending to settle finally in the country when the war was over. Now, despairing of the lost cause, a good many of these men deserted. The movement to desert was much more general among the Canadians. They went off in droves. On the whole they had fought well. Some of the French officers, indeed, speak ill of their Canadian allies, but the truth seems to be that they had been useful in a somewhat irregular way. They did not fight well in the open. But their patience, their activity, their hardiness made an officer on the French side call them the best militia in the world. (Johnstone, iii.).

When, however, the French had retired from before Quebec, the Canadians seem to have concluded that the cause of France was finally lost. They were acute enough to know that, if the struggle was to be prolonged, it would not be on their account, but on that of the French officers, thinking of their own military careers in Europe. Accordingly, with or without leave, the Canadians trooped away to their homes. On May 21, Lévis wrote in his journal that nearly all the Canadians had left him, and that the officers, instead of checking their men, had set them a bad example.

The Canadian militia consisted chiefly of farmers. They were sorely needed at home in the month of May, and this excuse was urged on their behalf. When the French officers would have dealt sternly with the deserters, and made threats of wholesale executions, Vaudreuil, as we have seen, would not allow this severity. The governor's boast of what he could do with his 'brave Canadians' had become a byword in the army. He was always sure that, when really needed, they could be relied upon; he understood the difficulties of their position and protected them from the consequences of military law.

The uncertainty and misery of a hopeless campaign were prolonged by the inactivity of the British. They lingered at Quebec and showed no signs of a forward movement. Murray was, in truth, waiting for more troops and for the development of the campaign against Montreal by the deliberate Amherst. Meanwhile, day by day, the forces of Lévis in the interior were being reduced to a pitiable condition. Perennial famine haunted the French camps. As the summer wore on,

Lévis wrote that he would soon have nothing but bread for the troops, and that it would not be easy to get even bread. He cast longing eyes on the maturing harvest, but he could not forbear asking whether the French would be there to gather it. So many officers had died, or had been wounded or made prisoners, that Lévis had not enough to do the necessary work.

Daily the equipment of the army grew worse. Little powder was left, and the artillery was so hopelessly weak that it was impossible to defend effectively points on the river where otherwise it would have been easy to harass, if not to check, the advance of the British ships. The army was short of both muskets and bayonets. 'The troops, except (the regiments of) La Sarre and Royal Roussillon, are entirely naked,' wrote Lévis to the Minister of War on June 28. Some of the men, of course, marched barefoot. The destruction of boats, when Lévis began his retreat, proved a disaster of great moment, for, though urgent efforts were made, it proved impossible to replace them.

The lack of boats meant that the return towards Montreal must be made by land only, and this worked a double evil. It led the troops through the Canadian villages, where they committed depredations on the inhabitants, and it added to the difficulties of movement, for there were few bridges, and boats were necessary to cross the rivers. With only a few carpenters left, Lévis could build hardly any new boats. To take their place his men constructed rafts which proved an unstable means of transport for troops and stores across the swift Canadian streams. By June Lévis had learned that France had refused to honour the drafts on her treasury made from Canada in 1759. This spelled ruin for nearly everyone concerned. Even the officers of the regular army had been paid in these drafts. They had borrowed money upon them and would now be overwhelmed with debt.

Lévis issued a private circular letter to the commanders of battalions telling them what had happened and outlining a plan for appealing to the king to meet at least the drafts for the pay of the soldiers. But the Canadians, too, would be ruined by the action of the Court. Soon the French leaders found that the failure to redeem the ordinances was fatal. France had no longer any credit in Canada. Already the peasantry had more than enough of nearly worthless paper, and yet the French Army was without other money for purchases. The leaders were obliged to pledge their own credit for the supplies to be furnished to the troops. But, with a failing cause, this still proved poor security, and usually supplies could be obtained only under compulsion. When this failed, even officers sold their clothing for food.

Meanwhile Vaudreuil's wordy optimism never slackened, and Bourlamaque indulges in a little chaff at 'the long and fastidious dissertations of the personage'. Lévis was not so hopeful; he admitted that he had no means of checking a fleet of frigates and transports in an advance to Montreal, and that to meet this advance the French would have to abandon their frontiers. But he wrote simply:

> We shall use every means to save the colony, though our situation is so frightful that only a miracle can do it. . . . It is necessary to finish this business with honour and to delay the loss of the colony as long as we can.

He kept himself busy inspecting the danger-points, and his observations led him to conclude that the English would soon have 40,000 men in the heart of Canada.

A momentary gleam of hope cheered the French when news came that their fleet, so long hoped for, had reached America. Protected by the frigate *Machault*, the little convoy had left Bordeaux on April 10, and had taken more than a month to cross the Atlantic. On May 14 the *Machault* captured, in the Gulf of St. Lawrence, a British ship, and learned from her that a British fleet had already ascended the river. This was grave news, and a council of war decided that the French ships should take refuge far up the Bay of Chaleur at the mouth of the Restigouche River. Here they would have the help of about fifteen hundred Acadians expelled a few years earlier from their homes in Nova Scotia. On arrival the French sent word at once to Montreal. Lévis wrote in his journal on June 13:

> In the night we received news from France by a courier sent from Restigouche in Acadia where our ships destined for Quebec had stopped. (He adds, with a touch of bitterness). They started . . . just when they should have been arriving.

Vaudreuil was highly excited by the long-looked-for intelligence which had come, of course, overland wrote:

> At last we have the news from France which we have so long desired; what a pity that the ships which brought the news did not come earlier; we should now have been entirely at our ease. . . . The letters which I have received from the Minister assure me . . . that we shall have peace towards the middle of the campaign.

He concludes, with his usual irresponsible optimism, that the British cannot possibly send any further help to North America, and that France is about to make in Europe the most potent efforts to crush her enemy. (Lévis, *Journal*; Vaudreuil to Dumas, in *Report on Canadian Archives*, 1905, i.).

The arrival of the French convoy did not disturb the plans of the British or arouse in them anything but exultation. British commerce had suffered much from French privateers. During the war more than two thousand British ships were captured by the French, while the British took less than half that number. Even in the year 1759, so disastrous to French power on the sea, the French had captured 812 British vessels. The explanation is that British prey was abundant, for, unlike the French, the British had a vast sea-going commerce which offered easy conquests to privateers.

It was the parallel of the situation during the civil war in the United States, when the South, with almost no ships on the sea, was able, by means of a single privateer, the *Alabama*, to inflict ruinous loss on the extensive shipping of the North. The French had managed to take a good many vessels laden with stores for Quebec. Le Blanc, a much-dreaded privateer, had haunted the waters near the mouth of the St. Lawrence and inflicted heavy loss on the trade of the British colonies. Now the time had come for the British to ruin what remained of French naval power in America.

When news of the arrival of the *Machault* and her convoy reached Halifax and Quebec, a squadron set out from each place eager to be the first to deliver the crushing blow. Captain Wallis left Quebec, with five ships; Captain Byron, grandfather of the poet, left Halifax, also with five ships, himself leading in the *Fame*. Fortune favoured Byron's squadron. The Restigouche River empties into the Bay of Chaleur, a long and narrow arm of the sea. The upper waters of the Bay are so shallow as to be hardly navigable for large ships. The French convoy consisted of the frigate *Machault*, of thirty guns, two large store-ships, and some twenty smaller vessels, most of them prizes taken off the coast of New England by the enterprising Le Blanc. The French had pushed up the Bay to a point where the shallow water seemed a protection against the great British fighting ships.

Captain Byron, parted from his other ships by bad weather, arrived at the Bay in the *Fame* five or six days before they came up. His first exploit was to capture an armed schooner, but her forty-seven men escaped to the shore. Afraid to take his large ship up the Bay, he anchored and sent boats some dozen miles farther to learn where the French lay. Though the channel proved to be extremely narrow and difficult, he resolved, in the end, to bring up his own ship. The attempt nearly proved fatal; he ran aground and for a time was in imminent danger of being boarded by the French. But after nine or ten hours of hard work he was again afloat. His other ships now appeared, but two of them ran aground before they could reach him.

The *Repulse* and the *Scarborough* were, however, able to come on, and they and the *Fame* advanced up the narrow channel which the French had tried to block by sinking some ships. In spite of grounding a dozen times, the *Fame* at length opened fire on a shore battery. Its defenders ran away at once, and the British then landed and not only destroyed the battery but set fire to the adjacent village of Restigouche containing some two hundred wooden houses.

The French frigate and transports were still out of reach, pressing farther and farther up the Bay, but, as the British observed, running often aground. By lightening two of his frigates as much as possible, Byron was able to follow the enemy, and, in the end, he came within range. Then followed a duel between the British ships and the French frigate, which lay close to a shore battery. The duel lasted for two or three hours. The French fought well and were determined that the frigate should not fall into the hands of the British. The day went against them. They abandoned the *Machault* after taking off the wounded and setting her on fire. The British took, in all, twenty-two vessels, laden with cargoes valued at not less than two hundred thousand pounds.

Even in these ships was evidence of the profound corruption which affected Canada: horseflesh and putrid meat had been sent out. The British removed from the store-ships wine, brandy, and all else of value, and then burned the whole convoy. It was a disastrous end of France's effort to aid her perishing colony. The losses on the British side were only four killed and nine or ten wounded, while the French had about thirty casualties. The British did not take a single prisoner, for the French crews landed and escaped. As Byron's victorious squadron came down the Bay, he met Captain Wallis, just arrived with his squadron from Quebec and eager for a share in the struggle. He had, however, come too late and could only turn back to Quebec with the news of one more British triumph over the French upon the sea. (Byron's Report to Colville, July 14, 1760—Manuscript in Canadian Archives; *Relation de la Navigation de la petite flotte partie de Bordeaux pour Montréal*—Newcastle Papers, British Museum, vol. 226).

Meanwhile Murray had been making himself secure. He obliged the Canadians to level the works which Lévis had raised to menace Quebec, and he warned them by proclamation to expect rigorous treatment for any acts hostile to the British. It was no empty threat. On May 29 Murray seized, in the parish of St. Michel, on the south side of the river, a captain of militia named Nadeau. After taking the oath exacted by Murray, this man had joined and induced others to join the army of Lévis, and now Murray caused him to be hanged in his own village. (It is characteristic of Murray's tender heart that he is said to have provided at a later time at his own expense for the education of Nadeau's son).

Soon after the retreat of Lévis, Murray drew up his army outside the walls of Quebec. It was, in truth, rather a pitiable array, for of the seven thousand left in the previous autumn only about fifteen hundred men were now left fit for duty. But Murray told them that their task was nothing less than the total conquest of Canada. They faced it cheerfully enough. Hundreds of worn, sick men were eager to take their places in the ranks as soon as possible. Murray sent invalid soldiers to the Island of Orleans to recuperate; for invalid sailors the church at the Point of Levy was turned into a hospital.

Great tasks still awaited the army. When, on May 30, the British had held a solemn thanksgiving service in Quebec, their gratitude had sprung as much perhaps from a lively sense of triumphs to come as of those already attained. But waiting had proved necessary. The British Ministry had decided, early in 1760, that the former French stronghold of Louisbourg in Cape Breton should be totally destroyed. Even the harbour was to be so ruined that never again could it be useful to an enemy. The destruction would release the considerable garrison still holding Louisbourg, and a good many of these troops were to be sent to help Murray. But to destroy the massive works at Louisbourg took time, and aid to Murray was long in coming.

Time was also required for the recovery of the sick at Quebec, and for the deliberate Amherst to begin his advance on Montreal. Murray chafed under the delay and cursed Amherst's slowness; Malartic, who sat at Murray's table, declares that he heard Murray, in his usual impulsive and somewhat extravagant style, threaten to hang some of his officers who were trying to justify the impassive deliberation of the commander-in-chief. Not for two months after Lévis retired could Murray begin to advance on Montreal. The French thought that the long delay was part of a deep-seated plan to advance when the harvest was ripening and when the Canadians would wish to remain at home to gather it.

Murray's forces were in motion before the news of the destruction of the French squadron reached Quebec. Amherst had mapped out a complete plan of campaign, and this plan Pitt had studied and approved. We know that, during these strenuous days of war, Pitt worked with fiery energy and so devoted himself to his tasks that he gave up even the usual attendance at Court. Nothing is more striking than the precision in regard to detail of this great minister who was carrying on a world-wide war and might well have left detail to the professional military man. He knew, however, that in military operations detail is everything. He must have studied closely the existing maps which showed the situation in America. The generals send him diaries of their doings and he follows their movements.

The situation of every obscure post is clear to him. He knows where boats will be needed and writes anxiously to Amherst to make sure that those used in the previous year are being properly cared for and that the building of new ones is looked after. He knows what dangers lie in the path of British success and points them out clearly. But he rarely finds fault and he never scolds. He chose men whom he could trust and he trusted them. He was not superior to the popular view that France was England's natural enemy, and he exulted in her disasters. When, in November 1759, Hawke delivered his crushing blow to the naval power of France, at Quiberon Bay, Pitt wrote to Amherst a glowing account of the 'signal and glorious success' and of 'the consternation and dejection' of the enemy. He was resolved so to prostrate France that never again could she assail England.

British defeats and victories stirred his deepest emotions. With Wolfe's victory England, as a whole, had dismissed Quebec from its mind. That game it thought was won. But, until France's power in America was completely crushed, Pitt was anxious. The defeat of Murray on April 28 filled him with sadness, the retreat of Lévis, not many days later, with joy. He then wrote to his sister Hester:

> Join, my love, with me in most humble and grateful thanks to the Almighty. The siege of Quebec was raised on the 17th of May, with every happy circumstance. The enemy left their camp standing, abandoned forty pieces of cannon, &c. Swanton arrived there in the *Vanguard* on the 15th, and destroyed all the

French shipping, six or seven in number. Happy, happy day! My joy and hurry are inexpressible. (*Chatham Correspondence*, ii. 45.)

With such a leader the generals in America were bound to plan something far-reaching. All through the winter, Amherst, stationed at New York, had been busy with the bringing together of an army so great that the result could not possibly be doubtful. It is amazing that New France, with her scanty population, should so long have fought the British. Her peasantry, however, were organised into a very effective militia, they were accustomed to despotic leadership, and they did what they were told. New France was united. The British colonies, on the other hand, were divided. They were jealous of each other and of their own independence. The citizen farmers coming together in their dozen legislatures were somewhat prone to stand by their own views of the problems of an Empire and to reject the insistent urgency of Pitt.

For the most part the colonial levies raised for the campaign of 1759 had been disbanded and had returned to their homes. To secure new levies Amherst must correspond with each governor. Each governor must, in turn, lay the general's demands before the legislature of his province. The talk of peace which the French so persistently indulged in was common also among reluctant legislators as an excuse for inaction. But the zeal in some quarters was admirable. Massachusetts, under her enthusiastic governor, Pownall, one of the most ardent Imperialists of the eighteenth century, led the van and made promise of help so generous that Pownall was able to write:

> It has been hitherto the Merit of this Province to stand foremost in the King's Service but here they stand alone.

Massachusetts was to put 2,500 men in the field. New York promised 2,680, New Hampshire 800, and so on. The remoter colonies were less zealous. The Legislature of Pennsylvania insisted that, whatever the menace to other colonies, Pennsylvania was in no danger, and, in spite of Amherst's protests, the colony would promise only 150 men.

In 1900, when the British colonies sent contingents to South Africa, the mother country paid and equipped the regiments. In 1760, the colonies did better, for they undertook not merely to muster but also to clothe and pay their men. Arms, ammunition, tents, and food were, however, to be supplied by Great Britain. Pitt wrote somewhat peremptorily that the king *expects* and *requires* colonial help; yet he promised that the colonies might be compensated by the British Parliament for their outlay. In the end they put into the field what were for them considerable armies, and to do so they incurred heavy financial obligations. But, of course, they were carrying on a war at their own door and for their own safety.

Pitt had urged Amherst to be ready by the first of May to begin his campaign. The colonial levies were, however, not to be hurried. Amherst left New York on May 3 to proceed up the Hudson River, and, by way of Albany and Schenectady, to advance ultimately to the shores of Lake Ontario. Three armies were to close in on Montreal, one from the east, one from the south, and one from the west. The French could not break through the cordon which surrounded them, and they must either surrender piecemeal or be driven in upon Montreal. We may surmise that a single army advancing on Montreal in great force by way of the St. Lawrence would not have proved less effective.

A slow enveloping movement was, however, in accordance with Amherst's deliberate and thorough methods. He took one great chance—that the British fleet would reach Canada before the fleet from France. Had this not happened, had the French recovered Quebec and been able to hold it, Amherst's attempt on Montreal might well have proved disastrous. Bourlamaque, perhaps the ablest officer on the French side, calls the advance by way of Lake Ontario a foolish chase, and says that Amherst undertook it only to prove that if Montreal had not fallen in the previous year it was not his fault but Gage's.

Plans on paper, made remote from the scene of action, can very rarely be carried out. This plan, however, worked admirably. Since Amherst had blamed Gage for his failure to clear the Upper St. Lawrence of the French, he now undertook this task himself. His delays were many. Not, as had been hoped, in May, but in July, some ten thousand men were laboriously advancing through the wilderness from Albany to Oswego, not far from the point where Lake Ontario discharges into the St. Lawrence, there to embark and descend the great river to Montreal.

At the same time more than three thousand men, under Colonel Haviland, were to advance by Lake Champlain, the route which Amherst himself had used in the previous autumn. Haviland was to keep the French at Isle aux Noix in a state of constant alarm and thus conceal the chief menace, which was from Amherst's overwhelming force. A third army, under Murray, was to advance from Quebec. The movements were so planned that the three forces should arrive before

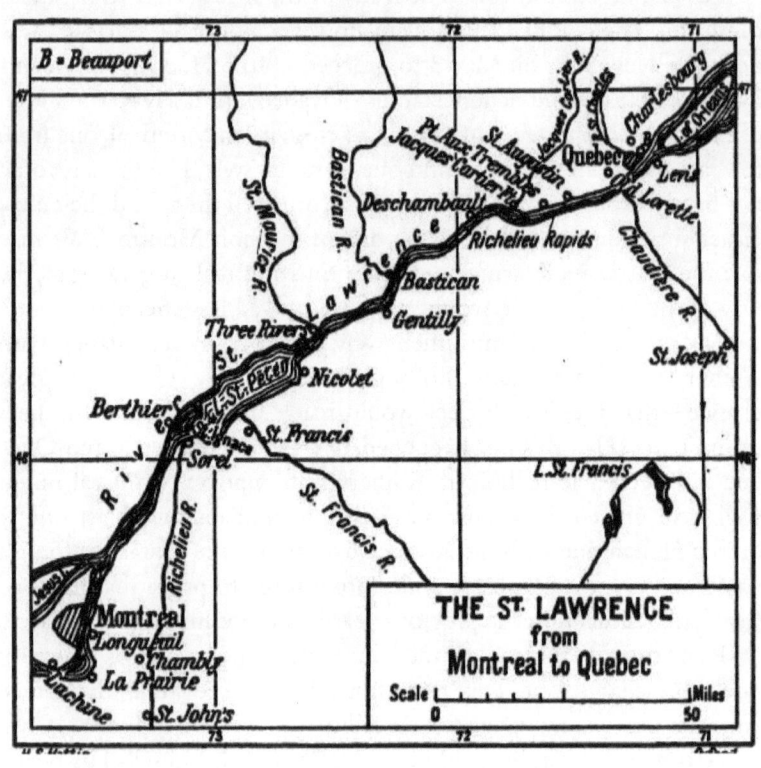

Montreal at the same time.

It was Murray's advance that the French leaders watched most anxiously. The really decisive movement was, indeed, that of Amherst; but Amherst, far up in the wilderness of the interior, could not be watched, and only vague rumours of what he was doing reached the French. They now knew that if the British should decide to take a fleet up the river they could do little to stop them. An army they were ready and more than willing to fight, but a fleet they could only watch impotently from the shore. Murray intended simply to ignore the French land forces. He was safe on the ships. If the French wished to remain in his rear they were free to do so, for, should Montreal fall, any further efforts to hold Canada must collapse. Murray hoped that the French would surrender to him before the advance began. Malartic wrote to Lévis on May 26:

> He wished, I think, to pump me this morning, he asked me what you intended to do, and said that it was impossible for you to save the colony. You would only ruin it by holding together your army.

Murray told Bellecombe, a French officer at Quebec, that he would grant easy terms if the French would capitulate. When Bellecombe answered with some spirit that the English would have to do some more fighting before they took Canada, Murray retorted that the French Army could not live on air. The French were, however, able to keep up a long, losing campaign, and the war could be ended only by an elaborate campaign.

Murray managed so to keep in touch with Amherst's plans that he knew the proper time to set out. In the end he started without waiting for the reinforcements from Louisbourg. They would, however, follow him quickly. Colonel Fraser was to remain in command at Quebec, and both Murray and his second in command. Colonel Burton, were to go up the river with the army. Officers and men who had gone to New York and elsewhere to recruit their health now returned. Some others were able to leave the hospitals at Quebec. But three thousand sick and wounded remained, and, in the end, Murray could array for active service only about twenty-five hundred men of all ranks.

Officers and men, really too ill for such service, none the less begged to be allowed a share in the final glory of the conquest of Canada. They had borne, they said, the burden and heat of the day, and now, it seemed, they were to be left at Quebec and deprived of their reward; the glory, due to them, others would secure. But Murray was firm and gave strict orders to his officers not to take with them any one unfit for full duty in the field. So insignificant seemed the French power for attack that Quebec was left defended by only 1,700 men fit for duty; but, of course, some ships remained, and, in case of need, others could hurry down the river to the rescue.

On July 11 the baggage of the troops was put on board the transports. Lévis, with his army half starving, heard with hungry desire that the British were taking a prodigious quantity of food supplies. On the 12th Murray reviewed his force. Next day at five o'clock in the morning the right brigade embarked and at five in the afternoon the left did the same. The men had just received a part of their pay, long overdue, and had been guilty of some irregularities, but, in spite of this, the embarkation was made in good order. At three o'clock on the next morning, the 14th, everything was ready; the fleet weighed anchor and began its momentous advance. The array on the St. Lawrence was imposing. Four British men-of-war provided the escort. The men-of-war, floating batteries, and transports, made up a fleet of some eighty vessels. Considerable fleets had often sailed up as far as Quebec, but this was the first time that one had set out to attack Montreal. The array made a profound impression upon the people who surveyed its advance from the shore. Lévis wrote on August 7:

> The *habitants* are frightened to death at the sight of the fleet, they are afraid that their houses will all be burned.

Some of them already knew by experience what the British could do in this respect.

On the first night the fleet anchored opposite Pointe aux Trembles. On the 15th it was before Jacques Cartier, the stronghold which the French had held during the winter. The fort stood on a bold eminence, and an abattis of felled trees, stretching down to the water, made assault from that side almost impossible. The garrison fired some shot and shell at the ships. But the channel was far away, near the south bank, and the fleet passed on untouched, leaving the fort in the rear. Murray now showed that he intended to do precisely what Lévis most dreaded—to advance to Montreal without attempting to fight on land. Dumas, who commanded at Jacques Cartier, was instructed to follow Murray up the river. Vaudreuil had written:

> If the enemy should decide to penetrate to the heart of the colony and to leave you where you are, you will not hesitate, in

such a case, to withdraw your outposts, to summon the militia of your neighbourhood ... and to proceed to join M. de Longueuil and the forces which he will have assembled at Three Rivers. (Vaudreuil to Dumas, June 4, 1760: *Report on Canadian Archives*, 1905, i.).

Vaudreuil added that if the British should try to land at Three Rivers they were, in his accustomed fine phrasing, to be resisted even at the cost of the total annihilation of the French defending force.

The British rarely ventured to land on the north shore, but on the south they repeatedly threw out parties of rangers. This was a challenge to the Canadians. However, weary they might be of the contest, they could not refrain from the guerrilla warfare in which they excelled. Now they had an occasional brush with the British. Sometimes the rangers marched on shore for days together, advancing with the fleet. On leaving Quebec Murray had issued a proclamation saying that Canadians who laid down their arms had nothing to fear. He required only an oath of neutrality. On July 25 Captain Knox describes a scene that was often duplicated:

> The parish of St. Antoine have this day laid down their arms, and taken the oath of neutrality; as the form of swearing is solemn, it may not be improper to particularise it. The men stand in a circle, hold up their right hands, repeat each his own name, and then say,—
> '.... Do severally swear, in the presence of Almighty God, that we will not take up arms against George the Second, King of Great Britain, &c., &c., or against his troops or subjects; nor give any intelligence to his enemies, directly or indirectly; So Help me God.'

The oath was mild enough and Murray insisted that it should be scrupulously observed. From time to time he himself went ashore. Since he knew French well he could speak to the people in their own tongue. He told them that, while the cause of France was hopeless, the might of Britain as shown in her ships, artillery, and other equipment was resistless. He added that he would in no way molest the persons and property of the men who were attending to their duties, but that he would burn all the houses from which the men were absent. This resolution caused extensive desertions from the French Army. Many of the militia returned to their parishes in order to avert the destruction by the British of their houses, should they not be there. In village after village the whole male population took the oath, saying, in some cases, that they were glad to have the excuse of Murray's demand for so doing.

Some Canadians, however, showed irreconcilable hostility, and Murray blamed the clergy for this attitude. To a priest brought before him he said:

> The clergy are the source of all the mischiefs that have befallen the poor Canadians, whom they keep in ignorance, and excite to wickedness and their own ruin. No doubt you have heard that I hanged a captain of militia; that I have a priest and some Jesuits on board a ship of war, to be transmitted to Great Britain: beware of the snare they have fallen into; *preach the Gospel*, which alone is your province.

Early in the advance up the river the French sent a party of Indians to the south shore to harass the British with their barbarous methods of warfare. The result was a stern message from Murray, sent under a flag of truce to the officer commanding at Deschambault, that if the savages were not instantly recalled, and if they committed any barbarities, no quarter would be given even to regulars and that the country would undergo military execution wherever the British landed.

Along the river the houses were numerous, Captain Knox says:

> From the Island of Coudre, below Quebec, to that of Montreal, the country on both sides of this river is so well settled, and closely inhabited, as to resemble almost one continual village; the habitations appear extremely neat, with sashed windows, and, in general, washed on the outside with lime, as are likewise their churches, which are all constructed upon one uniform plan, and have an agreeable effect upon the traveller.

When the British landed and entered the houses which, from the river, looked so charming, they suffered disillusion, for the peasantry were, Knox declares, 'intolerably dirty'. As the fleet advanced farther from the regions about Quebec desolated by war, the condition of the people improved. Knox says:

> I have been in a great many farmhouses since I embarked on this expedition, and I may venture to advance, that in every one of them I have seen a good loaf, two, or three, according to the number of the family, of excellent wheaten bread; and such of the inhabitants as came on board our ships, from time to time,

in order to traffick disdained our biscuits, upon being offered refreshments. . . . Notwithstanding all that has been said of the immense distresses and starving condition of the Canadians, I do not find that there is any real want.

Black cattle, sheep, and pigs seemed numerous, and sometimes this plenty was too great a temptation to the British seamen allowed to go on shore. On one occasion they pillaged houses and offered violence to some Canadian women. The result was a stern threat from Murray that death by hanging would be the penalty for a repetition of the offence. The men had more innocent diversion in fishing and in paddling the Canadian canoes. To the British sailor these were a great novelty. He knew little of their use and would sometimes stand up in them to fish, with the inevitable result of an upset. The current was very swift and a good many soldiers and sailors were drowned as a result of their own carelessness.

The point on the river probably most easy of defence was Deschambault, some nine or ten miles above Jacques Cartier. There the Richelieu Rapids made passage difficult, for the channel was shallow and full of rocks, which at low tide appeared above the surface. Powerful batteries at this point could have checked an ascending fleet. Murray had, indeed, planned to seize this place in the spring so as to make impossible the further ascent of French ships which might reach Quebec. (Murray to Amherst, by Lieutenant Montresor as messenger, March 3, 1760—Canadian Archives).

The French had placed a battery in the church at Deschambault, and this began to play on the British ships as they tried to work their way up the channel. Adverse winds helped the French to delay for about ten days a part of the fleet. A lieutenant and three privates were killed by their fire. But, owing to bad powder and to bad guns, the resistance was really weak, and when, on the 26th, there was a favourable wind, the fleet sailed on without further injury. At no other point on the river had the French the slightest chance of retarding the British advance. Indeed, though the ascent of the St. Lawrence involved difficult and intricate navigation which taxed the skill of Captain Deane, the officer in command, not a single ship was lost or even damaged during the entire journey.

Day by day as the fleet advanced it was 'politely attended', as Knox expresses it, by a French force which marched along the north shore abreast of the ships. The French feared that the British would try to land at Three Rivers, the most important place in Canada, after Quebec and Montreal. Here M. de Longueuil was in command, and he with Pontleroy, the engineer, had long been busy preparing for defence. It was the capital of one of the three subdivisions of Canada, and the French considered it a garrison town of great importance. Knox, however, calls this 'open straggling village' a 'wretched place', and notes with satisfaction that part of it lay so low on the north shore as to be an admirable object for bombardment. He saw what strikes visitors to French Canada to this day: the poor wooden houses of the inhabitants in vivid contrast with the massive stone church and convent buildings. The place was defended by extensive entrenchments and redoubts, as Knox says:

> Indicating an intention to have disputed every inch of ground with us, if we had made a descent there, which it may be presumed they expected.

It was here indeed, that Vaudreuil had said that rather than let the British land the French must die to the last man. But the British had no thought of landing. The Canadians, as distinguished from the French, invited them to do so in what seemed no unfriendly way. When some armed British boats went forward to examine the channel before the town, a body of Canadians drawn up on the bank called out to them, 'What water have you. Englishmen?'

The reply was given with true British brusqueness: 'Sufficient to bring up our ships, and knock you and your houses to pieces.' The answer of the Canadians showed the temper to which some of these unfortunate people had now come. A man, supposed by the British to be an officer, called out that the Canadians, if left alone, would offer the British no annoyance, and ended by inviting the officers to come ashore and refresh themselves. Two channels led past Three Rivers, that near the north shore commanded by the batteries of the town, that on the south side out of range. The ships passed quite safely by the south channel. The day—the 8th of August—was clear and pleasant, and Captain Knox, who had an eye for beauty, thought that:

> The situation on the banks of a delightful river, our fleet sailing triumphantly before them, in line of battle, the country on both sides interspersed with neat settlements, together with the verdure of the fields and trees, afforded, with the addition of clear pleasant weather, as agreeable a prospect as the most lively imagination can conceive.

The French troops, who seemed to number about two thousand, lined the works as the British ships filed past.

Their light cavalry, who paraded along shore, seemed to be well appointed, clothed in blue, faced with scarlet; but their officers had white uniforms.

Knox, aided by a glass, discerned among the troops fifty naked savages with painted faces. Even at this, the most carefully defended spot on the river, the French could only stand impotent on the bank and see the hostile fleet pass. It mattered nothing to the British that Three Rivers, like Jacques Cartier, was left in their rear, untaken. Even its defenders soon abandoned it to march along the north shore in the wake of the advancing fleet.

When the fleet reached Sorel at the mouth of the Richelieu River, a new embarrassment appeared for the French defenders. Haviland was advancing down Lake Champlain to the head of this river. Would Murray try to ascend the river and catch as in a vice the fort at Isle aux Noix, which would be assailed at the same time by Haviland from the south? This was what the French most dreaded and what they were resolved, if possible, to prevent. Bourlamaque, now in command at Sorel, was puzzled. Lévis was moving from post to post and the couriers were kept busy. Even though paper was now hardly to be had, Bourlamaque sometimes sent to his leader three letters in a single day.

On August 12, impotent on the shore at Sorel, Bourlamaque watched the long array of ships file past. It was useless to fire upon them, he said, as he could do no real damage. He could only count the ships, and write to Lévis how many there were: five ships with three masts, nineteen with two, ten with one mast, twenty-one armed *bateaux*, and a seemingly endless number of smaller craft. What should he do? he asked. He could not for ever keep marching his barefooted men along the shore to points where the English might possibly land. He had only seven hundred troops, and three hundred and fifty of them were militia, not well-disposed. He had no one to look after the stores, no secretary even for the necessary clerical work, no smith to repair damaged muskets. If he had had one or two naval officers they could have told him what to expect from the movements of the British ships. He wrote:

> I am worn out, I have no one on whom I can depend, I can get no sleep.

It is interesting to contrast with this despairing utterance the thoughts of the British officer, Captain Knox. On this same day, August 12, Knox describes in glowing terms the scene which he surveyed as the ship approached Sorel:

> I think nothing could equal the beauties of our navigation this morning, with which I was exceedingly charmed; the meandering course of the channel, so narrow that an active person might have stepped ashore from our transports, either to the right or left; the awfulness and solemnity of the dark forests with which these islands are covered, together with the fragrancy of the spontaneous fruits, shrubs, and flowers; the verdure of the water by the reflection of the neighbouring woods, the wild chirping notes of the feathered inhabitants, the masts and sails of ships appearing as if among the trees, both a-head and a-stern ... formed, all together. .... an enchanting diversity.

There were other things to please a British officer, for while the fleet lay before Sorel it was joined by a second squadron bringing two regiments from Louisbourg, long expected by Murray. Lord Rollo, its leader, had not tarried at Quebec, but had hurried up the river to join Murray's expedition. Opposite Sorel is the island of St. Ignace, and here the troops were landed that the transports might be cleaned and aired. The strip of water separating them from the mainland was an adequate protection from attack. Since the male Canadians seemed to be absent serving with the French Army, the British took freely as the spoils of war what provisions they could find in the houses.

The Canadians in this district had seen as yet no real war, and they had not learned, what those near Quebec had learned, how sternly the British would punish acts of hostility on the part of the civil population. A church at Sorel had been fortified under the direction of the *curé*, and many of the male inhabitants in the neighbourhood were in arms. A stern lesson seemed necessary. Accordingly, on August 22, about two in the morning, a British force under Lord Rollo dropped down the river from the island of St. Ignace, and, landing a little below Sorel, began the work of devastation. They burned the houses of the men who were absent from home, but spared the others. This destruction was the result of the same policy that Wolfe had carried out near Quebec. Murray wrote to Pitt:

> I was ... under the cruel necessity of burning the greatest part of these poor unhappy people's houses. I pray God this example

may suffice, for my nature revolts, when this becomes a necessary part of my duty.

It was effective. Bourlamaque wrote to Lévis at six in the evening of that very day:

> Protests and menaces are unavailing to keep the inhabitants of this parish from giving up their arms to the English. At this moment they tell me that twenty men of the company of Cormier are going off with their muskets. I am writing to M. Denos to try to stop this by announcing that I will burn down the house of the first man who does it.

Fifty or sixty Canadians, sent from Montreal to take some vessels down the river, abandoned them and ran off to their homes, and a company of militia broke out into open pillage in their own camp. They declared, says Rocquemaure, in command at St. Johns, that they would stay with the French Army as long as it suited them, some until Tuesday, some until Friday, and that then they should go home. Since whole companies were guilty, punishment was really impossible. It was useless, Bourlamaque says bitterly, to write to Vaudreuil about any misdoings, of the Canadians. The governor gave no heed, and would probably write to the Court that Bourlamaque had two or three thousand Canadians who were doing wonders. These poor people had meanwhile a hard fate. If they went away from home the English burned their houses, on the supposition that they were serving with the French; if they stayed at home the French threatened to do the same thing, on the supposition that they were not fighting for their country.

By this time Isle aux Noix had become untenable. Already, on August 2, Bougainville, in command there, wrote:

> I expect the enemy to unmask tomorrow a great devil of a battery, which is hardly a musket-shot from us.... They have made immense abattis .... It doesn't matter: we shall do our best.

On August 9, three vessels, representing the vanguard of Haviland's force, appeared before the place, and soon shot and shell were pouring into it pitilessly. Bougainville had done what he could; he had made elaborate works and entrenchments and had stretched booms across the two branches of the river enclosing the island. But the British carried on a furious bombardment, and they managed to work round with some mortars and cannon so as to attack the fort from the rear. They pushed up their works so close that they were able to kill soldiers on the ramparts with muskets. Moreover, Bougainville was likely before long to be face to face with famine. The seven or eight oxen which he had were killed by the British fire. The river was full of fish, but the British fire made it impossible to resort to this source of supply.

Bourlamaque thought that Isle aux Noix should be abandoned; so did Vaudreuil; but Lévis, who wished to prolong the fight and to delay surrender, opposed retreat until the very last moment. He ordered La Pause, an able and tactful officer, to send forward, if possible, help to Bougainville from St. Johns, a few miles lower down the river towards the St. Lawrence. On August 3 La Pause could hear firing at the distant fort. It was raining heavily. The Canadian scouts would not volunteer to carry dispatches to Bougainville, and, in the end, Noguères, an officer of the Royal Roussillon Regiment, was obliged himself to undertake the task, and but one Canadian could be induced to accompany him.

On August 25 a critical event happened. The British suddenly pushed forward some cannon and opened a hot fire on the five French ships which lay at the foot of the island. The ships were riddled by the fire. Some of the sailors escaped by swimming to shore, the rest surrendered. After the protecting ships had been captured, the British would soon break the boom, or at least carry across boats so as to attack the fort from points below as well as above the island. They could also go down the river and attack St. Johns and other places. Lévis was still most anxious to hold the fort. He had written on August 19 to Bougainville:

> I count much on your post to prolong our defence and to do honour to our arms. The place could not be in better hands.

Later he sent a verbal message through La Pause, at St. Johns, that Bougainville should hold out. But Vaudreuil was of a different mind. On August 26, when the news of the capture of the ships reached him, he wrote to say that if Bougainville could not check the advance of the British down the river, or was in danger of being captured, he should spike his cannon and retire. Lévis, he said, knew the purport of his letter. Bougainville was sorely puzzled what to do. He held a council of war on August 27, and they reached a unanimous decision to retire.

This had become no easy task, for the British were now encamped above and below the fort on both banks of the river. Bougainville planned a ruse. While withdrawing his men he would keep up the appearance of strenuous defence. Some forty invalids, under a colonial officer, La Borgne, were to continue firing the seven or eight pieces of cannon as long as ammunition lasted. Meanwhile the retreat would be effected. At ten o'clock at night all the available boats were gathered at the chosen point and silently the garrison crossed to the mainland. The plan succeeded.

The British did not learn of the retreat until noon the next day. Then La Borgne, who kept up a vigorous fire, had no more ammunition, and he raised the white flag. Meanwhile Bougainville was marching through the forest towards Montreal, as he thought. He had counted on Indians as guides, but they had deserted a losing cause, and, without guides, he lost his way. From midnight to midday the army toiled through frightful swamps, only to find in the end that it was still near the British camp before Isle aux Noix. Bougainville now tried to reach St. Johns, a few miles down the river from Isle aux Noix, and at four in the afternoon his bedraggled force arrived at a clearing not far from that place. The Chevalier Johnstone, who took part in this terrible march, writes:

> I was so overcome with fatigue, and so totally exhausted, not being able but with the greatest pain to trail my legs, that I thought a thousand times of lying down to finish my days; but the fear of falling into the hands of savages connected with the English, and the idea of the cruelties and torments which they exercised over their prisoners, making them die under the cruellest sufferings, at a small fire, . . . the terror of that gave me from time to time new strength. . . . . I have very often found myself in . . . painful and fatiguing positions but never in any where I experienced so much suffering as in this cruel journey.

The weather was very hot, and when he reached the river and had sufficiently recovered, he plunged in, still wearing his uniform, and remained for more than an hour with only his head above water. The French lost twenty-four men on the march.

La Pause, at St. Johns, was distressed when he heard of Bougainville's retreat. Since but few men had been lost at Isle aux Noix, he thought that greater sacrifices should have been made to support the glory of the French arms, Bougainville's answer to these reflections was a demand to be judged by a council of war. La Pause himself had now to retire, for no one at St. Johns, not even the officers, wished to fight. He postponed his retreat to the last moment, that he might help to rescue the poor fellows lost in the woods. But when, on the night of the 29th, the British began an advance in force on St. Johns, the French set it on fire and marched the dozen miles to La Prairie, opposite Montreal, Misfortunes did not come singly. Just at the same time word was received that Fort Lévis, far up on the St. Lawrence, had fallen to Amherst.

The Indians, alert to see how the wind was blowing, were now treating independently with the British and deserting the cause on which their own misdeeds had brought such discredit. On September 2, Lévis met some of them at La Prairie, opposite Montreal, on the south side of the river. While he was haranguing them a messenger arrived to say that the Indian tribes had made peace with the British. At once the savage audience ran off without listening further. The moment the Indians who had negotiated the peace with the British had completed their work they gathered on the beach opposite Montreal, and brandished knives and hatchets and shrieked their war-cry, in token that they had now become the enemies of the French. The British did not find that their new allies mingled well with their own savages. While Murray was occupied, apparently at Longueuil, with the French Indians, two Mohawks entered the room. They gazed intently at the others and then dashed at them with fury. When separated the two groups continued to mutter reproaches and threats. The Mohawks recalled outrages by their old enemies and swore that 'the cowardly dogs' should pay for it.

> We will destroy you and your settlement, root and branch; . . . our squaws are better than you; they will stand and fight like men—but ye skulk like dogs.

At this the French chief raised what Knox calls 'a horrid yell'. Murray kept the peace only by threats of stern chastisement from Amherst if any violence was done.

The French *débâcle* was now almost complete. Place after place near Montreal surrendered to the British. Lévis could not hold together his forces. Knox wrote on September 3:

> The regulars now desert to us in great numbers, and the Canadian militia are surrendering by hundreds.

> Those who did not surrender deserted in bands and ran off to their

homes. Even when they did not desert they refused to obey orders. Roquemaure says on September 3:

> I gave orders to M. de Bellecour to lead his mounted men to Longueuil, but not one would follow him. The militia attached to the Royal Roussillon battalion refused to march.

Even the regulars went off half a dozen at a time. The officers harangued the troops and appealed to their honour, but with little effect. Everywhere was raised the cry for 'Capitulation'.

Meanwhile Murray was pressing up closer to Montreal. By September 4 he had disembarked most of his troops on the island of Ste Thérèse, near the lower part of the greater island on which Montreal stands. From this point he could easily land in force on either the north or the south side of the river. Haviland was advancing steadily from St. Johns to Longueuil, immediately opposite Montreal, and news had come that Amherst was near on the upper river. The word now went forth on the French side that all the regiments should close in on Montreal. Their forces on the south bank crossed the river as best they could, and by September 3 the sadly diminished ranks of the dispirited army had been reunited in that place.

Chapter 7

The Fall of New France

The complicated plan of bringing together at the same time and at the same place three armies, each faced by a resolute, if weak, foe, was working out admirably. Amherst's movements had been the slowest and the most protracted. He had arrived at Albany, from New York, early in May. But, as we have seen, his colonial levies came in only slowly, and a long two months passed before it was worthwhile for him to go on to Oswego, the point on Lake Ontario where he intended to embark his forces. At Oswego Colonel Haldimand, an efficient officer, was in charge of the preparations. Even after Amherst arrived, it was still another month before his force was ready to set out. Far up near the west end of the lake the British held Fort Niagara, and from the St. Lawrence to the Mississippi they were masters. Detroit, on the route from Lake Erie to Lake Huron, still held out for France. The posts in the north-western country France also retained. If, however, Montreal fell, the sources of supplies for these posts would be cut off and they would fall to the conqueror without a further blow.

For months Colonel Haldimand had waited at Oswego, making ready for the great enterprise. During the weary time of preparation. General Gage at Albany had sent on to his brother officers what news he could glean in America and also welcome supplies of magazines from Europe. While Haldimand waited, winter had become spring and spring summer; and now summer itself was wearing away. Slowly the motley battalions of regulars and provincials came in and made the little fort a busy scene. On July 23 Sir William Johnson arrived, leading some hundreds of Indians. Their knowledge of the forest might have made them useful as scouts in this wild country, but the information which they gathered was often worthless. For week, they had been bringing in wild rumours of the arrival, not of a French but of a Span-

GENERAL GEOFFREY AMHERST

ish fleet in the St. Lawrence. Spain was still at peace with England, but a general in a remote wilderness could not be sure of this, and the rumour caused some slight disquiet.

If anyone could control the Indians it was Sir William Johnson. He had lived long among them in the colony of New York and knew thoroughly the half-childish ways of these wild sons of the forest. The tribes of Iroquois, with whom he came chiefly in touch, respected him and usually obeyed him. But the remoter tribes, with whom, during the past months, the British had been carrying on laborious negotiations, were less easy to manage. Amherst himself loathed the practices of his savage allies. When they had the chance they would sometimes dig up even buried corpses in order to scalp them. 'Firmness with these gentry is very necessary,' Amherst wrote at this time, and, in spite of their sulks and threats when crossed, he held them in check and would not permit any of the outrages that the French officers, from Montcalm downwards, had not prevented.

The great camp on Lake Ontario could in time muster more than ten thousand men. The primeval forest came down to the shore of the sparkling lake, spreading away to the horizon, seemingly vast as Ocean itself. The fort with its surrounding clearings formed but a slight break in the sombre monotony of forest that hedged it in. Food was sometimes scarce and bad, and insanitary conditions caused heavy mortality. While there was no corruption on the part of contractors such as we hear of on the French side, we get an occasional hint that the shrewd colonial traders were not too scrupulous in their methods. In this isolated spot the life of the soldiers was tedious, and it is not to be wondered at that some should plan to desert. The provincial troops suffered especially from home-sickness, and a good many of them tried to run away. It was not easy, however. Some offenders were caught and brought to trial, and the penalty of desertion was death.

On July 29 we have a grim order from Amherst. Eleven men are condemned to be hanged for desertion, but one of them, John Jones, is to be pardoned if he will accept the alternative of acting as executioner to the other ten. These are to prepare for death, and when they have gone through their devotions one of them is to be hanged. Amherst's justice was tempered with mercy, for he ordered that, at the moment when the remaining nine thought themselves on the verge of the grave, they should be pardoned, with a stern warning never to desert again. It was a mode of punishment likely to be impressive to the lines of soldiers drawn up round a hollow square to see the majesty of the law vindicated.

Perhaps hardly less impressive was the review of the troops for which Amherst issued an order on August 3. For the complex manoeuvres of a showy parade there can have been little space on the stump-strewn and somewhat hilly shore of Lake Ontario. The main thing was to see that the men were well equipped for their uncertain tasks in descending the river to meet the foe. Along the shore of the lake and on the banks were lying the hundreds of '*batteaus*' and 'whale-boats' necessary to carry ten thousand men on the long journey to Montreal.

The might of Britain on the sea was represented by a fleet of two ships under Captain Loring, the *Onondaga* and the *Mohawk*, three-masted merchant vessels of the type known as 'snow'. They were well armed. The *Onondaga* carried four nine-pounders, fourteen six-pounders, and one hundred seamen; the *Mohawk*, sixteen six-pounders and ninety seamen. Some three weeks before Amherst himself set out from Oswego, he had sent them to seek, and, if possible, to destroy two French vessels which had the hardihood to appear off Oswego on July 20. But for some time, even with the best pilots to be procured, the vessels could not find a channel, and the delay was such that, instead of going down the river before Amherst, they set out only after he had begun his advance.

Even by August 10 all the boats were not ready. Amherst, however, determined to start with the regulars and the artillery, leaving General Gage to follow with the colonial troops. On the morning of the 10th, therefore, the army embarked at daybreak. The route was at first along the shore of the open lake. These vast inland waters can be as tempestuous as the sea itself; this day the lake was in an ugly mood and one boat was lost. On the whole, however, all went well. General Gage soon followed with the colonial forces, and by the 12th all were in the comparatively safe waters of the St. Lawrence River, on that flowing tide which swept for many miles past forest-clad banks and occasional clearings on to Montreal itself, the end of the journey.

In all the world, perhaps, there is no other river so majestic. It discharges the waters of half a dozen mighty lakes, and its broad current is in very few places less than a mile wide. At its beginning it wanders through hundreds of islands, the famous 'Thousand Islands', at the present day dotted with summer residences. Then it plunges into swirling rapids, full of peril for small boats. At the foot of the last of these, nearly two hundred miles from the head of the river, the little

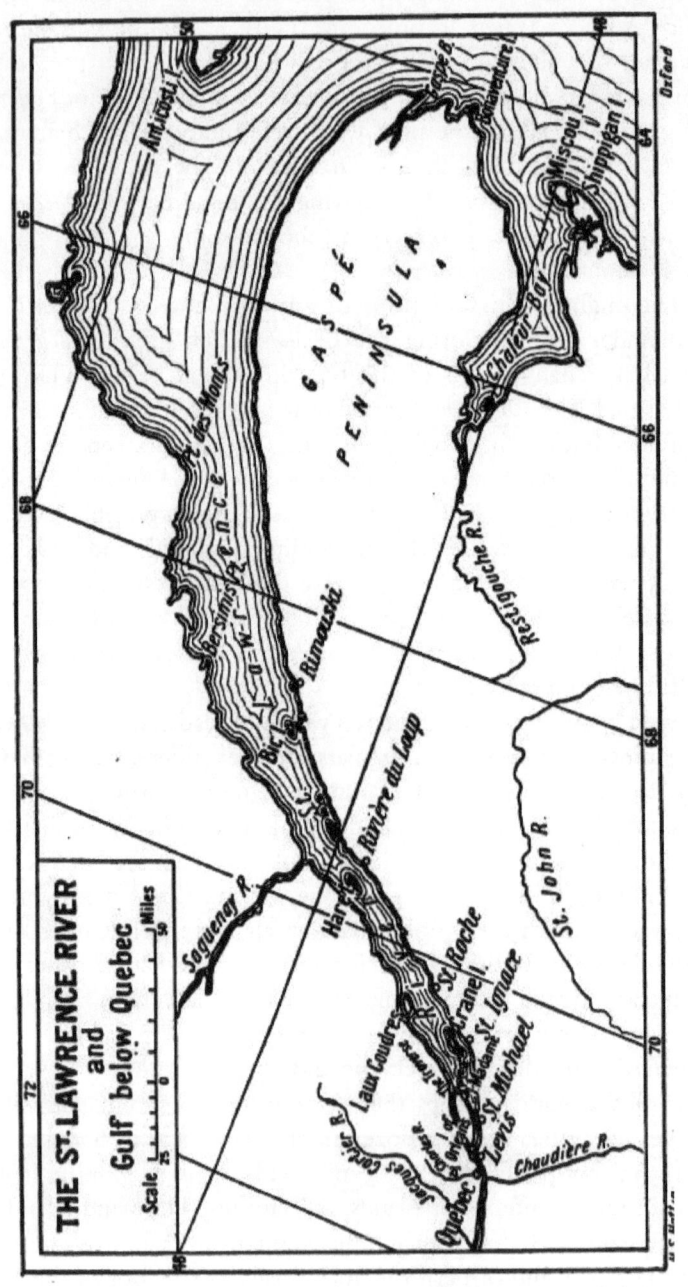

town of Montreal had grown up. The task of Amherst was to take his great force in small boats along those many miles of river. He had three problems to solve. The first was to overcome the French force which he should find barring his way at Fort Lévis, near La Presentation, now Ogdensburg, some seventy miles from the entrance of the river.

As his second task he would then have to pass through the rapids, the beginning of which Fort Lévis guarded. Last of all he must crush the French Army awaiting him at Montreal. So overwhelming was his force that the military tasks were really easy. Yet there were some uncertainties. The two armed French vessels were hovering near Fort Lévis and they might work havoc in the flotilla of small boats; moreover, the actual strength of the French force barring the way was quite unknown to the British, though it could not be formidable.

Fortune favoured Amherst.

Just at the time when he was drawing near Fort Lévis, one of the French vessels ran aground and was so much damaged as to be rendered useless. When an Indian brought in this news on the 15th, Amherst hurried on with his small boats, hoping to capture the other ship while her companion was disabled. He met her at daybreak on the 17th, trying to pass up the river towards Oswego. The British attacked her with five rowing galleys armed with artillery. Since it was calm, the small boats could move freely, while the large ship lay motionless and almost helpless. There was a sharp fight, but the French ship soon gave in, and she and her hundred men, under an officer named La Broquerie, were taken at slight cost.

On the same day Amherst occupied La Présentation, which had been evacuated and practically destroyed by the French. It commanded not merely the trade by the St. Lawrence from Montreal, but was also convenient of access to the very heart of the colony of New York. Here for some ten years the Abbé Picquet had carried on a flourishing mission, chiefly to the Iroquois Indians. The *abbé*, half priest, half politician, had thrown his whole heart into the work and had dreamed of establishing the sway both of the Church and of France over all the lands bordering on Lake Ontario. With a statesman's foresight he had chosen this important strategic point. He had worked zealously among the Indians, had lived like one of themselves, and had led hundreds of them to give their adhesion to the Roman Catholic faith. He had not changed their mode of warfare.

The British found in the Indian habitations at La Présentation many human scalps. This sight especially incensed the Mohawk allies, and they burned the chapel. The Indians at La Presentation showed a disposition to make terms with Amherst, and the Abbé Picquet's dreams for their future were doomed to complete failure by the British occupation. La Presentation has now become prosaic Ogdensburg, a thriving American town, with scarcely a memory of the days when it was a cherished outpost of France in North America.

Five miles down the river from La Présentation lay Fort Lévis. Here, during the previous winter, the French engineer, Desandroüins, amidst manifold discouragements that nearly drove him out of his mind, had toiled to make a strong post. In the end he had asked for work elsewhere. Then hither to take command had come in March Pouchot, who had held Niagara until it fell to the British. We have the story of his hardships told by himself. He had left Montreal on March 17 to go to Fort Lévis. In the earlier campaign he had lost his personal equipage at Niagara and now was without the common necessaries. Yet, as he declares, when he was about to set out on the ice to go to his post, the Intendant Bigot refused to supply him with even the blanket that he asked for. Obviously he was not in the ring that was working with Bigot, and all that he obtained from the king's supplies for his own needs was a keg of wine. Nevertheless, he was now resolved to make a stern fight. Lévis had indeed a dim hope that Pouchot could so delay Amherst as to permit the main French Army to defeat Haviland and Murray in turn before Amherst arrived.

To leave Pouchot serenely alone in his little island fort would have been wise policy for Amherst. Murray had left untouched the French at Jacques Cartier and at Three Rivers, when he ascended to Montreal. Amherst could pass down the river by the north and south channels unharmed from the guns of the fort, leaving Pouchot to bombard the air if he liked. But Amherst would leave no unconquered foe in his rear. Accordingly, on the 18th, when Murray and Haviland, already near Montreal, were chafing at the delay of their chief, he made elaborate plans for assaulting Fort Lévis. The captured French vessel anchored within range of the fort. One British column rowed down past it on the north side and another on the south side.

On the first day Pouchot found himself completely invested. On the second day Amherst made preparations for attack as elaborate as if he had been besieging a vital stronghold. He began to construct land batteries on points commanding the fort. His two vessels, which had been delayed at Oswego, now appeared at last, and he had three ships at anchor at advantageous points. He spent day after day in these tasks, and not until August 23 was he ready to open fire from all his batteries and to close in on the fort with his vessels. Even on that day he did nothing decisive, he wrote to Pitt:

> For the going down of the vessels to the fort was not effected in the manner I could wish, and I determined not to pursue my plan that day. (Amherst to Pitt, Aug. 26, 1760).

For another and still another day he continued his bombardment, gradually dismounting the French guns with his fire, until at last, on the 25th, Pouchot, caught like a rat in a trap, surrendered at discretion with his three hundred men. He had made a brave fight and had inflicted some loss on his assailants. Even after the surrender, Amherst still lingered at the fort which he now renamed Fort William Henry. On the 26th he took time to write an elaborate letter to Pitt describing what he had done and enclosing lists of everything found in the captured stronghold. Then he busied himself in making repairs to the fort and to his boats. Not until the 31st was he ready again to set out. An army of ten thousand men had been kept occupied for two weeks in reducing a fort containing three hundred.

Amherst sent to New York the prisoners taken at Fort Lévis, and retained only the pilots, who would be of service in meeting the dangers of the river. With justice, as the event proved, he dreaded the descent of the rapids. He questioned the captive Pouchot anxiously about the perils, and we may be sure learned nothing from that astute officer which would be very reassuring. On the morning of August 31 the army was once more afloat. That day they rowed twenty miles and passed through two rapids which Amherst thought 'more frightful than dangerous'. The next day he was not so fortunate.

As his boats neared the Long Sault Rapids, a little above the present Canadian town of Cornwall, he put ashore covering parties to save his force from possible ambush by the enemy. The boats passed down the rapids in single file, and the experience was exciting enough. The rapids were full of choppy waves which curled over the edge of the boats. These took in water so freely that some of them were swamped, and a corporal and three men of the Royal Highlanders were drowned. The next day, September 2, the army rowed the twenty-four miles across Lake St. Francis, an expansion of the St. Lawrence. That night there was a great storm, and on the next day the weather was so bad that the army remained in camp. Montreal was now not far off. In it the French Army was concentrated, and Murray and Haviland were advancing rapidly to meet their leader before its walls.

The 4th of September was fine and well fitted for the most ticklish part of Amherst's task, the passing of the series of rapids which include the Cedars and the Cascades. Disaster awaited him. He had the pilots from Fort Lévis; he had also some Indians expert in river navigation. But these pilots were not sufficient in number for the hundreds of boats. None of them spoke English, and the British steersmen hardly understood perhaps the directions given to them in a strange tongue. At any rate the boats did not keep at a proper distance from each other. Some of the men at the helm lost control, and the tossing boisterous waves wrought havoc with their prey. When night fell the whole force had not yet passed down, but already sixty-four boats had been dashed to pieces, among them seventeen laden with artillery, and no less than eighty-four men had been drowned. The long row of dead men seemed a dire penalty to pay for lack of skill in meeting the dangers of the river. The next day, when greater care was shown, the remainder of the army passed down with ease.

The army was now encamped on Isle Perrot, and Amherst waited the whole of the 5th to repair his boats. Looking across Lake St. Louis, the British could see the houses of Lachine, and Montreal itself was now not twenty miles distant. Isle Perrot was well peopled, but the inhabitants had run off into the woods and abandoned their houses. Some of the men who lived on the island had served with the French forces up the river and they were now in great fear of retribution from Amherst and his savage allies. But he treated kindly those who were captured or came in, and restored them to their houses, when once they had taken the oath of fidelity to King George. 'They seemed as much surprised with their treatment as they were happy with it,' says Amherst. They had, indeed, been told by Vaudreuil that they could hope for no mercy from the cruel and pitiless English.

Soon after daybreak on the morning of the 6th the army was again afloat for the last stage of the advance on Montreal. There still remained the terrific Lachine Rapids before Montreal could be reached by water. These were, however, impassable for '*batteaus*' and whaleboats; accordingly, Amherst landed at Lachine and marched overland the short distance from that point to Montreal. Though some mounted French volunteers had followed him along-shore, when he started from Isle Perrot, they made no attempt to oppose his landing. In fact, he was soon pursuing them. At three o'clock on the afternoon of the 6th the head of his column appeared before the feeble walls of Montreal. That night the British Army encamped on the open plain before the town, and the general was busy bringing up his artillery with a view to a speedy bombardment. A powerful British fleet lay in the river nearby. The sight of a man-of-war with fifty guns was one of the sensations of the day at Montreal; nothing of the kind had ever been seen there before. Had it alone opened fire it could soon have ruined the town.

Resistance to the British forces was hopeless. On the 7th Haviland arrived at Longueuil on the south shore of the river, and the French officer Malartic looking across from Montreal saw numbers of the inhabitants hurrying to that village in order to take the oath of fidelity required by the British as the condition of leaving the people undisturbed in their homes. From the east, too, the British were closing in. Murray landed his forces on the island of Montreal, also on the 7th, and began his march upon the town.

The country people seemed delighted to welcome him. Crowds of Canadians flocked to the British camp, and they brought horses and saddles for the officers, horses for the artillery, and carts for the luggage. As the army marched towards the town, the people lined the road, offering pails of milk and of water to the soldiers and expressing courteous regrets that they had no better liquor for the officers. The priest and nuns of a convent which the troops passed stood at their door and told the British that they were welcome. Progress was slow, for in the previous night the last of the French battalions had retired into Montreal, destroying the bridges behind them. The delay was such that before Murray's column could appear in front of the walls of Montreal Amherst was already treating for its surrender.

As Murray approached, Vaudreuil had tried a little ruse. Suspecting that Amherst was of sterner stuff than Murray, and knowing Murray's love of glory, the governor had sounded him as to the terms of surrender which he would give, and thus become the conqueror of Canada. Murray, however, answered that, since Amherst was so near, it was with him that Vaudreuil must treat. Each side had seen the inevitable and understood pretty well what terms were possible. On the night of the 6th-7th Vaudreuil summoned the principal French officers to attend a meeting at his quarters in Montreal.

With British columns in sight, the tap of the British drum in their ears, and the roar of British cannon likely to begin at any time, the business was urgent indeed. The *intendant*, Bigot, read a memorandum outlining the condition of affairs in the colony. The inhabitants of Montreal, fearful of massacre if taken fighting, now refused to arm, and under cover of night they had already begun to cart away their effects by wagon-loads. The Indians were joining the English; the Canadians had deserted entirely; so also had many of the French regular troops; and those now in the ranks numbered only about 2,400. The situation was desperate. Bombardment might reduce Montreal to ashes in a single night. For its defence Lévis had only six pieces of artillery. Food and ammunition were scarce. The disparity in numbers, too, was overwhelming. Vaudreuil believed, or, at least, said, that there were thirty thousand of the enemy to face.

In such a situation Vaudreuil urged that capitulation was necessary. To this the military officers agreed, if honourable terms could be secured, and Colonel de Bougainville was named to go early in the morning of the 7th to Amherst, to propose a suspension of arms until October 1; capitulation was to follow at that date should news of peace not arrive in the meantime. If Amherst would not grant this, terms of surrender were to be proposed. Amherst writes that on the 7th 'in the morning two officers came to an advanced post with a letter from the Marquis de Vaudreuil, referring me to what one of them, Le Colonel Bougainville, had to say. The conversation ended with a Cessation of Arms 'till twelve o'clock, at which time the Proposals came.' (Amherst to Pitt, September 8, 1760).

Amherst would not listen to the French plan to suspend arms until October 1, but he was ready to discuss terms of surrender. These Vaudreuil had long meditated upon, and he now had ready an elaborate paper guarding carefully the civil and religious interests of the Canadians and also providing that the French army should be accorded the honours of war.

Political and religious questions Amherst was prepared to treat in a generous spirit. He did not forget that already Canada was practically British territory. Of course Vaudreuil asked for more than he expected to receive. Amherst would not promise that the Canadians should always be governed under French law and that they should pay no new taxes. Vaudreuil's demand that the vanquished people should remain strictly neutral in any war between Great Britain and France Amherst brushed aside with the comment that they must become the subjects of the British king. He refused, too, the absurd demand that, even should Canada remain British, the King of France should have the perpetual right to name the Bishop of Quebec.

He would not agree that the Church should retain its right to levy the tithe, but the right was afterwards yielded by the British Parliament. Though he gave the communities of nuns special protection, he would not promise to the Jesuits, Récollets, and Sulpitians, the three orders of priests working in Canada, anything in regard to their privileges. They must await the pleasure of the king. Their, and all other rights of property were, however, to be respected. The new subjects were to enjoy equal privileges with the incoming British in respect to commerce. They were to be free to remain in Canada or to withdraw, and if they chose to withdraw some were to be helped to go to France. They were to enjoy full liberty for their Roman Catholic faith. Vaudreuil had said that if the British were successful the Canadians would be deported from their homes. This poignant fear Amherst removed; they were never to suffer the fate of the Acadians and to be carried away, against their will, to the British colonies or to England. The Chevalier Johnstone, fighting on the French side, says that the terms granted by Amherst were 'infinitely more favourable than could be expected in our circumstances'.

Amherst was resolved, however, that the French Army should make one great expiation. It was the general belief in the British Army that the French had allowed, and even encouraged, outrages by their Indians. After Braddock's defeat in 1755 the French had joined the Indians in scalping the fallen British. After Montcalm's victory at Fort William Henry, in 1757, scores of disarmed British prisoners had been massacred by the savages, and some of the French officers had been slack in their efforts to prevent the atrocities.

A few days later some British prisoners had been brought by Indians to Montreal, and there, as Bougainville says, 'at two o'clock in the afternoon in presence of the whole town,' one of them had been boiled and eaten by the savages, and his fellow Englishmen had been obliged to partake of the horrid feast, (Kerallain). While high-minded French officers like Montcalm and Bougainville bitterly denounced the Indian practice of scalping, Vaudreuil, no doubt because he was a Canadian long familiar with savage warfare, was, as we have seen, not greatly shocked at it, and he constantly reported to the French court the number of scalps taken in the border struggles. Lévis, too, had been weak in checking the Indians.

There is no doubt that on the British side, too, guerrilla captains like Rogers had waged war exactly as their Indian foes waged it. Even Wolfe had permitted scalping when the enemy were Indians or Canadians dressed like Indians. But, in the regular operations of war, the British had held the Indians sternly in check. Amherst disliked them and punished them with something like avidity. At Montreal, when he caught an Indian in the act of stealing, he promptly hanged him. Amherst wrote to Pitt that:

> Not a peasant, woman or child has been hurt by them (the Indians) or a house burnt, since I entered what was the enemy's country.

The Indians were not allowed to commit 'one single act of savage barbarity', writes a non-commissioned officer triumphantly. (Amherst to Pitt, September 8, 1760; Quartermaster-Sergeant Johnson, in Doughty, v.).

Nothing more astonished the Canadians who saw Amherst's army at Montreal than his strict control of the Indians. Far other was the tale on the French side. Vaudreuil had been, in truth, afraid of his own Indians, and he still showed fear of the race. Among the most insistent terms which he now drew up were those by which the British were to guarantee protection to the French from the cruelties and insults of the savages. In regard to this Amherst wrote on the margin of the proposals:

> There never have been any cruelties committed by the Indians of our army and good order shall be preserved.... Care shall be taken that the Indians do not insult any of the subjects of his most Christian majesty. (Articles 9 and 51 of the Capitulation).

Resolute himself against savage barbarities, Amherst was now resolved to punish the French for their slackness. He would not yield the honours of war to the defeated army. They must simply surrender and must not serve again during the war.

These terms were hard indeed. It was the custom of the time to grant honours of war to a garrison which surrendered before an assault was made. Moreover, the provision that the French officers and men should not serve again during the war might mean that for years they should have no military employment. The French protested vigorously. When Vaudreuil received Amherst's terms, he sent Bougainville back to ask for some mitigation. Lévis declared that the terms were intolerable, and he too sent Colonel de la Pause to make representations to Amherst. But, though La Pause was a man of rank and reputation, Amherst would not listen to his attempt to justify the protest of Lévis. He sternly ordered him to be silent and declared that:

> He was fully resolved, for the infamous part the troops of France had acted in exciting the savages to perpetrate the most horrid and unheard of barbarities in the whole progress of the war, and for other open treacheries, as well as flagrant breaches of faith, to manifest to all the world, by this capitulation, his detestation of such ungenerous practices, and disapprobation of their conduct. (Knox, ii.).

He wrote in reply to Lévis:

> I cannot alter, in the least, the conditions which I have offered to the Marquis de Vaudreuil, and I expect his definite answer by the bearer on his return.

That night at 7 o'clock the officers of the French army again held a council of war. There was clamorous indignation at Amherst's stern terms. They involved for these unfortunate men not merely military disgrace but also something like starvation, for if they could get no employment they were likely to become idle pensioners when they returned to France. In the night La Pause was sent back to ask that at least the prohibition to serve might apply only to America. But Amherst would not yield one jot. On the receipt of the last peremptory message from Amherst, the officers demanded that Vaudreuil should break off the negotiations. It was unheard of, they said, that an army should make such terms before the place it was defending had been assaulted; they should either march out against the British as Murray had done at Ste Foy, or they should await an assault on Montreal and fight to the last. If either of these courses should prove to be impossible the officers asked permission to withdraw to St. Helen's Island, in the river near Montreal, there to fight until at least honourable terms could be secured. Lévis wrote to Vaudreuil:

> We have still enough ammunition to fight if the enemy wishes to attack us sword in hand.

It is not easy to estimate the sincerity of these protests. The British men-of-war could easily have destroyed the defences of St. Helen's Island, as the French officers must have well understood. Lévis and others were thinking of their future military careers and probably hoped that this brave talk would soften the disgrace of a humiliating surrender. But Vaudreuil had no military glory in view, and he had to listen to other clamour besides that of the military. The multitude of refugees in Montreal flocked to implore him to save them and their goods by quick surrender to the British. These, and these only, would be strong enough to check the danger of outrage from the savages whom the weak French Army could not now control. (Letter of M. Bernier, *Commissaire des Guerres*, to M. de Crenille, Lieut.-Gen., September 12, 1760; quoted in Malartic, note).

Vaudreuil admitted the inevitable. Amherst's terms must he said must be accepted; this was a duty he owed to the ruined colony. The British general had named six o'clock on the morning of the 8th as the time for the final answer, and soon after that hour he received a letter from Vaudreuil complying with his stern demands. New France had at last fallen, and Britain had won half a continent.

Amherst sat up late on the night of the surrender. Major Barre was to leave at once for England with dispatches, and there was much to report. To his friend, Major-General Joseph Yorke, Amherst wrote, in spite of weariness, a brief account of his work:

> I have as much pleasure in telling you Canada belongs to the king as I had in receiving the capitulation of it this day, from the satisfaction I know it will give you. The French troops all lay down their arms, and are not to serve during the war; their behaviour in carrying on a cruel and barbarous war in this country, I thought deserved this disgrace. I have suffered by the *Rapides* not by the enemy. I entered the inhabited country with all the savages and I have not hurt the head of a peasant, his wife or his child, not a house burnt, or a disorder committed; the country people amazed; won't believe what they see; the notions they had of our cruelties from the exercise of their own savages, drove them into the woods; I have fetched them out and put them quiet in their habitations, and they are vastly happy. I can't tell you how much I am obliged to you for your good letter to me; but though 'tis three in the morning of the 9th, and I have not slept these two nights past, I would not let Major Barré go away with my dispatches without telling this news to you.—Yorke, *Life of Lord Chancellor Hardwicke,* iii.

To assert possession of Montreal on behalf of the British Army, Amherst promptly sent Colonel Haldimand, a Swiss by birth, an officer who knew the French language thoroughly and who afterwards was Governor of Canada, to hold one of the gates of the town and to repress any beginnings of disorder. Amherst promptly issued to his troops an order in which he said:

> The Marquis of Vaudreuil has capitulated; the troops of France, in Canada, have laid down their arms; they are not free to serve during this war; and the whole country has submitted to the dominion of Great Britain. The three armies are all entitled to the general's thanks on this occasion, and he assures them he will take the first opportunity of acquainting His Majesty with the zeal and bravery which has (*sic*) always been exerted by the officers and soldiers of the regular and provincial troops, and also by his faithful Indian allies.

He added a note of warning as to the lawlessness and outrage likely to occur at such a time:

> The general is confident that, when the troops are informed this country is the king's, they will not disgrace themselves by the least appearance of inhumanity, or by any unsoldierlike behaviour of seeking for plunder; but that, as the Canadians are now become British subjects, they may feel the good effect of His Majesty's protection.

Amherst meant this last injunction to be taken seriously. A British soldier caught in the act of pillage was promptly hanged.

On the day after the surrender the inhabitants of Montreal saw a memorable illustration of the fortunes of war. One by one the French battalions marched to the Place d'Armes and there surrendered to the custody of the British the weapons used in the long struggle. One set of trophies Lévis was resolved that the victor should not have, and, on the 8th, when he saw that Amherst intended to compel a humiliating surrender, he ordered the colours of the French regiments to be burned. Amherst, writing to Pitt on September 8, had promised to send him soon the French colours as glorious trophies. Perhaps he did not realise that it is one of the strongest traditions of the French Army that flags must not be given up to the enemy.

As recently as in France's last great war, that with Germany in 1870, one of the most indignant charges against Bazaine, who surrendered at Metz, is that he did not burn his flags rather than let them fall into the hands of the victors. When Amherst demanded the French flags, both Vaudreuil and Lévis declared that, owing to the difficulties of a country where there was so much forest, the colours had become useless and had been destroyed. Amherst insisted that the two leaders should give him their word of honour that this was the case, and they promptly did so. It was, of course, true that the colours had been destroyed, but the French leaders were certainly not frank in their reply to Amherst.

It may be doubted whether the French officers resented more the sternness of Amherst or what they considered the too-ready acquiescence of Vaudreuil in the British demands. Yet he had acted wisely. By surrendering before an assault was made on Montreal, he had procured favourable terms for the Canadians, whose desolate country, after further resistance was hopeless, assuredly deserved some consideration. They might return to their homes without penalty, and they were now certain of protection to their property and of the free exercise of their religion. But, because Vaudreuil was himself a Canadian, he was suspected by the French officers of sacrificing the interests of the army to those of his own people.

When, on the day after the surrender, he gave a dinner to Amherst, not a French officer would accept his hospitality. Nor would they accept courtesies from Amherst himself. Relations between old acquaintances were strained. At Quebec Malartic had seen much of Murray, but now he could accept Murray's hospitality only after securing special permission. Murray, he says, overwhelmed him with compliments on the resourcefulness of his countrymen; the French, Murray said, had covered themselves with glory in defending through six campaigns what the British ought to have taken in one.

When, on September 9, Lévis reviewed his little army for the last time, there were present 1,953 soldiers and 179 officers; in the hospitals there were besides 241 sick and wounded. No less than 927 were absent from their regiments. Some, indeed, were absent on service, but 548 had deserted or disappeared. It was a somewhat pitiable showing. At Jacques Cartier and Three Rivers there were still small garrisons, and a handful of French soldiers remained at Detroit and Michillimackinac, distant posts in the interior. All who surrendered were to be sent home at once. The married officers and private soldiers were to have accommodation for their wives and families. In addition to the military, a few civilians, chiefly the officials of the French government in Canada, had the right of carriage to France. These French subjects were not numerous, and allowing for women, children, and servants, probably four thousand would be a liberal estimate of the number now to be embarked in Canada for their return home.

It was not unnatural that the defeated army should desire to get away as quickly as possible. In the terms of capitulation, Vaudreuil had stipulated that his whole force should be embarked for France within fifteen days. Though this was a heavy undertaking it was possible to carry it out. More than fifty transports had come up the river with Murray's forces and were now available for this new task. Moreover, there were other transports at Quebec. The days following the capitulation saw busy scenes. The British had wished to send some of the French regiments to New York, there to be embarked. To this, however, Lévis would not assent, for he was sure that on the journey to that distant port many of his soldiers would desert and be lost to France. He now kept his disarmed battalions in their own quarters and drew up elaborate regulations for their governance during the voyage.

The troops embarked at Montreal were not to be allowed to go ashore at Quebec except under the strictest regulations. Lévis prescribed the measures to be taken on board for preserving both health and discipline; and he counselled officers and men to study great reserve in their communications with the British who were to carry the army back to France. He promised, and he kept his word, that he would spare no labour, on his return to France, to secure for these brave and unfortunate men the payment of the drafts on France which represented their hard-earned wages during the many months of war.

Vaudreuil had stipulated that, until he embarked, he should continue to occupy unmolested his own excellent house in Montreal, the property of his family. He also arranged that the most comfortable ship available should be provided for himself, his wife, servants, and suite, and he and Bigot took special care that they should be allowed to carry away their papers without examination by the British. Two ships were to be provided for Lévis, his chief officers, and their suites; and they too were to carry away their papers without examination.

******

Lévis preserved carefully a mass of correspondence, and in later years, when Governor-General of Artois, he occupied himself with arranging it. In 1888 his great-grandson, Comte Raimond de Nicolay, presented copies of these papers to the Government of the Province of Quebec on condition that they should be printed. This *Collection des Manuscrits du Maréchal de Lévis* is of great value for the history of the period. Upon the *Collection* much of the present volume is based. The editorial work on the documents is very defective.

******

It was also provided that Bigot, the *intendant*, should have a ship for himself and his suite. It is perhaps significant of the quantity of luggage and of papers which Vaudreuil and Bigot were taking away that three flat-bottomed boats were placed at the disposal of each of them for conveying their effects to the waiting ships. A similar courtesy was denied to Lévis and his staff until they explained satisfactorily the disappearance of the colours. Amherst had heard gossip that the flags were still in existence, and he threatened to search all the baggage before it was embarked if they were not produced. As we have seen, however, the colours had really been destroyed.

After three or four days spent in the preparation of the ships, the work of embarkation began on September 14. We can picture the water-front of the little frontier town alive with the movement now going on; the troops of France in their worn and faded uniforms marching to the points assigned to them to enter the boats; the many spectators, in the idle days of transition, eagerly watching the dejection and the exultation that the events of war must always bring in varying degrees to its votaries. On the side towards the swift river five gates opened through the wall. The quays were inadequate and some of the ships could not be brought near the shore. This made embarkation difficult. By the 16th, however, nearly the whole of the French Army was afloat and on its way down the river. Rearrangements were to be made at Quebec, where lay other transports.

Colonel de Bougainville, the handy man of the French Army, had been sent in advance to Quebec to superintend the work at that point. On the 17th Lévis himself set out from Montreal in the ship assigned to him, but Vaudreuil and Bigot lingered a little longer to complete necessary business. On the 15th a crier went through the town to notify all who had demands for payments to apply to the *intendant* at once. At the same time the governor and the *intendant* issued a joint statement assuring the Canadians that the King of France would not fail, in time, to redeem the paper currency now worthless in their hands. The business affairs of France in Canada were, as far as possible, closed, and a commissary was left behind to settle what was still left open.

On the 20th Vaudreuil took ship for his troubled voyage home, and on the 21st Bigot did the same. During three weeks some twenty or more British transports laden with French soldiers were making their way down the river. Some of their names—*The True Briton, The Fanny, The Mary and Jane, The Sally, The Hannah, The Abigail,* and *The*

Young Isaac—must have sounded strangely in French ears. One vessel engaged in this service had a notable history. It was *La Marie*, which alone had escaped from the British during the fight with Vauquelain. She had now become a British transport.

A few weeks earlier Captain Knox had delighted in the bright sunshine and the entrancing beauty of the river scenery as he passed up to Montreal. Now, however, nature was as unkind to the defeated army as war itself had been. We have a detailed narrative by Malartic of the journey, and his experiences were similar to those of the French army as a whole. It was on September 16 that Malartic embarked in a schooner with a part of the regiment of Béarn. The next day the ship ran aground in Lake St. Peter and lay helpless for more than twenty-four hours. She had set out without good pilots, and with such an inadequate supply of provisions that, after two or three days, those on board were obliged to send foraging parties ashore to seek bread and vegetables among the inhabitants.

Soon after passing Three Rivers, on the 19th, the ship encountered a heavy storm from the north-east, which made progress almost impossible. On the 22nd she ran aground again and smashed one of her small boats. So incomplete was the ship's equipment that no hammer or nails could be found on board with which to attempt repairs. The soldiers went ashore freely and a good many deserted. The ship crept on slowly in spite of the storm which lasted many days. Not until October 5, nearly three weeks after leaving Montreal, did she reach Quebec. During this tempest we hear a plaintive note from the Intendant Bigot, storm-bound at Batiscan, near Three Rivers.

Madame Péan, the Pompadour of Canada, is, he says, bored to death by the monotony of life on the small ship, and is moreover sea-sick; he himself is also miserable from sea-sickness. He had provided luxuries for his own party on the journey, but he complains that the company is half-starved, in defiance of the sacred obligations which Great Britain had assumed to feed the French leaders as well as her own officers were fed. Lévis, too, was not without female consolation on the voyage, and he also complains of straitened quarters and hard fare. Vaudreuil had an even more serious quarrel with fortune. His ship struck a rock on the way to Quebec and he was obliged to abandon her.

The troubled journey to Quebec was not a promising beginning for the longer voyage. In some cases, there was now a hurried transhipment. Malartic was given only one hour to get himself and a considerable body of the regiment of Béarn on board a British snow and to be afloat again. Lévis pressed the British to give the French Army adequate accommodation, but the result did not prove satisfactory. A number of vessels, disabled by the terrific storm, could not go to sea; and, in consequence, the remaining ships were somewhat crowded, Lévis declares, however, that the English were rigorous in not allowing more than one man for each ton of a ship.

The impoverished French officers had no money to buy from the traders, now swarming at Quebec, any luxuries to ease the hardships of the voyage, and, for the most part, they could secure only the fare of the common sailors. The season was far advanced and haste was necessary, for, in the late autumn, the St. Lawrence route is dangerous. Obviously there was no time for niceties in regard either to the equipment of the ships or in the order of sailing. At first Lévis was resolved to be the last to set out, but in the end he was obliged to sail when his ship was ready and to leave Bourlamaque in charge.

The voyage proved tempestuous. Off Louisbourg the storms were so frightful that the ship of Lévis lost a mast and, for two hours, it seemed certain that she would sink, Malartic describes the way in which his ship was now becalmed, now lost in fog, on the St. Lawrence. At one time she came into collision with a larger ship and nearly sank. After passing out into the Atlantic between Cape Breton and Newfoundland, she was still five weeks in reaching the shores of France. Since luxuries were wholly wanting, there was joy when they met in mid-ocean a great Dutch vessel from Surinam. Her aged captain was completing his 66th year of voyaging, but he was still acute enough to sell them rum, sugar, and coffee at a high price. We may wonder where the impoverished French officers, returning to France almost penniless, secured the money to pay for these luxuries.

At length, late in November, they cast anchor in the harbour of La Rochelle. Lévis arrived next day, and the other transports came straggling in. Though the weather had been bad and the ships, in some cases, crowded, the health of the whole army was surprisingly good on the voyage. Lévis says that he brought back only 1,500 or 1,600 men. The rest had preferred to remain in the colony, and the captive French leader had been powerless to check this desertion. A good many of the French-Canadians of the present day must have in their veins the blood of the soldiers of Lévis.

Under the plea of needing rest, Lévis waited at La Rochelle for five or six days. He wrote to the Duc de Belle-Isle on November 25:

'I have disembarked only this moment, I should have wished to be able to leave for Versailles at once, but the fatigues and also the dangers which I have undergone in the voyage just completed oblige me to take five or six days for the recovery of my health.'

The real cause of delay was, perhaps, the lack of money to go to Versailles. He was soon aided by his powerful connexions, but other French officers were not so fortunate, and the poor reward of some of the grizzled veterans of the Canadian campaigns, when they returned home, was a lapse into hopeless poverty. Those who brought the paper money with which they had been paid in Canada found it quite valueless in France. When they demanded relief they were often sent unsatisfied from department to department.

Each department said that it was the business of another: The Controller-General referred the matter to the Department of Marine, and M. Berryer, the head of that department, said the claims must go to the Department of War or of Finance. The unfortunate men who had suffered great hardships for their country may well have thought that it was better to starve amid the perils of a campaign than ingloriously at home. Doubtless many of them were heart-sick enough in France to regret the life in the Canadian wilderness where, though half-naked and half-fed, they could still do something for the honour of their country.

For the defeated leaders, fate had varying fortunes. Since crimes may be forgiven only to success, shame was in store for the discredited plunderers of the colony. In the France to which Bigot, Cadet, and a dozen others had so longed to return in affluence, they found a stern reception. The loss of the colony had caused general indignation, and the government was only too glad of the excuse of alleged fraud to find scapegoats. When Bigot presented himself at Versailles before Berryer, the Minister of Marine, he was greeted angrily with the charge that it was he who had lost Canada by his criminal plundering of her resources, and that the rigours of justice awaited him. Vaudreuil, too, met with a stormy reception. He wrote from Brest on December 10 a plaintive letter to excuse his conduct and to explain the loss of the colony. But his words did not avail.

By the king's command he was censured for surrendering Montreal, in spite of the protests of Lévis, and he was one of the many persons accused of fraud. Twenty-three were sent to the Bastille, among them Vaudreuil, Bigot, Cadet, and Péan. There they remained, at a daily cost to the king of a hundred and sixty-four *livres*, for about three years, until final judgement was rendered. Durance in the Bastille involved, for at least the well-to-do class, less rigour than the Paris mob supposed when it destroyed that famous prison some twenty-five years later. Vaudreuil had his negro servant with him and a supply of books, and he was allowed to take exercise in the open air. We get glimpses of Bigot and Péan also with servants in attendance. The prisoners were permitted to have tobacco and wine. A surgeon attended twice a day upon one of them who was ill. Special permission was accorded to Bigot, Cadet, and others to go to mass. Assuredly they had need of repentance.

The trial was not begun until more than a year after the fall of Canada. The case came before the Court of the Châtelet. Twenty-seven judges, named for the trial, were engaged fifteen months in the examination of the papers. The proceedings attracted the attention of Europe. The accused persons numbered fifty-five, and each of them prepared a *Mémoire* in his own defence. That of Bigot runs to nearly twelve hundred printed *quarto* pages. He traversed the whole ground of his term of office in Canada, and denied boldly that he had been a party to any fraud. He attacked Cadet as the chief criminal in the affairs of New France. He declared too that Vaudreuil, his superior in rank, was, for that reason, more responsible than he for any seeming official collusion in fraud.

Bigot so traduced the memory of Montcalm that the mother and the widow of the dead soldier petitioned the court to impose a fine on the former *intendant* for the libel. Vaudreuil answered the charges with dignity. His lineage he declared should have placed him above the suspicion of sordid fraud; he had been wholly occupied with military matters; he had not been concerned with finance and had had no interest in contracts. He defended with eloquence the officers of the regular army, dead and living, who lay under suspicion. It was to him, he said, that these poor men, who had shed their blood for France, had the right to look for defence. They were now the victims of base calumny and he should himself be base if he, did not stand forth as a witness to their talents, their virtues, and their innocence.

Judgement was rendered in December, 1763. The prosecution asked for Bigot a punishment truly mediaeval—that, clad only in his shirt and placarded as a thief, he should be made to kneel before the principal gate of the Tuileries, with a rope round his neck, and to proclaim aloud his own guilt, and that, after this, his head should be struck off. He was, of course, found guilty, but a sentence less severe was imposed upon him. He was to pay a fine of 1,500,000 *livres* and to suffer the loss of all his goods by confiscation. It is not clear how, with his goods confiscated, he was to pay the fine. In addition, and worst of all, when we remember his dream of a life of luxury in France, he was condemned to perpetual banishment.

Cadet was banished for nine years from Paris, and, since his stealings were on a colossal scale, was ordered to restore six million to the king's Treasury. Varin had to pay back 1,600,000 *livres*, and he, too, was banished. Péan was condemned to restore 600,000 *livres* and to remain in prison until he did so. He paid the money at once and was set free. Lesser rascals were also punished, but two of the worst, Deschenaux and St. Sauveur, seem to have escaped because they had chosen to remain in Canada.

Fortune seemed to treat the plunderers of Canada with rigour. The government instructed its servants to hunt out the stolen property in all the provinces of France. There was something like a scramble among persons of rank to secure the silver plate of Bigot, his soup and *entrée* dishes, his wine-coolers, his candlesticks, and dozens of other objects of luxury. Some of the criminals, now penniless, and unable to pay their fines, remained in jail, and we hear from their destitute families piteous appeals to the king for help. The way of transgressors was hard for some, but not for all.

The sentence of banishment upon Cadet was soon cancelled. In 1764 he was granted permission to go to Canada. After his return he purchased extensive lands in France. He had the hardihood to claim from the French Government no less a sum than 9,000,000 *livres*, as due to him. He was prosperous for a time, but his mania for speculation, and perhaps, too, for sport, since he was fond of good horses, in the end brought ruin. He died a bankrupt in 1781. His two daughters married into two of the oldest families of France. (*Un Munitionnaire du Roi à la Nouvelle-France, Joseph Cadet, 1756-81*. Par A. Barbier. Poitiers, 1900).

For Bigot we find no less a person than the Bishop of Blois interceding in 1774, and, though we know little of his later career, it seems that he was allowed to return to France and to end his days there with some appearance of prosperity. It is worth noting that the France which dealt so gently with some of these guilty men, was, at the same time, relentless towards an innocent man who had tried to build up her empire. After a brave struggle, the Comte de Lally had been defeated in India and carried a prisoner to England. When allowed to return to France in 1761, he was sent to the Bastille, a fellow prisoner of the accused men from Canada. By faults of temper Lally had made enemies, and it was now charged that he had sold Pondicherry to the English. There was no real evidence against him, but he was sentenced to death. This brave and innocent Frenchman, handcuffed and gagged, was taken in a dung-cart to the scaffold and executed with every accompaniment of horror. Cadet, a real criminal, became a *seigneur* in France, and but for his own bad judgement might have ended his days in luxury.

Among those who were declared guiltless of fraud in Canada we are glad to find Vaudreuil. He was liberated in December, 1763. Choiseul wrote to him in the following May to express the king's pleasure that his conduct had been found without reproach. He received a pension of 6,000 *livres*; and he also received what he greatly prized, the Grand Cross of St. Louis, which carried with it a further pension of 6,000 *livres*. Drafts on the French Treasury which he held had not been honoured, and without his pensions he would have been poor. His later years were sad. His brother, a distinguished admiral, died shortly before the verdict of acquittal; so also did Madame de Vaudreuil; and he was left a lonely old man. He wrote to a friend in March, 1764:

> I am well convinced of the instability of human affairs and should be indifferent to life but for the kindness of relations and friends.—To M. Duchesnay. Manuscript in Canadian Archives).

He lived on until 1778. Perhaps posterity has been a little unkind to the memory of the fussy, ineffective, but well-meaning governor who loved Canada with all his heart and spared himself no labour in the interests of the ruined colony.

★★★★★★

The family of Vaudreuil, an ancient house of Languedoc, preserved for more than a hundred years the governor's papers which he carried back to France from Canada. Their study might have put his work in a better light, but in 1871, when the family *château* was about to fall into the hands of the Germans, Vaudreuil's papers were destroyed to save them from the invaders. There is a mediaeval rhyme:

Les Hunauds, les Lévis et les Rigauds
Ont chassé les Visigoths;
Les Lévis, les Rigauds et les voisins

Ont chassé les Sarrasins.
Rigaud is the family name of Vaudreuil. The association of his family with that of Lévis was thus very ancient.

✶✶✶✶✶✶

The lot of Lévis was happier. His connexions were very influential, and, like the rest of the French world, he paid court to Madame de Pompadour. His friends made representations at the British Court in order to remove the prohibition to serve in the French Army before peace was made. Lévis himself protested that he and the other French officers had treated generously their British captives and had done their utmost to prevent Indian outrages in America. In the end Pitt cancelled the disability placed on Lévis to serve again during the war. The action was hardly pleasing to Britain's ally, Frederick the Great, who soon found Lévis taking an active and distinguished part on the French side in the campaigns in Germany.

After the war closed he was named Governor of Artois. He became Marshal of France and Duc de Lévis, and died at the age of sixty-seven, in 1787, just before the Revolution began. Two years later, in 1789, when the Revolution broke out, his body, buried at Arras, was torn from the grave and his bones were scattered. The Revolution swallowed up many of his family. He had married a wealthy lady after his return from Canada, and his widow and two of his three daughters perished on the scaffold during the Terror.

His son, a deputy for the *noblesse* in the States-General of 1789, fled as an *émigré* to England and lost his property. He returned to France with Louis XVHI on the fall of Napoleon and had the honour to become a member of the French Academy. His father had died on the eve of the first fall of the Bourbons, and he died in 1830, just before their second fall. His son, the last Duc de Lévis, born in London in 1794, died without issue in 1869 in the arms of the Comte de Chambord, the Bourbon claimant to the French throne. (Hauteclocque, *Le Marshal de Lévis, Gouverneur-Général de l'Artois*, Arras, 1901).

The most conspicuous lieutenant of Lévis, Bougainyille, was extremely fortunate in his career. He was born in 1729, and early showed a varied range of talents. In 1754 he was Secretary of the French Embassy in London. Already, when he went to Canada in 1756, he had published a treatise in two volumes on the Integral Calculus, had been made a Fellow of the Royal Society of England, and, to please his family, had become also an advocate. After his return from Canada in 1760, he secured leave from the British Government to serve in the existing war, and he took an active part in the campaign on the Rhine in 1761. He was offered the post of Governor of Cayenne, but declined it because he had another project in mind. Britain with her navy, stronger now than the combined navies of the rest of Europe, needed only, it was said, to master the South Seas in order to establish that universal monarchy which was supposed to have been also the ambition of Louis XIV.

Bougainville planned that France should be ahead of her in the South Seas. When already thirty-four this scholar and soldier began the life of a sailor. As soon as peace was concluded in 1763, he set out, a naval captain, on an adventure as coloniser and discoverer. He founded in the Falkland Islands a French colony which, however, the protests of Spain soon obliged France to withdraw. But in 1766 Bougainville set out again, and this time penetrated into regions more remote and made important discoveries of hitherto unknown regions in the South Seas. By 1769 he had completed a voyage round the world, two years before Captain Cook, who had also served in Canada at the time of the fall of Quebec, returned from his famous voyage.

Bougainville commanded the first French squadron to go round the world. His *Voyage autour du Monde*, published in 1771, showed close observation of nature and won a prodigious success. He had a share in the crushing defeat of the British at Yorktown in 1781. We are impressed with his versatility when we find him commanding a naval squadron at Brest in 1790. He soon retired from scenes of war, however, and under Napoleon became a Senator of France. He died in 1811, shortly before the fall of the Empire.

There are not wanting indications that, next to Montcalm himself, the most efficient of the soldiers who served on the French side during the war was Bourlamaque. He was the intimate personal friend of Montcalm, who unburdened his mind to him with self-revealing frankness. Bourlamaque was less intimate with Lévis, and it is quite clear that the quiet, painstaking, hard-working soldier had not too much confidence in the military genius of his superior officer. No one could doubt Bourlamaque's courage and honesty; he had a high sense of dignity, and gossip and slander left him alone.

At the time of the capitulation, Bourlamaque, who was very poor and had no other means of livelihood, begged Amherst to except him from the prohibition to serve again during the war. Both he and Lévis declared that they had given no countenance to the outrages by the savages. Bourlamaque had, indeed, risked his life more than once to save British prisoners. Amherst proved inexorable, but, a little later, the British Government removed the prohibition from Bourlamaque, as they did from Lévis and Bougainville. On returning to France, Bourlamaque, with other officers, was invited to serve in Malta, menaced at that time by the Turk. He did not live long enough to win further distinction. He was sent as governor to Guadaloupe and died there in 1764.

The fate of the brave sailor, Vauquelain, was tragic. It is said that even when a certain duchess begged Berryer, the Secretary of the Navy, to do something for the heroic seaman, the minister was obdurate. There were so many people of good birth, he said, who wanted places that he had nothing to spare for any one not noble; it was true that Vauquelain was a hero, but what could one do? Since Vauquelain had been trained in the merchant service, he should now go back to it. Better counsels, however, soon prevailed. In 1761, Berryer himself retired from the navy, much to the advantage of that service. The Duc de Choiseul took his place and infused new life into French naval policy. In 1763 Vauquelain was sent on a mission to India with the rank of an officer in the Royal Navy. Great was the tumult among the officers of noble birth at this appointment. There is much obscurity about the later events. This, however, is certain, that on Vauquelain's return from India, in 1763, he was assassinated when only thirty-seven years old.

We get glimpses of a few others who played their part in the war. Ramezay was attacked savagely because he had surrendered Quebec, He begged for leave to publish a defence, but this was refused on the ground that it would only cause others to explain themselves and perhaps to contradict him. Only a hundred years later was the defence of Ramezay published, when the old controversies had long been dead. Though the unfortunate officer was miserably poor he was allowed a pension of but 300 *livres*. By 1771 he had died, apparently while serving in Cayenne, and his widow was then petitioning for help for herself and her children.

Some of the French officers lived to take part in triumphs over the victor who had humbled them in Canada. Desandroüins, the engineer who had built Fort Lévis, was, like Bougainville, at Yorktown in 1781, when a British army under General Cornwallis, many times more numerous than that of Lévis at Montreal, was forced to surrender. At Yorktown the French fleet had, for the moment, the command of the sea, and played the same decisive part that the British fleet had played in the St. Lawrence. It is, indeed, well to remember that the victor of

1760 was the vanquished in 1781. France had proved but feeble in Canada against a foe who revealed boundless energy, but France was not exhausted. Before the Seven Years' War ended, a plan for reviving the navy was making great progress under the energetic lead of Choiseul. The agitation resulted in an active campaign for help and in liberal gifts for the fleet. The estates of Languedoc offered a ship; trade guilds, chambers of commerce, great capitalists, took up the question. Even the clergy voted a million. In all 14,000,000 *livres* were contributed.

Canada, however, France had lost for ever. As soon as Montreal fell the British reached out to grasp what was to prove in the end more important than the territory they had actually occupied. At points of vantage on or near the great lakes of the interior, at Detroit, St. Joseph, and Michilimackinac, the French flag still waved. These places commanded that great west, destined to provide homes for so many millions. Amherst sent Major Rogers at once with two hundred rangers to occupy these forts. In accordance with the terms of the capitulation, Vaudreuil wrote letters to the *commandants* ordering them to transfer the posts to the British. It was at these places that the corrupt ring in New France had reaped such great profits.

But, in spite of these evils, the French had attached to themselves a good many of the Indian tribes. These did not like the change to the British, and mutterings soon began. Did the victors, they asked, then claim that, by a paper signed at Montreal, the whole western country, the country owned by the Indians themselves, should suddenly become British? Naturally the French did nothing to check the misgivings of the savages. The result, two or three years later, was an outbreak under the chief Pontiac, which caused a barbarous frontier war.

It was in accordance with the methodical accuracy of Amherst that, as soon as he held Montreal, he should have set to work at once to find out how many people lived in the country which he had conquered. On October 4 he sent a report to Pitt on this subject. There were, he said, 108 parishes, inhabited by 76,172 people, of whom 16,412, or more than one person in five, were enrolled in the militia. It is not possible now to verify these figures. They do not include the Indians in the country or the French in the interior. On the other hand, they probably make no allowance for the wastage of the war. It is, on the whole, doubtful whether there were more than 70,000 persons of European origin dwelling in the vast regions which now fell to Britain.

Yet only after six severe campaigns had their country been mastered. At this time, as one hundred and forty years later in South Africa, it was made clear that a people reared in the hardening conditions of pioneer life, accustomed to the use of arms, fighting for their homes on their own ground and scattered over a great area, could hold out for a long time against overwhelming numbers.

Not many of the Canadians went back to France. The people who crowded into the returning ships in the autumn of 1760 represented chiefly the classes whose occupation was gone in Canada—French soldiers and officials of the French Government. It is true that some of the landowners left Canada. In the first pangs of defeat there were, of course, men who despaired of their country and were resolved to abandon it. In all, however, little more than a hundred of the Canadian *seigneurs* left the country. When they knocked at official doors in Paris they always received smooth words.

The French Government showed much sympathy for the sufferers and continued for many years to bestow largess upon needy families. But men accustomed to be masters in Canada were unwilling to fill the role of beggars in France. It might, after all, be easier to gain a livelihood on the banks of the St. Lawrence than on the banks of the Seine, and some of them recrossed the ocean. In any case, whatever a few *seigneurs* may have done, the farmer, the real producer in Canada, never thought of leaving the country, and remained to keep strong the traditions of the social life of old France.

The British took up the task of governing Canada with their usual energy. As soon as their flag was raised over Montreal, they sent parties to survey the St. Lawrence from Isle Perrot downwards to Quebec. The French, Amherst says, had made little use of the river for water carriage, and, until the previous year, when their ships had been forced to ascend it to escape from the fleet of Saunders, they had not known that large vessels could come up to Three Rivers and Montreal. Amherst sent Colonel Burton to be governor at Three Rivers; General Gage was to stay at Montreal; Murray was to remain as Governor at Quebec. Sir William Johnson departed with his Indians, after they had received such trinkets as Johnson thought necessary to satisfy their childish tastes.

Amherst ordered the works at Isle aux Noix to be completely destroyed, and everything of value in the fort was taken to that solid fortress which he had built at Crown Point. He himself soon went to New York. Three weeks after Montreal fell he wrote to Pitt that

Canada was as quiet and secure as any other portion of the king's dominions.

The dispatch sent to Pitt by Major Barré announcing the surrender of Montreal reached England on October 3. The news was received with joy, but the public had expected it and did not go into the transports that marked the unexpected news of Wolfe's victory a year earlier. Three weeks passed before, on October 24, Pitt wrote to congratulate Amherst on his success. With a great display of capital letters Pitt expressed 'the universal applause and admiration' at the outcome of 'that masterly plan, which you had, with such unwearied application and diligence, formed.' The terms of the 'Capitulation of Montreal are highly becoming the Humanity, Magnanimity, and Wisdom of His Majesty'. By this time, however, Pitt was thinking of other plans. Further efforts must be made against France, and his active mind was already occupied with the problem of a renewed attack on the French islands in the West Indies.

France still retained, too, a footing in the North American Continent, for the lower portions of the Mississippi remained in her possession. Pitt pressed Amherst to secure any information that might aid in further attacks on the French. He did not realise that a crushing blow to his own power was about to fall. On October 25, the day after Pitt wrote the letter to Amherst, King George II, a model of regularity, rose as usual at six and drank his chocolate. At a quarter past seven, a servant, hearing a noise in the king's room, rushed in and found that he had fallen and was lying dead on the floor. His death meant the end of Pitt's rule. The new king, George III, meant himself to rule and would have no servant all-powerful, and the end of the sway of the great minister was not far off.

Pitt, however, was still minister and was still all for war. But war soon wearies those who bear its real burden. In the spring of 1761 the new military levies, on which Pitt insisted, caused at Hexham a riot so serious that forty-two persons were killed. One obstacle to peace was that Pitt had taught the nation to expect the complete humiliation of France, he said:

> Some time ago I would have been content to bring France to her knees: now I will not rest till I have laid her on her back.

Yet France, as we know, was far from being completely exhausted. The young king, George III, did not share Pitt's views, and showed at once another temper. In the draft of the king's speech to be read at the opening of Parliament in November, 1760, the war was spoken of as 'bloody and expensive'. Owing to Pitt's protest, the war was called instead 'expensive, but just and necessary'. To attack the war remained, however, the policy of the king and his friends. Pitt was received coldly at court, and it was clear that he was no longer the real master.

Not a jot, however, did Pitt abate in his ambitions or resolve. France must be trampled in the dust. She set great store by the Newfoundland fishery, largely because it was a nursery for her seamen, but Pitt declared that she must give up any share in it. During negotiations for peace in the summer of 1761, Pitt, who had recently recovered the use of his right hand, said that he should regret this recovery if he should use the hand to sign any document that left France a shadow of right not merely in Canada and Cape Breton but even in Newfoundland. France was equally determined.

Choiseul declared that he would be stoned in the streets of Paris if he gave up the fishery, and he simply refused to listen when the question was broached. France now secured a new ally, for in August, 1761, she signed a treaty with Spain by which each country guaranteed the possessions of the other. The treaty was secret, but Pitt got wind of it and urged the British Cabinet to declare war on Spain and use British sea power to occupy Cuba and the Philippines before Spain was ready.

Most of Pitt's own colleagues were alarmed at his aggressive policy. These ambitions for worldwide empire, said Hardwicke, the Lord Chancellor, would alarm other nations and cause them to unite against the ambitions of Britain as they had united against those of Louis XIV. On one occasion, at least, a meeting of the King's Council to debate the problem of peace lasted for six hours. Pitt banged the table with his fist, declared that he would not be responsible for what he did not control, and threatened to resign if his will was not done. We may doubt whether the peers who then governed England had ever before been addressed in this style. Nearly all of them, including Pitt's own nominal leader, the Duke of Newcastle, were opposed to an extreme policy. Newcastle had raised the money for the war, while Pitt had spent it with a lavish hand.

In the spring of 1760, when Pitt had been aiming his final blow at Canada, Newcastle had declared that Britain could not stand the strain for another year. At this Pitt had flown into a violent passion. 'In short, there was no talking to him,' wrote Newcastle at the time. Now, however, some of Pitt's colleagues talked to him. Hardwicke believed that Pitt was trying to make his own resignation inevitable. He had led the nation to expect so much that now he could not be a party to a peace that was reasonable without losing his popularity. When his colleagues voted against him in regard to the proposed attack on Spain, he carried out his threat and resigned on October 5, 1761. Only one minister, Earl Temple, his brother-in-law, retired with him.

Thus ended the sway of the minister to whom, more than to anyone else, it is due that Canada and India are today British. Even a hostile king did what honour he could to the great minister. He was offered the post of Governor of Canada, with a salary of £5,000 a year. We must not suppose that anyone thought Pitt would go to Canada to govern on the spot. It was intended that he should remain in England and be governor only in name. The offer to create such a post shows, however, that Britain was resolved to retain Canada. Pitt refused this honorary post, refused, indeed, to take any office or any title. But he accepted a pension of £3,000 a year, and, though he would not himself become Lord Chatham, he allowed his wife to be made Baroness Chatham. The acceptance of these favours tied his hands. It was a very mild Pitt who criticized the policy of the new ministers.

Even with Pitt out of office, the war did not end at once. The new leader was the Earl of Bute, and events were too strong for him and the young king. They found themselves obliged to make war on Spain, the new ally of France. Even with this added enemy to meet, the matchless weapon for war which Pitt had forged did its work. Men whom he had inspired remained in the Cabinet. The British fleet continued to be superior to all the other fleets of Europe combined. In 1762 Britain took both Cuba and the Philippines from Spain. She took Martinique from France, and shattered the last remnant of French power in the West Indies. But the new ministers almost regretted these successes, since they served to show that Pitt had been right. This is not the place to pursue the story.

George III and Bute wanted peace, peace at almost any price, though Britain was the victor. Bute tried to negotiate peace with Austria behind the back of his own ally, Frederick the Great. He cut off from Frederick the subsidy which had supported 60,000 Prussian troops. He abandoned the war in Germany with no regard to the safety of Hanover, the apple of the eye of George III. In November, 1762, the king's speech referred to the 'bloody and expensive war', the words rejected two years earlier through Pitt's urgency. George III bought a majority in the House of Commons who would vote for peace; in a single morning £25,000 was paid in banknotes to members of the House of Commons to secure their support. The measure of the king's grasp of the far-reaching problem of peace, as it affected Canada, is perhaps to be found in his remark that in North America France would make the Mississippi the boundary and would demolish all the forts on the *Ganges*. (Yorke, *Life of Lord Chancellor Hardwicke*, iii.)

It is not impossible that, in view of the resolve of George III to have peace at almost any price, France might have retained Canada. The British had conquered Guadaloupe, one of the French West India islands, before they had conquered Canada, and voices were now raised to urge that, if some of the conquests must be given up, it were better to yield Canada than Guadaloupe. With a much larger population than Canada, Guadaloupe was a better market for British goods:

> Pray what can Canada yield to Britain .... but a little extension of the fur trade? Whereas Guadaloupe can furnish as much sugar, cotton, rum, and coffee as all the islands we have, put together.

Britain was warned that to take Canada and drive France from North America was to make inevitable the loss of the English colonies. As soon as these had no need of the support of the mother-t land against a foreign neighbour they would demand independence. (*Reasons for Keeping Guadaloupe at a Peace, preferable to Canada,* London, 1761—Pamphlet in Canadian Archives).

When, in the summer of 1762, France sent a naval force to Newfoundland and captured St. Johns, the French ministers talked as if that island now belonged to France and as if the reconquest of, Canada was not impossible. The navy of France was certainly reviving under the strong lead of Choiseul. She could not, however, hold St. Johns when the British realised what had happened. Nor was it clear that she even wished to recover Canada. The frauds of Bigot and Cadet were much in the public mind in 1762, and Canada seemed like a bottomless pit in which France had already lost vast sums to no profit.

When Berryer had heard of the loss of Canada he had shown satisfaction because there would be a charge the less. Voltaire, the master-spirit in the French literary world of the time, declared against retaining Canada, which would only be an eternal cause of war and of humiliation. When the public was clamouring for peace he said:

> I am like the public; I care more for peace than I care for Canada, and I think France can be happy without Quebec.

Montesquieu said:

> The effect of colonies is to enfeeble the country from which they are drawn without peopling those where they are sent.—Lacour-Gayet, *op. cit.*

France was, in truth, sick of colonial adventure, and, with hardly a pang, was ready to give up Canada.

The Treaty of Paris was signed on February 10, 1763. To the ministers responsible for British policy for the moment it hardly mattered that the Duke of Bedford, who negotiated the Treaty at Paris, went much beyond his instructions in admitting the French to a share in the fisheries of North America. France thus obtained what Pitt had declared she should not have; she continued to hold the rights in Newfoundland which had remained to her under the Treaty of Utrecht. These rights were interpreted to mean the exclusive use of the west shore and became at a later time the source of angry disputes.

France secured also two islands near Newfoundland, St. Pierre and Miquelon, but undertook not to fortify them. Canada 'with all its dependencies', Cape Breton and all else in the vast region about the St. Lawrence and the Great Lakes, passed to Britain. The Mississippi River was to be the western boundary, and Britain was to have everything east of that river except the land about the town of New Orleans. The peace was such that neither country had much reason to be pleased with its rulers. In France it was not the king, but the king's foe, Frederick the Great, who was praised by the indignant populace. When, to commemorate the peace, an equestrian statue of Louis XV was put up with four allegorical figures of virtues at its base, a wit wrote:

> *Grotesque monument, infâme piédestal:*
> *Les vertus sont à pied, le vice est à cheval.*

In England, too, the public was not pleased. The storm of anger raised by the Treaty forced Bute to retire. But George III remained, to wreck an empire in the years to come.

Of the leaders on the British side during the struggle, Amherst, as was perhaps fitting, had the most prosperous career. He received the thanks of Parliament and became Governor-General of British North America, a term which then included the colonies destined soon to become the United States. Amherst, whose chief merit was his quality of slow thoroughness, found himself face to face in 1763 with a situation requiring skill which he did not possess. Then the western

Indians, who, under the chief Pontiac, had formed a league in protest against the British claim to own their country, attacked settlers and soldiers and committed many brutal outrages.

Amherst had always despised the Indians, and he now raged against what he called their despicable and inhuman villainy. In his savage anger at their methods he himself made the barbarous proposal to destroy them by distributing among them blankets tainted with small-pox. The victor who denounced at Montreal the methods of the French had assuredly stepped down from his pedestal. Amherst returned to England in 1763, leaving Gage to direct the war against Pontiac. Amherst was made Governor of Virginia, but of course had no thought of going to Virginia to govern.

When the Jesuit order was abolished, George III granted to Amherst their great estates in Canada, but the Chancellor refused to sign the patent, on the ground that, since Canada had been bought with the blood and treasure of the people, the Jesuit estates were their property and not that of the sovereign to give away. Amherst long treasured a grievance over his failure to get these lands. He became Earl Amherst and Commander-in-Chief of the British Army. The seat of his family in Kent is still known as Montreal.

Murray's connexion with Canada was more vital than that of Amherst. He remained as governor at Quebec for five or six years and played a considerable part in the early period of British rule. Though he wrote to Pitt after the fall of Canada to say that he was a poor soldier of fortune without a friend at Court, he yet managed, in some way, to acquire at least six great *seigniories* in Canada, and he appears to have become in time a man of substance. The siege of Quebec was not the only one which he had to endure from a French army. In 1781, when he was Governor of Minorca, the French laid siege to the island. His force of two thousand men was, in time, terribly reduced by scurvy and other diseases, and, when almost none of them remained fit for duty, he was obliged to surrender. Lévis, who was still living, must have noted with a certain satisfaction this humiliation of the enemy who had baffled his own attacks.

Gage, who succeeded Amherst in the command in North America, played a part in the early stages of the revolt of the British colonies. He had returned to England, but he was sent out to Boston in 1774 as Governor-in-Chief. His first task was to put military pressure on the colonists who had recently shown their anger at the tax on tea by throwing cargoes of tea into Boston harbour. When Gage found the colonists arming, in fear, as they said, with astute humour, of war with France, and sent to seize their arsenal at Concord in Massachusetts, they attacked his force at Lexington and thus brought on the first battle of the revolutionary war. The Battle of Bunker Hill which quickly followed was the result of orders from Gage. He soon returned to England, and took no further conspicuous part in affairs.

More important than any success or failure of individuals was the destiny of the conquered colony. New France had fallen and it had deserved to fall. The cause of failure was not that the French had no genius for colonisation. On the contrary they fitted in admirably with conditions in the New World. They took naturally to the life of the forest and were good hunters and good woodsmen. They were not good farmers, in the sense of knowing much about soils and about the rotation of crops, but they knew how to wrest a livelihood from mother earth in the hard conditions of pioneer life.

It is still true that the tenacity of the French-Canadian to hold what he has and to press on into new fields is a cause of jealous alarm to his rivals of British origin in Canada. Not because of his lack of vigour, but because of the tyranny and corruption of those who ruled did the life of the colony languish. The author of the pungent *Mémoires sur le Canada* declares that posterity would not believe the tale of what he himself saw. Those who governed showed slight regard for law. Patronage did everything; merit was persecuted; so-called justice was sold. The people were under a stern military rule and had no shadow of political rights. The old regime in the mother-land of France was, we may be well assured, not wholly evil, and it certainly meant well by the colonies.

The officials in old France took endless pains with the tangled affairs of New France. They were paternal in their counsel and admonitions. All was dependent, however, not on them, but on the man on the spot; and the man on the spot, named by favour and not by merit, ruined the colony. When a clever rascal was sent across the sea, it was not easy to know that he was doing evil. Democracy has its faults; it is often extravagant, inefficient and corrupt; but those who appeal to it must, at least, create some kind of public opinion, and they must profess virtue, however much they may disdain to practise it. Democracy, too, is many-eyed to see and many-mouthed to denounce what it dislikes. It is incredible that if the people of New France had controlled their own affairs they would have borne ills which involved their ruin and sapped all devotion to the mother-land.

The Canadians had remained densely ignorant. The *coureurs de bois* who ranged the forests, the hardy men of the axe who cleared the ground that they might sow and reap, had learned much of the cunning of nature, but they knew nothing of books. Probably not one in twenty of those who served in the one hundred and seventy companies of militia could read or write. Owing to the work of the convents the women, then as now, in French Canada were better educated than the men. There was not a newspaper in the land, and outside of the two or three large towns there were practically no books except books of devotion. Oddly enough the Canadians were freer in respect to the conduct of the business of the Church than of the State. The people of the parishes had a real voice in electing those who administered the temporalities of the Church, while in civil affairs they had as yet no shadow of political liberty.

For a time, it was expected that the Canadians would become not merely British in political allegiance but also in outlook and spirit. The Bishop of Quebec, Monsignor Pontbriand, had died during the summer of 1760, those last dark days of New France. For a time, the British would not permit the appointment of a Roman Catholic bishop. There was to be a Protestant Bishop of Quebec, and sanguine people were sure that in time the Canadians would accept the Protestant faith. It was a naive hope which had never even the beginnings of realisation. The Canadians had many reasons for wavering in their devotion to France, for they had been cruelly harassed by the secular power. The Church, however, had been their steadfast friend. The priests in the parishes were devoted men, mindful of the sacred duties committed to them. They had, it is true, no thought of religious liberty.

It is almost amusing to read of the excited alarm shown by the *curés* at the idea that a Protestant might appear among their flocks; that would be a contagion worse than any plague of physical disease. No Protestants, however, appeared. New France had remained Catholic to a man. Her people had not the education or the taste for religious speculation, and the Church was to them the universal mother. The fall of French power only deepened their devotion. In the days of adversity, the priests had words of consolation for an afflicted people. With the old secular authority gone and the new one not yet known or trusted, the Church was the one institution which remained deeply rooted in their traditions. Her rulers wisely accepted the new regime. Prayers in the language of France for 'our most gracious sovereign

Lord King George' were offered in the churches from the first days of the conquest, as they are offered still.

The British soon found that the Church was their best friend in securing the allegiance of the people. Murray had not long been governor at Quebec before he was urging the British Government to rebuild the ruined cathedral at Quebec and to encourage the religious communities. In the end the Church regained her old privileges, and to this day she collects the tithe from her members with all the sanction of law as she did when Canada was under the Bourbons.

On the civil side, too, there was reason for the Canadians to be content with British rule. No longer was commerce in the control of corrupt monopoly. Traders from the British colonies arrived at Montreal with the army of Amherst. As soon as the place surrendered, Amherst sent notices broadcast inviting the colonial merchants to occupy the new field opened to their enterprises. They were quickly flocking to the chief centres, and the Canadian farmer benefited by the wider competition. It is true that he needed little from commerce, for he built his own house, made his own wagon and most of the other things which he used, while his wife clothed the family in garments home-woven and home-made, with no call on the outside world. Still he bought something.

The British goods were cheaper and better than the French had been, and the frugal Canadian housewife soon had the potent argument for British rule that under it a scanty store of money would go much further than it had gone in the days of the old regime. There was, moreover, no longer a Cadet to descend upon a parish and plunder and despoil in the name of the king. The British paid for what they needed in good yellow gold coin and not in the worthless paper money with which Cadet had paid when he paid at all. Moreover, the shadow of war was now removed. After the surrender of Montreal, the military levies ceased, and the farmer could remain at home, to till his fields and harvest his crops. The former rulers had often shown little regard for legal rights.

Now persons with a strong sense of law were in control. There were doubts for a time whether Canada was under French or under British law, but the victors at least recognised that it was under law. The capitulation, too, gave rights which the vanquished claimed and the victors acknowledged. Canada, it is true, remained under military rule for some years, but it had always been under something like a military regime. The British military courts judged in accordance with the laws and customs of the country and took counsel from those who were versed in the practices of New France.

The shadow of Bigot's finance hung long over Canada. Traders, farmers, even officers in the army held the ordinances, the equivalent of present-day banknotes, which he had issued in his own name, promising to pay sums ranging from a few to a great many *livres*. The Court of France refused to pay not merely this fugitive money but even the drafts which he had drawn on France during the latter part of his administration. Murray estimated in 1762 that 80,000,000 *livres* were still owing. We can imagine the anxiety of the man who had in his strong-box, let us say, 50,000 *livres* of this money, and remained in doubt whether it might not be worthless. Everything depended on what the French Government would do. While the war dragged on it delayed and did nothing. Holders of the paper money journeyed to France from Canada in order to present their case. They were sent from one official to another, but could get nothing done.

Meanwhile the money sold sometimes for one *per cent*, of its face value. When peace was concluded in 1763 the question had not been settled. In 1766 a Convention was concluded between the British and the French Governments to the effect that British holders of the paper money should receive up to, but not after, October 1, 1766, 50 *per cent*, of the face value of their bills of exchange and 25 *per cent*, of the face value of their ordinances. This, however, did not apply to the French holders. We find the Marquise de Montcalm begging for payment of money due to the general, and for years we get glimpses of needy officers urging their claims. France's promises to pay were thus not fully honoured and many Canadians suffered.

The Canadians had been told that the British would inflict upon them every outrage and would deport them from their homes as they had deported the Acadians. The vanquished people found instead a security and a justice to which they had long been unaccustomed. The kindliness of the new rulers astonished the Canadians. During the war the British had already shown, indeed, a most creditable magnanimity. In the autumn of 1759 the bankrupt French Government withdrew its accustomed allowances to the French prisoners in England, who numbered about twenty thousand.

A public subscription was taken up for them, and within a few weeks the British public had contributed funds sufficient to reclothe this considerable army. Smollett says:

It was one of the noblest triumphs of the human mind.

During the winter after the surrender of Montreal, when a good many Canadians were in a half-starving condition, the British soldiers gave cheerfully from their scanty means a day's pay in each month to relieve the distress of their former enemies. The reconciliation was in consequence rapid. It was not long before many of the Canadian militia officers who had fought against the British were proud to wear the British uniform. In 1762, as we have seen, a French squadron appeared in Newfoundland, captured St. Johns, took nearly five hundred British vessels of all kinds, and inflicted damage on British shipping to the extent of a million sterling.

An advance to Canadian waters seemed possible. General Haldimand says, however, that, had such a squadron appeared in the St. Lawrence to reassert the claims of France, it would have caused consternation among the French inhabitants of Canada. They did not wish to be disturbed in their new allegiance. A recent observer, tThe anonymous author of *Milices françaises et anglaises au Canada*), says:

> Never in the history of nations did a province change its nationality with *less* of a shock. For this there are various reasons; the isolation of New France; the development of an independent colonial spirit; but above all the wisdom and tact of the conquerors.

The war in South Africa, one hundred and forty years later, was followed by a reconciliation equally rapid. Britain, to be busy, soon after 1760, in taxing unwilling colonists and forcing them on to revolt, was Britain at her worst. She was at her best in the large tolerance shown in the moment of victory in Canada. Her conduct at such a crisis goes far to explain the secret of her dominion.

www.ingramcontent.com/pod-product-compliance
Lightning Source LLC
Chambersburg PA
CBHW030227170426
43201CB00006B/138